Honourable Rebel

the memoirs of
Elizabeth Montagu
later Elizabeth Varley

with a Foreword by Etienne Amyot

ISBN 0 9523386 10

Printed and bound in the United Kingdom for
Montagu Ventures Limited
Beaulieu, Hampshire SO42 7ZN

Elizabeth Montagu has asserted her rights under the Copyright, Designs
and Patents Act 1988, to be identified as the author of this work

Set in Adobe Garamond with chapter numbers in Rosart

HONOURABLE REBEL

CONTENTS

EDITOR'S NOTE

In 1999, just as Christmas Eve was turning into Christmas Day, the village of Beaulieu became engulfed in water from an overflowing Beaulieu River. Heavy rains had coincided with a very high tide and several homes around the river's edge were flooded, one of these being the Mill Race, the home of my aunt Elizabeth. In the days that followed, I found myself sorting through a lot of wet papers, books, film scripts and photographs, some of them very old. When I showed the dried-out documents to my aunt, I quickly learned that each held a story. She had written her memoirs some years before, but finding so many remnants from her past life prompted me to look at the unpublished manuscript. I soon realised that 'Liza' (as we all called her) had a fascinating story, but it was also clear that the memoirs were incomplete, and so I set about completing the task with her.

We usually got together on Sundays for tea, after which I would go through a section of the book, asking her to clarify various things, and expand on others. Quite often, she would then come out with new reminiscences, many of which we incorporated into the text. My task, which started as an exercise in light editing, became so fascinating that I was soon drawn into doing additional research. This turned up much useful information and served to fill a few gaps where Elizabeth's memory eluded her. After about two years' work, just as our task was nearing completion, Elizabeth suddenly became ill with cancer. She faded fast, but mercifully, was able to spend her final weeks at peace in her own home.

So, with great sadness, Elizabeth's memoirs are being published posthumously. In preparing the final manuscript, Elizabeth and I were assisted by many people whose contribution is acknowledged over. Where factual accounts are given, every effort has been made to check the information given; however if any reader should discover inaccuracies, or have additional information, I would be pleased to hear from them.

Finally, two special thank yous. First my gratitude to Graham Weston for his interest in, and support for, this project. Second, I would like to recognise the contribution made by my father, Lord Montagu, as it was he who persuaded Elizabeth to write her memoirs in the first place. RM

Inputting: Nicky Deering and Jane Box

Research: Jane Box and Susan Tomkins

Editorial assistance: WN J Howard and Tim Horn

Editorial advisor: Ailsa Camm

Assistance and advice: Lord Montagu, Lady Chichester, Mary Clare Horn, Tim Horn, Robin Pleydell-Bouverie, Betty Haywood, Silvia Combe (nee Coke), William Pease, Emma Page, William Davies, Françoise Pitt-Rivers, Claudia Maconic, Martha Turinas, Fred Norris, Nanny Nelson, Viv Heathcote-Hacker, Newton Webb-Bowen, Margaret Elsworth, Robert Hill, Donald Buka, Etienne Amyot, Susanne Trachsler-Lehmann, Julia Varley, David Valentine, Jill Chandos-Pole, Iris Goldsworthy, Laure de Margerie-Meslay, Oscar Yerborough, David Prime-Coote, Ted Thomas, Barbara Steward, Elizabeth Louvain, Peter Kamber, Peter Lemmey, Nick Lera, Tania Alexander, Charles Drazin, Lord Teynham, Elena Sandoz (nee German-Ribon), Lord Tweedsmuir, Sir Edmund Fairfax-Lucy, Rosella Voremberg, Stan Seaman, Douglas Gregory, David Etheridge, Jim Maxwell, Ursula Schellenberg, Jean-Francois Thibault.

Libraries and Picture Libraries: Beaulieu Estate Archive, British Library, BBC Written Archives Centre, BBC Photograph Library, V&A Theatre Museum Library, British Film Institute, New York Public Library, Canal Plus, British Film Institute, Marconi plc, National Portrait Gallery, San Michele Foundation, Hulton Archive, Norman Parkinson Archives, The Sheffield Library, Timepix, Praesens Films, The Courier-Journal.

For full picture credit list, see page 502.

Ralph Montagu, Editor

Text appearing in a typewriter font on a tinted background denotes that the passage is an excerpt from one of many letters written by Elizabeth to her close friend Renata Borgatti. Where undated, they originate from the mid-1930s.

FOREWORD
by Etienne Amyot

Elizabeth and I were both born in the same year – 1909 – a long time ago. We first met in the winter of 1929, also a very long time ago. In the years which followed that first meeting, I had endless opportunities to discover the extent of her many, sometimes astonishing, gifts. She was an accomplished musician, a writer and translator of distinction and acted important roles on the London stage with famous stars. She was on the boards of music festivals, involved with the creation of a great new orchestra, the Philharmonia, and worked on films both here and abroad, notably *The Last Chance* and *The Third Man*. But perhaps her finest and most personal achievement was her English libretto for Liebermann's *School for Wives*, an opera which was performed in America and all over Europe.

All these varied talents went somehow with her personality, for she possessed a magical quality which captivated everyone meeting her for the first time. She could literally charm any bird off any tree, and with that charm deal successfully with the most intractable situation. Her beauty and elegance ensured that all eyes turned to her whenever she entered a room. But when one got to know Liza better it was her sense of humour and entrancing laughter which one most came to love her for. Totally devoid of the inane class distinctions of her youth, she was as much herself to the dustman as to the richest Duke. She was born in what is, or rather was, called 'the purple'. It was a state she ignored and had no patience with. I once asked her what she considered the most important thing we could be born with. I imagined she would say intelligence, having such an abundance of it herself, but this wasn't her answer. "Character and quick thinking" was her reply.

Her ability to use these assets is well illustrated in this memoir – a story of an exceptionally rich life in which she put her energy into so many different fields of work. Notwithstanding the diversity of her career, there was a common thread running through everything Elizabeth touched: this was the passion she exuded, both in her work and in the relationships she formed. She befriended an extraordinary variety of people, all outstanding in their fields and pre-eminent during a momentous period in European history. For those of us who knew Elizabeth, it is a pleasure to re-live some parts of her life through these charming reminiscences. And for those who didn't know her, this self-effacing account cannot disguise the fact that the writer was a remarkable person who deeply enriched many lives.

Etienne Amyot
Cranmer Court, London SW3
August 2002

Myself at the House in the Wood. The lady holding me is probably Nurse Elstol, who is recorded in my baby book as the person who witnessed my first crawl!

I

The Shock of Being a Girl

In September 1909, the birth of my mother's long-awaited second child should have been greeted with a fanfare of trumpets. It was nearly twenty years since the birth of her first child, after which eminent gynaecologists had ruled out the possibility of any further conceptions. But at the age of forty-three, my mother proved them all wrong when she became pregnant again. My father was convinced that his prayers would now be answered with the delivery of a son and heir, and, wishing to ensure that both mother and son had the best medical attention available, he prepared for the event by renting an expensive house just off Hyde Park Square in London[1]. So when I, a girl, appeared at 11.30 on the morning of Sunday 26th September, the news was almost too much for my father to take. Profoundly shocked, he left my mother at the house and moved to the Ritz.

The people of Beaulieu must have shared my father's bitter disappointment, but they never let me feel it. Indeed, as I became conscious of my surroundings, I had every reason to be grateful. Just four years prior to my birth, my father had inherited the Beaulieu Estate from his father, and it was now my good fortune, or lucky accident of birth, to be growing up in a beautiful place. Whilst Beaulieu had been in the family for generations, it came to my grandfather in a most unusual way: in 1865 he was given the Hampshire estate as a wedding present by his father, Walter Francis, 5th Duke of Buccleuch. Even from an exceptionally well-endowed landowner, this was a most generous gift for a second son whose eldest brother would usually inherit everything, but Walter Francis had a special affection for Henry, and the acres that he bestowed on him were carefully chosen. In addition to Beaulieu, he was also given land in

1

Clitheroe, Lancashire, which produced a useful income from its coal mines. On the death of his mother in 1895, Henry also received the family dower house, Ditton Park, near Windsor. Wisely Henry chose Beaulieu as his permanent home, and in 1885 Queen Victoria granted him a barony, making him Lord Montagu of Beaulieu. His wife, Cecily Stuart-Wortley, youngest daughter of the 2nd Baron Wharncliffe, would have been considered a suitable match for the second son of the powerful Scottish duke, the only possible objection being that Stuart-Wortley blood contained the odd rogue gene! However she soon rose in favour when she gave birth to an heir, John, in 1866, followed by Robert in 1867, and Rachel in 1868. Her fourth child, James, was born in 1873, but died the following year.

When my grandfather took over Beaulieu in 1866, he found a tightly-knit community, largely independent of the outside world. To the south lay the waters of the Solent, to the east the Beaulieu River and to the north the sparse heathlands of the New Forest. Only on the western side was there a continuation of cultivated land, with a scattering of country dwellings. The 10,000-acre estate consisted mainly of farmland and forestry but included the villages of Beaulieu and Buckler's Hard, and one of the few privately-owned rivers in the world. At the head of the estuary stood the family home of Palace House, an imposing stone edifice facing the village across the mill pond. Milk, cream, poultry and eggs were supplied from the Home Farm, while sleek pedigree cattle grazed the lush green parkland. And for those members of family who enjoyed sport, there was plenty of game to be shot in the woods and fish to be caught in the river. To my Scottish grandfather and Yorkshire grandmother, Beaulieu must have been a paradise after the harsher climates of the north.

By today's standards, the newly created Lord and Lady Montagu of Beaulieu lived in grand style, but by Victorian standards my grandfather adopted a relatively informal approach to life, typical of the great Scottish border families amongst which he grew up. This easy attitude increased in my father's time, and is the secret of the special relationships we have enjoyed in Beaulieu for well over a century. Of course, I was aware of our position and responsibilities in the village, accepting these without any feeling of superiority. Even when I was still a small child, my father took immense pains to explain to me the background of our presence in *Bellus*

My Mother and Father outside Palace House

Beaulieu High Street looking north – note the scattering of cow pats on the road

Locus Regis, and to teach me the history of this ancient holy place which was our home. He would tell me about the three centuries of monastic occupation and the abbey's dissolution in 1538, after which Henry VIII sold the estate to our ancestor Thomas Wriothesley, 1st Earl of Southampton. Referred to locally as 'The Palace', the family home was converted from the great gate house of the abbey, with 18th and 19th century additions giving the house its Scottish baronial appearance.

Although my grandfather Henry died on 1905, my grandmother Cecily, the dowager Lady Montagu, was still living at Palace House at the time of my birth. Keen to establish a family home of his own, my father had a new house built about a mile north of Palace House, called The House in the Wood, but it wasn't too long before my granny moved to London and we were able to take up residence at Palace House. Up to 1914, my memories of Beaulieu are of a bucolic calm; everyone seemed to know one another and were always friendly and helpful, even to the 'foreigners' from neighbouring villages.

Despite the relative isolation of the estate, Beaulieu was by no means a dull place for a child; there were plenty of exciting things to do, and the red brick properties in the village included a variety of useful shops.

Beaulieu High Street looking south – the aproned Mr Winsey standing outside his shop

Approaching from Palace House, one's first glimpse of the world beyond the garden came as you passed through the arch of the outer gate house. This was where the main road crossed the river, bordered on the Palace House side by the village green, known as the Timbrells. Here, cattle would often be seen browsing as they ambled from the village farmyards back to the meadows, leaving a splattered trail of cow pats behind them. A more impressive sight was that of the coastal barges as they came up the river from Southampton. The appearance of these splendid vessels with their russet coloured sails usually signalled the delivery of coal for the Electric Light Station; this was landed opposite the Timbrells at Palace Quay, just a few yards away from the generating plant.

After crossing the river and passing the mill and Montagu Arms Hotel, the first shop you encountered was Aldridge's the newsagent on the corner of the High Street with Lyndhurst Road. It was here that I bought my comics, *Puck* and *Rainbow*. This was a great rallying point where villagers got together and stood around gossiping. Next up the street was the busy Manor Office, and on the opposite side of the road, Winsey's, one of Beaulieu's two grocery stores[2]. Despite the filthy state of the shop, I liked the portly Mr Winsey because he was always full of jollity and gave me sweets. From time to time, the store was invaded by a horde of Romany gypsies from their camps at nearby Penerley and Ipley. Despite the dreadful stench that always accompanied them, I would watch fascinated as they stocked up on sugar, flour, lard and other basics, paid for with great rolls of dirty banknotes. I was also captivated by their extraordinary garments, and the women who carried their babies in a papoose on their backs. Their pale, grubby, runny-nosed children made me ashamed of being so much better-off, but I loved hearing them talk excitedly in Romany.

In contrast, Mr Stevens' store[3] was more up-market, very clean and a little more expensive. My nanny would go shopping there and have seemingly interminable chats with Mr Stevens whilst I had to stand by her side. On one occasion I became very bored, and, looking down, saw a box of chocolate biscuits stacked just off the floor. On and on they talked, as grown-ups do, and eventually temptation overcame me and I sneaked my little hand in the tin. Mr Stevens saw me and gave me a terrible reprimand: he said that stealing was a serious offence and threatened to call the village policeman. What was more, the biscuit would have to be paid for – I would have to ask my father for the money! I shall never forget it, and I never stole again.

Fortunately for me, there were plenty of other shops to visit. One of these was Norris's Saddlery, which seemed to be able to deal with anything from shoe repairs to supplying patent remedies for farm animals; the place always had a delightful smell of leather. Another was the Dairy & Haberdashery, run by the elderly Misses Cockerel, and then at the far end of the street, Haywards, the 'high class family butcher'. But there was more to Beaulieu village than retailing. The high street saw a steady stream of horses being marched along to Mr Payne's blacksmith and wheelwright shop opposite the village school. Every farm had horses and most people relied on them for local transport, so there was invariably something happening at the forge, which held a special fascination for me. I loved watching the glow as Mr Payne's assistant, Frank Bailey, pumped the bellows, heated up the shoes and hammered them on the anvil. Then, with a great hiss, the red hot shoe would be plunged steaming into a bucket of water and nailed onto the horse's hoof. The smell of singed hooves made me very concerned for the animals but I soon realised that they didn't mind. Teddy Payne was also the village parish clerk and undertaker – a

Mr Payne's smithy and wheelwright shop

wonderful combination – and when his mother died in 1922 he also took on the Post Office which she had been running.

In addition to the village traders, there were a number of striking, larger than life personalities who kept the estate running and everyone on their toes. First and foremost was David Kitcher, the Head Forester, who later became Head of the Estate Works Department[4]. An ebullient character with a loud voice and red hair, he had a first class brain, great energy and Herculean strength. A man of absolute integrity, he was one of my father's most trusted and dependable employees.

Another important figure was Mr Wadley, who was in charge of the Electric Light Station. Mr Wadley was a small, clean-shaven man, a great personality and the chief authority on all matters electrical. The installation of electric light in Beaulieu had been an innovation of my father and the sound of the station generator throbbing away in the evening was very comforting as I nodded off to sleep. Mr Wadley also ran the Estate Fire Brigade, and on one occasion I was taken to see them in action. The fire was at Bunker's Hill Cottages on the edge of the village; it was already dark and the spectacle of this inferno was quite a sensation.

The Beaulieu Band. Tom Gregory is on the left edge of the large drum

The Rev Robert 'Daddy' Powles and Teddy Payne outside Beaulieu Abbey Church

One of my own favourites was Mr Gregory, the Estate's Head Carpenter, with his white apron and enormous black walrus moustache. Standing opposite the vicar in the choir stalls, he played a silver cornet at matins on Sundays. Mr Gregory was also the master of the Beaulieu Band, whose magnificent uniforms and gleaming instruments always made an impressive sight. I well remember lying in bed on a Sunday evening as the sound of the band playing outside the church floated across the east lawn and through the night nursery window.

But the man I remember best was our Vicar, 'Daddy' Powles, who had an extraordinary aura about him. He was always sartorially immaculate in his pale grey morning coat (white in summer) topped with a large broad-brimmed hat to match. He wore white gloves and exuded a delicious scent of rose geranium. His neat white beard and piercing eyes gave him the appearance of an Old Testament prophet as he strode majestically through the village armed with an ivory-handled walking stick. The Reverend RF Powles christened me, taught me the catechism and helped to prepare me for confirmation, but what impressed me most of all were his contacts with the 'other world'. He would talk quite naturally about the long-dead monks from the Abbey – apparently good friends of his. On Christmas Eve he would hold a candlelight mass for them, locking the church doors to ensure that his ghostly congregation would not be interrupted by live human interlopers.

He also let it be known that he was always accompanied by two large dogs. He would tell of how a strange woman had left these dogs in his keeping at Curtle House while she paid my mother a visit, but she never returned to claim them. (At the time, my mother and father were living at The Lodge, a large house in its own grounds only a hundred yards from Curtle House.) Apart from Daddy Powles, no one had ever seen a hair or whisker of these canine phantoms, but we all believed in their existence. The Reverend Powles told how they had once saved his life when he was making haste to Buckler's Hard on foot. It was a dark and stormy night and when he reached the point where the path descends from open fields into woodland[5], the dogs had growled a warning to him not to proceed. The next morning he discovered that the stream which ran through the wood had swollen and swept the footbridge away – had he gone ahead, he might have been drowned. Even now as I stroll round the cloisters on a

Myself aged about four years old

quiet summer evening, I fancy I catch a hint of rose geranium on the air, and half expect to see Daddy Powles walking towards me.

One of the vicar's devotees, almost a lay curate, was Aimée Cheshire. A lady with 'a decidedly unconventional artistic and musical nature',[6] Miss Cheshire lived with her Alsatian dog in a flat at one end of the Domus[7]. She liked to receive visitors and on one occasion invited the two Miss Campbells, residents of Penerley Lodge on the north-western edge of the estate, to tea. On arrival, the two spinsters found that Miss Cheshire had already been joined by a man dressed in a monk's habit. Sitting quietly in the corner, he smiled politely but said nothing. When Miss Cheshire produced the tea, the sisters were indignant to find that the monk was not offered anything. Later, they related this story to others and the explanation must have surprised them. Miss Cheshire would regularly talk of the ghost monks, and this had obviously been one of them. Like the Reverend Powles, she was personally acquainted with the abbey's former brethren, and often referred to them by name. I remember her once complaining that the squeaking of Brother John's boots kept her awake at night, and she did "wish he would do something about it". As far as the

Myself in the 'dog cart' outside Palace House in late 1912

Campbell sisters' story was concerned, the only surprise was that they had actually seen someone, as the monks were invisible to the rest of us.

Living three miles from the nearest railway station at Beaulieu Road meant that we were reliant on the animals of the Palace House stables for transport. For short trips, I was carried in a special basket which was strapped onto Neddy, our grey donkey. Neddy was crafty, stubborn, intractable, greedy and absolutely adorable. He was also very bright, and capable of outwitting anyone. When he was asked to ascend even the mildest slope, his breathing became heavy, his ears drooped and his legs threatened to buckle. But as soon as we turned around to go home, these distressing symptoms would magically disappear, leaving Neddy as fresh as a daisy. On slightly longer journeys, such as a trip to picnic on the sea shore, Nanny and I were driven by Wallis, a smart, liveried groom in an equally smart green governess cart drawn by our tricksy Forest pony Tommy.

Quite unexpectedly, I found myself with animal responsibilities of my own when I won a silver-haired fox terrier in a raffle at the Domus. My father was none too pleased, but he could hardly make me give him back. My terrier turned out to be the first of a line of dogs, the next being Ming, a one-eyed Pekinese from Battersea Dogs' Home given to me by my relation Nellie Stuart-Wortley[8]. A former Gaiety Girl with a vivacious personality, Nellie lived nearby in Palace Cottage and was much respected in Beaulieu. Later I had Chinkey, another Peke who would go off hunting with my father's two black Labradors. When they returned, bedraggled and exhausted, my father always blamed Chinkey for leading his dogs astray – this was one of the things that got him really angry!

Whereas my father was largely a realist, my mother was a romantic and more at home in the mid-Victorian age in which she was born than the turbulent early years of the twentieth century. She was very beautiful, tall and slim, with a swan-like neck and long elegant hands. A talented pianist, she was welcome in any company with her good looks and wry sense of humour. So in most ways she was the exact opposite of my father, but in the early years of their marriage they had been very much in love. Occasionally I would ride in a motor car with my father, but those early cars failed to make much impression on me. I am sure that my mother also preferred horse-drawn transport, but she loyally stood by my father as he enthusiastically experimented with the perils and vicissitudes of the motor car. Despite his inexhaustible appetite for adventure, my mother cared about him deeply, and was rightly filled with apprehension for his safety. She even became a contributor to his transport magazine, *The Car Illustrated*, although I am sure she would have preferred to sit at home at her piano.

The Car Illustrated was produced in London from my father's office at 62 Pall Mall. Here, George Foster Pedley was his right-hand man, Eleanor Thornton his personal assistant and Jane Clowes his secretary. But this was a small staff compared to those employed at Beaulieu, where life in Palace House was similar to that enjoyed by most upper class families before the Great War. The house staff consisted of a Butler, two liveried Footmen, a Head Housemaid, three Housemaids, a Cook, two Kitchen Maids and a Scullery Maid. These were supplemented by a Nanny and Nursery Maid to look after me, and at least a dozen men in the gardens and at the stables.

I always suspected that the servants had 'special food' because I used to pass the Servants' Hall on my way back from my walks with Nanny, and,

"Me and my teddy bear"

My father and me going to the wedding of my cousin Dor Forster in June 1914

peeking in, would see great joints on the table – a stark contrast to the dull nursery food awaiting me upstairs. In fact, the servants ate in two different groups according to their status. The 'lower orders' had their meals in the Servants' Hall under the watchful eye of the Head Housemaid, whilst the senior staff ate in the north-western turret. This was the Housekeeper's room and if one of my father's guests brought his own valet, he would eat seated to the right of the Housekeeper whilst a visiting lady's maid would be placed to the right of the Butler.

With such numbers of people to supervise, the heads of department enjoyed considerable prestige and were held in special regard by family and staff alike. One of these was the Butler, George Pleasant. Nicknamed 'Pascha' Pleasant, he was an impressive figure, not least because he wore a red Egyptian fez given to him by my grandfather Henry following one of his overseas tours. Another was the grand Head Coachman, Mr Gooderson. One of his grooms, Frank Wallis, later became the family driver but at the time it was Teddy Stephens who was my father's faithful chauffeur and mechanic.[9]

So in terms of servants, we lived a life of some luxury, but in terms of comfort, we definitely did not. The monastic chill which pervaded Palace House prevented it from ever being a cosy home. On entering the front hall, one found a billiards table which served as a handy surface on which to leave your coat. Next one passed through a door in a partition screen which divided the hall from the staircase, but if the visitor expected greater warmth on the other side, he was to be disappointed. With so many lofty rooms, the house was virtually impossible to heat. The largest room was the dining hall where the position of the fire place, on one side of the long dining table, meant that you were either roasted alive or, if seated at the outer extremities, left to freeze! The adjoining lower drawing room was even worse, and so damp that a green slime formed on one of the walls. Only in the library, with its slightly lower ceiling, could one be reasonably certain of some warmth.

Long flights of stone stairs were the lot of the servants and also of those in the nursery. The first floor nursery quarters, under the direction of Nanny Stevens, were largely separate from the rest of the house. Sometimes I was allowed to visit my father and mother in the dining hall after eating my

The south side of Palace House – the nursery is on the far right (first floor)

own breakfast in the nursery. Inclined to spoil his young daughter, my father would feed me sardines or allow me to run along the dining table. More often, however, I didn't see the grown-ups until after tea. In those days, upper class children were rarely seen or heard by their parents but visiting the estate tenants with my mother, I saw an altogether different picture. There would usually be a roaring fire, and even if the room was a bit smelly, everybody was friendly and cheerful. I remember envying the children in their crowded parlours, all 'hugger-mugger' but warm and relaxed. *Real* families, I thought. Then I would go back to bleak Palace House where I was the only child.

Mornings were usually spent on walks with Nanny. In the garden, the thing I most enjoyed seeing was the horse-drawn lawn mower in action. Skilfully guided by a man sitting high up on the machine, the horse patiently plodded across the velvety surface with its hooves securely enclosed in great leather boots. Beyond the garden, woodland trails, estate tracks and the quiet local roads offered plenty of scope for hearty exercise. Every detail of those routes became etched on my mind, each with its own character and associations, forming a network that defined my little world. At midday I would be sent to rest before lunch, which was at one. All my meals were taken in the nursery, with food sent up in warmers from the kitchen at the other end of the house. Nanny deliberately antagonised the Cook – a dragon of a woman – so we got the most awful food: an endless diet of flaccid whiting with its tail in its mouth and gritty spinach. My father wasn't always happy with the food either: he liked his meat well-seasoned and very underdone, and there would be a big row in the kitchen if it wasn't done to his liking. On one occasion, my mother decided that some venison, which had been hanging for weeks, was past consumption and had it buried. On his return, my father was so incensed that he ordered it to be exhumed and roasted!

My afternoons were generally spent out of doors, and although I was allergic to horses, there was nothing I loved better than mooching around the stables, where I was sometimes allowed to polish the elaborate harness with *Bluebell* brass cleaner. On the north side of the stables there was a small orchard[10] with a stream running through it. Bucolic and untouched for centuries, this was where my mother kept her beloved bantams and chickens. Here, I was allowed to help collect the eggs and feed the birds, the only useful jobs I ever got to do, the rest being the domain of the servants.

Tea was at four, and the fresh cottage loaves and butter we had were sometimes the best meal of the day. The next bit was less fun, as I was dispatched from my warm, friendly day nursery to walk alone along the dark, spooky corridors to visit my mother downstairs in the drawing room. For these occasions, I was dressed by Nanny in a stiffly starched dress with a scratchy collar, my lank red hair was combed and tied up with blue ribbons, and my feet were forced into tight patent leather shoes. At Palace House, the nursery was at the far east end of the modern, Victorian wing, while the grown-ups' social life took place mainly in the ancient monastic part, a considerable distance away. Once I had left the well-lit nursery corridor, the frightening part of the journey began. My father had a mania for turning off lights and the house was therefore full of shadows. I had to pass several Gothic arches, each hung with heavy velvet curtains which held untold terrors; if there was a wind, they would move mysteriously as if concealing some dreadful menace. So I was down the stairs in a flash to the safety of the lower drawing room, where my mother would be sitting to the left of the fireplace.

"She's a very quiet child," guests would say as my mother took me on her knee and gave me a hug. She knew why. Although I loved seeing my mother, my appearance in the drawing room seemed to be treated as a form of entertainment, which I didn't enjoy. Sundays were particularly awful as there were bound to be extra people to tea, and they were usually complete strangers to me. No doubt my parents were proud to show me off to their friends, but the whole thing was a bit of a pretence, especially as I had already been given my tea in the nursery. However, I would dutifully play with my tea set for about half an hour until Nanny arrived to collect me for a bath and then bed. My daily wash took place in a tin hip bath in the night nursery, where Nanny and I slept. Sitting upright in this awful tub with most of my body above the water line, it was difficult not to shiver: little wonder I was always getting coughs and colds. Then came the part I most dreaded – bedtime.

If you were lucky enough to have a really good Nanny to look after you, nothing could have been better. But if you were not, and your Nanny was positively unpleasant, the isolation which was your lot for most of the day delivered you helpless into the hands of a tyrant. Nanny Stevens was of the latter kind; sadistically inclined, aggressive and rough, she inflicted a great deal of real physical and mental cruelty. I remember vividly how she would put me to bed, and then, about a quarter of an hour later, creep into the room, lean over the bed and glare at me. If I wasn't asleep but just lying there 'doggo', she would hiss "I know you're not asleep, Miss Elizabeth; I know you're just pretending!" With this, she would lift me out of my warm bed, carry me into the adjoining turret room and proceed to beat me. I learned not to cry and never told my mother. The staff at Palace House must have known how badly my Nanny treated me, but they kept their silence – in those days, well-to-do mothers were not expected to be close to their children. My mother's ignorance was certainly not due to negligence or a lack of affection, for in later years we became very close.

Done up in my best party dress for a studio portrait with my mother

My maternal Grandmother, Victoria, Marchioness of Lothian

2

NORTH OF THE BORDER

Despite the disappointment I caused by not being born a boy, my mother's family at Monteviot particularly welcomed my arrival. Latterly, my mother had been sad and lonely, and it was felt that the advent of a child whom she could love and care for might bring some warmth and happiness back into her life. Her mother, my grandmother, was born Lady Victoria Montagu-Douglas-Scott, and as daughter of the 5th Duke of Buccleuch grew up at Drumlanrig near Dumfries (my father and mother were first cousins). In spite of her ducal background, she was essentially a country girl and was brought up tough, so that when she married the 9th Marquess of Lothian and moved to Monteviot, the lack of ordinary creature comforts, such as heating and hot water, would not have worried her. But tragedy stalked her married life; first she lost her husband, then her eldest son Willie was killed in a shooting accident in Australia. Finally, her second son, Robert, was confined to Edinburgh with mental problems. As a result, she had special reason to welcome us, since my father – her nephew – had almost become a surrogate son and was her blue-eyed boy. The house was always spruced up when he came to stay and this welcome was maintained throughout the years we visited Monteviot, which became my favourite place on earth.

If Palace House was sometimes frigid and remote, Monteviot was exactly the opposite. Situated 12 miles north of the border in Roxburghshire, Monteviot was the seat of the Marquesses of Lothian, but my grandmother now lived there with her second husband, Bertram Talbot. Standing a few hundred feet above the Teviot, a tributary of the Tweed, it was not so much a house as a conglomeration of houses. These were of all shapes and sizes,

*Monteviot in September 1913. Judging from the amount of
activity in the garden, it must have been an Indian Summer*

with an 18th century farm house at the centre and many later additions,
all connected by tin-roofed passages – a veritable rabbit warren. There were
few creature comforts, no heating, no bathrooms and no electricity, but it
didn't seem to matter. There was one formal wing, ponderous and
Victorian, which housed the servants' quarters, the nurseries, three guest
rooms and the dining room. All this grandeur ended abruptly in a jagged
wall which descended balefully into the garden, a testimony to the point at
which my grandfather had run out of money. As a former Secretary of State
for Scotland[1], he was not a particularly imprudent man, but his hobby of
growing orchids and drilling coal mines near his other home, Newbattle
Abbey, near Dalkeith, soon drained the Lothian coffers of all available cash.

Monteviot was a paradise for children. There was the river with its boats,
canoes and fishing, and there were also opportunities to play croquet,
tennis and squash. Importantly, there was also lots of delicious food. For
me, the Order of Merit went to those splendid Scottish breakfasts and teas
with their porridge, baps, scones and bannocks – far better than the

'Monteviot, steeped in sunny beams, Smiled down on Teviot's winding streams.'
(from Walter Laidlow's 'A Summer Ramble on the Teviot')

nursery food at Beaulieu. My grandmother insisted on a strict code of
behaviour at breakfast; porridge should only be eaten with salt, and
preferably whilst walking around, so woe betide the unfortunate guest who
scattered sugar on it. In other matters, however, my grandmother was
surprisingly tolerant. As long as we appeared punctually at meals looking
reasonably tidy and clean, she left us to our own devices. She wanted us to
be happy, but would quickly show disapproval if we quarrelled. In
retrospect, it seems strange that although we were often on the river, she
never once enquired whether we could swim, nor did she caution us when,
armed with razor-sharp axes, billhooks and choppers, we disappeared into
the forest on wooding forays. Her confidence in us seemed justified, as we
would always reappear unharmed. We loved and respected her, for she
radiated great serenity, and of course we never doubted her wisdom. She
was later afflicted by deafness and failing eyesight, and sometimes seemed
a little remote, but her sense of humour, courage and glowing Christian
faith carried her through to the age of 93. She typified the best of the
Victorian age.

Myself (left) with two cousins in the garden and
Aunt Margie (inset) playing her violin outside the house

Whereas at Beaulieu I felt like an only child (my sister Helen was nearly 20 years my senior and had left home), at Monteviot I found myself one of a tribe of grandchildren. These were the offspring of 'the aunts' – Mary, Helen, Victoria and Isobel. Each was a considerable personality, especially their elder sister Aunt Margie who had never married and still lived at Monteviot. In her youth, she had proved so talented that her professor in Vienna wrote to her parents recommending that she take up the career of a concert violinist. My grandfather was so appalled by this suggestion that he summoned her home forthwith and locked her violin in a cupboard. Poor Aunt Margie! However, she was not completely thwarted and formed a family quartet in which Aunt Mary played the viola, Aunt Helen the cello and my mother the piano. These aunts, some of whom lived well into their nineties, were a great joy to me and became friends for life. Like my mother, they all possessed a wonderful wry sense of humour and always seemed to sparkle. Aunts are very important in one's life; one should always remember that!

As far as I can recall, there was only one negative aspect to Monteviot, and the Borders generally, and this was the prevalence of spooks. I was reasonably used to such things at Beaulieu, but the Scottish breed was

Myself and two cousins test the strength of the house donkey.
The lady on the right is probably my mother

different – they were much more sinister and frightening. As a child, I had several paranormal experiences, some of which, I was to learn later, could be matched to historical events. The one I remember most vividly occurred when we went out for an afternoon picnic on the Cheviot Hills east of Monteviot. Before tea we decided to play a game of prisoners; with about a dozen children in the party we were just the right number. We had ten minutes to hide before the game began, so each of us went in search of a really good hiding place. I found a burn beside which was a hanging rock concealing some form of cave. I climbed inside and found the space much larger than I imagined – this was ideal! I was rather pleased with myself for finding such a good hideout, but as I waited, a sense of fear and doom descended on me. At first I tried to shake it off, but it just got worse until eventually I had to run out. I was immediately spotted and taken prisoner, but that feeling from the cave stayed with me. Some time later whilst leafing through a book in the library at Monteviot, I came across an account of a how a horde of English raiders massacred the Kerrs (the Lothian clan) after they took refuge in a cave. Reading on, I realised from the description that the cave was the very one in which I hid briefly during that game of prisoners. The anguish of my Kerr ancestors evidently still resided in that dark, dank cavern.

A frightening experience of another kind had a happier outcome. Nanny Stevens usually travelled with us to Scotland, but Monteviot seemed particularly prone to dramatic thunderstorms, of which Nanny had a pathological fear. At the first flicker of lightning she would collect all the nursery cutlery, glass and mirrors and hurriedly hide them away in a huge domed trunk which sat in the passage. Insisting that thunder was the 'wrath of God', she would then climb in after them, taking me with her. I can still recall the horror of being shut in the trunk with this awful woman, until, on one occasion, my mother discovered us both. Taking me to the drawing room, she held me up to a large bay window and tried to explain this frightening phenomenon. "Don't worry darling; it's only the angels rolling their boxes about before they go on holiday!" My mother's discovery had finally revealed that her daughter's nanny was, to say the least, a bit strange. She departed soon afterwards, bound for a mental home – at least that was what I liked to believe.

Unfortunately, my mother's next choice was not much better. I had a particularly favourite teddy bear, who had lost most of his fur, but the new nanny didn't approve of me carrying him around with me. She hadn't been with us very long when she turned on me. "What a horrible filthy thing! You can't carry that around with you!" She seized my little bear and slung it on the nursery fire. I loved that bear as you would love an animal and burst into bitter tears. For me it was like a living thing and I shall never forget the awful grief I felt.

By the age of four, I was old enough to know that, in my short lifetime, we had always spent the summer months at Monteviot. What I could not have understood were the events which would soon disrupt this routine. 4th August 1914 should have been a day like any other, so I expected little of interest when I perched myself at the nursery window. From here I could look over the front door and down the drive, watching for any interesting activity below – perhaps the arrival of an elegant carriage drawn by beautiful horses, or the gardeners raking the gravel into intricate patterns. But this day turned out to be most unusual: so many carriages arriving, so much hustle and bustle. I asked my mother what was happening, but there were tears in her eyes. It had something to do with the Kaiser and war with Germany. I didn't understand it at all, but sensed it might spell trouble for our beloved German *Fraülein* whom our Lothian grandmother had

Outside the front door of Monteviot with my mother, circa 1914.
In those days, horse-drawn transport was very much the norm

engaged to teach the family German. My mother was devoted to her, and
she visited us at Beaulieu several times, but within a few days this kindly
soul had to depart for Germany amid tears and lamentations. Later I was
taught to hate the Germans, but it was all rather puzzling, as the only
German I had known was our kind *Fraülein*.

The outbreak of hostilities meant an immediate return to Beaulieu, and
while I was not to see Monteviot again for eight years, my mother had left
her old home for the last time. So we said farewell to the Cheviot Hills and
headed south in a frenzy of excitement. My father, acting as Director of
Organisation, Special Constabulary in London[2], was already in uniform;
everything around us seemed to be changing, and it didn't take long for
people to realise that life would never be the same.

My Uncle Harry & Aunt Rachel Forster (above)
and their youngest son 'Wag' (right)

3

UPHEAVAL

The temporary loss of Monteviot was somewhat compensated for by the introduction of London into my life, where my Uncle Harry and Aunt Rachel had a delightful house in Hans Place, a stone's throw from Harrods. My uncle, Harry Forster, was an able and hard-working politician whose devoted wife was involved in anything and everything that would help her husband in his work. Uncle Harry was a strikingly good-looking man, a superb helmsman, a first class cricketer[1] and someone who always radiated good humour. Aunt Rachel was also good-looking and highly intelligent. My father's only sister, she could appear rather formidable at times, although I soon found her to be one of the most warm-hearted and truly remarkable women I knew. She had two daughters, Dorothy and Rachel (known as Dor and Ray), and two sons, John (known as Jack) and Alfred (known as Wag, short for Scallywag).

Dor and Ray were many years older than me – real grown-ups – and I remember feeling very privileged to be allowed to see them before they left for Buckingham Palace dressed in all their presentation feathers and finery. Hans Place must have been an exceptionally happy house until the 1914 war, when, like millions of other homes, it was struck by tragedy: Jack was killed in action just six weeks after the war started, Dor's husband Harold was killed in June 1918 and Wag returned seriously wounded from the final advance, four weeks before the Armistice. As he convalesced at Hans Place, I spent many hours talking with this humorous, charming and intelligent young man. But his condition worsened and he was taken to hospital where he died of blood poisoning in March 1919. The man in the next bed was the sculptor Cecil Thomas, who on his recovery made Alfred the subject of a bronze effigy which forms the war memorial in Exbury Church[2], just 3 miles from Beaulieu.

Hyde Park was only minutes away from Hans Place and we regularly went there for fresh air and exercise. At Albert Gate there was an old lady who sat with an enormous bunch of gas-filled balloons; how I longed to walk along with one of these tugging at my hand but I was always told to make do with one of the cheap ones filled with ordinary air. I was no more successful with kites; lots of children brought them to fly in the park, but my nanny considered them to be common, so I never had one. Fortunately, I was allowed to sail my model boat on the Serpentine, which gave me great pleasure. As an exceptional treat, I would accompany my aunt on shopping expeditions to Harrods, and these might include a visit to their toy department, an Aladdin's Cave of marvels. Once, in a moment of generosity, she bought me an expensive scooter with proper handlebars and a bell; no present, before or since, has given me such a thrill. Anxious to try it out, I rode it around the house leaving tyre marks all over the carpet! I was in big trouble! Another vivid memory of Hans Place was the Zeppelin, which appeared, mysterious, silvery and beautiful, in the night sky during an air raid. Standing in the street in our night clothes, we watched in awe as it was picked out by the searchlights. We were not afraid, it just seemed such fun.

When I was in London, I would be taken to visit my grandmother Cecily, the Dowager Lady Montagu, who lived in a small but elegant house in Tilney Street, Mayfair. This granny, who always wore black, was regarded by most of the family as more fearsome than a jabberwocky, but I knew her as a kindly old lady who spoilt me with large quantities of sticky cakes.

I saw little of my father during the war years. On 26th September 1914 (my fifth birthday) he was gazetted to take command of the 2nd/7th Battalion of the Hampshire Regiment, and on 12th December departed with his 800-strong force for India. The following April he was summoned to join the General Staff of the Indian Army as Inspector of Mechanical Transport. It was possibly during his next home leave that my father asked me to help with a top secret experiment on the old golf course, down on the foreshore of the Beaulieu Estate. We met two high-ranking military men who had doubtless chosen this spot for its remoteness. They produced

My paternal grandmother, Cecily, Dowager Lady Montagu

two strangely-shaped boxes made of slatted wood and gauze, each painted with different patterns and measuring about three feet in length. Holding one of the boxes over my head, I was instructed to scuttle about between the gorse bushes, stopping and starting as ordered. Then they got me to try the other one. Comical as it may sound, the exercise was conducted in the utmost seriousness. It seems that they were trying to assess the effectiveness of different camouflage patterns for a new secret weapon, which I later recognised as the tank.[3]

My father in the uniform of a Colonel in the Hampshire Regiment.
He was promoted Brigadier-General in 1918

Another excitement arose when my father took me up to the Royal Flying Corps base on Beaulieu Heath. His uniform probably made it easier for him to request a flight, although the pilot was evidently a bit concerned about the combined weight of a small girl and her father. Fortunately he was persuaded not to worry, and I was taken up in the rear seat of the biplane, sitting on my father's lap. This was my first ride in an aeroplane, and I remember being fascinated as we flew over Southampton Water and then back over Beaulieu.

In December 1915, my father packed his bags for another tour of duty in India. After crossing the Channel, he travelled overland to Marseilles to join the P&O liner *SS Persia*. He was due to complete a report for the Indian Government and therefore arranged to take his personal assistant, Miss Eleanor Thornton, with him for part of the voyage. It was planned that she would type up the reports and then leave the ship at Port Said whilst he sailed on to Bombay. But there was more to this arrangement than would have appeared to all but his closest friends. My father and Thorn were also lovers, a situation which was apparently accepted by my mother who was on friendly terms with her. In a letter sent just before his departure, my mother told her husband that she was glad that Miss Thornton was going with him, and implored him to take care of his health. Such was my father's enthusiasm for whatever he was doing that he was prone to exhaust himself; my mother evidently hoped that Thorn would help him to get some rest on the voyage. Sadly, she was never able to complete her task. At 1.15pm on Thursday 30th December 1915, the *SS Persia* was torpedoed and sunk 71 miles south-east of Cape Martello, a promontory on the south-eastern coast of Crete. After over 30 hours either in the water or perched on a badly damaged lifeboat, my father was one of those lucky enough to be picked up alive. Out of over 300 passengers and crew, more than 130 had perished. My father's survival was at least partly due to his wearing a Gieve inflatable waistcoat, an early form of lifejacket designed to be worn with ordinary uniform.

Tragically however, Thorn was lost to the sea. She had been my father's Personal Assistant for 15 years and had helped him tremendously throughout the pioneering years of the motoring movement; he was devoted to her and he felt her loss bitterly. I would miss her too – she was a very beautiful and charming lady to whom I had taken an instinctive

The SS Persia leaving Malta on 29th December 1915, one day before she was sunk

liking. But as long as the words Rolls-Royce symbolise the very best, Thorn will be remembered. In her earlier years, she had modelled for the sculptor Charles Sykes who, on my father's advice, was commissioned by Rolls-Royce to create a special mascot for their cars. Whether Thorn actually posed for Sykes as he created Spirit of Ecstasy is not certain, but there is little doubt that she was the inspiration for the figure that has graced every Rolls-Royce radiator since 1911.

At Beaulieu, first word of the sinking came on Saturday 1st January 1916, the newspapers declaring that many of the passengers and crew had been lost. On the Sunday, a provisional list of 158 survivors from four life boats was published, but my father's name was absent. There now seemed little hope that he had survived and *The Times* duly published his obituary on the Monday. The news that my father, a man of such vitality, was dead, was met with disbelief. My mother was grief-stricken, and I remember sitting on her knee, both of us howling with sorrow, unable to console ourselves. But our vicar Daddy Powles knew better. He had seen an apparition of my father standing on the bridge over the river, just where the two men would often stop to pass the time of day. Soon after, the vicar visited my mother who was confined to her bedroom. "I spoke to his Lordship, but he wasn't able to reply," explained the vicar. "That means he can't be dead." Such was my mother's faith in God, and her trust in Daddy Powles, that she knew his account must be true, and we started to believe that all was not lost.

On Tuesday 4th January, my mother received another telegram: a fifth lifeboat had been picked up, and my father was one of the 11 men on board. He was alive after all and in a Maltese hospital recovering from his ordeal. She was elated and all Beaulieu rejoiced with her. I can't remember much about that day, but the memoir written by my father's friends Laura Troubridge and Archibald Marshall recalls the moment beautifully:

> The people of Beaulieu, who had mourned John not only as the Lord of the Manor but as a son of the soil and a brother of each one of them, gave themselves up to whole-hearted rejoicing. A stranger who visited the place on the Tuesday the news arrived and was unaware of the close links binding the owner of Beaulieu to his village friends and neighbours had recorded his bewilderment at the local excitement. The Beaulieu Band paraded through the thoroughfares playing appropriate tunes from 9 a.m. and the windows were be-flagged, while apart from these semi-official demonstrations each individual reacted to the news as if to some personal good fortune.

On the same day that the news reached Beaulieu, my father was propped up in bed writing to my mother. The pencilled letter was only rediscovered after the publication of my father's biography in 1985, and is such a remarkable account that I have included it in the appendices of this book. Soon after, he had the rare opportunity of reading his own obituary in *The Times*, written by his old friend Lord Northcliffe. After two weeks in Malta, he travelled back to Beaulieu by hospital ship. Arriving at Palace House with his arm in a sling, my father was pale and wan, and clearly the worse for his ordeal. It was unlike him to be still for long, but the disaster which struck in the Mediterranean had temporarily taken the wind out of him. It wasn't just the physical injuries that pained him but a deep melancholy after losing Thorn. For a few weeks he was unusually quiet and pensive, but his physical and emotional energy gradually returned, and by late January he was working again on matters of mechanical transport for the Indian Army.

On 1st February 1916, news arrived that my father's younger brother Robert had died, but not in any kind of military action. My Uncle Robert's bright red face, great nose and alcoholic breath had never endeared him to me. Stinking of brandy, he would pick me up and slobber all over me; no doubt he was showing affection but I took a profound dislike to him. Robert had been a brilliant undergraduate at Oxford but was something of a 'ladies' man' and was fatally drawn to liquor – it must have been that bad Stuart-Wortley blood! My father and Aunt Rachel had done everything they could to help him, but to no avail, and he died of an alcohol-related illness. Following the cremation in London, my father took his brother's ashes to be interred at Beaulieu. After leaving the train at Brockenhurst, he suddenly remembered that the casket was still on the luggage rack. An anxious call was put through to Bournemouth station, where Uncle Robert was eventually found and re-despatched to Beaulieu, the dear departed's final journey being as a piece of lost luggage!

By 1916, most of the household staff had gone to fight in the war and Palace House had become an impossible place to live in, so later that year, it was decided that my mother, my governess Miss Mary Knott ('Bunny') and I should move to a smaller, more convenient house. For reasons which remain unclear, Tunbridge Wells was recommended as a good area in which to hunt for furnished accommodation, so there we went, initially staying at the Spa Hotel. It was here in safe, sleepy Tunbridge Wells, that the full horror of what was happening in Flanders was brought home to me. We had arrived at dusk, and while the others unpacked, I glanced out of the window and spotted something that instantly attracted my attention. Outside on the common there stood a strange contraption, like a monstrous gallows, from which a number of bodies hung, swinging gently in the wind. I was very frightened and hardly slept that night. The light of day brought an explanation no less horrible than what I had imagined. This part of the common was used for young recruits to practice their bayonet drill. They would line up, and after a barked order from the NCO, would rush forward uttering fearful guttural screams and bury their bayonets in the entrails of the hanging sandbags. I was an imaginative child, and it did not take much effort to realise the implications. The Western Front now seemed very close.

After a brief stay in the Spa Hotel, we found a four-room house on the outskirts of Penshurst in Kent. Our new home, 'Petersfield', was reasonably well furnished, not far from the shops, and though cold, was not as damp as Palace House. My mother had very little money at her disposal, and with the exception of Bunny, we were without staff. However, she insisted on doing all the shopping and showed herself to be an excellent housewife and cook. Following our arrival in Penshurst, my mother visited the butcher

My mother and myself

and introduced herself. The proprietor was most impressed to think that
Lady Montagu of Beaulieu would be opening an account with him, but his
pride was somewhat dented when she ordered a sheep's head. This was the
main ingredient in what became a regular dish, based on an old recipe
from Monteviot. I thought it delicious, especially when served cold, but
Bunny wasn't so sure.

> Sheep's Head Pie: The sheep's head to be scalded, not skinned – put on to
> blanch. When blanched, add weak broth. For 2 heads put 3 carrots, 3 onions,
> 1 bunch parsley, (2 sticks of celery), 3 leeks on to boil 8 hours, until the bones
> come freely from the meat. Place all upon a large dish and season well. Then
> put it in a pie dish, pass and skin the liquor free from grease and reduce in to
> one third of the quantity and then pour it over the meat. When cold, cover
> with puff pastry and bake it.

Anxious to ensure that my education was properly organised, my mother
enrolled me in the PNEU[4] scheme which provided a syllabus for my classes
at home. She also gave me my first music lessons and passed her love of
music to me, a love that has never diminished. There was an upright piano
in the sitting room, and, to save electricity in the evenings, my mother
would improvise on it for hours, illuminated by the flickering light of the
fire. She was a natural composer and it was around this time that she wrote
some alternative music for the hymn *Guide Me O Thou Great Redeemer*.

Despite some carefree moments, long shadows hung over everything. Each
morning the newspapers carried ever-lengthening casualty lists and details
of new disasters. Daily I would see soldiers on their route marches along
our roads, the young men looking grey and strained; even those on leave
seemed to have forgotten how to smile. Food rationing was biting deep
and there was little or no entertainment. These were grim times, but it
helped all of us, children included, to realise the vital importance of
human relationships and the evanescence of material things. However, in
my own innocent way, I took the war effort very much to heart. 'When
you come back you will find me in soldier's clothes and you will not know
me…' I told my father, in a letter from Penshurst[5], adding 'I have got five
War Savings Certificates so I am helping my Country'.

In April, my father returned on leave from India. Visiting our little house,
he gave me his light-coloured tropical tunic and cap, with which I was

Ditton in happier days

thrilled. Suitably attired for military action, I went out into the garden and dug a series of defensive trenches in the herbaceous border! My mother was none too pleased, but my father had rather more weighty matters on his mind. In March, the government had served a compulsory purchase order[6] on Ditton Park, our property near Windsor, which was urgently required by the Admiralty. As all 60 rooms in the house were fully furnished, and contained many treasures, this 'order to quit' presented grave problems. My mother, Bunny and I travelled up to Ditton to sort out the contents as best we could. When we had stayed at Ditton before the war, staff abounded, the lawns were like velvet and grand carriages stood in the stables. Now everything was different; the house was dusty, bleak and cold, the lawns ragged, the gardens overgrown with weeds and the stables empty. Only the front drive retained its former glory, its verges lined with a forest of beautiful snowdrops – spring must have been late that year.

My father had tried to sell Ditton before without success[7], but the Admiralty's compulsory purchase at a price deflated by wartime conditions

Myself outside the front door of Ditton

was a most undignified and unsatisfactory end to our ownership of a lovely property. Today, standing midway between London Airport and Windsor, Ditton Park must be worth millions, but in 1917 the war was going badly and the Admiralty needed moated Ditton to test marine and aircraft compasses, so this charming family home had to be sacrificed to the all-important war effort. I would miss my stays there, for the house always seemed warmer than Palace House, and I so enjoyed our walks to Datchet.

It was impossible at that time to arrange a proper sale of the vast quantities of valuable furniture, pictures and other treasured possessions, so my parents wisely decided to donate a good deal of these to various national museums, the Victoria and Albert Museum being one. This still left a good deal to be moved to Beaulieu. It was very difficult to find private transport, but one of my father's best friends in the motoring world was Tom Thornycroft, whose factory in Basingstoke was manufacturing lorries for the army. He immediately offered his help and sent a fleet of test vehicles to convey our possessions from Ditton to Beaulieu, making Palace House look more like a furniture repository than a home. Amongst the things which found a prominent place in Palace House was the massive elm table from the servants' hall and the false bookshelf door from Ditton's once splendid library.

We didn't stay at Penshurst for more than a year, but Palace House with all its extra furniture remained a difficult place in which to live. My memory is a bit hazy, but I do recall living at The Lodge for a while, and this may have been towards the end of the war. In those days there was a large conservatory greenhouse on the north-east side of the house, filled with splendid hyacinths. We also spent some time at the family beach house, called The House on the Shore, where Lady Hilton Young, widow of the explorer Captain Scott, came to stay with her son. Peter Scott and I did -lessons together with my governess, and also devoted much time to nature studies on the foreshore of the estate. I was very keen on collecting birds' eggs, but Peter was horrified and he begged me not to do this. He showed me how I could look at birds' nests without doing harm, identify them, and perhaps make a sketch of what the eggs looked like – but never handle them. We built up a tremendous friendship on that basis; he was a sort of professor figure to me and I followed him like a slave, learning something new every day.

Myself on the south lawn of Palace House c1918 when there was no one to cut the grass

My mother and I returned to Palace House in the early summer of 1918, at about the same time as my father completed another tour of duty in India. I missed the intimacy and cosiness of 'Petersfield' and The Lodge, but now we had two land girls living in Palace House to help with the heavier chores, such as humping logs. Attired in the then familiar Land Army uniform, these 'girls' were somewhat misnamed, as one of them, Mrs Bradley, actually had a daughter, Joan, who was the same age as me. With the home fires burning again, Palace House was tolerably comfortable, and I had the company of someone of my own age. In the village, I made a number of friends through joining the Brownies and later the Girl Guides. One of these was my patrol leader, Ena Crouch. Our activities were organised by Miss Dent who lived in a gypsy caravan at the back of Godfrey's Farm with her golden retriever, grey Persian cat and white hen. She loved entertaining us to tea with cakes and fortune-telling, something she no doubt learned from the forest gypsies.

Companionship of another kind came from the two sons of our head gardener, Mr Aldridge. They were slightly younger than me, but we enjoyed climbing trees and sailing our toy boats in the Mill Dam. They also became my willing accomplices in raids on the apple stores and the strawberry patch. My father's most prized fruit was the nectarine which Mr Aldridge cultivated with great care, with the aim of having something ripe for his Lordship's homecomings. On one occasion he caught me stealing a nectarine and was furious; he took the matter up with my father, but his reaction was simply one of mild amusement! From then on, my relationship with the small and curious-looking head gardener was somewhat strained, but I still enjoyed my forays into his domain.

Sadly, when my governess discovered that I had been playing with the Aldridge boys, she put a stop to our association on the grounds that "they are not the same class as you, Miss Elizabeth". I was very confused, as the only definition of class I knew came from schooling, and since I was educated at home, I couldn't see how a clash of 'classes' could arise. Fortunately, there were still the solitary pleasures of tree-climbing and I prided myself that there wasn't a tree in the garden which I hadn't climbed. The evergreen oaks on the south side of Palace House were my favourites and I would spend hours hidden up among their branches, where no one could find me. The trees also formed an important part of my imaginary world in which I acted out serial plays with myself. The cliff hangers came when I had to go inside for tea, but I would say to myself, "Well, we've got to that point now – just before the Duke of Monmouth got captured at Sedgemoor – I must remember that," and the next time I would go out and carry on. Whilst I was quite happy without companions to play with in the garden, I was not completely without friends of 'the right class'.

In Dock Lane, on the east side of the Beaulieu River, Joyce Anstruther became a great pal of mine. Her mother, Dame Eva Anstruther, was a bit of a mystic and claimed a special knowledge of Pan, ancient Lord of the Forest. She didn't mix much with other Beaulieu people, and her house, Pan's Garden, was very different to anywhere else I had been. Most striking was the very large and curiously ornate chimney piece, which appeared to serve as an altar to Pan, of whom there were statues throughout the garden[8]. Joyce was some eight years older than me, but I was flattered to have her attention and felt safe to tell her about my garden fantasies. She had a wonderful imagination and later wrote under the name of Jan

In the saddle of my horse 'Alice'

Struther, creating the Mrs Miniver character who became so famous during the second world war.

After the Armistice on 11th November 1918, the village gradually returned to its usual routine and welcomed back its surviving sons from the war. Perhaps to honour those who were not returning, it was decided to burn an effigy of the Kaiser on a huge bonfire outside the local pub, the Montagu Arms. I was fascinated as the flames consumed the hated Prussian Emperor, right up to his formidable moustache. For me, it was a slightly frightening experience but I remember holding the hand of my father's new Land Agent, Captain Widnell,[9] who gave this account of the proceedings:

> Watching the bonfire and listening to the speeches was an interested crowd, among whom, in my mind's eye, I can still see a small girl, just turned nine years of age, with lovely, long, well-brushed auburn hair. She was dressed in a bottle green coat and skirt... The little girl's companion was a bright young lady who carefully supervised her small charge. To take the smaller of the two figures first, Elizabeth was the younger of Lord Montagu's daughters by his first wife, Lady Cecil Kerr, whilst the escort was her governess, Miss 'Bunny' Knott, a considerable figure in the household of the day.

But any rejoicing was to be short-lived, as the country would now experience one of the worst plagues of all time – Spanish Influenza. More people died in this epidemic than were killed in the four years of war; indeed very few escaped the scourge. Beaulieu was no exception and many in the village and in Palace House were laid low. At the time, we had my Aunt Mary and Uncle Harry Kidd and their daughters, Betty and Molly, staying for Christmas. This gave rise to a tense undercurrent as I knew my father heartily disliked Uncle Harry. On Christmas Day the church was full of British and American soldiers who were stationed in a local camp, and many blamed them for bringing the epidemic into Beaulieu. Hospital nurses were summoned to look after us day and night, but, when I developed symptoms, my mother tended to me in her own bedroom, holding my hand and mopping my brow.

Dipping in and out of consciousness, I was completely unaware of another crisis taking place around us. My cousin Betty recalls that as Christmas drew to a close, a housemaid put some old decorations on the library fire, which started a fire in the chimney. The clouds of smoke alerted people in the village before we were even aware of what had happened and the estate fire brigade was called out. There was some panic when the fire spread into the roof as it might have been necessary to evacuate the sick, but the blaze was eventually brought under control.

Meanwhile, my condition had been so bad that I wasn't expected to live, but after a few days I came out of it and returned to full health. However, my mother then fell victim to a particularly vicious attack from which she never completely recovered. Ironically, it was my poor mother who was the subject of a huge row between my father and Aunt Mary. She took a poor view of my father's flirtations with other ladies and encouraged my mother (her sister) to take a firmer line. His behaviour had been a worry to my mother for some years, but my father regarded his sister-in-law as a bad influence on his wife and forbade my Aunt Mary ever to return to Palace House!

By now, my father was busy re-opening the Estate and his business interests in London, but following the outbreak of Spanish Influenza, my mother had become a semi-invalid. Her health had been deteriorating for some time and my father would become increasingly irritated when she wasn't well enough to go out with him. The distress she felt made me angry with him, especially as he hadn't been at home much to care for her, but it was eventually decided that she should go to Bournemouth where the sea air was supposed to have restorative effects. So off we went to stay at a small but comfortable hotel overlooking the sea, while my mother's favourite sister, Aunt Margie, was summoned from Scotland to look after her. For me this was a happy time as I was close to my mother and could amuse myself in the park where I sailed my toy boat. But best of all, my Aunt Margie took me to concerts at the Winter Gardens where I vividly recall hearing the violinist Fritz Kreisler and the singer Dame Clara Butt. Unfortunately, my mother was still very weak and as my father considered the atmosphere of a sickroom bad for a child, he arranged for me to go to a boarding school near Hindhead in Surrey. My mother reluctantly had to accept his decision. The fact that my father had never seen the school must have worried her, and my agonised letters during that summer term of 1919 cannot have helped.

Lingholt was probably suggested to my father by Blanche Brucelow, a non-resident governess who tutored me at Palace House from time to time. I liked Blanche and stayed with her family in London but the fact that her sister Constance taught part-time at the school was not in itself a recommendation. Lingholt had no modern sanitation and was in many ways Dickensian; three earth closets among thirty girls, no heating, and some indifferent teachers. Desperately homesick for my mother and constantly bullied, I remember the summer of 1919 as being one of hopeless misery, all except for one unforgettable event. The Government had decided to hold a Peace Day in the summer of 1919, and various celebrations were organised. One of these was to be the lighting of traditional beacons throughout the country, including one on Gibbet Hill, just a few miles from Lingholt. Still desolate and grim, this high hill towered above the flatlands and was obviously a splendid place to light a great bonfire. We schoolgirls stood around it in the dusk and solemnly watched as one by one other beacons flashed like great torches into the night sky. It was a magical moment.

When we broke up at the end of that summer term, I returned to Beaulieu to find that my mother had been moved to a private hospital in Bournemouth. I was allowed to visit her a number of times, and could see

The girls of Lingholt School. I am sitting in the front row

her growing visibly weaker. Then came our last meeting, when she told me in rather gentle Victorian language that she was going to die. She took me in her arms and we looked long into each other's eyes. Then she kissed me goodbye. I left that hospital room never to see her again.

My father seemed to be at Palace House less and less in those late summer weeks. On the afternoon of Saturday 13th September he was out on the Solent in his boat *Wild Duck*, and I was alone in the house when the telephone rang at around teatime. At the age of almost nine, there were few things that frightened me more than the telephone, but, as instructed, I lifted the heavy earpiece and took the message. It was the hospital in Bournemouth asking for my father. I haltingly replied that he was out, but the voice just continued, "Well, will you please tell his Lordship when he returns that his wife passed away this afternoon...".

I put back the receiver, ran out into the garden and sat in my favourite tree by the river. I was stunned by what I had heard, and too sad even to cry. I wondered desperately how I was going to break the news to my father. I think I also dimly realised at that moment that my childhood had gone forever. But the memory of my mother, so sensitive and gentle with her wry sense of humour, elegance and great musical talent, and the unstinting warmth and affection she always gave me, has never faded. She was only 53.

My mother outside the front door of Palace House

*Some time after my mother died, I was sitting alone in the 'Outdoor Room'
(a conservatory on the south side of the house which no longer exists) reading a paper
after lunch. Looking out through the west window, I saw my mother standing outside the
front door: her face was absolutely clear and she was dressed in a familiar mauve suit
with a black seal fur. There wasn't time to reason; I simply dashed out through the
courtyard and onto the grass bank which runs around the edge of the house, but when I
turned the corner she was gone.*

Of all those I have cared for most in my life, I know that my love for my mother was the most enduring and total love of all. I still feel a deep regret that she had to leave me so early, for she was the best friend I ever had.

The following Tuesday, my father and I had the painful ordeal of the funeral, held in a packed Abbey Church. Despite the presence of close family and friends, the mourning was primarily that of a father and his youngest daughter, as the *Hampshire Advertiser* poignantly observed.[10]

> Few restrained their tears and nothing roused their sympathies more than the sight of the bronzed and kindly-faced peer – a fine example of British nobility – and the pathetic little figure (the Hon Elizabeth Scott-Montagu) clad in a simple white dress touched here and there with black, who clasped his hand as they entered and left the church.

I didn't like the dress I had to wear that day, but far more distasteful was the appearance of Arthur Clark-Kennedy, the husband of my sister Helen. She had married this sinister-looking Scotsman three years before[11] in New York and this was the first time we had met him. Walking across the lawn to the church, he grasped my hand and, pulling me along, told me to call him 'Brother Arthur'. I was seething with resentment and took an immediate dislike to him.

My sister was a strange character. At the age of nineteen, she had cut adrift from Beaulieu and announced her intention of 'going on the stage'. My father was horrified, but, in an effort to make the best of a bad job, sent her to the Royal Academy of Dramatic Arts[12]. Helen was bored to tears in this ordered and hallowed institution, so after collecting a sheaf of black marks for unpunctuality and non-attendance of classes, she departed to become a Gaiety Girl with George Edwardes, a leading producer of music comedies. 'Titled Girl Defies Family: Joins Chorus' proclaimed one of the tabloids. Such was the embarrassment for my father in having a daughter on the stage that he tried to persuade Helen to adopt 'Ellaine Cecil' as a stage name, but this was short-lived. After she had appeared in several musicals, my father made one more effort to help her in what he regarded as the right direction, and got her a very small part in *Trilby*, a play at His Majesty's[13]. This was arranged through his friend the impresario Sir Herbert Beerbohm Tree, but again Helen became bored and returned to the chorus line. Up to this point, she had been allowed to collect half-a-crown from my father's office every week, but after deserting *Trilby* they had a terrific row and he cut her off without a shilling.

Undaunted, Helen continued to appear in musicals but in December 1914 the show for which she was rehearsing, *Tonight's The Night,* was cancelled due to the war. Fortutitously for Helen, the production's Actor-Manager George Grossmith arranged for the show to move to New York, complete with its cast. 'Gaiety Company Arrives – Daughter of Lord Montagu one of the chorus girls' reported the *New York Times*[14]. The American stage opened up new opportunities for Helen, who went on to appear in a succession of New York shows. The next, *She's In Again,* was a marital farce in which Helen was cast as a maid. Despite only playing a small part, she was the subject of considerable attention as she was required to appear fleetingly in a bath tub – her bare shoulders exposed! In the summer of 1916, Helen returned to London to appear in *Half-Past Eight* at the Comedy Theatre but the lure of the United States was too great and by October she was back in New York. Here, she joined the chorus of *The Century Girl,* a show co-produced by Florenz Ziegfeld at the Century Theatre with many of the scenes and sequences following the style of his famous Follies.

Despite Helen showing some signs of success in her career, my father was not impressed and my mother was deeply worried. Her letters usually included pleas for money, for she was hopelessly extravagant, recklessly generous, and, as a result, usually deeply in debt. In December 1917, my father paid Helen a visit while passing through New York on his way back to India. He went to see her in a show, but not wishing to hang about the stage door, left a note inviting her to supper at the very grand Hotel Plaza. Helen eventually turned up at the front desk of the Plaza and asked for Lord Montagu. As chorus girls usually dressed outrageously, I imagine the reception clerk misunderstood the situation. "Your *daughter* is here, my Lord – shall I send up some champagne?"

Both my mother and father tried to help Helen, but it was hopeless. My mother even sold her pearls to get money to her, but, not wanting my father to know, bought some imitation replacements. The money quickly went the same way as the rest, and it was only years later when my stepmother went to have the pearl necklace valued that she discovered they were fake!

My sister Helen

The west and south sides of Palace House. The west window of the 'Outdoor Room' is in the stepped section of wall between the front door and the round house on the right

Helen standing alongside her maroon Citroen Six, outside Palace House

Helen's marriage to Arthur Clark-Kennedy on the other side of the Atlantic has always been a bit of a mystery. Family tradition has it that each assumed the other to have money and when, on their wedding night, they discovered that neither had any savings, they parted company never to meet again. However, in a long letter to my father dated 26th May 1917, Clark-Kennedy presented a somewhat different picture. Whilst the words of a man described by my mother as 'hopelessly plausible' have to be read with caution, it would appear that the marriage probably endured for several traumatic months before the couple parted.

Clark-Kennedy explained that his late step-mother was Charlotte Cust, a niece of the 5th Duke of Buccleuch, and that he had regularly visited Bowhill and Drumlanrig. Arriving in New York whilst en-route to his 'mining interests' in Colorado, he claimed to have taken pity on my eldest sister, who he could well have read about in the press. It was certainly true that since arriving in America, Helen had been the subject of a steady stream of newspaper articles, not about her theatrical prowess, but the fact that she, a daughter of an English peer, was on the stage.

Clark-Kennedy possibly saw an opportunity in this for himself but told my father that he wished to save Helen from the scandal of being in the press. It is difficult to believe that his attempts to take Helen 'in hand' were motivated purely by his concern for a fellow family member; however he claimed that his consent to marriage was the only way he could get Helen to promise to give up drinking and behave herself. As anyone who knew Helen would have predicted, the promise, if made at all, was short-lived. At the time, however, Helen must have seen some advantage in the union; perhaps the prospect of having someone to pay her bills. But if Clark-Kennedy hoped for long-term rewards from Helen or my father, he was to be disappointed, as was Helen in him. She told of how he was a compulsive gambler and even reclaimed a mink coat he had given her as an engagement present, so that he might pawn it on their wedding day!

Clark-Kennedy wrote of bringing his bride back to live a respectable life in Britain but, in the event, sailed home on his own. Helen soon exhausted her savings and when an outbreak of influenza caused the New York theatres to close, she ended up penniless. After eight years in the United States, Helen finally returned to England in July 1923. My early memories of her were extremely hazy, but I certainly wasn't expecting the person who stepped off the train at Beaulieu Road Station. My sister was now a peroxide blond and spoke with an American accent! As sisters, we were basically fond of each other but shared few interests. She deplored my liking for serious classical music, and when I went on the stage, my choice of straight theatre was pure boredom to Helen. However, she taught me the facts of life which no one else was prepared to do, and told me some of the best blue jokes I've ever heard. She was naturally musical and had the rare gift of perfect pitch. How she used to suffer when I played everything in E flat major, regardless of the key in which the song was written. Noel Coward allegedly did the same!

A little while after Helen had returned to England, my father decided to get her a divorce in Edinburgh[15], her husband being a Scotsman and divorce proceedings cheaper north of the border. The cruel irony is that Arthur Clarke-Kennedy died the following year[16]. My poor father; if only he had waited a little longer! Meanwhile, Helen tried to resume her stage career, but ended up playing the piano in London pubs and clubs – something she actually did very well. Drink continued to be a great weakness and she lost her driving licence after hitting a policeman in Shaftesbury Avenue. Clambering out to apologise, she excused herself with the words: "So very sorry, officer, but I thought you were a lamp post".

Playing tennis with Silvia Coke on the front lawn

My father outside the front door of Palace House, wearing his favourite old tweeds

4

'Little Feller'

I loved my father dearly and was always fascinated by him, but our relationship was fragmented. For much of the time he darted unpredictably in and out of my life, but there were periods when events forced him to stay put at Beaulieu and be more reflective. The first of these followed the sinking of the *SS Persia*, when we became much closer. There had never been any doubt of his affection for me, and despite my being born a girl, he decided to make the best of a bad job. I became his 'Little Feller', was treated as a boy and, after Helen had been disinherited, became the heir to the Beaulieu Estate.

My father was a remarkable man, and one who, despite his conventional education at Eton and Oxford, would strike out in a thoroughly unconventional fashion. This began when he got a job at the London and South Western Railway's Nine Elms depot so that he could learn about locomotive engineering; he later became a qualified engine driver. After this phase, he was attracted to Fleet Street and journalism, to him far preferable to the drawing rooms of Mayfair and its social life. Of course, this was much deplored by his aristocratic relations, particularly those north of the border.

Despite retiring from the army in November 1919, my father's involvement with a plethora of causes and ventures meant that he had to spend much of his time in London, but he would always return to Beaulieu for the weekend. Very often on a Saturday morning, he would call Captain Widnell at the Manor Office and we would drive 'round the manor' in his 12 hp Delage. This was his way of keeping tabs on his estate, and, as the tour proceeded, my father would deliver a commentary on the people, places, buildings, drains, ditches and wildlife we passed, with 'Widdie' taking careful note of any instructions. Later, in 1923, the author HV Morton visited Beaulieu whilst writing *In Search of England*. Devoting several pages to the estate, he described one of my father's tours of inspection.[1]

> We entered a motor-car. We rushed to a gamekeeper:
>
> "Hallo, Jim!" (Do this; do that!)
>
> We rushed to a boatman:
>
> "Hallo, Tom! How's the baby?" (Do this, and why have you done that?)
>
> We rushed to a farm:
>
> "Hallo, Jack!" (The fence must be mended!)
>
> So we went on over 10,000 acres, "the lord" proving how he loved each one of them: his river with its reedy banks; his bird sanctuary; his heronry; his woods where the deer hide; his fields where the pheasants whirr and bang from the grass; his old house with its roots in the reign of King John; his thatched cottages; his timbered farms. ... All the time his sharp eyes roving over the fields, taking it all in, missing nothing. "When people in London ask me why I don't play golf," he said, "I tell them that I play Beaulieu!" A very good old game too.

For many months after my mother died, I assumed responsibility for looking after my father and did my best to make him feel less lonely. Hartford Hole was his favourite fishing spot, and I would spend hours with him by the river standing motionless as he cast an expert line over some wily, fat sea trout. When he got a bite, he'd play it for a time and then it was my job to get out the landing net. This could be very tricky and on one or two fearful occasions I messed it up and the fish got away. How he shouted at me! Fortunately, I was relieved of these duties when my father's friend Lord Buckmaster gave me my own fishing rod, a splendid one from Hardy's of Pall Mall. Now I was subjected to a different kind of scrutiny as my father made me practise casting on the lawn of Palace House. Placing a half-crown down on the grass, he instructed me to cast at it, directing my line to exactly where I wanted the fly to fall.

I never felt bored in my father's company; he had a wonderful sense of

The Library in Palace House – the only warm room in the house

humour, and, while encouraging my interests in every way, he also tried to stimulate fresh ones. We would often walk through the woods or along the shore, and it was on these walks that I picked up much invaluable nature lore. He had a child-like obsession with streams and drains: whenever he saw water building up where it shouldn't be, he couldn't resist clearing the blockage with a stick and channelling the water in the right direction. He fervently believed in acquiring general knowledge, and after church on Sundays there would be a session of questions and answers. These included in-depth meteorology and reciting, in order, the names of all the railway stations between Brockenhurst and Waterloo. This really was useful as I was regularly sent to London and even Scotland by train on my own. He also encouraged me to read, and another of my Sunday rituals was to sit in his library chair before lunch, reading his weekly column in *The Observer*.

Turning to books, he was amused by my favourites: *Black Beauty*, *The Secret Garden* and of course, *Alice in Wonderland*. I vividly remember my excitement when he announced that we were going to have tea with the *real* Alice! I was thrilled. My heroine apparently lived at Cuffnells, a house near Lyndhurst just a few miles away. When we arrived, we were greeted by a very pleasant and friendly lady, but she was grey-haired, shortish and rather stout. Where was Alice? I asked myself. When I discovered that she had grown up and was now the elderly Mrs Hargreaves, I was shattered!

Although I was still only ten years old, my father now regarded me more as an adult than a child, and treated me accordingly. There were no more nursery meals and I now sat primly at the long refectory table with the grown-ups, meeting remarkable people. For me, this was a happy and most stimulating time, but my attempts at adult conversation must have made me a precocious little horror! I remember chatting easily to such eminent men as Lord Buckmaster, then Lord Chancellor, Owen Seaman, the editor of *Punch* and John Buchan, who had married my relation Susie Grosvenor[2]. Their daughter Alice became one of my greatest friends, and when I went to stay with her family at Elsfield near Oxford, I felt I was stepping into another world. Being a fellow Borderer, I liked to think of John as a kinsman, especially after he talked to me about *The 39 Steps* and *Greenmantle*, into which he evidently put a good deal of his own knowledge and experience. Assuming responsibility for my literary education, he drew up a reading list and would never allow me to leave Elsfield without a book or two – it might be EM Forster, HH Munro or one of his own. Their comfortable Cotswold stone house was lined with books and at weekends it was a favourite meeting place for talented Oxford undergraduates. Of these, I particularly remember Quentin Hogg, later to become Lord Hailsham.

At Beaulieu, my father's very best chum was the genial Sir Thomas Troubridge BT, a charming amateur archaeologist who had taken up residence at Old Ways, half a mile north of Palace House. In the words of Captain Widnell[3], Sir Thomas was 'a large, cheerful and garrulous man, greatly interested in everything in the countryside and knowing an immense amount about it'. A regular shooting and fishing partner to my father, Tommy loved his food, and would regularly come down to Palace House for a second breakfast after his first one at home. His wife Laura was a tremendous listener and became a great confidante to me in my teenage years. An author best known for her book on etiquette, her writing produced enough income to keep them both, which was just as well as the easy-going Sir Thomas rarely turned his mind to work.

Alice Buchan

Guests at Palace House included quite a number of beautiful and glamorous ladies who would float elegantly through the house while I eyed them with suspicion. My father was one of the most gregarious of mortals, and being alone, except when out of doors, was anathema to him. For a while I took it upon myself to protect him from suitors – particularly Eve Cadogan and Madge Limby who were both regular guests – but my hostility to the latter must have been poorly disguised, as one conversation with her outside the clock house ended with Mrs Limby slapping me across the face!

Knowing that my father would be quite a catch for someone, I was neither surprised nor upset when my father told me that he would be marrying again, the lady being a Miss Pearl Crake from London. This development caused some resentment in my mother's family, who felt that the timing of the wedding, less than a year after her death, was a little hasty. To some of the 'old guard', who were loyal to my mother, the Crake family seemed rather bourgeois and not quite good enough, but I took a favourable view of my father's bride-to-be, the Crakes being an honest and healthy addition to a rather effete, rascally old family! Pearl was kind, friendly and pretty and I liked her from the first. And what did she think of me? In her diary, on 7th July 1920, she wrote:

> John brought little Elizabeth to see me at 11.30. She has come up from school for one night especially to see me. She is a perfect darling, red hair, blue eyes and a beautiful complexion - aged 10. We both fell in love with each other. John had to dash off to meetings but she stayed with me till 1. She lunched with mummy and then Mrs Lubbock fetched her and took her to be fitted for bridesmaid, etc.

It was evident to everyone that my father was deeply in love with Pearl; Palace House soon lost its gloom and people in Beaulieu seemed to smile again. She was a very attractive and vivacious young woman with a tremendous sense of duty, which made my father very happy. One of the most touching symbols of Pearl's affection for my father was that she kept and framed the seat tickets from the occasion in Hyde Park when he proposed to her. These sat on her dressing table for the rest of her life.

Their marriage on 10th August 1920 spelled the beginning of a new era for all of us. The service was held at St Margaret's, Westminster, with

Miss Pearl Crake, soon to become Lady Montagu and my step-mother

My father's marriage to Pearl with myself as one of bridesmaids

Daddy Powles officiating. It was a grand affair and even my role in the proceedings was reported:

> The chief bridesmaid will be the 10-year-old daughter of Lord Montagu, the Hon Elizabeth Douglas-Scott-Montagu, who will be followed by six other bridesmaids ... all wearing cream shadow lace dresses over under-dresses of pink ninon, with wreaths of different coloured flowers. They will carry sheaves of pink carnations and natural-coloured ostrich-feathered fans mounted on mother of pearl handles, the feathers of which were a gift from Cecil Rhodes to Lord Montagu... A reception will be held at 25 Belgrave Square, lent by Sir Charles and Lady Seely, and the honeymoon will be spent at Beaulieu.

In addition to all the usual speeches, my father proposed a toast to his best man, Harry Forster, who was about to depart for Australia with my Aunt Rachel, to serve as Governor-General[4]. It would be over five years before we would see them again.

Whilst my father and Pearl enjoyed their honeymoon, I was sent to spend

Picnic in the New Forest. Left to right are Bunny Knott, myself,
Pearl, my father and Jane Clowes, my father's secretary

a fortnight on the *Shenandoah*, a beautiful three-masted schooner which
was being leased by my father's friend Mr Anderson. Escaping all those
who usually supervised my life, this was my first real taste of freedom!
Embarking at Southampton, we sailed west to Dartmouth and then turned
south for the Brittany coast. Crossing the Channel, we sailed into some
very stormy weather and as the last adults dashed heaving for their cabins,
they left a large green bottle behind. Someone said I should take a drink
from it if I felt queasy. By the time I had finished its contents I was
completely oblivious to the storm – champagne was a wonderful antidote!
The days that followed in St Malo were great fun; the grown-ups set off
each morning to tour the area, leaving me to play on the 118-foot boat.
The crew were very attentive and would haul me up the mast in a rope
basket for a bird's eye view of the harbour.

A few days after my return, I was re-united with Bunny Knott. She had
departed rather abruptly after the war – I suspect my father had been
flirting with her and my mother would not have approved – but now Pearl

Bunny Knot and myself ready to run the 'Bran Tub' at the Church fête

encouraged Bunny to pay us visits. I think this suited Pearl, as she knew that I was close to Bunny, and possibly hoped that having a Holiday Governess for me would reduce the demands on her to be an attentive stepmother! On this occasion, Bunny took me down to Bodmin to stay with Lord Vivian, whose daughter Gwennie was about the same age as me.

As Pearl became established at Palace House, she set about sprucing up the place and its inhabitants, making it the well-organised and lively home that it had been before 1914. My father must have offered a measure of resistance, as he loved to wear his oldest clothes and had a positive aversion to pinstripe suits and town clothes generally – I don't think they looked right on him either. Courageously, Pearl decided to take me in hand as well, and on 2nd December I received a visit from her at Lingholt, with my father in tow! Such interest had never been lavished on me before. Her diary entry was as follows:

> John and I started down to Hindhead in the car at 12 and arrived at Morlands Hotel at 1.30 where we had Elizabeth out to lunch. She is looking so well. Then at 3 we went to Lingholt to her school. Miss Batchelor [the Headmistress] and John gave a magic lantern slide lecture on aviation to the girls and boys from two other schools; we then had tea there and I was shown all over the school by Elizabeth.

The Links School

Although she didn't say anything at the time, my stepmother was evidently appalled at what she saw – and probably smelt. The contents of the earth closets were emptied daily into a pit in the garden, and if the wind was blowing the wrong way, the stench was truly awful. Pearl made enquiries, probably with her friend from Romsey, Mrs Wilfred Ashley, and decided that The Links at Eastbourne would be a more suitable establishment for the education of her stepdaughter. Mrs Ashley's daughter Mary was there already. The Links was a small and exclusive school which offered an excellent education and certain other advantages: the headmistress, Miss Jane Potts, had been governess to Princess Alice, Countess of Athlone. In Pearl's eyes this gave The Links considerable social status, but I soon discovered that Miss Potts was a real dragon – I was terrified of her!

Back at Beaulieu for Christmas, I was saddened to find the house without my favourite member of staff. 'Mother Graham' had been employed as housekeeper and companion to me after Bunny departed in 1918, but Pearl decided that she was no longer needed. In large houses, staff often had more time to become friends to the owners' children than their parents, and so when one of them left it could come as quite a loss. Fortunately, I was later able to visit Mrs Graham at Chequers where she was housekeeper for Stanley Baldwin, but this came to an end when she

Fred Norris outside the mill

was dismissed for allegedly stealing the housekeeping money. My father felt terribly guilty as he had given her glowing references, but we knew nothing of her gambling tendencies when she was at Beaulieu[5].

There were changes in the village too. In 1920, Mr Fred Norris, who ran the saddlery in the high street, and was one of my father's favourite tenants, took over the lease of Beaulieu Mill. The tall and rangy miller with his wing collar and dingy coat was never seen without his trademark bowler hat; flour-stained and battered, it was his protection against the many low beams inside the mill. In the high street, a new business was established in an old army hut just south of the Manor Office. This was Mr Wells' bicycle shop, where my father bought me my first bicycle. Like most of the stock range, it was second hand and very beaten up; my father evidently felt it was

Captain Widnell and David Kitcher

good enough for me to learn on but I never got anything better. I even had to save up my pocket money for a pump, basket and bell.

With Pearl came periodic visits from her widowed mother, Mrs Clara Barrington Crake. When my father was courting Pearl, some people presumed that he was making overtures to Mrs Crake, who was more his age, but this was decidedly not the case, and he dreaded it when his mother-in-law came to stay. A fearsome-looking matriarch, she was very demanding and the first to complain when the servants got something wrong. "Darling Mummy" as Pearl always referred to her, was only three years younger than my father, but that was where the similarities ended. Whilst he never stood on ceremony, she expected formality, and where he was unconcerned about a person's background, to her class was everything.

Mrs Crake, myself and Pearl

As my step-grandmother, she never hesitated to tick me off whenever she saw fit, or to pronounce on the suitability of my friends if they weren't quite 'top drawer', as she termed it.

Mrs Crake would visit Beaulieu for indeterminate periods, during which time my father would become increasingly irritable. After a week or so he would start employing tactics to unsettle her. The first of these was to ensure that wherever she was in Palace House, there was always a chilly draught; as soon as she complained, my father would attentively rush off and close the offending door, only to open a window somewhere else. When this failed to work, he would take to carving the meat on the dining table. Positioning the dish near to Mrs Crake, he would attack the joint with great energy, flicking bits of under-cooked meat in her direction. His target was her cleavage, and his aim with the carving knife was surprisingly accurate. Profuse apologies always followed, but my father would always be ready with the time of the next train, should she ask.

Another regular guest was Pearl's younger sister Gladys. Whilst Pearl was a very dutiful stepmother, she was never one to give a motherly cuddle, but Gladys would put me on her lap and show real affection. Unfortunately, her husband Cyril Cubitt with his smooth, slightly condescending tone was not to my father's liking; he put up with him but would make his feelings quite clear to me once we were out of earshot of the rest.

Pearl may have succeeded in bringing her relations into Palace House, but my father would never countenance the giving of cocktail parties or inviting people for drinks. My poor stepmother must have suffered terribly; this was the great cocktail era and she had to go through all those years as a young bride without throwing a single cocktail party! Despite these trials, Pearl's marriage to my father revived hopes that he might finally produce a son, but when she gave birth on 4th October 1921, my father found himself with yet another daughter! Christened Anne, she was followed by Caroline over three years later, on 13th February 1925.

After my first summer term at The Links, I came home an enthusiastic cricketer. I was so keen that between 1921 and 1924 I captained my own team called 'Miss Elizabeth's Eleven'. Mostly drawn from friends who lived on the estate, the team courageously took on other local players, including Edward Cadogan who later played for Hampshire. But even cricket

Myself, aged 12, with my new half-sister Anne

seemed temporarily unimportant when, in July 1922, film director J Stuart Blackton chose Beaulieu as the location for *The Gypsy Cavalier* – an historical drama set vaguely in the 18th century. The male lead was taken by the French boxing champion Georges Carpentier, with the young and striking Flora le Breton the leading lady. Other principal roles were taken by a Miss Mary Clare (after whom my youngest half-sister was later named), Nell St John Montague, Rex McDougal, and the three Maclaglan brothers, then well known for their boxing exploits.

The arrival of these luminaries, not to mention the crew with all their equipment, caused great excitement in our usually sleepy village. Stuart Blackton also arranged for his latest film, *The Glorious Adventure*, to be screened in the School Hall, which had just been converted into a cinema. Among the guests that night was His Highness the Jari Sahib of

Caroline and Anne with my father and Tommy Troubridge (right).
My father affectionately summed up his dearest friend when he said
"Tommy knows everything about everything which doesn't matter!"

Nawanagar, Rangi Singh, complete with two Indian attendants. Whilst this must have aroused considerable interest amongst the audience in the village cinema, such visitors were not so unheard of at Palace House as my father had made many friends in India.

The following two days[6] were undoubtedly the most dramatic of *The Gypsy Cavalier* shoot. Creating a chase scene, the director wanted a stagecoach carrying the heroines Flora le Breton and Mary Clare to cross the riverbed, as if it were a ford. As in all good dramas, the coach was to get stuck mid-way, just as a fictitious dam wall was blown up. A torrent would then engulf the coach with the ladies stranded inside, and our hero Georges Carpentier would come to the rescue. I watched the entire shoot from the Timbrells (the village green beside the river), together with the rest of Beaulieu who lined the river's edge to spectate.

Before the cameras rolled, the sluice gates had been shut to accumulate as much water as possible. Despite warnings from David Kitcher, who was in charge of the sluices, the ferocity of the current was rather more than the crew and actors had reckoned on. When the gates opened, the horses started to panic, and their owner, Mr Frampton of Home Farm, had to wade in and hold them in case they tipped the coach over. Mary Clare's character jumped into the water and the horses were detached, but Flora le Breton had to remain put, for her character, Dorothy Forest, couldn't swim!

The next stage, featuring the heroine's rescue, required a mock coach to be positioned in a deeper part of the river, with the water now up to waist height inside the carriage. Directing from the Timbrells, Stuart Blackton seemed delighted with the torrent, which almost carried the prop and its contents away, but was more concerned with getting his shots than about the welfare of his leading lady. By the time he had finished, the water had virtually submerged the coach; as she clamoured to get out, the expression on Le Breton's face suggested that she was no longer acting. The heroine was in the icy water so long that she fainted, with the result that Georges Carpentier really did have to swim out and rescue her, adding considerable drama to the scene.

Most summer weekends were spent with my father on the river or at sea, and in June 1922 he bought a new motor boat from Thornycrofts, the Southampton-based boat-building firm owned by his friend Tom Thornycroft. Our trips in *Cygnet* – which I was allowed to steer – often involved social engagements with the owners of splendid yachts visiting the Solent: Lord Inchcape in his steam yacht *Rover*, Lord Dunraven with his 170-foot motor yacht *Sona*, and the Duke of Sutherland in *Maori*, to name but three. But the only yachtsman who really interested me was the debonair Guglielmo Marconi, who we took to Cowes so that my father could introduce him as a new member at the Royal Yacht Squadron[7]. His own yacht, *Elettra*, particularly interested me. The 220-foot steamer had a crew of 30 and was fitted out as a floating laboratory, from which he carried out many of his radio experiments. The good-looking Marconi had a house at Eaglehurst near Beaulieu and was a good friend of my father's. He always brought me chocolates and I was fascinated by his Italian accent; not surprisingly, I developed a bit of a crush on him! One day during

Crowds line the river's edge during the shooting of 'The Gypsy Cavalier'

Flora le Breton shortly before her rescue from the mock coach

Guglielmo Marconi in his laboratory on board his yacht 'Elettra'

Cowes Week, he came to lunch with us; most of the conversation consisted of lofty scientific talk, but then my father mentioned a strange experience I had had a few days previously.

It had been a hot evening and I was lying awake in bed when I suddenly became aware of some singing outside my window. Coming from the direction of the abbey ruins, it had the quality of a badly tuned-wireless. The music was slow and repetitive and I wondered if it might be the gypsies who lived in the forest nearby. As the noise became louder, my Pekinese started howling. I knew that the Romanies crept into the gardens at springtime to steal the daffodils, but now I began to imagine that they had come for a more sinister purpose. Confused and a little frightened, I hid with Chinkey under the bedcovers and eventually got off to sleep. The following morning, Tommy Troubridge was having one of his customary second breakfasts with my father. I told him what had happened the previous night and he asked me to sing a little of what I had heard. He immediately recognised it as a Gregorian chant sung by Cistercian monks.

I was very embarrassed at having my story told to the eminent

Relaxing in the ruins of the Chapter House of Beaulieu Abbey

Mr Marconi, but after giving me a long searching look, he smiled: "Look, John, I don't believe in ghosts, but I do believe your daughter's story." Then he gave us his explanation. "When you drop a stone into a pool, it makes concentric rings on the water, and those rings, theoretically, go on for ever. Sound waves behave in much the same manner, so Elizabeth probably managed to 'tune in' to such a wave. She actually heard those medieval monks, not ghosts!" By this time, we were all listening in absolute silence. "In the same way I truly believe that one day we shall be able to discover the secrets of history, and even hear Christ giving the Sermon on the Mount..." I remember thinking this explanation was wonderful and adored Marconi even more!

Not very long after this, my father purchased his first wireless, no doubt encouraged by Mr Marconi. The set, an enormous box with lots of Bakelite knobs and dials, was installed at the bottom of the front staircase in Palace House. At first, one's listening was done through headphones, but a speaker was later added, allowing a number of us to gather round. Pearl complained that the apparatus, surrounded as it was by a clutter of wires, disfigured the hall, but it became a preoccupation of my father and he was always fiddling with it, blaming someone else if it went wrong. I was forbidden to touch it, but later had my own crystal set in the nursery.

Another aspect of my childhood was performing duties with Pearl and my father, who was still grooming me as heir to the estate. These included giving Christmas presents to the children of Beaulieu School at their annual party, presenting prizes at the children's fancy dress party at the WI Hut and attending the Audit lunch at the Montagu Arms. The latter was originally given for tenants in recognition of their rent being paid, but it became a goodwill gesture to the many people on the estate for whom my father felt affection. I was also expected to accompany my father when he went shooting: my abiding memory is of trying to restrain his badly-trained Labrador Bess with one hand whilst struggling to carry the pheasants she had retrieved in the other!

On 1st September 1922, we set off from Beaulieu on a motor trip to Scotland. Holidays of this kind were invariably mixed with business appointments for my father, in which Pearl and I were expected to take an interest. At the time, my father was promoting a scheme to build a London-Birmingham-Manchester-Liverpool motorway, and so our route to the north seemed to be planned around this. We made numerous stops to meet County Surveyors and were even taken on a tour of the Brunner Mond Chemical Works at Northwich[8] to see bicarbonate of soda being made – all very educational! Six days later we finally arrived at Monteviot, where I was to spend a week while my father and Pearl did other things. This was the first time that either my father or I had been there since the death of my mother. Keen to make a good first impression, Pearl flung her arms around my grandmother, little realising that the austere and undemonstrative Marchioness never embraced anyone. The family onlookers were frightfully amused, but once she got over the shock, my granny was very welcoming to Pearl. For me, it was lovely to be back amongst my mother's family in their Scottish home. Now almost 13, and able to play the piano, I was allowed to play the organ in the beautiful family chapel, where I would sit practising for hours. At other times I would spend a happy afternoon with a book on the river, discovering the joys of poetry. Sadly, the summer holidays came to an end all too quickly, and I soon had to prepare myself for school.

Left to right: Aunt Margie, Nigel Gosling (son of my Aunt Victoria), my Grandmother, her second husband Bertram Talbot, myself and my father at Monteviot

Despite all the advantages of a schooling at The Links, there was something stifling about the place. Accompanied by my friend Rachel Ray, I was constantly getting into trouble for unladylike behaviour such as climbing trees or running along the top of walls. Bored with petty rules, I was becoming rebellious and the threat of expulsion loomed. So in the autumn of 1924, my father arranged for me to move to a larger school, St Margaret's, Bushey, where I was to be very happy and never bored. One of my best friends there was Penelope Chetwode, later to become the wife of Sir John Betjeman; another was my distant cousin Silvia Coke whose father[9] lived at Sowley House near Beaulieu. There was never a dull moment when they were around and both of them would visit me in the

Pearl, Anne, Mrs Crake, Bunny Knott and myself in Boldre Wood, 1926

Myself (top left) as a member of the St Margaret's tennis team

holidays. As teenagers, Penelope and I would go on ghost hunts, and on one occasion we sat up all night in the Oak Bedroom[10]; alas, the spirits failed to appear but we enjoyed gorging ourselves on 'bull's eyes'.

My time at St Margaret's coincided with a change in my sporting preferences as cricket gave way to the more ladylike game of tennis. I also loved playing lacrosse and soon got into the school team, eventually becoming captain. My father was so impressed that he gave up a day's shooting – a big sacrifice for him – to see us play against Roedean. It was a cold, wet and miserable day, but he stoically stood on the touchline, the only father there. Fortunately his suffering was not in vain as our team won and I was awarded a big lacrosse champion's badge – I was very proud of that. When not on the sports field, I continued with the piano studies which my mother had started me on. Music was something I seemed to do well at: I got a first class in music theory at the London College of Music and, soon after, started conducting a small orchestra at school.

On 9th January 1926, my father held the first of what would become an annual dinner for his inner circle of friends and family. The Beaulieu Brotherhood was, in the words of Captain Widnell, a 'ceremony of endearment and the kindliest intent, which would shine clearly through an aura of humorous effect'. As Beaulieu had been a Cistercian foundation, my father used monastic titles, making himself Abbot (or Prior), Pearl Abbess, Captain Widnell Scribe, and Mrs Crake (most appropriately) Mother Superior. Other members were termed brothers or sisters. Held in the lofty dining hall of Palace House, the dinner, cooked by Mrs Triggs, consisted of Consommé, Fried Fillets of Sole, Roast Saddle of Venison, Roast Swan, Cold Roast Pheasant, Plum Pudding, Mince Pies and Cheese Straws. This was followed by oath-taking and the issuing of Beaulieu Brotherhood sashes of red and green made by Beaulieu's dressmaker, Miss Preston. It was all a bit of a nonsense, but my father had been through such hell in the war, and this was his way of making up for it with his best friends who shared his love for Beaulieu. The evening finished in the Upper Drawing Room where I entertained the Brotherhood with some of my piano playing[11].

In late August there was great excitement when an archaeological dig in the abbey led to a most unexpected discovery. Three stone coffins had already been uncovered, none of them particularly remarkable, but one of them had a large crack through its base. I remember watching as a metal probe was carefully guided through this opening and continued down for some distance before it stopped with a dull thud. This was repeated several times, and the probe always stopped at the same depth, well below the underside of the stone coffin. A major excavation was then carried out, revealing an oak coffin, all of 7'6" underground.

It was known that royalty and noblemen were buried within the nave of abbeys in stone coffins, but this one was crudely made in wood, and hidden under the stone tomb. The sense of mystery increased when the skeleton's height was calculated to be a 6'3" man[12] and it was found that the skull had a prominent hole in it. This was all the press needed to turn the discovery into a murder mystery and *The Daily Express* of 26th August ran the 'Beaulieu Abbey Discovery' story on its front page. The news prompted large numbers of people to visit the abbey, including Sir Arthur Conan Doyle, who lived nearby in Minstead. The author was intensely interested in spiritual matters and was accompanied by a lady with long flowing clothes, who, as a medium, made her own investigations. Initially unsuccessful, they were rewarded on a second visit when the medium saw a figure with a golden crown rise up out of the ground.

The archaeologists, headed by BG Lampard Vachell, were not able to draw any firm conclusions, but the event was notable in that it was probably the first occasion that publicity had boosted visitor numbers to the abbey, which had been open to the public since 1910. At the time, we regarded this front page splash with a mixture a mild disapproval and faint amusement, but in another 50 years, press coverage would become one of the main ways of promoting Beaulieu as a visitor attraction.

Sitting with my father and his labrador Bess

My father with his long awaited son, Edward

5

COMING OUT

On 20th October 1926, some very important news was brought to me at school, in the middle of a history lesson. I was summoned to the telephone in the school office, where I was told that Pearl had given birth to a boy. To that date, I had been the heir to the estate, but Edward's arrival made me very happy. I knew how much my father wanted a son to inherit his title, and I was very relieved that I would no longer be expected to take on the mantle of responsibility. The following month there was an arrival of a different kind when my father's secretary, Jane Clowes, moved from London and took up residence in the Mill Race[1] at Beaulieu. Unlike her former colleague, Eleanor Thornton, 'Plain Jane' was in no way the object of my father's affections but she was devoted to the family. Her relocation allowed my father (whom she always called 'Chief') to do more of his office work from Palace House, but Jane also became invaluable to Pearl and helped out with various family activities.

The winter term of 1926 was my last at St Margaret's. In the sixth form I had passed the Junior Cambridge exam with a distinction in English and desperately wanted to go on to Oxford, but Pearl's influence prevailed; I was to go to the Villa Brillantmont in Lausanne to learn Domestic Science. I felt rather let down by my father, but he adored Pearl and generally went along with what she said. And so on 17th January 1927, I was taken to Victoria Station where I met the formidable Headmistress, Mademoiselle Heubi, who escorted me with several other English girls over to Switzerland. The months passed and in March my father, who loved touring the Continent in his Rolls, visited me with Pearl. They saw how I was learning to cook the *cordon bleu* way and excelling as a member of the

85

Above: myself with friends at the Villa Brillantmont in Lausanne
Right: enjoying my first visit to Italy
Below: The kitchen at the Villa Brillantmont where we learned to cook

Baba, Elspeth, Billy and Penelope Whitaker at Pylewell Park,
one of the local houses to which I was regularly invited

hockey, lacrosse and tennis teams. Soon after, I went on a two-week tour
of Florence and Venice with several other girls. This was my first real
exposure to Italian culture, for which I quickly developed an appreciation
and a desire to come back for more.

On returning to England in June, I took up tennis with renewed
enthusiasm. Most of the local gentry had tennis courts, and so we were
regularly visiting each other's houses for friendly matches and social
gatherings. My tennis-playing friends included Silvia Coke from Sowley,
Sarah Ryder from Durns, Ruby and Betty Bolton from The House in the
Wood, Dick and Tony Du Cane from The Rings, Arthur Godfrey from
Hides Close, and Pamela Bowes-Lyon from Whitley Ridge House,
Brockenhurst. I also took part in a range of competitions, most notably the
prestigious Bournemouth Juvenile Tournament. When I played in the
New Forest Six, my 'mixed double' partner was Fitz Malmesbury[2]; he
stayed at Palace House when the match was at Brockenhurst, and I stayed

at Hurn Court when the game was at Christchurch or Bournemouth. Once we even played as substitutes for Hampshire!

Before leaving the subject of the local gentry, I cannot resist mentioning the contradiction in attitudes between two different households in Hartford Wood. For as long as I could remember, I knew that Harford House should be avoided at all costs, as the nefarious occupants were unmarried and living in sin! But the neighbouring property, The Rings, was also lived in by an unmarried couple, the distinguished Sir Leslie Scott and Mrs Du Cane, with whose sons I played tennis. Whilst I never challenged the received wisdom of ostracising one family and accepting the other, I did form my own theory. Mrs Du Cane was so exceptionally unattractive that it was impossible to imagine any carnal intent on Sir Leslie's part; he must have accepted Mrs Du Cane and her sons into his household out of pure Christian charity!

After one more term at Brillantmont, I returned to Beaulieu via Paris, where I met up with Bunny. We spent four marvellous days sightseeing and Christmas shopping, but the pleasure of returning home was somewhat dented when Pearl announced that she had made plans for me: I was to be groomed as a debutante for the 1928 season which would culminate with my presentation at Court. This started with a Coming Out dance for me, given at Palace House on 3rd January. The evening commenced with a relatively small dinner for my own house party, after which the 180 guests for the main party started to arrive. 'Darling John, who hates this sort of thing, rose to the occasion so splendidly', noted Pearl in her diary. 'We kept it up till three and everyone said they had enjoyed themselves enormously…'. The proceedings were also reported in the local paper:

> The upper drawing room was converted into a ballroom, and dancing was kept up with the greatest enjoyment from 9.30 pm till three o'clock, the music being provided by Pickett's Orchestra. Supper was served in the beautiful and historic dining hall, and the dance was an enjoyable success, the charming young debutante being the recipient of the heartiest congratulations and good wishes.

Whilst the real Season was yet to come, there was a respite, as my father always made a trip to the South of France between February and Easter. This time, the party included Mrs Crake, a back-seat driver if ever there was one, and my friend Silvia Coke; my father's mechanic, Teddy

March 1928: Relaxing with friends in Valescure (Silvia Coke is centre left)

Stephens, and Captain Widnell followed in a two-seater AC. Pearl, who was pregnant, made her own way by train, accompanied by her maid, Miss Gravestock.[3] Departing from Beaulieu on 3rd February, my father drove us through the wintry French countryside in his beloved open Rolls-Royce Phantom I. A sleek monster painted in racing green, it was fast, reliable and guaranteed to impress the locals. However, we quickly learned that turning up at a hotel in a Rolls strangely inflated the prices. My father eventually overcame this by parking around the corner and sending me off to enquire about room rates in my best schoolgirl French. Since I was not too smartly dressed, the *patron* must have taken pity on me and I always got a good price. Only then did my father bring the car to the front, much to the chagrin of the hotel proprietor!

This was not the only example of subterfuge which took place using this car. On a previous visit to France in August 1924, my father decided to visit Cîteaux Abbey, from where the Beaulieu monks had originated. Since the Cistercian order forbade women to enter the abbey precincts, my father hid Pearl and me in the back of the car and covered us with rugs. Only when the monks had taken him inside did Pearl and I venture out to take a look round the abbey's exterior.

Arriving in Valescure on 11th February, I found the Riviera both tedious and artificial, but was able to play lots of tennis and even won my match in a competition. I also won some money when Pearl took me to the St Raphael Casino, but it was a visit to the cinema which had the most lasting effect on me. The film was the now famous *Napoléon* directed by Abel Gance, by the end of which I had fallen completely in love with the late French emperor. From then on, I avidly collected books, pictures and anything that referred to my hero.

We returned to Beaulieu in mid-March, and now the serious party preparations began. Pearl planned that I should go through all the 'deb' hoops, and, despite my misgivings, even arranged to take a special house in London to be used as our base during the season. Such was the scale of the operation that a lorry with all our luggage was sent from Beaulieu to 22 Egerton Gardens, with Bunny and five servants despatched by train. Arriving on 1st May, I was launched into a seemingly endless succession of carbon-copy dances together with their equally carbon-copy suppers. There were also girls' lunches and teas, including one which Pearl organised for about 40 of my friends. We even had a clairvoyant, which added a little interest to the proceedings!

In preparation for my presentation at Court on 23rd May, Pearl had taken me to the fashionable costumier Zinias to have a special dress made. Following a number of fittings, I was finally able to show it off to the family before leaving for Buckingham Palace. Pearl wrote:

> At 7.45 Mummy, Joan W, Sylvia W, Gladys, Aunt Netty and Miss Samuel and lots of friends came to the drawing room to see Elizabeth and Rachel in their court dress and train. Elizabeth looked awfully nice wearing a white chiffon and silver lace frock, and silver lace train lined with pale green chiffon. She wore a crystal necklace given her by John, and a diamanté bracelet by Rachel, and a white fan by me. Rachel luckily got the 'Entrée' which makes all the difference, so they didn't leave till 8 then went on to be photographed by Alice Hughes.

I was presented to Their Majesties George V and Queen Mary by Aunt Rachel, who, as the wife of a former Governor-General of Australia, had the right to the coveted *Entrée*. This privilege allowed us to enter Buckingham Palace by the side entrance, thereby avoiding hours of queuing in the Mall. Another advantage was that you were presented in the first batch, and could then retire to enjoy the splendid supper especially reserved for the élite. Despite these perks, my father was not in a good mood; he disliked these high society antics and had put on weight since he last wore his scarlet dress uniform – it was uncomfortably tight. After a cursory greeting he turned his back on me to pursue a conversation with Winston Churchill, whose daughter Diana was also making her curtsey. This long and protracted ceremony was a trying ordeal for débutantes, and I was terrified that I would fall flat on my face at Their Majesties' feet, but it all went to plan, and Pearl was evidently delighted:

> Elizabeth absolutely loved her 'Court' last evening and wished she could have it all over again – I knew she would after the first nervousness had worn off. Rachel and two other ladies were asked to be taken into supper by the diplomatic corps and Elizabeth and two other girls found themselves following on in the Procession behind the King and Queen and diplomats, and finally being offered supper by the Turkish Ambassador and Austin Chamberlain!!, which was the most awful fluke and luck for E.

I think that Pearl got more pleasure out of hearing about it than I did taking part; I still shudder at the thought of the pale green chiffon and those uncomfortable ostrich feathers. Despite her determination that I should do the season, my stepmother couldn't actually take part as she was heavily pregnant with Mary Clare, who was born on 9th June. As a result, I had to be farmed out to various hostesses, and make my way in society as best I could. Kindly, Mrs Crake, who lived in South Kensington, did her bit to look after me as well as attending to her expectant daughter.

When going to parties overnight, I was often allowed to take Pearl's maid 'Gravey' (Miss Gravestock), who made a number of my dresses. She was a most devoted ladies' maid, but her dresses hardly equalled the London and Paris fashions which most debutantes were flaunting. Although fashionable weekly magazines such as *The Tatler* featured me as a popular debutante, the serious moon-faced girl with her long red hair in a bun and dowdy home-made dresses attracted few admirers. Indeed, I had to work hard not to become that object of ridicule, a wallflower, who, lacking a partner, would sit forlornly on one of the little gilt chairs scattered around the ballroom. Then came a miracle in the shape of a handsome Coldstream Guards Lieutenant, Evan Gibbs. He seemed to like me enough to ask me to dance at every ball we attended and we became very close. For a while, we were unofficially engaged, but it didn't last. The final event of the Season was on 4th July when Aunt Rachel gave a dance for me at

*All done up in my court finery, but hardly brimming with
confidence or enthusiasm, I pose for a portrait by Alice Hughes*

42 Bryanston Square, the London house of her daughter Dor Pease[4]. On reflection, the season of 1928 turned out to have some good aspects in that I was able to spend time in some really magnificent and historic houses, but I was thankful when it was all over.

Sensing how much I disliked all the society rigmarole, and probably to cheer me up, my father introduced me to an entirely new interest. That summer he bought me my first motor car, a two-seater Morris Cowley. This second-hand vehicle, which cost £100, was not so much a gift as an advance on a legacy I was due to receive on my twenty-first birthday from Lord Northcliffe. In fact, I hardly knew the Fleet Street peer, but he was a long-standing friend of my father, and his wife was a kind and generous godmother to me.

My father, always at the forefront of the motoring movement, insisted that I should have a proper grounding in the workings of the motor car and enrolled me at the Mansions Motor School. Located near Victoria Station, the school was a noisy, dirty place, but it was great fun. I was their only woman student and wore the regulation oil-smeared dungarees and cap. In the evenings, my father would quiz me about what I had done, but the course was thorough and equipped me to do minor repairs and service my own car for years. There was a bonus too, for as my hands and nails were permanently ingrained with black engine oil, I was declared unsuitable for the hated dances and parties.

When it actually came to driving the car, my father tried to act as my instructor, but he was an impossible teacher, so I asked the more patient Teddy Stephens to take his place. More often, however, I was left to practise on my own, using the tracks around Hartford Wood. Being at the wheel of my own car was absolutely marvellous; never had anything given me so much pleasure. At the time, I was also very keen on golf, so one of the immediate benefits of my new-found freedom was to be able to make regular trips to the nine-hole course at Rollestone near Blackfield. Driving back, I dreaded the long dip at Ipers Bridge where I tried to get as much speed as I could down the incline, in the hope that I could avoid changing down on the way up; there was no synchromesh and much as I practised, double-declutching was a hit-and-miss affair!

In August, there was great excitement when Queen Mary decided to pay us a visit – the third in as many years. Their Majesties would come to the

Queen Mary and my father walk towards the Master Builder's House with Prince George and myself following at a respectful distance

Solent each year during Cowes week, staying on the royal yacht, but whilst the King was sailing, Queen Mary preferred to return to the land. My father would collect her from Cowes in *Cygnet* and take her over to Buckler's Hard where she came ashore. On 10th August 1928, she visited us with her son HRH Prince George, Lady Shaftesbury, Sir Henry Verney and Admiral Sir Charles Cust. The local press recorded the event.

> The visit was quite a private one, and beyond the villagers, the Queen's arrival was only witnessed by a few residents who had heard that Her Majesty was expected. They, however, raised a hearty cheer as the party drove off to The House on the Beach[5], and the cheers were repeated when the hotel chef appeared at a side door, and, waving his headgear, 18 inches high, shouted further hurrahs.

> Lord Montagu presented his agent, Captain Widnell, and his bailiff, Mr Kitcher, to the Queen. Some amusement was caused by the appearance of 'Neddy',[6] the Buckler's Hard donkey pet of the village, who wandered down the pathway to the pier and then leisurely walked behind the Royal party as they proceeded to the Master Builder's house. Neddy is the friend of all. He wanders in and out of the cottages as he pleases, and when the presentation ceremony was in progress, made friends with members of the Royal party, who petted and made a fuss of him.

Three Cheers for the Queen as she departs for The House on the Shore

Following lunch at the House on the Shore, the Queen asked to be taken for a drive in the New Forest. The royal convoy consisted of two cars, but Her Majesty did not stand on ceremony and travelled in the front seat of the first car with my father. He put her completely at her ease, no doubt giving the Queen a running commentary on the lore of the Forest, about which he was so knowledgeable[7]. I travelled in the second car with Prince George, who, at the time, was courting 'Poppy' Baring. The Queen did not approve of this liaison, and by insisting that her son should travel with her, she made sure that he was deprived of an afternoon with his lady friend in Cowes. As if this didn't irritate him enough, the Queen then instructed him to jump out and open the gates which we encountered as we drove through the forest. I think she got a sly amusement out of seeing her son used as a runner, and he was furious!

After a drive which included a stop at Ladycross Lodge[8] and the Verderers' Court in Lyndhurst (where my father served on the bench) we returned to Buckler's Hard. Here the royal party took tea at the Master Builder's House which had been converted into a hotel and was run by Mr and Mrs Foster Pedley. But the Prince remained disconsolate; Captain Widnell observed how he sat by the window, gazing mournfully across the river![9]

Queen Mary was notorious for visiting stately homes, expressing a liking for something, and then expecting her host to offer the item to her as a gift. She departed from many a grand house with furniture, paintings and ornaments – a fate we escaped, but only just. During a previous visit to Palace House, she stopped at a portrait of our ancestor Monmouth, which she seemed to admire. "I don't think we have a picture of him in the Royal collection," she said thoughtfully. "Well, Your Majesty, I don't suppose you would," responded my father with a respectful irony. She got the point and, slightly embarrassed, moved on. It would never have done for the leader of a rebellion against her ancestor James II to have his portrait at Windsor!

In November, my father sent me off to Paris with Baba Whitaker, my friend from nearby Pylewell Park. The idea was that we should practise our French and learn about French culture, but my thoughts turned immediately to Napoleon, with whom I was still obsessed. We stayed at the Hotel Imperial, Rue Christophe Colombe, where we were put under the strict supervision of our chaperone, Mademoiselle Caraux. This very worthy lady, dressed entirely in black, took us to all the great sights as well as a wonderful musical show called *Mariette* with Yvonne Printemps; I enjoyed it so much that I saw it three times! But the real attraction was Les Invalides, Napoleon's tomb, which I had yearned to visit ever since I saw the Abel Gance film in Valescure. Baba and Mademoiselle Caraux would patiently wander around outside whilst I stood looking down on the Bonaparte tomb, reverentially communing with my hero. I think my father hoped that the trip would help me to get Napoleon out of my system, but I came back even more in love with him!

July 1928: Pearl with Mary Clare in her christening robes

My friends may have been classified as 'long-haired intellectuals', but I couldn't wait to have my hair cut short – a long fought-for freedom, as my father loved my long strawberry-blonde hair

6

Long-Haired Intellectuals

The London Season left me bored and frustrated: I was becoming dangerously restive and on the brink of becoming a rebel again. This was not helped when Pearl found me reading Dostoyevsky's *The Idiot* and confiscated it on the grounds that it wasn't suitable! She tried to keep me 'on track' by sending me to hunt balls and dreary weekend house parties, but I was like a fish out of water. Fortunately, I could escape to my Aunt Rachel and Uncle Harry, whose friendly rambling house just a few miles from Beaulieu overlooked the Solent. Lepe House was to become a second home to me during the Thirties, just as my Aunt Rachel wished it to be. Life there was very different from that at Beaulieu, and as I was intellectually very curious, I found the company at Lepe both agreeable and stimulating. Ray Pitt-Rivers (Aunt Rachel's younger daughter) became a close friend, as did her two sons Mike and Julian as they got older. Rachel too was the perfect aunt, treating us all as civilised, mature and much-loved human beings.

By now, I was also old enough to choose my own friends, many of whom were characterised by Mrs Crake as 'long-haired intellectuals'. These included the film editor John Goldman and Eton-educated John Heygate who had just written *Decent Fellows*, a sensational novel about his old school. It was considered very shocking. Good-looking in a raffish kind of way, he once came to tea at Palace House with two of his friends, Evelyn Waugh and his attractive wife Evelyn (known as 'She-Evelyn'). At tea, Waugh seemed bored and monosyllabic, whilst his wife and Heygate tried rather too hard to compensate, which contributed little to the success of the visit in Pearl's eyes. His mood was explained soon afterwards when

'She-Evelyn' left her husband for Heygate; a much-publicised elopement which confirmed Pearl's view that I was keeping the wrong company. Fortunately she never knew that I had spent a whole weekend with the guilty couple, living happily in their cottage near Brighton. The cottage was unbelievably cold, damp and primitive, but I have hardly ever enjoyed a weekend more, nor felt so daring and sophisticated!

If my step-mother's tastes were not the same as mine, I certainly inherited my father's love of motoring and developed a real taste for the internal combustion engine. I would drive fast and furiously, ignoring the risks and loving the independence that motoring gave me. I also counted myself lucky to have friends with their own aeroplanes, and greatly enjoyed my hair-raising trips with them. Later, I took flying lessons myself, but after four lessons I had to give up through lack of funds. However, it is odd to remember how freely and happily one could wander around the skies in those days, even over London.

Despite his huge energy and capacity for ceaseless work, my father's health was now in decline. The concerns which my mother felt for her husband over ten years before were now becoming apparent to Pearl. He had been suffering asthma attacks for many years; then, in October 1928, he underwent treatment for an enlarged prostate gland. Doctors advised surgery but this was postponed when he developed pleurisy in his left lung and then caught 'flu. Despite Pearl's optimism, my father was not his usual ebullient self and he underwent strange bouts of melancholy while he waited for a room to become available at Miss Lancaster's clinic in London. Finally, a message arrived saying that he could be admitted on Monday 18th February. It was a cold winter and the weekend before his departure was dominated by problems of frozen pipes. As their own house was without water as a result of the freeze, Tommy and Laura Troubridge came down from Oldways and stayed with us – my father would have been delighted to have their company. Palace House also had problems with burst pipes, but the freeze did allow us the delights of tobogganing and skating. I remember my father watching intently as I skated around the frozen pond in the church meadow, taking it all in, as if he were saying a final goodbye to his beloved Beaulieu.

Lepe House at the mouth of the Beaulieu River, overlooking the Solent

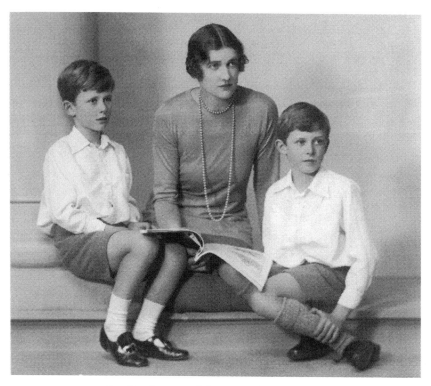

Ray Pitt-Rivers with her sons Julian and Mike

Sunday 17th February 1929: The last photograph taken of my father at Beaulieu, one day before he went into hospital. From left to right are Mary Clare, Pearl, Anne, Edward, my father and Caroline. Despite my father's ill health, Pearl's diary entry recorded a day of considerable activity:

The most divine day, 26 degrees of frost and mixture of St Moritz and Riviera – quite hot in the sun. Little Caroline went to church for first time. She was so good. 1st Sunday after she was 4. The same age as Anne went. Had 20 mins skating on Church Pond before lunch. After lunch John and I went by car as far as Culverley and then walked through snow as far as Beaulieu Road – then back through Ferney Crofts and Culverley – went in to see Mrs Kingsmill Coke, a few minutes. The Rolls joined us there – we then walked home across the Mill Dam. 1st time it has been frozen over since 1895. We came across some interesting old photos taken by John's father that year. Nellie SW dined.

My father's operation at 29 Wimpole Street on 20th February went to plan but we knew that his recovery would be slow. Pearl telephoned daily reports through to the Manor Office at Beaulieu, where bulletins were displayed in the window. On 2nd March, he showed the first real sign of improvement when he asked for the papers and later had a quail for dinner, but complications arose soon after. First he developed bronchitis, then heart problems were diagnosed. Pearl spent long hours at his bedside, with Helen and myself visiting him every few days, but there was no disguising his weakening condition. I was further alarmed to find that he was being cared for by a nurse with a heavy cold. On 27th March, the doctors confirmed that he had developed an abscess of the lung and another operation was deemed essential. Strangely, even at this stage I didn't realise how serious the situation was: Easter was approaching and Helen and I made our way to Beaulieu for the weekend.

On Easter Saturday[1], Helen and I were sitting on the lawn at Palace House surrounded by daffodils, when I noticed my father's secretary, Jane Clowes, walking towards us. As she got closer I could see that she was very distressed. Weeping, she told us that our father had died. We couldn't believe it at first; it seemed impossible that this vital, amazing man who had exuded such warmth and vitality had ceased to be.

A great deal has been written about my father, much of it concerning his role as a pioneer motorist, but he was a many-sided personality who was completely unrestrained by any notion of conventionality. He had a wonderful sense of humour and an almost inexhaustible energy which drove his passion for an extraordinary range of interests. My own most cherished memories are those of a quiet man who loved spending hours fishing by the river, walking through the woods, or at the helm of his motor cruiser in fair weather or foul. Above all, he deeply loved his Beaulieu – and the people of Beaulieu loved him. He left a huge gap in all our lives.

Prior to the funeral[2], my father lay 'in state' in the upper drawing room where people could pay their last respects. As a former monastic chapel, the setting was very fitting and the room was beautifully decorated with white lilies, azaleas and hyacinths. Touchingly, he had inspired such loyalty that there was a queue of tenant farmers wanting to keep a candlelight vigil over their late master, now covered with a large white ensign. It was terribly solemn and impressive. When it came to bearing his coffin to the church, the men of the Estate were almost fighting to volunteer, and they had to perform their task in relays. The funeral service was taken by our own dear vicar assisted by our friend the Rev Tubby Clayton, with the address given by the Bishop of Winchester. Whilst the Bishop and Daddy Powles were the greatest of friends, the Abbey Church was, ecclesiastically speaking, a 'peculiar', and not under the jurisdiction of the diocese. Accordingly, the vicar, who regarded himself as the successor to the former abbots of the abbey, processed after the Bishop. This little display of local autonomy would not have surprised the many Beaulieu people in the congregation, but for those from further afield, it emphasised how Beaulieu remained a little kingdom of its own. My father was laid to rest in the family burial ground within the Abbey Cloisters, alongside my mother who had died ten years before.

The loss of my father left Pearl understandably shattered, but she had four small children to care for, numerous Estate responsibilities and death duties to pay. So she dutifully soldiered on, perpetuating the devotion to service to Beaulieu which she had learned from her late husband. Meanwhile, I made a rather superficial *sortie* into politics, becoming chairman of the local Junior Imperial League, the equivalent of today's Young Conservatives. I did this not out of any profound political conviction but because it was something to do. In the run-up to the election of 30th May 1929, I found myself attending a number of local political meetings and volunteered to do some canvassing in East Boldre, just beyond the Beaulieu manor boundary. Inhabitants of this village tend to see themselves as different from Beaulieu people, and I was soon confronted by Arthur Vardy, the local threshing machine contractor, who attacked me with a torrent of verbal abuse. Mindful that East Boldre was originally a squatters' settlement outside the feudal control of the Montagus, I had learned a lesson – that venturing into a Labour hotbed wearing a blue rosette was inviting trouble!

After the Christmas of 1929, it was agreed that Pearl deserved a good holiday and that I, now aged 20, should accompany her. So on 30th January 1930, we set sail from Liverpool on the *SS Orbita*, bound for Bermuda. The two-week voyage was filled with the usual programme of activities and, being a keen sportswoman, I was elected to the Sports Committee. After two weeks of tennis, ping-pong, bridge and fancy dress parties, we were met at Bermuda by our host in his official launch: Captain Reggie Holt commanded the Royal Navy's base in Bermuda, and he and his wife Evelyn ensured that we were well looked after. With the exception of a few official vehicles, there were no cars on the island and we went everywhere by bicycle. Our activities included swimming, sailing, fishing, golf, tennis, shopping, and – as was always the case in Pearl's company – a good deal of socialising!

After three weeks on this magical island, we boarded the *RMS Arcadian* for New York, and from there took an overnight express to South Carolina. Our destination, Aiken, had been colonised by more than a few millionaires and the townspeople were overwhelmingly social. 'E felt rather out of it...' noted Pearl after I returned from my first dinner party. Despite the beautiful countryside and the old colonial architecture, danger lurked in the most innocent-looking places. The first drama arose when I wandered into a picturesque water meadow; amazed at my stupidity for walking into a snake-infested area, the locals were almost speechless when I returned unscathed. Another excitement arose when I won a fortune at bridge, blissfully unaware of the unusually high stakes played at my table. When we got home, Pearl took a high moral tone and insisted I repay the money. However as this clearly presented certain difficulties, I was able to keep those lovely fistfuls of dollars! I had already been invited to play golf in Aiken, so I spent the money on a smart leather golf bag and a set of all-metal clubs. With my handicap at a respectable 12, I was able to visit the Palmetto Golf Club with the greatest confidence and style!

Our next stop was Washington DC. 'They have not really finished building yet, but in another 50 years it should be a great city...' noted Pearl after we viewed the capital from the top of the Washington Memorial. Finally we returned to New York for five days' sightseeing. We did the usual tourist round, visiting museums, theatres and even night clubs. In 1930, prohibition still cast its long shadow over America, but speakeasies were commonplace and evidently part of the social life of our hosts. Pearl's diary entry for 26th March shows that she would rather have taken me to the respectable Embassy Club dance, but our hosts had other ideas – it all seemed very daring!

We wanted to go to the Embassy dance but Mr Slade wanted us to all go to a 'low haunt' called 'Hollywood' on Broadway. We talked and talked if we should go or not – and would it be raided and should we be shot! And eventually at 11.50, carrying 4 bottles of champagne, we went there. We found a huge low room, thick with smoke and packed with people at little tables. About 20 young girls danced about with hardly a stitch on, one turn hurried on another – some good acrobats and roller skate artists – this show goes on continuously from 12-6! We all wanted to go to the Embassy but that shuts at 1.00. In the end we left at 1.50! We were to have gone to a play and dance after – however it was an experience – but Miss Pell and Miss Seares were very bored. Everyone brought their own wine and were drinking it *sans gêne* all round us – this is a prohibition county!

Once I had returned to Beaulieu, life seemed flat and pointless. I was longing for a real job, but the nearest I could get to it was taking part in some local amateur dramatics. One of these was a pageant of Hampshire History organised by the Women's Institute at Merdon Castle, Hursley Park[3]. Pageants were very popular at the time, and as an enthusiastic WI member, Pearl ensured that Anne and myself took part. Slightly more challenging was a play about the Borgias organised by Alice Buchan. Performing in front of an audience of about 50 in a London town house, I played the wicked duke, dressed in a splendid red velvet tunic and tights! For Pearl, however, amateur dramatics were only a brief diversion from her responsibilities at Beaulieu. Death duties posed a tremendous financial burden on the estate and it was decided that we should let Palace House for the summer to Mr and Mrs Reeve Schley, some well-off Americans. The rental included all the house staff, but Pearl still worried that £50 a week was a bit steep!

With the old summer retreat, The House on the Shore, already let, the family was given the use of Inchmery House on the neighbouring Exbury Estate. This was a kind and thoughtful gesture by the estate's owner, Lionel de Rothschild, who had been a great friend of my father, but I found the move from Palace House rather unsettling. Soon after, however, I received an invitation to spend a few weeks in Austria, and, not wishing to stay the whole summer at Inchmery, I accepted with alacrity. The invitation came from the elderly Baroness de Tuyll who planned to visit her son and daughter-in-law near Salzburg, and to make the journey had hired a private

Approaching the 'Leone' used by Baroness de Tuyll.
The aircraft had a cruising speed of just 110mph

Pearl, Anne and myself in the Dame Alice Lisle episode of the WI Pageant
at Merdon Castle. Pearl took the part of Elizabeth, Lady Montagu,
whilst I played Lady Harvey and Anne, Lady Harvey's daughter

My cousin Ray Pitt-Rivers (stage name: Mary Hinton)
As a working actress she became a role model for me

aeroplane. The party was to include several members of the de Tuyll family, but sensing our anxiety, the Baroness arranged for us to go on a local test flight from Hanworth Air Park, two days before our departure. The aircraft, a De Havilland DH61 called the *Leone*,[4] turned out to be a rickety crate held together, I was convinced, by sticky tape and sealing wax. Not greatly reassured, we returned on 13th August for the long flight to Salzburg. It turned out to be the most hair-raising aeroplane journey of my whole life and included two forced landings, one in a field just short of a Bavarian Alp! Had it not been for the skill of our pilot, Captain Schofield, an experienced aviator of Schneider Trophy fame, I doubt that we would have arrived at all. Needless to say, I made sure that my return journey was by good old-fashioned train.

My host and hostess, the Baron and Baroness de Tuyll, were a pleasant couple in their mid-fifties, whom Pearl and I had met on the ship going out to Bermuda. He was Dutch, she was Argentinian. Their large chalet near St Wolfgang was delightful, but I soon found I had little in common with the young Baroness, who was the most remarkable social snob I have ever encountered. She was in her element in Austria and collected aristocrats as other people collect butterflies. I felt I was back on the society treadmill. Indeed, in Promek Haus, it was easy to believe that you were living in the reign of the Emperor Franz Joseph – everyone was titled! However, the Baroness genuinely loved Austria and the Austrians. "They are all so charming," she would say, "from prince to peasant." Actually, I don't think she had ever met a peasant.

There were of course advantages, as I was able to go to the Salzburg Festival, where I saw operas, concerts, and dramas performed to a standard I had never before known. By now I was fast developing a taste for this German-speaking county, its music, theatre and Baroque architecture, and so when I was invited to repeat my visit the following year, I happily accepted. It was a fatal mistake, and underlined the maxim that one should never go back.

26th September 1930 marked my twenty-first birthday. After a tea party with all the family, a number of my friends arrived to take me to the Empire Theatre in Southampton where we saw the world famous Paul Robeson sing in O'Neill's *Emperor Jones* – an unforgettable performance.

Returning to Palace House, we had a jolly supper party and I made a little speech. The guest list included Baba and Billy Whitaker, Alice Buchan, Ray Pitt-Rivers and Tim Brooke, author of *Man Made Angry*. Then came the crowning of my coming of age, all thanks to Ray's introductions backstage: Mr Robeson and his accompanist Lawrence Brown arrived at Palace House and honoured us with a recital in the Upper Drawing Room.

Music was now becoming an important part of my life. Silvia Coke and her father Tom were both excellent amateur musicians and regularly entertained their guests to performances of chamber music. They also invited professionals and it was at Sowley House that I first heard the wonderful young violinist, Yehudi Menuhin. Even Palace House attracted the occasional big name, such as Dame Nellie Melba, who came to lunch and then gave an impromptu recital in the cloisters, with only the family there to hear her.

Despite having been turned down for two jobs, one on *The Daily Mail*, the other as a courier for Thomas Cook and Son, I continued to try my luck in London. Here the growing-up process included visits to night clubs such as Dougie Byng's The Kind Dragon, and late night parties where the fashionable 'truth game' would be played, a typical question being "are you a virgin?" My innocent upbringing at Beaulieu seemed a world away.

In the New Year of 1931, one of my older friends in Beaulieu, Lady Dent, asked me to be her driver so that she could take her car to visit relations in southern Spain[5]. Win Dent was highly intelligent, cultivated and well-read: a real English eccentric. She exuded a kind of frantic intensity which frightened many people out of their wits. She was a true blue Conservative, and when after a road accident she lost an eye, she replaced it with a collection of glass eyes, including one that featured the burgee of the Beaulieu River Sailing Club.

On boarding the ship for Gibraltar, I discovered that the captain had known my father. More remarkably, the deck steward, Martin, had been one of the crew of the *SS Persia* when it was torpedoed and had been in the same lifeboat as my father. Fortunately, we were no longer under threat from U-boats and our ship, the *Rajputana*, completed her voyage without incident. On arrival in Gibraltar we made our way to Government House, where our stay with Sir Alex and Lady Godley should only have lasted a few days, but I developed acute appendicitis and had to be rushed to the Naval Hospital. This was a strict but marvellous hospital where the Admiralty ruled that every patient should have a daily glass of port with their lunch.

Perhaps it was the magic of Andalusia in the spring that made me lose my head and my heart to the surgeon who had removed my appendix, a swarthy, good-looking Irishman called McVicker. During my convalescence, he would take me for drives deep into the Andalusian countryside, where we would sit romantically among the asphodels in the shade of some ancient cork tree. But it was a star-crossed affair, for he was many years older and married. Although quite innocent, this romantic interlude got me into trouble, and to stop any gossip, Lady Dent decided that we should leave straight away and continue our journey to Granada.

Win Dent's relatives, the Mostyns, lived in an attractive house, the Molino del Rey, which commanded a magnificent view of the distant city and the Sierra Nevada. Mostyn was the Resident Agent for this, the Duke of Wellington's estate in southern Spain. It was a large property which had been presented to the Iron Duke after the Peninsular War by a grateful Spanish nation for freeing them from the clutches of the Bonapartes.

When we left Gibraltar, I thought I would die of heartbreak and cried nearly all the way, but Granada seemed to have remarkable healing powers. I remember being entranced by the Alhambra Palace and the impressive Easter processions, which included the solemn *Silencia* with its strange hooded figures reminiscent of the Klu Klux Klan. So a week later, when I returned to Gibraltar to board a Japanese ship for Southampton, I felt that my troubles were over. But I found I was still in love, and on my return to London, went straight to Aspreys to send McVicker an expensive gold fountain pen costing far more than I could afford. When it came to matters of the heart, I had a lot to learn!

The ruined Chapter House of Beaulieu Abbey

The south and east sides of Palace House

This garden is at its best now. There are masses
of yellow and pink and orange azaleas which
smell deliciously and the rhododendrons are just
coming out — they are wonderful in the forest —
great trees of them — making the air heavy with
a queer bitter sweet scent. They grow wild — oh,
and by the way, I have found lily of the valley
too. There are tulips in the orchard among the
old gnarled apple trees — and wild forget-me-nots
and patches of brilliant polyanthus AND great
long COWSLIPS! The trees are just breaking into
blossom in the orchard — little tight clusters
of red and tender pink — and where the flowers
have opened, a hundred bees are hard at work.

There is something incredibly restful about this
place — such complete peace — a sort of
timelessness — an indifference to one's troubles
outside to make one indifferent to oneself.
London and city life seem so far away and
undesirable; it would be dangerous to stay here
too long. There is something infinitely exciting
in the sight of these old grey stones — old
twelfth century walls — covered with fresh spring
green … The two colours are so fragile — the
pale grey and the uncertain tender green — and
as I sit here I can see a cluster of delicate
pink single roses high up — above the gothic
window — at its highest point. They make a
sentimental contrast. I love this place very
deeply — and part of me is buried here — was
born here — and whenever I return — I feel
myself identified with it in some curious way…

Etienne Amyot

7

TREADING THE BOARDS

A year before my 21st birthday, I had met two people who were to become my dearest friends and have a tremendous impact on my life. Pearl had heard that a nice, artistic lady was renting the Duke's Bath Cottage at Buckler's Hard and to make this new tenant feel welcome, invited her to tea. The lady's name was Robin Rate and with her came a young pianist, Etienne Amyot, who we presumed to be French. When Robin arrived, not dressed in strange garments, wooden beads or sandals, Pearl was clearly delighted at her apparent conventionality. While she chatted to the new tenant, I started off in my best French to entertain the attractive fawn-like young man with his shock of light brown hair. But my conversational efforts were met with a blank stare and dead silence. Then he explained that he didn't speak a word of French; he was a South African from the Cape. We all had to laugh and the ice was well and truly broken.

This meeting led to a return invitation and many others thereafter. Luckily, Pearl hadn't realised that Robin and Etienne were 'living together' and when I first crossed the threshold of the Duke's Bath Cottage, cracking my head on a low beam, I walked into another world – a world which I rapidly adopted as my own. Robin Rate and Etienne Amyot were exceptional people. Robin had been christened Muriel, but it was a name she heartily disliked. She wanted nothing of the social round and had rented the thatched cottage so she could entertain her friends and escape from her rather oppressive family near Dorking. 'Mod cons' were notably absent from the Duke's Bath Cottage, which consisted of only two rooms and a primitive kitchen. However, she could put up quite a number of people using divans, and her skills as a cook were never in question.

The Duke's Bath Cottage on the banks of the Beaulieu River

Robin followed her own tastes in music and conducted The London String Players, a small and excellent string orchestra which she had formed herself. Etienne was also a professional musician. Six years younger than Robin and the same age as myself, he was a gifted concert pianist, obviously destined for a brilliant career. Having studied in Cape Town and then Berlin, he was now performing throughout Northern Europe, giving recitals and taking part in music festivals. I was fascinated to learn that he knew many of the musicians, writers and artists I admired, and quickly realised that we had a lot in common.

I remember my first exhilarating encounter with their friends, most of them highly successful in their own fields. These included Gwen Ffrangcon-Davies, Marda Vanne and Stephen Haggard, all stars from the theatre. Then there was Harry Jonas the painter and Jim Brownell, an ace pilot who would often arrive for the weekend in a small aircraft, landing in a field not far from the house – I found this very thrilling. Best of all, there was always music in the cottage as Etienne had a superb grand piano on which he would play to us in the evenings as we sat around a huge log fire. He would often perform Brahms and Schumann, composers I still associate with that happy period in my life; even after we went to bed the music continued from a chorus of nightingales in the trees.

*Myself (centre) with Gwen Ffrangcon-Davies (left), Marda Vanne (right),
and Robin Rate (below) in the garden of the Duke's Bath Cottage*

Etienne Amyot   *Basil Bartlett*

In London, I met a great friend of Etienne's, Basil Bartlett. Tall, good-looking and brilliant, he was also a baronet and appeared to be very well off. He had come down from Cambridge loaded with honours and was renting an elegant house in Fitzroy Square where he lived a life of great sophistication. Of course I fell in love with him, or thought I had, so when in the summer of 1931 he invited me to drive out to Salzburg with him in his new Chrysler, I was sorely tempted. After all, I was due to go back to the de Tuylls' at St Wolfgang, so it could have been very convenient. But, I asked myself, could I really do something so unconventional, so daring? I was doubtful. I discussed it with Basil and we eventually arrived at a compromise, one that I hoped would save my reputation.

I knew Etienne was in Munich, so I suggested to Basil that he should meet us in Frankfurt, our first stop on the route, and that he should serve as my chaperone from then on. This plan meant that I would have to live dangerously for the first twenty-four hours, which would include the sea crossing, but I was prepared to take that risk. So Basil and I set off for Harwich one day in early August in his gleaming Chrysler, and boarded the ship for the Hook of Holland. Of course we had separate cabins but it wouldn't have mattered as we had an appalling crossing and were both very seasick. Our journey from the coast to the Rhine, and then southwards to Frankfurt, took far longer than Basil had calculated. Driving through one of those dark, brooding, German forests, we ran into a violent thunderstorm and pelting rain. Basil, already weary, was finding driving in such conditions difficult, so I suggested we should stop at the next town or village and take shelter for the night. He replied he could not possibly do that as he had promised me that I would never spend a night unchaperoned. I pointed out that circumstances had changed and if we telephoned Etienne in Frankfurt and told him where we were, that would make it all right. But Basil insisted he was a man of honour who always kept his word. I was quite upset, but filled with respect for this honourable man. So we struggled on, eventually reaching Frankfurt at around midnight.

When we walked into the Frankfurter Hof and gave our names, an army of porters rushed out to carry our luggage, not into the lift, but up an imposing staircase to an equally imposing entrance. With a sweeping gesture, the Head Porter announced that we had been given the Kaiser Suite, and flung the double doors open. And Etienne? Etienne was there all right, reclining on a sofa in the room with a bottle of wine at his elbow. He looked relaxed and very elegant in a heavy silk dressing gown with splendid brocade slippers, but quickly jumped to his feet when he saw us. Basil then gave directions about the luggage, ordered our supper, distributed largesse and the lackeys departed.

The awful moment of truth came when I saw how our luggage had been distributed, with mine left standing in a small room, possibly intended for a valet, while that of Etienne and Basil was in the main room, dominated by an imposing double bed. I had never encountered affection between men before, but now, at the midnight hour, dead tired and completely bewildered, I realised that Basil was intimately attracted to Etienne, and from now on I was the one who would be the chaperone.

It took us four or five days to arrive at the Austrian frontier, by which time I had adjusted to the situation and even accepted it. My two companions helped me here, as they could not have been more charming, although I was always relegated to the back of the car and to small single rooms. Having crossed the frontier, we made our way via Salzburg to St Wolfgang, where Etienne and Basil booked into the famous White Horse Inn. Then they drove me up the hill to Promek Haus where Gypsy de Tuyll had invited us all to tea. In the course of the conversation it emerged that I had travelled unchaperoned from London to Frankfurt where I had picked up a second young man for the rest of the journey. A whole week alone with two attractive young men! The Baroness was horrified and drew her own conclusions. When the boys left for their hotel, I soon realised that my relationship with my hostess, never over-friendly, was now one of open hostility.

She clearly regarded me as a 'scarlet woman', an opinion which evidently got around town as I noticed a remarkable increase in attention and invitations that summer from the local young men – I had obviously gained a new reputation. My stay at Promek Haus was consequently not a happy one, and it was made crystal clear to me that my hostess was longing for me to leave. But the Salzburg Festival was now at its height, and as Basil and Etienne had invited me to several operas and concerts and there was nowhere else to stay, I stuck it out and was amply rewarded by attending some of the most splendid performances of their time.

The Salzburg Festival, the first of its kind, was already world famous and a Mecca for music lovers. That year I had the good fortune to hear Richard Strauss' *Rosenkavalier* with the splendid original cast, including Lotte Lehmann, Elisabeth Schumann, Maria Olzewska and Richard Mayer – an unforgettable experience. The Vienna Philharmonic was under such conductors as Bruno Walter and Wilhelm Furtwängler, so my unease at St Wolfgang was only of minor importance. When I finally left Promek Haus, I was never to see the de Tuylls again.

With the tempo of my social life accelerating, it was perhaps inevitable that I would find myself venturing into dangerous territory. Whilst I had met and mixed with an extraordinary variety of new people overseas, nothing could have prepared me for the encounters which lay ahead over the coming months back in England. Whilst I was never drawn to the sophisticated and decadent coterie of London society, I did get a taste of it when Alec Waugh accompanied me to a party in Regent's Park[1]. As the author of *The Loom of Youth*, Alec had sent shudders of horror down many respectable British spines, but there were no such sensitivities at this gathering. Our host was the art gallery owner and flamboyant 'queer' Arthur Jeffress, and the invitation stated that guests must be dressed in red and white.

The venue was the home of the dancer Maud Allen, who was a great friend of Etienne's. On entering the house, we found our host dressed in angora skin pyjamas and white satin tails with a huge muff of narcissi on his left forearm. The party must have cost Jeffress a fortune; his guests could stuff themselves to the gills with caviar and be sure that if they got drunk, it would be on the very best champagne. Before long, everyone was indeed drunk or stupefied, so we went upstairs to look around the house, but every door we opened revealed cavorting couples. Alec later described the party as a watershed for the bright young things who packed the house that night; it was the end of an era and there would never be anything quite like it again. Intended to be the most decadent of parties, it probably achieved its aim[2], but despite the glitter and the sexual antics of some of the guests, I found it strangely hollow and boring.

Alec escorted me to the party not just as a good friend, but also as an ardent suitor. In his memoirs, he described how he arrived at the party half in love with me and, blissfully unaware of the high drama around him, left three-quarters in love! He was unlike his brother in every way; neither was conventionally good-looking, but while Evelyn still boasted a good head of hair, poor Alec had to suffer early baldness. We remained close for quite a time until he finally accepted that I would never marry him. I remember going to Waterloo on a foggy winter morning to bid him a final goodbye. He was about to leave on the boat train to Southampton, and, surrounded by his trunks and tropical gear, we were tongue-tied and tense. Waiting impatiently for the whistle to blow, I remember thinking that such scenes don't just happen in films, and so ended this rather sad episode in our lives.

The weekend following[3] the red and white party was spent in the apparent security of Palace House. It was the end of November, Pearl was away and I had invited some friends to stay; it should have been an innocent, carefree time but actually marked the beginning of a whirlwind love affair. The romance started happily enough but culminated in near-disaster when I tried to kill myself with an overdose. Fortunately, I came to my senses soon after and called a doctor. Of course, no sensible person would have entered into such a relationship, foreseeing the inevitable outcome, but as I could tell no one, I had no one to advise me. Whom could I tell that the object of my affection was a member of my own sex, a leading West End actress called Marda Vanne? Whom could I turn to? I had never felt more lonely and desperate than during those winter months.

Some instinct told me that work would be the best cure for despair. So on impulse, I applied to become a student at the Royal Academy of Dramatic Arts, like my sister Helen. But first I had to pass an ability test. This meant that I had to learn set speeches from Shakespeare and Congreve, which I would deliver before a small audience from the stage of the main RADA theatre. I sent immediately to one of my new friends, Gwen Ffrangcon-Davies, and asked for help. Gwen was starring as Elizabeth Barrett-Browning in *The Barretts of Wimpole Street*, so it was rather cheeky to ask her, but she reacted wonderfully and coached me so well that I must have amazed my auditioners.

The Principal of RADA was Kenneth Barnes[4] and my first interview with him in the spring of 1932 was a little odd, consisting mainly of awful warnings that I should not follow the example of my sister Helen, who, two decades earlier, had shocked RADA with her behaviour. But her actions as described by Kenneth Barnes seemed quite harmless to me: not turning up for classes, or turning up for them late and then going to sleep. It was alleged that this sleepiness was caused by 'dancing the whole night through', probably in low company – in fact she suffered from a glandular deficiency but this was only diagnosed some time later. Fortunately, I managed to persuade Mr Barnes that I would be a conscientious student, would never be late and would always stay awake, and so he offered me a place[5].

In 1932, life for a student at RADA could be a mixture of intense boredom, seething intrigues and general confusion. But if you were seriously-minded, there was a great deal you could learn and most of this was admirably taught. One of the troubles during my time there was the vast preponderance of girls over men, so it was inevitable that because of my height, I often found myself cast as a man. In fact, in one of our more important productions, I had the intense pleasure of playing the Dauphin in Shaw's *St Joan* – great fun!

Marda Vanne

Portrait by Madame Yevonde

Among my fellow pupils, there were several who would later make their names on the West End stage; they included Frith Banbury, Ida Lupino and Rachel Kempson, who later married Sir Michael Redgrave. There was also a fellow former 'deb', Diana Churchill – a few terms at RADA were still a useful 'filler' for aristocratic daughters between school and marriage! In my own class, I struck up a close friendship with a demure young lady called Vivian Hartley. Vivian was soon to marry the handsome young lawyer Leigh Holman, and not long after she emerged on the West End stage as Vivien Leigh, enjoying her first great success. In Vivien's company, there was never a dull moment – she had charm, wit and an endless store of blue stories.

In October 1932, I made my first appearance on the West End stage in *Well Gentlemen*, a one-performance courtroom drama at the Cambridge Theatre. It was staged by the 'G Club', which occasionally put on plays, and I was offered the part by a friend of Etienne's, Gladys Wheeler. A couple of months later, after the RADA's end of term show, I was contacted by the manager of the Newcastle Repertory Company, Mr McCormack. He had seen something of my work and told me he would like to discuss a possible engagement with his company. I hadn't yet completed the recommended three years at RADA, but a contract – a real job – was something beyond my wildest dreams! Next day, after several cups of tea at the Piccadilly Hotel, I signed a contract with the Newcastle Rep to play the juvenile lead or *ingénue* parts, starting on 1st January 1933 at a salary of £1 a week. I was, at last, an actress, and I was euphoric.

When I told Mr Barnes about this, he was very upset. "But my dear Miss Montagu, it is far too soon to start your career, you have still so much to learn." But I remained firm. He shook his head sadly. "I'm afraid you will live to regret this decision." But I still think I did the right thing, for it is surely better for a young player to appear before live audiences and experience the rough and tumble of the theatre first-hand than to remain in the sheltered climate of a drama school.

Returning to spend Christmas at Beaulieu, I thought my family might have been impressed by the news that I had landed my first job, but I was mistaken. Helen's theatrical career had confirmed everyone's worst fears, and now it seemed as if I might be heading the same way. Undeterred, I started planning my journey north. I would travel in my own car, a turquoise blue Essex 'Super Six' drop-head coupé, very grand but also very second-hand. With wintry weather on the roads, it took me two days on the Great North Road to reach Newcastle, which gave me plenty of time to reflect. It was, of course, wonderful that I was now a professional. There would be no more wandering around not knowing where I was heading and I was determined to make a success of my new career. But I was fully aware of the difficulties ahead, and wondered how, with so little experience of this new and strange world, I would cope.

When I arrived in Newcastle, I went straight to my theatrical digs which had been arranged for me by the management. My landlady turned out to be a voluble, good-natured soul who was proud of her no mod-cons bedsits. The only hot water came from a primitive kettle on the gas ring, but the bed was comfortable and there was always an excellent fire with a scuttle full of coal. My room was wallpapered with yellowing photographs of 'actor laddies', some in make-up and costume, whom I judged, from their fulsome tributes "to the best landlady in the North", had been my predecessors over the years. I paid 5/- a week for this room – a quarter of my £1 a week salary.

The Playhouse, Jesmond, home of the Newcastle Repertory Company, bore little resemblance to a theatre. Perched on the edge of a chasm known as Jesmond Dene, its stage door opened onto a void below which, if a blizzard roared in from the north, whooshed snow straight onto the stage. I will never forget the astonishment experienced by all when, during a performance of *The Admirable Crichton*, Eric Portman and I found large snowflakes drifting across our tropical island. The theatre was an unattractive, squat building but it could accommodate large audiences. For a minor rep, the cast and the performances were generally of a high standard but conditions were definitely substandard. On Saturday nights the Tynesiders would come in drunk and show their enthusiasm by heckling us. Back-stage, there were no dressing rooms and no heating, and if you left your greasepaint out, the rats would eat it. I soon learned to keep mine in a tin box.

As I had joined the company just before the year-end, I found myself involved in the customary New Year's Eve festivities, including a party given at the mansion of a rich industrialist. We had been given strict instructions to enter the house by the tradesmen's entrance; we were, after all, only 'theatricals' and should therefore know our place. Inside the house, everything was of an appalling vulgarity, including a purple grand piano, but our host gave us lots to eat and drink for which I was grateful. My diet in Newcastle consisted mainly of sardines, bread, treacle and fruit, healthy no doubt, but dull. On £1 a week, I couldn't afford much else.

I first appeared before a Newcastle audience on 9th January 1933 in a comedy thriller, *Well Caught*, the first of 14 plays in which I performed at the Jesmond Playhouse. For a southerner accustomed to the relatively mild climate of Beaulieu, the Newcastle winter seemed particularly bitter. I also learned about the other side of life, and more specifically what hunger and dire poverty meant, for this was the era of MP Ellen Wilkinson's Hunger Marches. A young and earnest clergyman wanted to show the world the terrible conditions suffered by these desperately poor people, and had written a film to draw attention to their plight. The cast of the Playhouse were approached to see if we could supply someone to play the lead role, that of a downtrodden housewife. I volunteered, and to make it more convincing, we shot this harrowing tale in the Tyneside slums using real homes, most of them by the river. I remember one poor and ailing family living in a house where every spring tide would flood their living room up to a depth of two feet. This was proved by the slime on the walls, and by the fact that out of a family of eleven, only two pale and rickety children had survived. Scenes like this, and contact with this hitherto unfamiliar world, made me an instant convert to Socialism, and basically a Socialist I have remained, although today it takes a rather different form.

As the routine of the Playhouse consisted of long morning rehearsals, twice-nightly performances and a new play each week, there was little time to study and learn one's lines. As a result, I developed a near-pathological fear of drying up that was to pursue me throughout my stage career. The worst case of this arose when I was right at the front of the stage and suddenly recognised the face of comedian George Robey, who was sitting in the nearest box. As I watched him leaning forward on his stick, with his distinctive eyebrows lowered, I became transfixed, but eventually snapped out of it and carried on. Fortunately it wasn't one of the nights when a talent spotter from London was in the audience.

One of these, the well-known actor-manager Leon M Lion, was about to stage a new play entitled *Beggars in Hell* at his own theatre, the Garrick in the West End. Unknown to me, he visited Newcastle, and not long afterwards I was stunned and very excited to get a letter from him inviting me to an interview in London. The audition involved reading a script on an empty stage while the management whispered among themselves. It was an extremely nerve-racking experience but I was eventually given the part – a quite considerable one – and joined the cast of well-known players which included including Ellen Pollock and Leo Genn. I was deliriously happily and the next day signed my contract at a salary of £3 a week. With this, I was able to rent a flat in Central London at 20 Hallam Street.

Beggars in Hell was a thriller about army life in a garrison town on the North-West frontier of India, and the first night was on Easter Monday, 17th April. Pearl came up to London specially to see me, and brought two bunches of Beaulieu daffodils to the stage door. In the theatre, she was joined by Ray Pitt-Rivers, Marda Vanne, Basil Bartlett, Etienne Amyot and the author Berta Ruck, all of whom had come to see my debut as a professional West End actress. Pearl's diary entry indicated that she approved of what she saw.

> We were all so pleased with her – we could hear every one and she 'made up' so well and looked lovely – and lovely dresses. She takes part of a girl of her own age, in a fort on North West frontier. So odd that her Daddy spent nearly all the war on the NWF. Went to her room afterwards as we all did – heaps of telegrams. After Elizabeth and I went to the producer Mr Leon M Lion's party – he was sweet to E – he put her through her part and is responsible for E's success… I do feel that my darling and Elizabeth's Daddy would be pleased with her success last night – he never minded the stage as a real profession and I feel sure Elizabeth is going to work and make really good.

Unfortunately, Leon M Lion ran into difficulty over his portrayal of an oily Sikh money-lender, a central character in the play. The reviews were all very favourable, but he came in for abuse from what today we would term the 'politically correct', and was under such duress that he had to close the play after a month. Fortunately, I wasn't out of work for long. The glamorous leading lady from *Beggars in Hell*, Leonora Corbett, was engaged to appear in AA Milne's new play, *Other People's Lives* at Wyndham's Theatre and she suggested that I should be her understudy. I soon learnt why understudying has such a poor reputation in the acting

Myself aged 23 as Nadine Browning opposite Frank Harvey in 'Beggars in Hell'

profession. Should the part you understudy be a leading one, you can be sure that they will try to engage some well-known name as a replacement; only in the event of an accident or sudden illness will you be able to take over the part. So you just sit around, night after night, reading, doing crossword puzzles, eating fish and chips and wondering what on earth induced you to take the job. When I first heard that Leonora would be leaving to star in the film of *The Constant Nymph*, I didn't expect to replace her, but miracles do sometimes happen, and I suddenly found myself playing the leading part in *Other People's Lives*. After a few weeks at Wyndham's Theatre, the play went on tour and kept me in employment for some time. This unexpected part helped my career a great deal; managers began to take note and from then on I was rarely 'resting'.

In the autumn of 1933, someone entered my life who was to have a profound and deep influence over me. Her name was Renata Borgatti, an Italian concert pianist whom I met at a lunch held at the Hampstead School of Music. She spoke excellent English, and I immediately sensed that here was an immensely cultured person, with whom I felt a close affinity. There was something about her that was exceptional, thrilling and inspiring. I have always had a truffle-hound instinct for acquiring knowledge and in Renata I saw a professor trying to get out. Apart from being a dedicated musician, her interests ranged over a broad spectrum. She counted numerous musicians and composers among her friends, but there were also painters, writers, poets, dancers, actors, singers and even royalty. In her company, I found myself mixing with these remarkable people and exposed to realms of knowledge which opened up new horizons. Always a trusted confidante, Renata taught me a great deal, and I especially remember her maxim that one should discard all thoughts of self-pity, whatever the circumstances. This, she maintained, was the most destructive emotion of all. I have always tried to follow that advice, and know that it saved my life on at least one occasion.

In early 1934 I was given a part in *Private Room,* with Kathleen Harrison and Basil Radford. The play started at the Croydon Theatre and then transferred to the Westminster Theatre, but before that run was complete I was offered a more important part in a new play by Lesley Storm. Staged at Daly's Theatre[6], *Dark Horizon* had me playing alongside Ernest Jay, Ann Todd and Marda Vanne. Despite the past traumas of our love affair, our paths continued to cross, and an underlying friendship persisted. Writing to her friend Gabrielle Enthoven[7], Marda observed, 'Elizabeth has improved. She works hard and is very keen…'. Not just keen, but on this occasion thrilled to have a lead role with a smart dressing room and my own dresser. Produced by Campbell Gullan, *Dark Horizon* was about a group of people living in London on the brink of war, threatened with

Arm in arm with Leonora Corbett

Myself in 'Private Room'

Marda Vanne and Gwen Ffrangcon-Davies, whilst staying at the Duke's Bath Cottage

bombardment and poison gas attacks. The final curtain saw all the players putting on gas masks, which sent a shiver of horror through the auditorium. The press notices were divided between those who recognised the writing on the wall and others who maintained that Hitler was a good guy. Unfortunately, box office takings were not good and the play closed after two weeks, perhaps because it told audiences what they didn't want to hear. Five years later, I often remembered this play, so prophetic in everything it portrayed except, thank God, the poison gas.

Marda now lived with Gwen Ffrangcon-Davies, her companion for many years, and I occasionally stayed at their house in Cadogan Gardens. Their relationship was one I could not resist describing to Renata[8].

> [Gwen] is extremely practical and a very unselfish and hard worker in the house – cooking and things but if there is a possibility of the cruder more unpleasant things, she becomes impossibly feminine and helpless. M is always taken in by it, for as a matter of fact Gwen is as strong as a horse! But she repaid our efforts by serving a really delectable supper, beautifully cooked. M had changed for the evening into a pair of black trousers, black patent leather shoes, and a Russian blouse and after Dinner she smoked two huge cigars!

In September 1934, I suddenly found myself being asked to take some screen tests for a series of forthcoming films. The most promising of these was *Escape Me Never* which was to star Elizabeth Bergner; I was tested for the part of a society débutante who stole Bergner's lover. I considered myself perfect for the role and so wanted to succeed, but the nervous excitement made me constantly sick and I didn't get the part. After weeks of happy anticipation, the refusals got me very demoralised. Money was also a constant problem: at one point I found myself cut off from the telephone and disconnected from the electricity, with threats of action from at least four firms. Fortunately, the family lawyer and my trustee Charles Nicholl came to my rescue and wiped the slate clean!

Later that year, I did at least secure a part in a BBC radio play, taking the part of Lady Minaret in *The Lady Sally*. This involved seven half-day rehearsals, so that we would be word-perfect for live evening performances on the National Programme on 12th November, and on the Regional Programme the following night. The people I met at the BBC were very friendly and after my usual daytime existence at home, working in the well-heated Broadcasting House really revitalised me. In addition to my main part, I played a Cockney boy, a hysterical woman in a theatre riot, a patriotic cheerer and a member of a crowd, all for a fee of six guineas. The 90-minute broadcast with a cast of 32, plus a 14-piece string orchestra, included several well-known radio actors of the day: Robert Speaight, Norman Shelley, Cyril Nash, Gladys Young, Noel Dryden, John Laurie, and Bruce Belfrage, who went on to become a wartime news reader. The following February[9], producer Peter Cresswell invited me back to play the Duchess of Devonshire in *Berkeley Square*, in which I was cast with Peggy Ashcroft, Carleton Hobbs, Lydia Sherwood and Marda Vanne.

It was around this time that I started one of the most serious love affairs of my life, an affair that was to last on and off for more than a decade. I had agreed to accompany Etienne to a grand lunch hosted by the wealthy Jenny de Margerie, whose husband Roland was First Secretary at the French Embassy. Son of the French ambassador in Berlin, and nephew of Edmond Rostand, creator of Cyrano de Bergerac, Roland was regarded by the Quai d'Orsay as one of the most gifted and intelligent men of his generation in France: he was destined to rise to the top of the ambassadorial tree, which he subsequently did.

Roland was not conventionally good-looking – his thick horn-rimmed glasses gave him a rather forbidding expression – but he had a brilliant mind, great charm and wit and a profound knowledge of literature and the arts which made him irresistible. Not long after our first meeting we became lovers, and during those pre-war years in London, we would often meet clandestinely. From Roland, I naturally learned a great deal about France and how the French thought, lived and loved. In those days I had a tendency to unpunctuality and he would wait for me in Hyde Park, sitting on a bench near his Embassy. I would turn up full of apologies, but Roland, completely unruffled, would assure me that any time spent waiting for me was a benison and a perfect way to relax. Long meetings were the staple diet of diplomats like Roland, and, bored by the proceedings, he would sometimes scribble me a little note. This one written from 10 Downing Street, postmarked 2nd February 1935, is an especially memorable example:

> The PM has a lovely grey curl on his forehead. Anthony Eden is too beautifully tailored for words. Sir John Simon does not show one single hair on his rosy skull – Mr Baldwin smokes an enormous pipe, and looks wise[10]. Happily, I do not see the French because I am sitting on their side of the tables.
>
> It is incredible to believe that all these people are discussing the future of Europe, because one feels that somehow, they are all too near of childhood, because of their youth or because of their age.
>
> Chère Elizabeth, c'est un tel plaisir de s'interrompre un instant, pour penser à vous et à cette fossette dans votre joue gauche, qui pare votre visage d'un second sourire plus secret.
>
> Affectueusement à vous – Roland

In February 1935 I found myself playing one of my ancestors, Mary, Lady Monthermer, in *Viceroy Sarah* at the Whitehall Theatre. An historical drama portraying the rise and fall of the Churchill family, the cast included Barbara Everest, Harcourt Williams and the lovely Irene Vanbrugh, who had known my father. I had appeared in the same play with Edith Evans during a one-week run the previous June, but this was a new production which would run for 157 performances. Being in a long run is not altogether a good thing, salary excepted, as you are out of circulation and

*Roland de Margerie (centre) in the French Embassy with the minister in London,
Roger Paul Jules Cambon, and the Ambassador Charles Corbin*

sometimes even forgotten. For me, however, the main difficulty was the
tedium of performing the same play every night, compounded by my
heartfelt desire to be with Renata, who was touring in Europe. She was an
enormous personality, with so much vitality and zest for life that when she
left, a thick dust settled down on those left behind. I penned a letter to her
almost every day, this excerpt from 7th March 1935 being typical of the
commentary I gave her on my life in London.

> I met Berta Ruck in the bus today; she looks as always quite incredible, but
> one can't help somehow liking her. She can make me laugh, and her books are
> so romantic, so lusciously second-rate, so wildly improbable that they are quite
> refreshing after the self-conscious intellectuality of some of our young well-
> known writers. She was going to a séance, and then to tea with Rebecca West;
> a lovely mélange! Well, darling, I suppose I must go to the theatre, and do a
> spot of work. At the moment, I am wearing a blue aertex shirt and a pair of
> old grey flannel trousers: not the accepted dress of a beautiful young actress
> perhaps; I think I had better change…

Berta Ruck was the Barbara Cartland of her day, who I had met through
Marda. A tall and affable lady of uncertain age, she was handicapped by a

particularly scraggy face. However, she paid me a great compliment when she gave me a cameo role in her novel *A Star in Love*,[11] using my own name.

In mid-March, falling receipts at the Whitehall Theatre prompted the management to organise a rather unusual publicity stunt. We had to perform the entire last scene of *Viceroy Sarah* in Selfridges department store in full costume and make-up, not to mention those awful wigs. To get on stage, we had to walk through the store in full costume as people gaped at us, and then yell at the tops of our voices to be heard above the clatter of tea-cups and old ladies fumbling with their parcels. The stage was very badly lit and the set was entirely strange to us, but in retrospect it was rather an amusing experience!

Fortunately, before *Viceroy Sarah's* long run finished, I was auditioned by CB Cochran for a part in his new play, *Mesmer*. I was ushered into an enormous room with a blazing fire, bowls of daffodils and a sleek black Steinway. The great impresario sat at a huge desk covered with an array of memoranda and telephones while a pageant of theatrical imagery looked down on us from the walls: Yvonne Printemps, Alexander Moissi, Max Reinhardt, Sarah Bernhardt and many others. Despite being somewhat under the weather and having difficulty in remembering what I had done before, I seemed to impress Cochran. "You're a very beautiful girl you know," he told me; I blushed, unutterably embarrassed, but got the part!

Mesmer was the true story of the unorthodox Doctor Mesmer, who cured a girl virtuoso of her blindness. The play was to be directed by the Russian director Komisarjevsky, with his wife Peggy Ashcroft cast as the blind Thérèse Paradis. Stephen Haggard played Mozart and the Austrian-born Oskar Homolka took the title role. Rehearsals started while I was still appearing at the Whitehall Theatre, which demanded an early morning start. However, keen to make a good impression with Cochran, I was always punctual. The set and costumes, all based on 18th century Vienna, were designed by Komisarjevsky who, being of the Russian school, was used to directing the visual aspects of the production as well as the acting. Initially, his quiet and efficient style of direction created an almost religious atmosphere in the theatre. However, as the date for the opening night came closer, the pace of rehearsals intensified, one finishing with poor Peggy Ashcroft in tears, her husband speechless with rage. We began to wonder how the production

ELIZABETH
MONTAGU and
MARGARET GASKIN,
two of the daughters of
"Viceroy Sarah," whose
story will be told in the
new play at the White-
hall Theatre next
Tuesday.

The Duchess of Marlborough played by Edith Evans, with Margaret Gaskin,
Andrea Troubridge, Christine Lindsay and myself as her four daughters

Renata Borgatti

could possibly be ready, as I explained to Renata on 25th April:

> My God, we are rehearsing now with a vengeance; all day, for hours on end, standing, standing, until I think my back has been nicely filleted and my feet have grown to elephantine proportions. I can't ever remember having worked so hard. These Russians! But he is getting great results, and he has so much imagination and keenness in him that it is always interesting and amusing work; it would be impossible to be bored. And how often is it possible to say that in the theatre! He has an amazing sense of pictorial effects and grouping, and his direction of people is extremely clever; he attacks them from a psychological viewpoint and immediately knows if they have the intelligence to accept his direction or not. If not, he leaves them more or less alone. The 'sets' will be most attractive; they are all more or less authentic and have a wealth of detail, such as great marble staircases running round the entire stage, a real fountain with water that really 'founts'; and as for stage effects, what we'll have will be all Komisarjevsky can think of and Cochran can afford! For one, they are building an organ into the theatre for one scene, and God knows what other ambitions they have!

Unfortunately, those ambitions brought problems. These culminated in the grand fountain malfunctioning, with water cascading all over the stage and into the orchestra pit. The show opened on 6th May at the King's Theatre Glasgow, but despite fairly encouraging reviews ('another outstanding study was that given by the Hon Elizabeth Montagu as Baroness Hascrky'[12]), Cochran decided that it was jinxed and cancelled the planned London opening.

I didn't know it at the time, but *Mesmer* was to be my last appearance on the British stage. However, I did undertake some voluntary performances of various classics in Wormwood Scrubbs Prison. Here, the law forbade theatrical performances as they were frowned upon as entertainment, but if we avoided costumes and make-up, and read our parts, it was considered all right. With rehearsals banned, performances tended to get out of hand and serious plays ended up as hilarious farces, to the delight of the very friendly prisoners. Despite the stench of urine throughout the building, I still regard this as some of the best theatre work I did. I often think that perhaps I should have continued with my stage career, which then looked quite promising. I really loved the theatre and have never found a job that gave me more satisfaction, nor a place of work where I was happier.

Approaching Beaulieu village from the south side, along Streeter's Lane

The Montagu Arms Hotel and behind it on the right, the Manor Office

Tonight — so differently — I walked back from the woods, through quiet lanes smelling of wet earth, between bare and dripping hedges and tall naked trees — where the rooks were sitting — high up on the slenderest twigs, cawing and clumsily fluttering. High overhead I heard the wailing flight of some swans going home to bed in the rushes by the river, and an orderly flight of wild duck silent and swift above me… Below me, in a little hollow, lay the village, with smoke curling from its chimneys and a flickering light in some of its windows, little red-roofed houses, higgeldy-piggeldy straggling down to the steel grey river that wound away towards the south through brown silent woods and pale green and yellow marshland to the open sea and the storm… There was a hardly distinguishable greyness that was the Abbey — and so it must have looked a hundred, two hundred, five hundred years ago… I had suddenly a feeling of peace and security, a certainty and at the same time, a doubt, of the permanence of things, and a knowledge that I belong to this place, and it to me, and a great pride that it was so … but it is so difficult to explain … I know that deep down, I really love England and above all, this particular corner of it. This place with its feudal atmosphere and way of living is an anachronism I know; the houses are old-fashioned and insanitary, but it is hard to be a socialist in Beaulieu, and the people are happy and averagely healthy, but I expect such an ideal state of things will soon pass; it must … but I shall always remember and love this peaceful old-fashioned way of living.

Relaxing in the forest – somewhere in Continental Europe

8

New Freedom

The premature end of *Mesmer* gave me the opportunity to make a change in my life. Much as I had enjoyed my two-and-a-half years on the stage, my horizons were fast expanding through the writers, musicians, artists and diplomats I had come to know. Moreover, I was becoming bored with acting, especially in long runs, and wanted the chance to travel more. I had already started to write short stories, and so in May 1935 I made the decision to leave the theatre and pursue a career in writing.

Meanwhile, my car, the Essex 'Super Six' two-seater, which had done thousands of miles, was becoming temperamental. With plans to do more travelling, I decided that the time had come to find a more reliable set of wheels. I knew that the dealers in Great Portland Street (known to motorists as 'The Street of the Forty Thieves') were suspect but thought there would be no harm in taking a look. Then I saw the car of my dreams: a Chrysler 'Straight Eight' with remarkably low mileage. The long, sleek American car didn't have a scratch on it and was for sale at a remarkably modest price. So I threw caution to the wind and that afternoon took delivery of the grandest car I have ever owned. It handled beautifully and I was happy as a bird.

Whilst I had greatly looked forward to showing Renata my swanky new car, by the time we next met, its novelty was wearing off. As I drove her to a concert venue in Folkestone I couldn't help feel a sense of unease, especially as it got dark. Not wishing to alarm Renata I didn't say anything until we arrived safely, but she had felt it too. On the return journey, we experienced the same eerie feeling, and by the time we reached London, we decided I should get rid of the car as soon as possible.

My Morris on one of its trips to Switzerland

I returned to the dealers who sold me the car, and probed into the history of the 'Straight Eight'. One of the salesmen admitted that its previous owners had developed a similar antipathy to the car. He had wondered if it might have something to do with an absurd story that a woman had been found murdered in it! When I tried to sell my white elephant, I could assure people that it had the most immaculate engine but they quickly made their excuses. It was either too long, too wide, too old or too flamboyant. The motor men offered me heart-breaking sums and when I showed my disappointment, they simply became more suspicious. Then I discovered that casting an eye over a new car, however small, had a miraculous effect on the price they were offering for my old one. So I opted to buy a tiny Morris 8, with all the latest innovations; dipping headlights, traffic indicators and a sliding roof! Having paid £132 on hire-hire-purchase, I was given a £60 discount on the value of the fiendish Chrysler, and was finally rid of the haunted motor car!

Despite my closeness to Renata and the continuing attentions of Roland, my departure from the stage seemed to coincide with a number of suitors coming my way. One of these was a British aircraft tycoon called Fred Sigrist. I well remember the strong impression he made on me when we first met. Sigrist was Managing Director of the Hawker Engineering Company and an entirely self-made man, and all honour to him for that. Thin, greying and wiry, he possessed inexhaustible energy and this somewhat compensated for his abrasive manner – he was the sort of man who 'didn't give a damn'. I must have appeared an attractive proposition from every point of view. He knew of my father's connection with, and interest in, engineering, and was most amused by the fact that I was a qualified motor mechanic.

I spent many evenings in his company, usually ending up at the Dorchester where caviar and champagne suppers became the norm. I loved to hear him talk about his work, aeroplanes, and above all, his early life, but apart from these topics, there was little we had in common. His status as a tycoon didn't rest easily upon him and he sometimes showed the kind of arrogance and insensitivity assumed by those not born to riches. I liked him, even admired him, but I knew I could never marry him. So one day quite amicably, we agreed to stop seeing one another, and after the usual champagne and caviar supper, said goodbye, never to meet again.

They say that 'diamonds are for forever', but they played little part in the next strange episode in my life, with the South African diamond millionaire John Bailey. When I first met John he had recently married an old friend of mine from RADA days, Diana Churchill, Winston's eldest daughter. Wishing me to meet her new husband, Diana had invited me to dinner one night at their house in Bayswater. It was a pleasant evening and they seemed happy enough, but some time later I heard that the marriage was on the rocks and that they were about to part. Then, a few months after the *decree nisi* was granted, came a telephone call from John – he wanted me to join him for dinner. I found this a little odd, but as there was no obvious reason to refuse, I accepted, probably out of curiosity. This turned out to be dinner for two, but John behaved impeccably and gave me no reason to suspect what lay ahead.

It cannot have been more than a few days later when John made his intentions clear: perfectly honourable ones too, for he asked me to marry him. I gave him a gentle but clearly negative reply, and was confident that I had settled that problem once and for all. But John Bailey was a tough nut and rarely took no for an answer; I must have presented him with a real challenge. His not very subtle tactics were those of 'storming the citadel', so from that moment on I was literally inundated with invitations, flowers and every kind of attention. I soon had to forbid him to give me expensive presents, threatening to return them forthwith. He then became quite crafty and even managed to persuade me to accept a second hand fur coat which, he said, would protect me from cold winds. Then an attractive piece of costume jewellery followed. It took me a full decade to discover that the stones that sparkled so prettily were, in fact, real diamonds. Similarly, the coat turned out to be Russian Squirrel, a rare and valuable fur.

Whilst Palace House had not been my main home for some years, I usually returned to be with the family at Christmas. Despite its distance from the world I now inhabited, it was still good to go back to my roots, a pleasure I shared with Renata in my letters:

22nd December 1935: It is just five o'clock, and I can just trace the outlines of the trees and the sheer wall of the old house against the deep blue of the sky – the maid is making up my fire and in a few moments she will draw the curtains and bring my tea, and this room will become again a little island of warmth and familiarity. I shall get up after tea, I think it will do me good, and I so want to see the children.

Christmas Eve: The house is silent – the children are asleep – their faces flushed with excitement of the morrow – a stocking filled to capacity – with thrilling bulges and knobs promising some wish prayed to Santa Claus earlier in the evening; they are the nicest children imaginable… I must go to bed; the fire has died down to a dull red glow, and the room is getting cold. It is now long after midnight.

Christmas Day: I still feel exhausted – Edward having woken me this morning at dawn – knowing that I had a football for him and that it was somewhere in my room! So after him scrambled three excessively energetic sisters, all bent on waking me and extracting from me their presents, and soon I was covered feet deep in brown paper, string, children and a dog which came in very muddy from the garden to join the fun! Of course, Edward insisted on playing football

Palace House from across the Mill Dam in winter

in my room, and to rescue my wireless from destruction as well the dressing table etc meant getting up – they thought that was a great joke! I've done my duty today though – twice to church, made lists of the children's presents, folded up miles of brown paper and string, pulled crackers, and eaten a gigantic Christmas dinner.

In the new year of 1936 I decided to join Ray's two sons on a skiing holiday. Aged 19 and 17, Michael and Julian Pitt-Rivers, were both exceptionally good-looking, charming and amusing, and were the only members of my family with whom I had a real rapport. Wishing to avoid the *après ski* crowd, we had chosen a guest house in Ehrwald, a pretty but remote village in the North Tyrol of Austria. Since Ehrwald only possessed one modest hotel and no winter sports facilities at all, it attracted few tourists. Despite my experience of skating on the frozen waters of Beaulieu, skiing was something new to me. Fortunately, the 14-year-old son of my landlady was an excellent teacher and I rapidly developed a passion for the sport. The sensation of flying downhill with the air rushing past my face was incredibly exhilarating and, following the coughs and colds of previous months, I felt incredibly well. Despite the sense of being magnificently isolated in our snowy eyrie, our holiday was punctuated by a series of dramatic dispatches from England. In the space of about a week, we learned that Pearl had become engaged to a Commander Edward Pleydell-Bouverie, then that my dear Uncle Harry Forster had died[1], followed soon after by the King[2]. Then a long telegram arrived from John Bailey. It announced that he and his valet would be arriving on the Arlberg Express the very next day and that I should book rooms for them at the best hotel. While I was puzzled and alarmed, my cousins found it a most amusing prospect.

John duly arrived, accompanied by his valet, an Al Capone look-alike, and a large quantity of luggage including a huge cabin trunk. I led the way to the hotel where John was to occupy their only suite, two small and stuffy rooms. While they unpacked, I went back to the slopes where I skied until we met for lunch. John had changed out of his travelling clothes into his usual London city slicker suit, over which he wore a splendid overcoat complete with sable collar. So when, after lunch, he insisted on accompanying me back to the slopes, he could not have looked more incongruous. He just wanted to see me ski, but in his pin stripe, smart black shoes and overcoat, sliding and slithering in the deep snow, he looked like a stranded whale. To extricate him from this embarrassing situation, I escorted him back to the hotel, promising to meet him later for tea.

This was to be no ordinary tea party. The management had laid on the usual high-cholesterol Austrian spread, but as I munched *Sachertorte*[3], John sat silent and preoccupied. Then suddenly he came to life, fumbled in his pocket for something, and broke the silence. "Do you know why I have come out to Austria?" I was beginning to suspect. Then suddenly he held up a small parcel, wrapped in tissue paper. "I wanted to give you this!" Inside the parcel was a little leather box, which he opened to reveal a ring, set with the largest diamond I had ever seen. He took my left hand and slipped it over my fourth finger. "Now we are officially engaged," he said, willing it to be true. I knew that whatever I said would be wrong, either by giving him false hope or wounding him deeply. So I compromised, agreeing that I would wear the ring while he was in Ehrwald, but when he returned to London he would take it back for safekeeping. But I insisted that we were not officially engaged. He handed over the box, on which my initials ES-M were tooled in gold, and appeared satisfied with the compromise.

Getting ready for another day's skiing with my instructor in Ehrwald

I kept my word, and for two days I walked around in the snow with a diamond nearly as big as a pigeon's egg on my finger. I was deeply relieved when I put it back in its box and saw John leave for London with it in his pocket. My cousins now teased me unmercifully, drawing up a list of the things I could afford to buy them once I became Mrs John Bailey: Julian would have a yacht whilst Michael wanted a smart new car! Of course there were those who thought it was about time I got married and couldn't believe my reluctance when the offers made to me came from such rich men. One of these was Robin Rate, who exasperated me with talk of a successful marriage, money, position and social eminence. "But Robin," I protested, "I am happy now, and happiness is difficult to find, especially if you seek it. Why should I throw it all overboard for something I'm not even sure I want?" Robin was undeterred; she didn't approve of me trailing all over Europe with Renata. Perhaps she was right by worldly standards, but I didn't see it that way, and Renata continued to be my closest confidante.

I was involved with John for nearly eight months, and gradually discovered that he was far from being the strong silent man he appeared to be, but a strange and complex character. On the surface, he was a spoilt playboy; he showed almost no interest in those things that mattered to me, so there was never a mention of music or the arts; in fact he was a complete philistine. But beneath his rugged face, scarred in active service, there was a confused and haunted man, unable to shake off terrible memories of the Great War. Sometimes when we went out for dinner in London, he would order large quantities of sandwiches and then, in his chauffeur-driven Rolls-Royce, take them down to the Embankment where they were hungrily devoured by the down and outs. Inevitably there came the moment when, bracing myself, I told him I would never wear his ring, and there could be no question of marriage. He took it well enough, and we parted and never met again. Not long afterwards I heard he had returned to South Africa and married a childhood sweetheart, and there he died, still relatively young.

Quite soon after parting from John, I saw his ex-wife Diana, who congratulated me on my decision. Where John had been studiously reticent about her, she had no such scruples, telling me what a lucky escape I had had. However, John had been very frank about his feelings for his father-in-law. He seemed to hate Winston, principally because of an awful wrangle over Diana's alimony. Churchill was, in his eyes, a money-grubbing, devious scoundrel and he hadn't a good word to say for him. The Bailey experience left me with a deep aversion to the idea of marrying money. This influenced my decision on three subsequent occasions; very foolishly, I must admit, as in two instances I could not reproach the gentlemen in question for anything worse than overflowing bank balances. Needless to say, my family and friends shook their heads, concluding that I was more than a little eccentric.

Back in London, I applied for an unusual new job at the BBC. Television was still undergoing trials, but in anticipation of its official launch on 2nd November 1936, the Corporation were looking for two new announcers to appear before the cameras. An incredible 1,122 people had applied, but I found myself on a short list of 17 with Jasmine Bligh and Elizabeth Cowell. The audition on the 19th February at Broadcasting House was conducted by the customary committee of BBC executives; the final sentences of their notes, still held in the BBC's archives, summed up their reaction to me.

> Person of enormous vitality and assurance and considerable charm. Very fair hair and pronounced features which would make her totally unsuited for television.

It seemed that my beaky nose let me down; I was disappointed but relieved too, as this meant I was still free and could continue my wanderings on the Continent.

I am always being dragged back to be the person I was four years ago, and when I try to rebel they exclaim rather peevishly — "Dear me, what a difficult child she is — she is getting above herself — we must sit on her for a bit".
13.2.1936

Renata

9

ETRUSCAN PLACES

I had longed to return to Italy ever since my school trip there in 1927, a desire which was re-ignited when I read DH Lawrence's *Etruscan Places*. Italy seemed to spell romance, a happy hunting ground for the eye, the mind and the appetite. When I learned that Renata was booked to do a concert tour in Italy, I tentatively suggested that I might accompany her and to my delight she agreed. We set off in late March, happy to leave the cold, murky north and progress southwards town by town, concert by concert, to Sicily where spring would have already arrived. After Milan, our first stop was to be Rapallo, where Renata was due to appear in a small music festival organised by the great poet Ezra Pound. The unspoilt little town on the Italian Riviera was also home to Renata's father, who lived there in retirement. Guiseppe Borgatti, the famous Wagnerian tenor, had sung in most of the great opera houses of the world, his home base having been La Scala in Milan, where Arturo Toscanini was resident conductor. Still very good-looking, he was now old and blind. "But I still sing," he stressed. Renata immediately went to the piano and to an audience of one he gave the finest rendering of Cavaradossi's great aria from the final act of *Tosca* that I have ever heard. It was very moving, a voice still pure, fresh and resonant, from an old blind man singing like an angel in a darkened room.

During our stay in Rapallo, Renata would spend the mornings rehearsing, while Ezra would take me for long walks to see the beautiful hills and coastline. He was a delightful and enormously stimulating companion, and loved a lively discussion about politics – although with Ezra it was nearly always a monologue. He declared himself a loyal admirer of Mussolini, but when I pressed him on Fascism, his answers were usually

Axel Munthe

woolly. He admitted that he was not very well informed about Hitler, so I tried to tell him all I knew about those Nazis north of the Alps. I spoke of the concentration camps[1], the persecution of the Jews and the burning of books; he appeared to be amazed, although I felt he was not particularly interested.

Happily our conversations were not confined to politics and ranged extensively over literary matters, where the depth and extent of his knowledge were astounding. I soon realised why this strange, ginger-bearded, gruff bear of a man could influence a whole generation of English-speaking writers, including Ernest Hemingway and TS Eliot, who called him *Il miglior fabbro*. Of course I soon fell under his spell and, by carefully avoiding politics, I found a truly wonderful teacher and was constantly aware of the poetry that was in him.

Ezra's festival was a modest success, and after it finished Renata suggested we break our journey and visit Capri for a few days, where we could stay with a lawyer friend of hers. Our host's residence, an eccentric modern structure, looked rather like a piece of Gruyère cheese, but had a breathtaking view of the Faraglioni, those great rocks which defy the sea. I had a preconceived idea of Capri, largely gleaned from Norman Douglas's *Siren Land* and Compton Mackenzie's *Extraordinary Women*. The latter had based his characters on people he knew, Renata being the inspiration for the pianist Cléo Gazay[2], but what I found bore no resemblance to their 'siren island' at all. I saw no 'extraordinary women', no 'flamboyant queers', and it was difficult to imagine any of the rather dowdy, respectable elderly ladies guilty of the proclivities mentioned in these books. Only in the ruins of Tiberius' villa did I detect a strange atmosphere, with echoes of the libidinous behaviour attributed to the island's inhabitants.

The main village was typical of the Italian Mezzogiorno, with a noisy village life centred around the small central square. Once outside this area, neatly paved paths led to trim villas, discreet but not beautiful. There was one resident whom Renata particularly wanted me to meet; he was an old friend and someone she knew I admired. The person in question was Axel Munthe, whose autobiography *The Story of San Michele* was a best seller. Now well into old age, the Swedish-born doctor lived in solitary retirement on Anacapri. According to his book, he was a man of many parts: medic, classicist, bird-lover, and a dabbler in the occult. Legend even had it that he had once been the lover of the Queen of Sweden. However, he decided that Capri was to be his last love, and he would dedicate the rest of his life to rescuing and preserving its unique bird life. Munthe elected to meet us in the courtyard of the villa where we were staying. It would have been impossible not to have been impressed by this tall, gaunt and unmistakably Nordic man in his flowing cloak, wide-brimmed hat and very dark glasses. His appearance might have seemed affected, but his friendly, natural and spontaneous approach soon dispelled that impression.

Munthe invited us to his house nearby, a rather dark and sinister place in a deserted part of Anacapri. His previous home, the Villa San Michele continued as a bird sanctuary, but he no longer lived there. "Sometimes I miss San Michele very much," he said sadly, "but alas, it is not possible to live there any more – my eyes, you see…" and he tapped his dark glasses. Later Renata explained that he was half blind, and that bright light hurt his eyes. After tea, he suggested that Renata should try his piano; it needed playing he said. Meanwhile he would like to talk to me; I was very flattered. He was an excellent conversationalist and we got on famously. Inevitably, I confessed to my great admiration for his book, and he seemed mildly amused and pleased by my comments, which he must have heard thousands of times.

It was only when I referred to his work as a young doctor at the famous Paris hospital, La Salpêtrière, that his mood changed. He sat bolt upright and his face darkened. "I expect you admire how I would sit, night after night, with the dying?" I replied that of course I did. "Well, don't. Do you know why I did that? Not out of compassion, but out of curiosity." He paused and I waited. After a few moments of silence, he continued. "I wanted to catch the actual moment of death, that's what I waited for through all those long nights. Sometimes it would happen, not every time, mind you, but many, many times." Suddenly the room seemed darker. "While they lay there, breathing their last, I would watch and wait until the death rattle stopped. Then very slowly, with a kind of gliding movement, another form would rise several feet above the bed, it was shadowy and indistinct, but identical to the body on the bed. It would hover there for a few moments and then, like the wraith it was, melt away into thin air!" He paused, then smiled disarmingly. "And like you, the nurses and doctors always praised my care for the dying. Of course I did care for them, but my long vigils had quite another purpose…"

He then changed the subject and began to talk about the problems with his eyes and his fear of blindness, but soon reverted to the subject of death. "Don't let me fool you, dear Miss Montagu, for though I may have been an observer of death, seen it and analysed it hundreds of times, I have never lost my fear of it." He paused, and then with a wry smile added, "And I'm still as curious about it as ever!" Suddenly Renata reappeared, and the subject was dropped. We ranged over other incidents in the book, his contact with his native Scandinavian trolls, for instance. He maintained that he had seen them, even talked to them. It was clear that he was a firm believer in the supernatural, but as I listened to him fascinated, I thought I could detect a hint of story-telling.

He then went on to elaborate an interesting theory, that phantoms are rarely known, nor do they materialise, in southern latitudes, since to achieve that state they need cool climatic conditions and a high degree of humidity. Consequently they are relatively unknown in the hot dry parts of the world but are a familiar phenomenon in northern Europe, especially Scandinavia and Scotland. I asked him if he had encountered any ghosts. "Oh yes, many!" he replied, "and Shakespeare did well to choose Elsinore!" Smiling, he continued: "Personally I prefer the company of those trolls who sit on the table beside my bed." I must admit I was compelled to believe him. When we had to leave Munthe in his gloomy house and so alone, we were left with a rather sad impression. This hitherto gregarious man and busy doctor, who clearly loved people, had now shut himself away from life to brood.

We regretted leaving Capri but the train journey south was a benison. Renata was to give five recitals in Sicily, in Catania, Syracuse, Agrigento, Taormina and Messina. Just the names of these legendary towns gave me a thrill. We arrived in Sicily at precisely the right moment, for all around us on the rocky hillsides and in the fields, pink and white blossom foamed, and there were flowers everywhere. It was also the time of the citrus fruit harvest, and, stopping at one small station we were showered with fat, sweet oranges out of a huge basket – a gift from the station master. Another unexpected pleasure was skiing on the slopes of Mount Etna: the snow may have been wet and soggy, but the breathtaking views and the great plume of smoke streaming out of the volcano's fearsome crater just above me made that day's skiing unique.

This Sicilian interlude was my first encounter with classical Roman architecture, and as usual Renata could explain and interpret everything we saw. It was also my first encounter with southern Italian musical taste. Unfortunately Renata, who was born in Bologna and brought up in Milan, had misjudged the expectations of her Sicilian audiences. Bach and Scarlatti seemed acceptable, but Schumann and Brahms were clearly rejected, with Debussy or Ravel leaving them very puzzled. The audiences were consequently rather thin.

The concert tour concluded in northern Italy, in towns whose names rang with history. When we crossed the Straits of Messina, it was a sparkling spring day but the flowering almond trees, mimosa and jonquils of the south now gave way to the foggy, dripping flatlands of the north where nothing seemed to flower but black umbrellas. But the Adriatic did its aquamarine best to cheer us up and the final concert in Fiume proved to be the most successful of the whole tour. The town had a solid musical tradition rooted in its Austro-Hungarian past, so that Brahms, Schubert and Schumann were warmly applauded by a capacity audience. Renata's tour had not been an outright success, but from my point of view it had been a wonderful experience, and one which still remains an amazingly vivid and pleasant memory. In particular, Fiume seemed caught in a time warp, with so much to remind one of Vienna and the Hapsburgs.

Exploring ruins in Italy

Caroline, Edward, Anne and Mary Clare in the gardens at Palace House

10

MEISTERSCHULE

On 2nd May 1936 my stepmother remarried and the cloud of sadness that hung over Beaulieu lifted. Her new husband, Commander[1] Edward (Ned) Pleydell-Bouverie, was brother to the Earl of Radnor and seemed to be just what Pearl needed. She had been desperately lacking a father figure for the children and so Ned, a distinguished naval officer with a commanding presence, was well placed to fill the gap.

The children were now of school age, and it was during my visits back home that I really got to know them. Anne, Caroline, Edward and Mary Clare were all bright, nice-looking and rumbustious children. Whilst there was a bit of an age gap between them and me, the deep affection and kinship I feel for them today has its origins in the games we played in the Palace House sandpit. Perhaps because of our common love of music, I was able to give Edward the time and understanding that he was unable to find from other members of the family. Despite having the title 'Lord Montagu of Beaulieu', he was a very shy and timid child, but he felt able to confide in me. On one occasion he particularly wanted to read me a poem he had written, but fearing that such expressions would be scorned by others, he swore me to secrecy. Only once we had concealed ourselves deep in a secret part of the garden did he read *The Wind* to me. Curiously however, he had no fear of boarding school, perhaps because it allowed him to get away from his governess and a very female-dominated household. On one occasion I remember him being particularly exuberant at bath time; when I asked him why he was splashing about with such glee, he told me it was because he was going back to school the following day!

161

Ned never succeeded in establishing a real rapport with his step-children, least of all myself. However, in the case of Edward, Ned devoted many hours to teaching him to shoot, for which he was grateful as this became a lifelong passion. Of course, being a step-parent is rarely easy, and Beaulieu must have presented considerable problems to Ned, now cast uneasily in the role of Prince Consort. As Pearl attended to 'matters of estate', she made constant reference to what my father used to do, spending many an evening at his old desk in the library. Ned must have felt excluded; as Pearl worked facing the window, he would sit in front of the fire, getting through a decanter of port in one evening. Pearl, discreet to the point of denial, never admitted to his emerging drinking problems.

On the international front, there were problems of an altogether greater proportion following Mussolini's invasion of Abyssinia. In May 1936, the capture of Addis Ababa effectively brought the war to a conclusion, but the League of Nations continued to advocate sanctions which achieved nothing other than to prolong diplomatic discussion. Up to the time of the invasion in October 1935, Italian Fascism seemed less horrific than German National Socialism, but now I began to think differently. On cultural matters, I very much identified with Italians, but when it came to foreign policy my outlook remained staunchly British. Whilst Renata may have been 15 years my senior, I didn't hesitate to give her the benefit of my analysis of the situation. Reviewing my letters, it is evident that my nationality had given me an unrivalled sense of fair play and justice over my Italian friend!

> 23rd May 1936: Because our Empire has been established for a very long time, I am unable to date my letter in the same way as you did yours. Quite apart from the fact that you haven't really got an Empire anyway, as it is recognised by no-one except yourselves. But in England, we regard your caperings and rejoicings with a very tolerant air – realising your Latin irresponsibility and temperamental habits… By the way, should you want any hints – very necessary – as you have certainly no ideas about it all at all on how to run an Empire – just write to us – we know how to do it so well. At the moment, Italy reminds us of a very parvenu nouveau riche – boasting of her new Rolls-Royce and her large country estate – stolen from some poor devil of an aristocrat who was forced to sell by some dirty trick.

24th May: My God, darling, what fun you must be having in Rome – according to the papers, everyone has gone quite crazy – and you have become an Empire etc – and apparently, Mussolini is reported to have said – the greatest Empire there is today. Nonsense – no comparison with ours. There is a distinctly acid flavour in the press here – and I hear there has been some distinct anti-Italian feeling at the Opera – so much so that the tenor – Signor Volpi – refused to take his calls after *Rigoletto* the other night. The truth is of course, that we have got ourselves into rather a mess, and can find no dignified way of getting out of it… I am anti-Sanction – but I DO think that your compatriots are behaving rather absurdly – and not in altogether the best of taste. I admire their victory – but I don't admire the boasting that has followed it.

25th May: I have not nearly exhausted my supply of Anglophobian arguments. Never mind, you have Abyssinia, and that is all that matters, and all you wanted – I imagine – for the moment… Everybody over here is very indignant that the Negus² is coming here – we don't want him a bit, although one paper came out with the story that he has accepted a contract for films and a theatrical engagement!!! Has my letter on the subject of the Anglo-Italian dispute dispersed your feelings about Mr Eden (I agree that *Paradise Lost* IS a good name!) that the poor man is not entirely responsible for sanctions? You and your countrymen are very unfair to him…

26th May: When one looks at the problem with unbiased eyes, one MUST realise that what Italy has done – has violated all the rules. She was so keen on the League – made Abyssinia a member – with a great song and dance about it at the time. Mussolini has always upheld the principles of the League VERY STRONGLY – so his action is very unforgivable and bare-faced. You say that it is very creditable that poor little Italy has dared to face up to the great strong British lion – but as I remember being told at school after a very defiant and bad breach of discipline, it is very easy to disobey. There is nothing particularly brave or original about it.

Despite these strictures and sincerely held views, I really longed to join Renata in Switzerland. Rather than visiting her on an extended holiday, I applied to go to study at Schloss Berg, the advanced piano school where Renata was deputy head. The school received aspiring concert pianists of all nationalities and also offered a haven to well-known artists who came to Schloss Berg to perfect their repertoires before concert tours. The master school was presided over by a really great piano teacher, Frau Anna Hirzel-Langenhan. I had serious doubts as to my prospects as a concert pianist, but

I was determined to try, and asked Frau Langenhan to accept me as a pupil.

Frau Langenhan, then in her sixties, was a great personality, a superb musician and an undoubted genius as a teacher. Exceptionally small and fragile-looking, her appearance was striking. Always dressed in long white dresses which flowed down to her delicate shoes, her fine features were topped by an astonishing *bouffant* of curly dark hair. I had heard so much about Frau Langenhan from Renata, but on meeting her, I soon forgot my nervousness and came to see her as a rather wonderful person: she had great humour, a kind, quizzical smile and the rare knack of making people feel their best, which boosted her students' confidence.

As a young woman she had excelled as a pianist, and recalled playing the Grieg Concerto at the Queen's Hall with Sir Henry Wood. But her promising career had come to an abrupt end when she was struck down by severe arthritis and had to abandon the keyboard. However, she fought back and was soon to become a teacher of international repute. Her first *Meisterschule* was in Munich but she later moved the school to Schloss Berg, deep in the northern Swiss countryside. In Munich, one of the many concert pianists who had sought her help was the young Italian virtuoso Renata Borgatti. Renata was basically self-taught and often undisciplined at the keyboard, but being ambitious was prepared to seek advice. So Renata, the wild and untamed Italian, who could play Debussy and Ravel better than most, went back to school. After several years of intense study with Frau Langenhan, Renata's exuberant performances became much more disciplined and Teutonic; some accused Anna of clipping her student's wings but Renata loved her teacher and adopted Schloss Berg as her second home.

To my delight, Frau Langenhan agreed to take me on as a pupil and I started at Schloss Berg in the early summer. The school was a large and rather odd house near Lake Constance, and on that first morning I decided to walk round the large garden. It was a warm, dry day, and through the open windows I became aware of an amazing cacophony of sound, with snatches of Bach, Mozart, Brahms, Rachmaninov and Debussy, demonstrating that my fellow pupils were hard at it. Each had a bed-sit with a piano where he or she would practise for up to ten hours a day, stopping only for meals. It was a near-monastic life, very simple and

Frau Anna Hirzel-Langenhan and her students. I am sitting on the far right

Me and Renata at Schloss Berg

lacking any form of distraction, but this mattered little to these dedicated musicians. Pupils at Berg could be of any age or nationality and ranged from an eccentric old lady of over seventy to a Swiss girl in her middle teens, but the common language had to be German. Among these, two became lasting friends: Dolly Roedern, a Roedean-educated German, and Beth Tregaskis, a South African journalist who had put her career aside in favour of music.

Some students were already showing remarkable talent and subsequently became leading pianists in Europe. But for Renata, Schloss Berg proved a mixed blessing. She loved teaching and had a natural talent for it, but it meant that she spent less and less time performing so that eventually her career as a concert pianist disappeared altogether. From time to time, there were visits from established artists, who would come to Frau Langenhan for advice. Among these I remember Edwin Fischer, Clara Haskil and Wilhelm Backhaus, and if we were lucky, these artists would play to us in the Concert Hall. Etienne was also an occasional visitor.

Back in Britain, a great drama was unfolding that would seriously disturb our peace of mind: the abdication of King Edward VIII. As winter closed in, we no longer listened to the music around us nor to the lowing of the cows in the fields outside, but sat crouched over an ancient radio, trying to glean from it every sad and dramatic detail. When the final act unfolded with the King's farewell speech on 10th December 1936, we burst into tears, finally convincing the non-British students we really were mad.

Frau Anna Hirzel-Langenhan

Schloss Berg

I remember Switzerland in early autumn as a country
of magic — of mists — colour — of golden days when
the sun shone from morning to night and yet never
seemed too hot to be unpleasant — of fields and
mountains and valleys sprinkled with autumn crocus
and cyclamen — and of a peculiar stillness when you
could hear the cattle bells two valleys away and
the shouts of children hundreds of feet up on the
mountainside. It is a country of exceeding
loneliness — whether winter with its glory of the
snows and dark trees, or spring when one has to
trample down lily of the valley and pheasant eye
narcissus, which smell so strongly they nearly
sicken me. Then summer — the wild flowers, gentians
on the higher slopes, the clearness of the air and
the incredible perfection of the landscape — with
its sudden blinding thunderstorms which roll over
the mountains and eerily echo down the valleys,
leaving a glistening, sweet-smelling and refreshed
world behind them. 15.9.1934

Studio portrait of me by Man Nell

II

Mannequins Mondains

I worked hard at the piano, but it was not long before I had to admit to myself that I would never be a Horowitz. So now I began to reconsider my previous ambition to write, and the possibility of journalism. Having followed widely differing trails across the Continent, I had learnt a great deal about Western Europe and was becoming politically aware. In particular, my journeys to Germany were not simply motivated by a love of music and architecture, but by an intense curiosity to discover all I could about Hitler's Third Reich. There was every indication that we were nearing the brink of conflict, but people still tried to behave as if everything was perfectly normal. Anything unpleasant was quickly brushed under the carpet, encouraged by such august newspapers as *The Times*. Anyone suggesting that the Nazis were up to no good was dismissed as a warmonger.

Fortunately, I could speak from a position of some authority as I had experienced the Nazi regime at first hand. The first time was in a *Bierhalle*, a large beer-swilling restaurant in Berlin, where burly members of the SA[1] were collecting in aid of the *Winterhilfe*[2]. The brownshirted thugs were very aggressive and I replied to their 'request' in less than polite terms. This may have been courageous, but it was also foolhardy. Whilst no further action was taken in the *Bierhalle*, the SA made enquiries about me and soon had a plain clothed investigator at the door of the house where I was staying. I wasn't so much afraid for myself, but realised that my hosts Count and Countess Roedern could be in trouble for their association with a suspect foreigner. I was taken down to the local police station for an interview, but I chose my words carefully and was soon allowed to leave.

The second occasion was when I had a tonsillectomy in Berlin's La Charité Hospital in the spring of 1936. The skill of my surgeon, Professor von Eicken, was not in doubt but his attitude, and that of the hospital staff, seemed typical of the whole Nazi outlook on life and death. After the operation was completed, von Eicken brusquely told me to walk back to my ward. Still reeling from the anaesthetic, I questioned whether I was really up to walking. "*Ist das nicht wiedermal typisch Englisch...*" he sneered, revealing his low opinion of the British. After such a put down, I had no choice but to show him that we were made of sterner stuff, and struggled to my feet. I later heard that von Eicken was one of Hitler's favoured surgeons, and after these and similar incidents I became more and more convinced that the whole Nazi regime was sinister and criminal.

Whilst I still enjoyed visiting my German friends, Paris was my favourite destination. Sometimes I would fly there for the weekend, or travel by ferry and train, but for longer visits I would take my car, not such an easy process when your automobile had to be craned onto the ship! Once the car had been unloaded at Calais, nothing gave me such a feeling of freedom as to be bowling along those straight French roads without any fixed timetable. I loved the anonymity of being in a foreign country, where no-one knew my name, destination or origin. When heading for Paris, I would try to arrive in time to see the city in the late afternoon light, the low sun reflecting on the Seine and the friendly splendour of Notre Dame glowing in a mist of pale rose. Being surrounded by the strange Parisian smells and sounds was very satisfying after the formal and reserved atmosphere of London. The Thames, grey, ruffled and oily, with the tang of rough vitality, seemed as masculine as the Seine was feminine.

Knowing that I could get good meals and reasonably priced accommodation, I would remain in Paris for months at a time. Very often these visits would coincide with Renata's concert engagements in the city, and she would act as a guide and introduce me to her many interesting friends. This arrangement was most advantageous to me, but not to Renata, who had to neglect her work, hardly touching the piano for days on end. We usually stayed among the artists and intellectuals at the Hotel de Versailles on the Rive Gauche. Despite the old-fashioned plumbing, the hotel was very friendly and within walking distance of the great seats of learning.

One of these, the prestigious *Sciences Po³*, had recently enrolled my cousin Julian Pitt-Rivers to study politics. A budding ethnographer, Julian was a very entertaining and stimulating person with whom I was delighted to share my knowledge of the city. One of our regular haunts was the Café des Deux (or the 'Café of the Maggots', as we called it), a favourite place of intellectuals and artists, where I introduced him to some of my friends. This was 'Paris between the wars', the Paris of Picasso and Hemingway, and indisputably the world centre of culture. It was also the city where you could buy banned books by James Joyce, Henry Miller and Radclyffe Hall, which you smuggled home in your sponge bag. But above all, I learnt so much about food, elegance and how to speak French easily and fluently. I was often daunted by the famous people I met, feeling hopelessly dowdy and inarticulate, but with time, I gained confidence and got by.

Renata had many friends among the musicians then living in Paris. One of these was Jacqueline Lévy-Despas, one of the famous *Les Six* group of young French composers. Now married to millionaire André Lévy, head of the well-known store *Uniprix*, she had become a considerable patron of music, financing talented artists such as Renata and the brilliant Czech pianist, Rudolf Firkusny. Jacqueline was a typical Parisienne; petite, gamine and always extremely articulate. Apart from her love of music, her passion was *haute couture*, having Jean Patou's sister as one of her best friends. Jacqueline must have spent a fortune at the distinguished House of Patou, and, given her natural good taste, she would always look tremendously chic.

Before the war, all the really chic clothes came from Paris couturiers: Lanvin, Chanel, Patou and Schiaparelli, but there were a few women who could wear these exclusive clothes without having to pay the usual horrendous prices. These were carefully selected from well-known personalities and socialites, to publicise Patou's much admired and elegant dresses – discreetly of course. When Jacqueline suggested that she might take my wardrobe in hand, I was only too delighted, and she put my name forward to become a *mannequin mondain*. Before long I found myself sitting on one of the spindly gilt chairs in the scented but airless rooms of the salon, undergoing long fitting sessions. The whole experience of having seamstresses busying around me with their mouths full of pins, taking in this, letting out that, filled me with a mixture of fascination and repulsion.

I had no choice in what they made for me, but was delighted to be able to appear in some really chic costumes, much to the amazement of my friends. Once, however, I made the mistake of wearing one of my Patou dresses at Palace House: I don't know whether it was jealousy on the part of my sisters, or a feeling that I was showing off, but it didn't go down well. Paris chic was not for Beaulieu!

When time permitted, Renata and I would make sorties out into the French countryside. The most memorable of these was a trip to Rambouillet, 35 miles south-west of Paris. It was a warm and cloudless summer's morning – perfect for soaking in the beauty of the Ile-de-France – and the happy impression I had of that day has never left me. We were on our way to lunch with the well-known painter Luc-Albert Moreau and his wife. There would be two other guests, one of whom, Renata promised, would be a wonderful surprise for me.

We were the first guests to arrive, and it was quite a time before another car drew into the yard. Two passengers alighted: a slim young man and a rather dumpy, middle-aged woman. Being a fervent admirer of her books, I immediately recognised the woman as Colette, the great French writer. I had pored over numerous photographs and articles about her in the past and could hardly believe my luck. She was just as I expected: a small, rather shapeless person who nevertheless moved with fluidity and assured grace. Her round sallow face was defined by penetrating eyes which twinkled with humour, an exquisitely shaped mouth accentuated by dark lipstick, and a halo of rather frizzy hair.

Before her arrival I had been chatting easily in French, but now I was silenced, feeling shy and awkward. Thankfully, Colette quickly put me at my ease and soon I found myself talking animatedly to my neighbour, the rather attractive Maurice Goudeket. Suddenly Renata jumped up from the table and announced that we should go out and shut the sunroof on my car, as there was thunder in the air. Puzzled, I followed Renata out into the yard. There was not a cloud in the sky but Renata was clearly upset. "Are you mad? Flirting like that with Colette's husband!" It was my turn to be upset. "I was not flirting, and anyway I had no idea that M Goudeket was Colette's husband. Why didn't you warn me?" Renata looked exasperated: "Oh you English!"

Colette with two of her cats

I followed her back into the house, and glancing apprehensively at Colette, was met with a ravishing smile and an easily detectable twinkle. Colette knew Renata of old and had guessed what had happened; from then on she seemed to pay me particular attention. The conversation somehow turned to the supernatural and she listened fascinated to my tales of ghosts at Beaulieu. Then the talk turned to cats, a recurring subject in her writing, and I learned to my delight that we shared a love of the whole feline race. I shall always remember looking at her as she exuded vitality, charm and charisma, and thinking "she is a cat" – she really is *La Chatte!*

Toscanini rehearsing the BBC Symphony Orchestra

12

THE MAESTRO AND FAMILY

I was now spending a good deal of my time on the Continent, but living overseas on only £23 6s 8d a month was sometimes expecting too much of my allowance from the family trust fund. From time to time, I would therefore return to England to pay my bills and do some work. Despite my long absences, I still had many friends in London, not least my cousin Ray. An actress and yachtswoman with exceptional good looks, she was a real sheet anchor, always trying to steer me safely through the troubled waters of my youth. After I gave up my flat at 20 Hallam Street, she allowed me to stay with her in Chelsea and 53 Bury Walk became my London base.

Renata had been performing at the BBC and it was through her that I met the Corporation's Music Executive, Owen Mase, who later became a good friend. At the time he was busy preparing for the first of the BBC's great Toscanini seasons. It was to form part of the London Music Festival, and by some miracle I managed to get in on the act, probably through Renata being Toscanini's goddaughter. Early in the summer of 1937, I was appointed Personal Assistant to the Toscanini family, an unpaid job, but one that carried with it the tremendous bonus of attending all the orchestra rehearsals.

Toscanini attracted huge interest and his six concerts featuring the BBC Symphony Orchestra were sold out on the day that booking opened. The Maestro arrived in London on 18th May accompanied by his wife Donna Carla, his eldest daughter Wally, her husband Count Emmanuele Castelbarco and their daughter Emanuela. The BBC had booked them a large suite at the Langham Hotel, which was opposite the Queen's Hall where the rehearsals and the concerts would take place[1]. I was duly presented to the Toscaninis, and quickly realised this would be no sinecure, for this was an extremely temperamental family.

Every morning for several weeks, I would watch the great conductor as he stood on the podium. Dressed in his black alpaca jacket with its stand-up collar, and his fine white hair combed back into a neat duck's tail, he looked rather like a priest. Sometimes he would sing tonelessly as he conducted but his hands were incredibly sensitive and his gestures eloquent and precise, denoting intense concentration and absolute authority. The rapt attention paid to him by the orchestra rarely wavered, but the 70-year-old Toscanini was notorious for his tantrums. We were only about a week into the rehearsals when he erupted into a major row with the orchestra. The BBC musicians sat impassively at their desks waiting for his rage to subside, but this calm only infuriated him more. Seizing the score on the desk, he tore it in half, and, flinging it to the floor, jumped up and down on it. After this amazing performance there was nothing left for him to do but to walk off the platform. There was dead silence, the orchestra remaining as quiet and restrained as ever. Then after a considerable pause, they put away their instruments and also left the hall.

The next morning, all seemed quiet and peaceful, despite a certain tension in the air. Toscanini mounted the podium, picked up his baton, and then, obviously taken aback, stood motionless as he looked down at what lay before him: a new, beautifully bound copy of the score he had demolished. He picked it up, leafed through it, and as he was very short-sighted, checked that his notes had been correctly copied onto it. Then, satisfied, he raised his baton to signal that the rehearsal should commence. During that season, he never threw another tantrum.

Donna Carla loved shopping in foreign cities, but her ample figure, poor sight and non-existent English constantly got us into trouble. She was very strong-minded and ruled her family with a rod of iron, the Maestro included. She even liked to make her presence felt at rehearsals; sometimes when the orchestra came to a particularly *pianissimo* passage, she would open her handbag, insert both her hands and furiously rustle about in it. The Maestro would visibly flinch, but aware of his wife's timeworn tactics, would stoically carry on. Another irritation to Toscanini was Furtwängler,

Toscanini with his wife Donna Carla (left) and daughter Wally (right)

who was in London at the same time, conducting a Wagner season at Covent Garden. I soon learnt that any reference to Furtwängler or Mussolini would result in some of the Maestro's most furious muffled growls. He was a leading anti-Fascist and a personal enemy of Mussolini's, while his arch-rival from Nazi Germany, Furtwängler, represented all that he most disliked in the art of conducting and the interpretation of music.

By now I felt accepted by the Toscanini family and invited them to Beaulieu for a weekend. The Maestro and Donna Carla declined, but his daughter, Wally and her family came in their stead and the visit was a great success. At the time, a heavily pregnant Pearl was staying in London at her mother's house, 29 South Street[2], where she gave birth to all her children. On 16th June, she and Ned celebrated the delivery of a son, christened Robin. His birth coincided with Toscanini's final concert at the 1937 festival; the event had been a triumph, but as soon as it ended the Maestro had to depart for Austria to conduct at the Salzburg Festival. I too left London in late July to join Renata, Etienne and Robin Rate at the Austrian spa of Bad Gastein. While they took the 'cure' in hot mud baths, I would write, with all of us travelling to nearby Salzburg for concerts. We managed to hear some marvellous music and while Bad Gastein itself proved most enjoyable, I planned to leave before the others as Wally Castelbarco had invited me to stay with her in Venice. Renata was very much opposed to me going as she questioned whether I would be able to cope with the highly sophisticated, decadent and sometimes corrupt society with which I would have to mingle. My reaction to this was, I suppose, predictable. At age 27, I felt supremely confident that I was sufficiently worldly and possessed the high degree of sophistication necessary to deal with any situation. It took less than a month for me to realise what an innocent I was.

It had been a full decade since I had last visited Venice. Then I had been a school girl, hell-bent on seeing all the sights from San Marco to the glass factories but having little contact with the inhabitants. This time was to be quite different. I was to be an insider, living with a prestigious Italian family. Despite the searing heat of mid-August, the impact of Venice when I arrived at the railway station was just as stunning as I remembered. Having left the train, travellers might expect to find a taxi rank, but to emerge onto a canal where a host of launches and gondolas were waiting was very unreal. It has all been said, written and filmed, but this first encounter still makes one catch one's breath. My late husband, never a man for clichés, later gasped and dryly remarked, "They should get the Dutch in – they'd deal with all that water…"

The Count and Countess Castelbarco lived with their daughter in a small, informal palazzo situated on a broad street, the Via dei Catecumeni, just behind the great church of the Madonna della Salute. Wally met me at the station and we took a private launch along the Grand Canal to the house. I was rather puzzled by the presence of two armed *Carabinieri* standing either side of the front door, but soon learnt that their presence was an outward sign of Mussolini's dislike of the Maestro and anyone connected with him. Wally merely laughed and said they gave her good protection against burglars. On entering, one was met with a wave of fragrance from great vases of tuberoses, which were everywhere. My bedroom proved not to be a room at all but an alcove at the side of the large salon. As a result, I couldn't go to bed until the last guest had departed, sometimes as late as 5am. By then, the temperature would usually have dropped a bit, but I still had to learn how to manage mosquito nets the hard way.

I was quickly initiated into a way of life that was entirely new to me, and it sometimes felt as if I was drowning in a sea of multi-coloured impressions. Wally was indefatigable in her pursuit of pleasure and people (although it was usually they who pursued her) and there was an endless succession of parties from very grand dinners to outrageous bohemian extravaganzas. But there were also serene hours spent on the Lido or sitting in the Piazza San Marco at sunset sipping an *aperitivo* as the gold gradually faded from the façade of St Mark's Basilica and the pigeons settled down to roost. Among my fellow guests that year were Wally's sister Wanda, her husband, the virtuoso Vladimir Horowitz, and the Contessa Ida Cavalli. On that first morning under Wally's roof, I was fascinated to hear Horowitz practising from a nearby room, something people said he never did, his technique and mastery of the instrument supposedly being perfect.

Of the many parties I went to, I particularly remember a grand banquet given by the vastly rich Count Volpi in his beautiful *palazzo* on the Grand Canal. The banquet was remarkable not only because of its distinguished guest list, but also for our host's meticulous attention to historical detail. The theme of the banquet was Venice at its apogee, so electric light was replaced by hundreds of candles perfectly illuminating the courtyard where we dined. Blacked-up boys dressed traditionally as Moors served us excellent food, while a string orchestra played discreetly from the wings; an unforgettable evening.

Another extraordinary party was given by the American celebrity Elsa Maxwell in a dance hall on an island near Venice. A 'homely pianist from Iowa', Maxwell's career as an actress and songwriter had been eclipsed by her reputation as 'the hostess with the mostest'. So when it became known that La Maxwell would be giving a special party, everyone was clamouring for an invitation. As a guest in Wally's household, I was one of the lucky ones, and on receiving the invitation learned that this was to be a fancy dress evening: men were to dress as women and vice-versa, in short a transvestite affair. This being Venice, no-one raised an eyebrow. Wally was vastly intrigued by the whole idea, and promptly set about organising costumes for her house guests. She decreed that Wanda and I should be dressed as rough sailors complete with a 'six o'clock shadow' on our chins. Wally herself stuck to the feminine gender, appearing as a convincing 'Madame' of a low class sea front brothel. But there was one 'gentleman' who really stood out from the crowd and that was Marlene Dietrich, flawless in top hat and tails.

Wally, of course, had her own very glamorous party that summer. If her guest list had been used in a name dropping contest, she would have won hands down. It included Emerald, Lady Cunard, whose name was associated with Sir Thomas Beecham, and Erich Maria Remarque, author of *All Quiet on the Western Front*. His mistress, Marlene Dietrich, was also there, leaning decoratively against the piano. Wally and Vladimir Horowitz were present as house guests, but it was Elsa Maxwell who sat at the keyboard, entertaining the guests. Her friend George Gershwin had passed away just weeks before[3], and there was great poignancy as she played *They Can't Take That Away from Me*, tears running from her eyes. The song was one of his final compositions, and although I hadn't heard it before, Elsa's incomparable rendering of it ensured that the melody never left my mind.

You didn't only meet *prominenti* at parties, you could bump into them at any moment as you wandered about the city. The Piazza San Marco always attracted them like a magnet, although some of the more sophisticated favoured a plush dive called Harry's Bar which served the strongest dry martinis in the western hemisphere. Among these *prominenti* was the American-born Princess Jane di San Faustino. The pale and excessively slim Princess would appear on the Lido clad in a strange black bathing dress which reached down to her ankles and her wrists, with black socks and gloves completing the covering. When she tripped delicately down to the sea she looked more like an enormous black insect than a human being. When I asked Wally if she was in mourning, she laughed: "No, she just doesn't want to get sunburnt!"

Despite the long shadow cast by Mussolini, that 1937 season in Venice was voted one of the most brilliant on record. Brilliant it certainly was, but primed by Thomas Mann's *Death in Venice* and Renata's Cassandra-like warnings, I soon sensed the decadence and corruption that lay behind the glittering façade. Then in late September the storm clouds started to gather over the Adriatic, and a thin grey mist drifted across the lagoon. Five days later, the rains came, heavy and relentless. The canals became dirty and dun-coloured, the golden brilliance was tarnished and everything dripped. It was indeed 'water, water everywhere', and I knew that it was time to go.

I returned to Britain to find public opinion marching under the banner of
'Peace in Our Time'. There were many who did not succumb to this myth
and it now seemed that we were a divided nation, with some professing
confidence in Chamberlain and others promulgating dark warnings. There
were bitter arguments everywhere, and to a large extent the press, ostrich-
like and negative, was singularly unhelpful. Most people tried to behave as
if everything was normal, so while priorities got sadly mixed up, the social
calendar was full.

The Hon Elizabeth Scott-Montagu embarks for the Northern Capitals. Wearing MATITA — as she usually does — here you see her in a canary and brown diagonal topcoat with its transparent buttons. Underneath is a plaided jumper in the same colours with a diagonal skirt.

13

PARTING OF THE WAYS

1938 started with a trip to Cortina d'Ampezzo in the Dolomites. The sun shone, the skiing was wonderful, but life in this fashionable resort seemed to be an extension of the *dolce vita* of Venice with much of the same superficiality. I longed to get away from it and return to work, but a shock awaited me as I travelled back to London on 12th March. Changing trains in Milan, I was greeted by placards screaming the Nazi invasion of Austria. Confrontation now seemed inevitable, and as the pace was quickening, I wondered how long it would be before the Nazis turned their guns on us in the West.

Back in London, I was increasingly moving in musical and literary circles, but still got the occasional request to appear in some glossy magazine as an actress. One of the most memorable was an assignment to model a range of *Matita* cruise outfits whilst posing on an ocean liner. Unfortunately, it was a freezing early spring day and the liner in question was a dirty old vessel undergoing a refit at Tilbury! The only consolation was the charm of the young photographer, Norman Parkinson, who coaxed me through the job and even had me lounging elegantly on the sun deck. It was only when my picture eventually appeared in the September edition of *Harper's Bazaar* that I realised that the wintry conditions for the shoot had been very appropriate: the clothes being promoted were supposed to feature me sailing for the 'Northern Capitals' of Scandinavia!

The summer of 1938 brought London one more unforgettable Toscanini season, and once again I found myself trotting around Harrods and Fortnum & Mason with the indefatigable Donna Carla. We now had an

183

established routine so there was no friction and few dramas. The concerts were again a great success and Toscanini had become a real star in London. Everyone concerned was jubilant and even Donna Carla smiled, but there was sadness too as the Maestro would not be going on to Salzburg. After the *Anschluss* Toscanini had declined to visit Austria, and from that point on the United States became his home.

Before she left London, Wally once again invited me to stay with her in Venice. Although we had now become good friends I accepted rather reluctantly. Venice still had its old magic, but everything in the summer of 1938 seemed to be in a lower key and there was less of the glamour and brilliance of the previous summer. My fellow guests this time were two agreeable Americans, Mrs Cobina Wright and her 17-year-old daughter Little Cobina; their enthusiasm and radiant happiness seemed to light up the house. Little Cobina was an outstandingly attractive young woman, and soon dozens of young men were appearing at our door. But as far as I could judge there was only one who mattered, a tall, blond, good-looking young man, quiet and shy, whose visits to the house became more and more frequent. I soon discovered him to be Prince Philip of Greece, then staying with his aunt, Princess Aspasia. However, when Philip proposed to Little Cobina she declined him, and the next time I saw the Prince it was in the cinema, on his engagement to Princess Elizabeth. Later, at the Royal Wedding, I read that among the guests were a Mrs Cobina Wright and her daughter Cobina from the United States, and in the years that followed, they remained close friends.

When I left Venice in September 1938, I decided to spend the autumn months at Schloss Berg where, no longer a student, I could function as an accompanist for pupils working on concertos. By returning to neutral Switzerland, and a music school at that, I thought I might escape the politics which permeated so many aspects of life in Italy, but I was wrong. Although Frau Langenhan had no real understanding of politics, she now adopted a stern attitude. To her, the National Socialists were the saviours of Germany and those of us who thought otherwise were merely prey to idle gossip and ignoble thoughts. Through one of her ex-pupils she invited Rudolf Hess to stay; "such a civilised and agreeable man," she said. Schloss Berg had a number of German pupils, most of them fervent Nazis, including a sixteen-year-old who had a serious crush on me. One day, as we walked in the garden, he harangued me on the virtues of National Socialism until I bluntly told him my opinion of the Nazis. He listened white and trembling: such was his fanaticism that I was transformed into his deadly enemy.

As tension between Britain and Germany increased, the Germans ruled that British visitors would require visas – a regulation we greatly resented. I had gone to the German Consulate in St Gallen to get a visa, and soon realised that I had chosen a bad moment to make the application. Only a few days previously, a young Jew had assassinated a German diplomat in Paris and this had provoked a terrible *pogrom* in Germany leading to the flight of many Jews into Switzerland. Waiting in a crowded room to see the Consul, I found myself among a number of these desperate refugees, some of whom had even swum across the Rhine. Bedraggled and shaking, some were still in wet clothes but buoyed up with the hope of getting the papers they needed to remain in Switzerland. We entered the Consul's office two by two, having duly filled in the necessary forms. As my application was for a visa, I had to answer a number of questions, including some concerning my racial origins as far back as my grandparents. Brusquely the Consul offered me a chair, making it clear that my Jewish companion would have to stand. Refusing the chair, I handed him my passport and the application form. He glanced at it, then quickly pointed out that I had failed to answer the question dealing with my racial descent. Stony-faced, I pointed out that such matters, where they concerned a British subject, were none of his business. He then started to shout at me, *"Sei nicht so frisch!"* (Don't be so impertinent!) By using the familiar mode of address, he delivered a clear insult.

At this point I lost control of myself and all my pent-up rage against the Nazis overflowed. Shouting abuse about Hitler, I reached out and with one grand gesture swept everything off the Consul's desk. This included a miniature Nazi flag and a large framed photograph of the Führer, all of which crashed down onto the floor in a heap of splintered glass. The Consul rose to his feet, picked up my passport, and with his eyes blazing left the room. The Jewish boy and I stood there for a moment, uncertain what to do. "You shouldn't have done that!" he said, trembling. He was right of course, for my angry protests would hardly be of any help to him.

Eventually, I was allowed to leave, but without my passport. This was to cause me maximum inconvenience, and earned me a reproach from the British Consular authorities, who deplored such incidents. I returned to London on temporary papers and then had to collect my passport from the German Embassy. Following the invasion of Austria, the German government had taken over Austria's consular buildings, and so I had to go to Belgrave Square, where my passport was handed back to me by Prince Bismarck[1] himself. He was surprisingly pleasant about it all, but his country's occupation of another's embassy (not to mention the *Anschluss* itself) had provoked widespread disquiet in London.

When I returned to Beaulieu, my grim first-hand knowledge of what National Socialism really represented seemed unreal in the peaceful tranquillity of the English countryside. That was the trouble, for in England life still appeared so normal, stable and carefree, in contrast to the subject of the Nazis and Jewish persecution, which was largely taboo. It seemed as if England was fast asleep. The Christmas of 1938 at Palace House followed the usual pattern with Ned and I getting into political squabbles; across the country, attitudes were hardening, with many families finding themselves divided.

However, there were lighter moments, such as when I took Edward to the Empire Cinema[2] in Southampton to see *The Crowd Roars*, a boxing drama starring Robert Taylor. Afterwards at the Cadena Café, he ate two complete meals of bacon, eggs and ice cream. On our return, the family were furious with me for exposing Edward to such a corrupt, adult film!

The dawn of 1939 saw little to celebrate, and the new year rejoicings seemed sad and hollow. It was probably because of this general discord that I became even closer to Roland de Margerie, who had been an important figure in my life ever since we met in 1934. He must have been under intolerable pressure as his opinions, always based on precise information and facts, were not always those of the Quai d'Orsay. Despite heroic efforts, he was unable to convince the British establishment or much of the press of the imminent peril facing us all. Despite this, he had some good friends in press circles, among them the distinguished journalist FA Voigt. With similar political convictions to Voigt's, Roland would often consult him on matters concerning the British press and public attitudes. Voigt was

Roland, his glasses in his hand

the diplomatic correspondent of the *Manchester Guardian,* an authority on German politics and one of the first British journalists to warn of the dangers of National Socialism.

I suspect that Roland had already suggested to Voigt that I might be useful to him, so he arranged for us to meet over lunch at the Hyde Park Hotel. By the end of the meal, Voigt had asked me to write a review for the prestigious monthly, *The Nineteenth Century and After,* of which he was editor. The next day a special messenger delivered a copy of Christopher Smart's *Rejoice in the Lamb*, a long magical poem written when the poet was already going insane. The discovery of the original manuscript had caused quite a sensation and it was now to be the subject of my review. I was so excited by it that I wrote a long and positive eulogy about this strange, haunting masterpiece. My piece was not a review at all, but as there was no time to alter it, I trusted to luck and, with a note of apology, sent it to the editor.

Two days later, 'FA' invited me to lunch. He made no mention of the Smart poem and I feared the worst. It was only at the end of the meal that he told me in a dead-pan manner that my piece would appear in the June edition as a major article, and he would be happy if I joined the magazine as a regular contributor. At first I was speechless, but when I left him that afternoon I realised that this day might be a major turning point in my career.

Voigt was an extraordinary man, and over the months I began to know him better, first as a respected editor and later as a personal friend. Born in Hampstead to German parents, he had something strange and indefinable about him. He was a tall but shy man with a quirky manner and a curiously untidy face. As Britain edged closer to war, his German descent could be a source of embarrassment for him, but for me he represented so much of what is most admirable in Germany. Moreover, being one of the team of the *Nineteenth Century* was delightful, as was writing the reviews and articles. The paper was enlightened, politically forceful and the standard of the writing remarkably high. There was a social side to my work too, notably lunchtime meetings with the editorial staff of other distinguished monthlies such as the *National Review*. These would usually take place at Rules, the excellent restaurant just off the Strand; in Rules there were moments when I could almost forget the awful things that were happening in Europe.

Frederick Augustus Voigt, better known to his friends as 'FA'

My network of contacts amongst the country's 'opinion formers' was quickly expanding and this was probably why my relation, Sheila Grant-Duff [3], the author of a widely acclaimed book on Czechoslovakia, invited me to her home in Kent for the weekend. The house party included Duncan and Diana Sandys, the good-looking Adam von Trott, Sheila and myself. At first sight it seemed an improbable mixture: Diana, Churchill's eldest daughter; a German diplomat likely to be loyal to Hitler; and Sheila and myself, both openly hostile to the Third Reich.

Surprisingly though it turned out to be a most enjoyable weekend, despite some extraordinary arguments. Diana, always too finely tuned to be relaxed, subjected von Trott to both awkward questions and provocative statements, all of which he parried most adroitly. It was not long before I realised that there was a tender friendship between Sheila and Adam dating back to their Oxford student years, so he was unlikely to be, as Diana insisted, a dedicated supporter of Hitler. I later learned that this weekend had been carefully planned with the object of opening a path for Adam von Trott to meet Churchill[4]. But I heard nothing more of von Trott until 1944, when I read of his involvement in the July Plot – the attempted assassination of Hitler. Later it was reported that he, together with most of the conspirators, had been arrested and executed as traitors. So perished a brave man who, as we now know, had already been in active opposition to Hitler before the war started.

Roland was delighted with my progress as a writer, and was now convinced I should consider becoming a full time journalist. He decided I should aim for the top, and so we carefully composed a letter to the Foreign Editor of *The Times* asking for an interview. I remember feeling that Roland was being over-ambitious, but amazingly, a reply came fixing a date for an interview. I was quite alarmed at the idea of setting foot in Printing House Square, but knew I must go through with it.

So clutching a bundle of articles and up-to-date reports written especially for the occasion, I entered the not very august portals of *The Times*. I had to wait several nail-biting minutes before Barrington Ward appeared, but from then on it was all very pleasant and businesslike. He asked me a host of questions covering various topics which I was able to answer to his satisfaction. A few days later, I found myself once more in Printing House Square to face a much more affable Foreign Editor. Then came the realisation that the impossible was about to happen; a job on *The Times* was about to be mine! Barrington Ward informed me that I would temporarily join the staff in the autumn, but before finalising anything, the Editor, Geoffrey Dawson, would like to see me at his house for dinner – his secretary would contact me. I wondered whether this was the standard procedure for new recruits to 'the Thunderer', but found it reassuring that this exalted editor took a personal interest in even his most junior staff. As I was about to leave, Ward added a curious remark: did I realise that I would be the first woman to work in his department since the turn of the century? With this he smiled enigmatically and ushered me out of his office.

The promised invitation to dinner soon materialised. Roland, jubilant that I was to have a position at *The Times,* was convinced I had found the niche best suited to my talents and also, with any luck, a job for life. It was a beautiful summer evening when I parked my car outside Geoffrey Dawson's flat near Hanover Gate, Regent's Park. Intent on making a serious impression, I brought a disturbing report concerning recent troop movements in Germany and other alarming developments – Roland had supplied the facts, so I knew my information was reliable. Dawson read it with obvious interest as we sipped our sherry, but did not, as I had expected, appear unduly concerned. Then he folded it, slipped it into his pocket, and gazing over the peaceful sunlit park, remained silent for a minute or two before turning back to me.

"You are sure you have got the facts right?" he asked. I replied I was. "And your sources, I presume, are impeccable?" I told him confidently that they were. Again he turned away to gaze at the trees in the park before abruptly rounding on me, but with an amiable expression on his face. "My dear Miss Montagu, let me assure you that at this moment I am far more concerned about the grouse disease in Scotland than I am about the European situation…" So spoke the Editor of 'the Thunderer' on 12th August 1939, a mere three weeks before the outbreak of World War II.

When I told Roland about Dawson's reaction, he was appalled. Now he was more convinced than ever that there was little hope that the British press, the Foreign Office or the government would heed any warnings, however dire. The hard evidence about Hitler's intentions was being consistently ignored, and further German aggression seemed both inevitable and imminent.

Etienne and Robin – soon to be married

14

DARK HORIZONS

The London of 1939 seemed more hot, stale and empty than usual, but despite the concerns of people like myself, normal life carried on until the very outbreak of war. Amongst the usual social round, however, I went to one quite remarkable dinner party. It was given by Count Albrecht Mongelas, a Bavarian aristocrat who, until the previous year, had been the London correspondent of the Berlin newspaper *Die Vössische Zeitung*. As he had never concealed his anti-Nazi views, he soon lost his job but had chosen to remain in London. Since Mongelas had acquired many English friends, his flat in Chelsea saw many a distinguished gathering, but on this particular evening his guest list was exceptional.

As I entered the room, I immediately recognised HG Wells with his current great love, the Russian-born Baroness Moura Budberg, by his side. Then, to my amazement, I recognised one of Moura's previous lovers, the diplomat Robert Bruce Lockhart[1], who had masterminded a plot to assassinate Lenin back in 1918. I remember wondering what on earth Mongelas was doing; bringing such a daring mix of people together seemed a recipe for disaster. Then I saw the great German actor Werner Krauss with his famous actress wife, Maria Bard. There was undoubtedly tension in the air, although everyone behaved with the greatest decorum. 'HG', who predictably took centre stage, made a great impression on me, while Bruce Lockhart said practically nothing, understandably perhaps. The German pair scintillated, and since the subject of politics was studiously avoided, the evening was an undoubted success. For me, the lasting importance of the occasion was meeting Moura, and soon afterwards I received an invitation to attend one of her famous 'Tuesdays'.

HG Wells and Moura Budburg at Claridge's in 1939

Born in the Ukraine, Moura was rated as one of the most beautiful and fascinating women of her time. Despite coming from a pro-Czarist family and being twice married to Baltic noblemen, she remained in favour with the Soviet authorities but eventually settled in London. Moura's beguiling charm and sexual allure were such that men fell hopelessly in love with her, and she doubtless used this to ease her passage into and out of many extraordinary situations. Moura's 'Tuesdays' had long been a tradition, taking the form of a weekly gathering for her various friends who would drop in for an evening drink. It was all very informal, but you could always be sure of meeting some remarkable people, usually from the stage and literary worlds. What brought these people together was their huge affection for Moura; they certainly didn't come for the drinks which never varied; it was always a tepid glass of orange squash topped with a generous splash of vodka.

Undeterred by the gravity of the international situation, I made another visit to Switzerland in mid-August. Etienne Amyot and Robin Rate had recently married in England[2] and were now on holiday, staying at Schloss Berg. On 23rd August we decided to visit Geneva, where there was a special exhibition of works from the Prado in Madrid. Full of happy anticipation, we set out with Robin at the wheel of her new Delage, the car being a present to herself. Having spent a very satisfying few hours in the Musée d'Art et d'Histoire, we came out to be greeted by men carrying sandwich boards, proclaiming that Germany and the Soviet Union had signed a non-aggression pact. It wasn't difficult to realise what this meant, as Hitler, no longer threatened in the east, could now concentrate on the west. As we walked along the Rue du Mont Blanc, we passed a large group of Jews huddled together, wailing and beating their chests: it was an unsettling scene, but even we didn't realise how prophetic their lamentations would prove to be. War with Germany seemed to have moved a giant step nearer.

We left Geneva immediately, but throughout the entire four-hour drive back to Berg we hardly spoke a word, gloomily preoccupied with our thoughts. Etienne was convinced he would be called up, and Robin was loathe to abandon her beloved car in Switzerland, so they decided to leave the very next day and make for the Channel ports. For my part, I decided to board the first convenient train, but I had to delay my departure when Julian Pitt-Rivers telephoned to announce that he would be arriving at Berg by car the next day. Julian had been studying in Germany at Tuebingen University and was full of strange, alarming stories and accounts of growing hostility towards the British. He was deeply relieved to have left Germany, and we concurred that we should return to England as soon as we possibly could. In Switzerland there was still a glassy calm, and at Berg we carefully avoided any mention of the political situation. However, the day before we left, Julian and I embarked on one of the most foolhardy and irresponsible acts of our lives. Julian had spoken of a large-scale mobilisation in Southern Germany, and in a moment of madness we decided to cross the frontier at Konstanz to see the situation for ourselves.

On the Swiss side of the frontier, a well-meaning customs official tried to dissuade us from entering German territory, but we were determined to carry out our plan. It did not take more than a few minutes in Konstanz to realise that a subtle change had come over the usually sleepy town;

Wehrmacht uniforms seemed to be everywhere. We decided to go to the station posing as ordinary travellers, and having parked the car, we wandered on to the platform. We immediately found what we were looking for, a dozen or so closely printed posters bearing mobilisation orders, regimental numbers and other details. We tried to memorise as much as we could until Julian spotted an SS officer on the opposite platform watching us intently. Seizing my arm, he whispered, "Let's get the hell out of here". The Swiss customs official greeted us with a wry smile. "You shouldn't have done that you know…"

Back at Berg, we realised how stupid we had been. When I rang Roland I received a thorough scolding. He was extremely angry at our puerile cloak-and-dagger operation, but carefully noted the details. Like Robin, Julian wanted to get his car, a Hillman Minx, back to England, and insisted we leave without delay. For him it was an easy decision, but for me it was heart-breaking. It seemed inevitable that everything Berg represented would soon be taken from me. The music, the strange magic of the place, and above all, Renata. This sudden severance from someone who was so dear to me was to prove one of the most traumatic experiences of my life, and despite Julian's efforts to cheer me up, I remained inconsolable.

As we drove westwards through the green and ordered valleys of Switzerland our predicament seemed more and more like a bad dream. But when we reached Basle and tried to cross into France, we were inexplicably turned back. Ignominiously we turned tail and drove back to Berg. Now seriously alarmed, Julian decided to leave his car there while we took a train to Paris, direct trains from Zurich to the Channel ports having ceased to run. This second leave-taking was an anti-climax, but still awful, and our journey to Paris slow and uncomfortable. On arrival we found the streets filled with men in uniform, but when Julian telephoned some of his Parisian friends they remained very complacent. France had not yet woken from her slumber. We stayed only two nights and then boarded an overcrowded train bound for Boulogne.

It was on our boat train that we got the first whiff of real panic, when someone rushed down the corridor shouting that the Germans had marched into the Bois de Boulogne. Shortly afterwards, he was followed by another man shouting even more loudly that the Nazis had attacked the

Channel ports and occupied Boulogne. Julian soon realised it was nonsense, but when we boarded the steamer at the docks, we looked around carefully just in case. There was not a single German in sight. As we stood silently on deck watching the coast of Normandy recede, we realised that not only had we left Julian's car behind with most of our luggage, but also a significant chunk of our lives. Seen from the taffrail, the past had never seemed so good, and the future never so unpredictable. The date was 1st September 1939.

When we emerged from Victoria Station that evening, we sensed a change, subtle and invisible, which seemed to have touched everything and everybody. It was not a joyous homecoming. In the streets there were certainly more uniforms to be seen, and some barrage balloons had already bulged into the metropolitan sky, but the trenches in Hyde Park still had to be completed. Julian and I went straight to his mother's house in Chelsea, where Ray welcomed us warmly. Although she seemed very calm and controlled, I sensed great anxiety behind her cool façade.

Ray had already contacted an ambulance unit and expected to be called up as soon as war was declared. She asked me whether I would like to do something similar, or did I merely intend to go on writing? It was a loaded question. My dinner with Geoffrey Dawson had been something of a watershed. I was grateful to him for the offer of a job on *The Times*, and often pondered over what might have been if I had accepted it, but his blinkered attitude had convinced me that I had to *do* something about the hideous international situation instead of just writing about it.

On the night of 2nd September, I dined with Roland at our favourite restaurant, the Monseigneur, which, like most restaurants that evening, was half empty. Roland told me what had been happening since I had left London. Then our conversation turned to such topics as the Maginot Line, the Siegfried Line, the Blitzkrieg and the Fifth Column – all soon to become household words. Finally Roland revealed his own plans. Despite being in a protected occupation, he would resign his Embassy post as soon as war was declared and join the *Diables Rouges*, a regiment attached to the Chasseurs Alpins. As he had never spoken to me of his intentions before, this came as a great shock, and I had considerable difficulty in hiding my distress.

All the events that preceded Chamberlain's Declaration of War speech have been chronicled, but the baleful atmosphere that hung over London is more difficult to put into words. The weather was unusually warm, so through thousands of open windows wireless sets crackled and blared as the latest news scattered across the city. Now at last we knew it would be war. But what kind of war? The final gas mask scene in the 1934 production of *Dark Horizon* now seemed highly prophetic; at that time, I had merely been acting a part, but might I now experience a repeat performance for real?

Everyone remained remarkably calm and simply concentrated on the practical side of it all. Up and down the country organisations such as the Red Cross, St John's Ambulance Brigade, Boy Scouts, Girl Guides and Women's Institute just rolled up their sleeves and got down to it. Everyone now agreed that Hitler was a particularly nasty fellow and that we should tell him so in no uncertain terms.

*At Beaulieu, an era came to end with the retirement of 'Daddy' Powles
on 1st August 1939. He had served as Beaulieu's vicar since 1886*

Julian and Michael Pitt-Rivers with their mother at Lepe

15

SIGNING UP

The morning of 3rd September 1939 saw Ray, Michael, Julian and me crouching round a small portable radio at Bury Walk. We had been told that the Prime Minister would address the nation at eleven o'clock. We waited in silence; it was a solemn moment, but when the declaration of war came, there was no rousing battle cry. In fact Chamberlain managed to sound more petulant than inspiring.

Ray was the first to speak, angrily and bitterly, remembering her two brothers killed in the previous war and foreseeing what could happen to her two sons. Julian and I were reproached for our anti-Nazi war-mongering, but we remained mute; what was there to say? Fortunately, the tension was broken by the banshee wailing of the air raid sirens, the first time we had heard them. This was followed by the sound of gas attack rattles wielded by the Chelsea air raid wardens. Ray, now perfectly calm, set about organising the necessary precautions. First, we stuffed cushions up all the chimneys and set about soaking blankets to cover the windows. Next a first aid box was produced and we slung our gas masks over our shoulders – we were prepared! Fixing dripping blankets to period windows is a difficult task, but Julian and I set about it with determination. Bury Walk was a Georgian house and the windows were loose and ill-fitting, so just when Julian was tucking in the final blanket, I lost my grip on the sash and it fell with a nasty thud onto his fingers. Julian gave a yelp of pain, but the incident broke the tension and we found ourselves laughing again. Of course the gas alert turned out to be a false alarm and Ray quickly contacted her ambulance unit.

When I met Roland that evening I knew that this would be the last time we would be together for many a moon. He had already contacted the *Diables Rouges*, who were stationed somewhere along the Maginot Line, and planned to leave for France the next morning. We discussed my plans, and he reluctantly agreed that I should abandon any idea of joining *The Times* and put my name down for some useful wartime organisation. He was very understanding, although I sensed he regretted my decision. On his side, he was giving up a brilliant career and a job he loved, but I was sure of his courage and knew that whatever he did, he would do it well.

It had been a hot and sultry day, and by nightfall lightning began to flicker. With his wife away in Paris, Roland took me back to a darkened Eaton Square and we sat at the window of his house, watching the storm clouds gather and the lightning flash. As he held me in his arms, the thunderstorm seemed charged with foreboding and dark portents. When we parted that night, I feared it might be for the last time.

By the next morning, with the air fresh and cool, family morale at Bury Walk had improved considerably. Ray had really enjoyed her first stint with the ambulance unit and suggested that I should join a similar organisation, the Mechanised Transport Corps. So I telephoned their headquarters and made an appointment for the next day. It was with considerable trepidation that I rang the bell of the MTC headquarters 33 Leinster Gardens. It was more or less what I had expected, a collection of bosomy, middle-aged ladies looking like a Women's Institute in uniform. The Commandant, Mrs Cook, was a toothy buxom lady of indefinite age who had served in Flanders during the Great War. She quickly sized me up, then, glaring at me fiercely, told me that I 'would do'.[1]

The Mechanised Transport Training Corps was formed in January 1939 out of the London Division of the Women's Legion (Mechanical Transport Section). The original object of the Corps was 'training women in all subjects necessary for service with the fighting forces, and with the Civil Defence organisation', although the emphasis was always on driving. Once war broke out, the training remit gave way to practical work, particularly ambulance driving and medical duties. We all served as volunteers, paying 10/6d a year for membership, but our voluntary status gave the MTC greater freedom from War Office bureaucracy[2].

Our Commandant, Mrs GM Cook OBE

My first task was to get a bus to the Army & Navy Stores, where I purchased my uniform. When I got home and unpacked my purchases, I decided to try them on. First the khaki cotton stockings, next the khaki skirt, shirt and tie, then the flat-heeled shoes and finally the tunic and cap. I looked in the glass and was appalled; no Parisian *chic* here. Even with my then reasonably good figure, I looked a frump. Later, Basil Bartlett took one look at me and commented, "At least now I know why they call them breast pockets…"

The autumn months of 1939 seemed to be endless – the 'Phoney War' was at its height. The weather was damp and depressing and I seemed to be living in a fog of uncertainty and frustration. I was stony broke and my health was far from good. Now living with Beth Tregaskis at her house in Swiss Cottage, I was well cared for but felt somewhat isolated. Most of my English companions were scattered, Renata was far away in Switzerland and my Italian and German friends from London had been interned on the Isle of Man as enemy aliens; aliens they may have been, but never enemies.

Learning how to defend ourselves with a ju-jitsu instructor

I soon found that the MTC took itself very seriously and recruits had to train hard. Waking up before dawn, often freezing, it was only when I left the house neatly dressed in my uniform that I would get a twinge of satisfaction from the thought that I was serving a noble cause! Daily drills and marches round the streets and squares of Bayswater were routine, all under the eagle eye of a fierce drill sergeant from the Irish Guards. As some of his squad were a little vague about which was their right and left, his raucous commands sometimes ended in chaos, reducing many an ex-deb to tears. Another hazard we faced was the errand boys on bicycles, who would follow us jeering and making ribald remarks when we got out of step. There were also hours of serious study, covering advanced map reading, first aid, convoy driving, stretcher drill, anti-gas precautions, and, somewhat surprisingly, ju-jitsu sessions; the exact purpose of which has remained a mystery to this day. Was it to repel the German soldiery, or to protect our virtue from the reputedly libidinous French? I will never know.

In the evenings, we attended car maintenance classes at a garage in Blackfriars. It was here that I got to know several of the girls with whom I

Examining the engine of our Ford V-8

would later serve: Elena German-Ribon, Joan Barker-Mill[3], Ronnie Monahan and Yvonne Macdonald. Mostly in their mid-twenties, all were attractive, resourceful and intelligent, but we soon recognised that Yvonne had special qualities. A blonde Anglo-Argentinian, Yvonne possessed powers of initiative and leadership which rapidly came to the fore. Utterly charming and strikingly attractive, she rarely failed to get what she wanted, especially as those in authority were usually men! She later published a memoir, *Red Tape Notwithstanding*,[4] for which I am most grateful as it has filled many of the gaps in my own memory covering our adventures during the first year of the war.

By the end of October I had passed my exams and was appointed secretary to the Transport Officer. Conscious that I had illegible writing, no experience of office work, and was not the tidiest person, I wondered what chaos I would bring. However, my tendency to catch coughs and colds made me glad to be in a warm office with plenty of cups of tea. The hours were long and I was now permanently in uniform, but I maintained an interest in matters cultural: 'FA' still had me doing work for the *Nineteenth*

Century, and there was solace to be found at the splendid National Gallery concerts organised by Dame Myra Hess, where Etienne was among the soloists. However, the fact that an era had ended became more evident every day: those sunlit uplands that had seemed to stretch endlessly into the future were now as much in the past as nursery teas and donkey rides. Most of all, I missed Roland and Renata, but we continued to correspond. Looking back on the letters of that Phoney War period, it is interesting to see what occupied our thoughts:

To Renata – 28th October 1939

> This morning I had my oral examination in the anti-gas course, and passed. It is strange how gas loses half its terror when one learns something about it. … Today, the news seems very ominous. V is very gloomy (he always is!) about Holland, but optimistic on the whole about the outcome of the war. We all are. Roland writes that he hopes that Hitler attacks the Maginot line, as they are so excellently prepared and the German losses – even if they did have some initial successes – would be so colossal that the German Home Front would almost certainly 'crack'. He was optimistic about the possible invasion of Holland too, but that was ten days ago… We are extremely satisfied with the performance of our RAF – our planes seem so much superior to the German ones, and our training is infinitely better and more thorough. Generally, we are optimistic but guarded in our optimism, as everybody realises that the war has yet to 'begin'.

From Roland – 15th November 1939

> I think it absolutely marvellous that the war should have made you into such a letter-writing person… but I am sorry to hear I owe some of your letters to colds or fatigue. Xandra Haig … tells me that Walter Buccleuch, under the new taxation, has to pay 18 and 6 out of the £! No wonder if he is a pacifist, his wealth may be one of the causes of our War – unconsciously he always took the appeasement line with Ribbentrop because he was afraid for his income, and Rib used to tell Hitler that "the vested interests of the British aristocracy would always prevent England to go to war." Be glad that you belong to the poorer branch of the family, no responsibility can fall on your shoulders in spite of the angry Pitt-Rivers group!

Keen that Renata should follow both the fortunes of my unit and those of the allied forces in general, I sent her a copy of the *Daily Express* war map, complete with little flags for marking the position of our lines. Such graphic representations of our conflict made war seem rather exciting!

Meanwhile, the MTC had been appealing for funds to create a mobile hospital for deployment with the French Army. Two wealthy couples responded and agreed to donate the ambulances we so badly needed. These were Brigadier-General Spears, whose wife was the writer Mary Borden and Sir Robert Hadfield, a steel magnate whose American wife had considerable wealth of her own. Later, that name would help to save my life, but more immediately I composed a report on the equipping of the Hadfield-Spears Unit, which *The Times* published on 16th November, 'from a correspondent'.

> The unit will resemble a modern British casualty clearing station in many respects but is completely mechanised, its staff and equipment and its 100 beds being transported by motors. Thanks to the generosity of Sir Robert Hadfield it was possible for Lady Hadfield and Mrs Spears (wife of Brigadier-General ELSpears MP) to supply the unit and present it to the French Army. During the Great War Lady Hadfield was in charge of a British hospital at Wimereux, and Mrs Spears of a French field hospital… In conjunction with the *Service de Santé Militaire* she is taking eight fully qualified British hospital nurses and 12 British women drivers recruited from the Mechanised Training Corps, who will be in charge of the vans and cars transporting the personnel.

Everyone wanted to be with the first MTC unit to go to France, but to be considered, you were expected to have your own car. I had been asked whether I would donate mine when I joined the corps, but had jibbed at parting with my new Vauxhall, so kept quiet about it. Now I wondered if I should have been more public-spirited, but as the departure date for the Hadfield-Spears Unit was repeatedly set back, another opportunity arose.

We heard that a Mrs Crawshay, based in Paris, was trying organise help for the refugees evacuated from Alsace, close to the Maginot Line. Yvonne spoke to her briefly on a visit to London; it sounded like just the kind of situation which we could assist with, but the letter of confirmation which Mrs Crawshay promised never materialised. Exasperated, Yvonne took matters into her own hands and managed to get both an exit-permit and a visa so that she might fly to Paris and discuss the arrangements with Mrs Crawshay in person. She returned a few days later having achieved her

Left to right: Ronnie Monahan, Elena German-Ribon, Yvonne Macdonald, myself, Mrs Edwards and Joan Barker-Mill

primary objective and made a number of useful contacts. The MTC's assistance was indeed required, and we had just a month to prepare!

I was desperate to be a member of the expedition, but once again the question of a car arose. This time, however, one of our training officers, Mrs Vestey, came to my rescue. She had recently raised the money to buy an ambulance, but was unable to go to France herself and allowed me to take it in her place. By now, Yvonne had been confirmed as expedition leader; this was no surprise as the venture was entirely her initiative, but I nearly fell off my chair when I heard that I was to be second-in-command, promoted to Ensign Montagu (the equivalent of a 2nd Lieutenant). How on earth had I suddenly become an officer? I guess it was because of my fluent French and the training my father arranged for me at the Mansions Motor School a decade earlier. Mrs Cook decided that we should keep our mouths shut and tell no one outside our immediate families. I was overjoyed and wondered whether the ju-jitsu might come in useful after all.

Leaning against the bonnet of our Vauxhall,
Yvonne Macdonald and I pose for press photographers

I soon found that the honour of being second-in-command had its drawbacks. With responsibility you also got the blame, and all the really boring work, of which there was plenty in the weeks running up to our departure. The worst part was dealing with large quantities of paperwork. Each of us had to sign a hundred and one forms, have extra identity photographs taken, and then spend many hours having them processed at the Passport Office. It seemed strange that going to the help of another country involved so much bureaucracy when the Nazi enemy had no qualms about simply 'walking in'.

The greatest problem concerned the transport of our cars across the channel. Yvonne decided that the best option would be to persuade the Army to help us; they were shipping hundreds of vehicles every day, and it didn't seem much to ask if they could include ours on one of their ships. Once she discovered the name of the colonel in charge of such matters, Yvonne wasted no time in driving round to the War Office to plead our case. She came back with a promise of help – it was just a matter of waiting

Front row: Yvonne Macdonald. Back row, left to right: myself, Mrs Edwards, (next person obscured), Joan Barker-Mill, Ronnie Monahan and Elena German-Ribon

for the sailing date to be confirmed! With this major obstacle overcome, our final task was to obtain the necessary visas and permits from the French Embassy. Fortunately, the ambassadorial staff could not have been more helpful: our passports were stamped with visas which permitted us to go almost anywhere in France and the Ambassador produced special letters requesting the authorities to give us every assistance.

Then came a set-back: Aunt Rachel wrote to my Commandant asking her not to send me to France – she said my health was not good enough[5]. It was true that I had been suffering with a cold, but I was still furious, and managed to convince the Mrs Cook that I was fit after all. One problem overcome, the next was altogether more serious: the War Office decided that it wouldn't ship our vehicles as we were not an officially recognised organisation. Undaunted, Yvonne adopted a different approach and asked the French Ambassador to write directly to the Minister of War, Leslie Hore-Belisha. A request made on behalf of the French government, we felt, would be difficult to refuse, and a few days later the good news came through that our vehicles would be shipped after all. Ironically, the

Commandant Coulon, the French Embassy's Assistant Military Attaché in London, inspects the MTC on the eve of our departure for France. Mrs Cook is on the right

Hadfield-Spears unit was still trying to organise their own shipping, but we could now plan for departure in early December.

Even with all the permissions in place, there was still much to do. We had to be prepared for both a severe winter and war zone conditions whilst being equipped to give whatever help the refugees might need. With this in mind, we went about collecting second-hand clothes, tinned foods, toys, blankets and anything else which people would give. On a personal front, we had our kit to assemble; lots of woolly under-garments, pullovers and warm gloves, together with the statutory tin hat, gas mask and first aid kit. We also had to get our inoculations updated and, in case the worst should happen, settle our affairs.

In anticipation of our departure, we were given some embarkation leave. Now permanently in uniform, I spent those final few days at Beaulieu. Attending church on Sunday, I was hugely embarrassed to hear the vicar mention my name in his prayers – it made me feel rather like a crusader off to the Holy Land! We were due to embark from nearby Southampton, but I was bound to secrecy because of the magnetic mines which posed a

A 30-YEAR-OLD woman motorist will drive along French roads next week at the wheel of an ambulance she bought out of her own pocket.

Nearly 20 years ago she travelled the same roads with her father, the late General Lord Montagu of Beaulieu, pioneer of British motoring.

The Hon. Elizabeth Scott Montagu, her fair curls tucked severely into her cap, told me yesterday:

"I'm one of the seven lucky girls chosen to go to France with the Mechanised Transport Corps. We are going to work in a reception area for evacuees from the war zone.

"This driving job will revive some of my happiest memories—I have driven thousands of miles over continental roads.

"My upbringing was "mechanised."

"My father gave me my first motor-car as a present for my 18th birthday, but only on condition that I first took a mechanical course at a motoring school."

Mrs. Yvonne Macdonald (left) Commanding Officer of the Mechanised Transport Corps, discussing details with the Hon. Elizabeth Scott Montagu.

Opposite an article headed 'We are buffeted, but the tides will flow in our favour – Churchill', this report appeared in the Daily Sketch on 7th December 1939. Whilst some MTC members did donate their own cars to the Corps, I was not one of them, but the story that I bought my own ambulance made good propaganda. Our seventh member dropped out before departure.

The members of MTC No.3 Unit. Top row: Yvonne Macdonald, myself, Mrs Edwards
Bottom row: Elena German-Ribon, Ronnie Monahan, Joan Barker-Mill

deadly threat to all shipping in the Channel. So I said goodbye to Beaulieu and, despite the Vicar's earnest pleas to the good Lord, soberly considered that I might never return. However, being an optimist, by the time I reached London I was in excellent spirits and rarin' to go.

One of my last evenings in London before leaving for France was spent with FA Voigt. He invited me to visit him at the flat where he worked, and casually asked me to marry him. I knew that this could never work, so I told him gently that his proposal had, alas, come too late as I was now totally committed to the war; my pen had given way to the sword, and I had to see it through. He took it badly and I left feeling sad and guilty. Fortunately, my mind was soon on other matters: Mrs Cook had arranged a parade of the whole Corps at Wellington Barracks on the eve of our departure, with the French Military Attaché taking the salute.

The MTC was now about 600 strong, and with the help of our drill sergeant, the Corps was able to put on quite an impressive display. With our adjutant, Lady Annaly, being the only staff officer to accompany her, Mrs Cook asked Yvonne and me to stand behind her as she took the salute. This was quite an honour, but Yvonne was simply relieved as she hated the idea of parading before a crowd. This was effectively the MTC's public debut and an important opportunity to draw the public's attention to our existence and the work we intended to do. The parade was covered both by newsreels and newspaper photographers, the story being that we were the first khaki-clad women to enter France since war had been declared. Unfortunately, women's units were simply not taken seriously and the tone of the press coverage was somewhat mixed. Rather than treating this as a good news story, some portrayed us as a lot of pretty girls with silk stockings and lipstick, insinuating we were more like *vivandières* than a serious-minded ambulance unit. Lipstick may not have been totally absent, but we were very serious about our mission, and in the weeks and months ahead, we were going to prove that.

Yvonne Macdonald at the wheel of the Ford V-8

16

CONVOY

After the pomp surrounding our parade the day before, our departure on Wednesday 6th December was a distinctly low-key affair. The journey to Southampton was our first experience of driving in convoy, a technique that had to be learned. The procession was led by our Commanding Officer in her Fiat, followed by Elena in her Vauxhall, Joan in her MG and Ronnie in a Ford V-8 van. At the rear were our two ambulances: the first driven by Mrs Edwards, a middle-aged NCO who had served in the previous war, with me bringing up the rear in a converted Buick. It was a peculiar-looking collection of vehicles that made its way along the A30 that morning, but we were thrilled to be finally on our way. Each vehicle proudly flew a Union Jack and the flag of the Corps whilst the ambulances, in grey livery, proclaimed the unit's official name: Mechanised Transport Corps No 3 Overseas Company.[1]

On approaching Southampton, I noticed a sign instructing 'All convoys report here', but the rest of our vehicles had already passed it, so I assumed that it didn't apply to us. Then a man leaned out from an overtaking car and yelled out something about the control post wanting us to stop. Our convoy training had taught us to stay together, and so as I pulled in, the rest of the formation followed. However, by the time Yvonne had stopped and walked back to find out the cause of the delay, the soldier at the control post had disappeared. Deciding it was all a misunderstanding, we continued, but just as we drew up to the South Western Hotel, a somewhat agitated despatch-rider pulled up with orders to return to the control post. It was mid-winter, the light was now fading fast and we were frozen from hand to foot; turning back was the last thing we wanted to do.

215

Lining up in front of our fleet prior to our departure from London.
Joan Barker-Mill is in the foreground, followed by Ronnie Monahan and then me.

Yvonne decided to stick to her original instructions and proceeded to report to Movement Control. Pacing about the South Western Hotel, I longed to make a local call to Beaulieu but I knew this was strictly forbidden as we were already 'under orders'. Eventually, Yvonne returned looking somewhat flustered; it seemed that we were not really expected but the full explanation only came after we had parked our vehicles in the docks. The reason that convoy control were so anxious for us to stop was that they had orders to turn us back: the Minister's consent had been withdrawn. The decision had been telephoned through to Mrs Cook, but some hours after we had left, so when we arrived at the hotel, unchecked, we presented the authorities with a somewhat difficult situation. Perhaps it was at this stage that the powers in the War Office began to appreciate our determination and relented – we would be allowed to go after all.

The following morning I woke up feeling awful, but was encouraged to learn that our vehicles were in the process of being loaded. Fortunately, our ship was not due to sail until three o'clock, by which time I had recovered sufficiently to march with the rest of the unit down to the quay. Our ship was considerably smaller than we had expected, but we were lucky enough to be allotted first class cabins. Then, with a flotilla of other ships, we pulled out into Southampton Water to lie at anchor off Portsmouth until darkness fell. Only then would it be reasonably safe to make the crossing to Cherbourg under the protection of a destroyer.

We all felt uneasy during the voyage, but Yvonne discovered a friend on board who introduced us to his colleagues, most of whom were doctors and medical staff. They turned out to be very agreeable company and after an excellent dinner, I started a good-humoured argument by asserting that all the great Scotsmen came from the lowlands. With several Scotsmen in our company, we were guaranteed a passionate debate, which I, being from a border family, was able to argue from a position of authority! Verbal engagements of this kind certainly helped to pass the evening, but when we retired to our cabin, the threats from planes above and submarines below started to play on our minds. To begin with, I was greatly comforted by my Gieve inflatable waistcoat, until I discovered, much to Yvonne's amusement, that sleeping with it inflated was almost impossible! In the event, we had a smooth passage and arrived at Cherbourg in the early hours of a cheerless winter morning.

Whilst the cars were craned ashore, Yvonne asked me to accompany her whilst collecting some *sauf conduit* cards which had been arranged for us by Mrs Crawshay – these would confirm the legitimacy of our mission to the French authorities. Walking through the streets, we encountered a lot of British troops, and realised for the first time that we were now in an almost exclusively male world in which uniformed women were quite a novelty. Most just greeted us with cheers and wolf-whistles, but then a platoon marched past us, and someone barked the order "eyes right". It took us a second to realise that we, as officers, now had to respond with a salute which we hurriedly gave – it was all rather flattering but Yvonne was highly embarrassed.

By noon our vehicles had been unloaded and we were ready to depart. Our ultimate destination was Châteauroux, a small town south-east of Tours, but that was a few days' drive away (see map on page 258). First we had to obtain some fuel, so armed with our letter from the French Military Attaché, we drove round to the British Army petrol dump. We had an anxious wait whilst they deciphered the letter, but then, to our relief, we were given enough fuel to get us to Tours. We could now start planning our journey and, referring to my Michelin Guide, we decided that our first overnight stop would be the Hotel du Gros Chêne in Flers. Delighted to finally be in France, we celebrated that night over a bottle of wine.

Before sundown the next day, we reached Tours. I had been to the city many years before when my father and I stayed at the Hotel de l'Univers. In those days, it was considered the best in town, and when we arrived I was delighted to find it much as I remembered. We knew that luxury hotels of this kind would not be an option once we were engaged in serious work so we decided to enjoy our creature-comforts while we could. The next day being Sunday, we stayed put, but there was still work to be done, obtaining more fuel. Asking the French Army for petrol seemed like barefaced cheek – we had no official status and therefore no right to it – but we had underestimated Yvonne, or rather the power wielded by an outstandingly attractive woman, and she duly returned with a fistful of coupons.

On Monday, we finally reached Châteauroux at about lunch time. We felt very confident and longed to start our work, which was just as well as there was an immediate request for a car and driver. Stoically, Elena volunteered whilst the rest of us checked in to the Hotel de Faisan. Here we learned that we were to be part of an organisation called *Le Comité International d'Aide aux Enfants de France*, which cared for French refugees displaced from Alsace-Lorraine. These people, of whom there were thousands, were in a desperate way. Their deportation seemed to have been a badly organised, insensitive and inhuman operation. Torn from their ordered homes, these wretched people had been dumped in the beautiful but undeniably primitive Charente countryside. They had left their comfortable houses to live in conditions of extreme discomfort, squalor and cold. Some of these unfortunates had been quartered in ancient farm buildings, damp barns and tumbledown sheds, which were neither warm nor clean. No provision had as yet been made for heating, although we were faced by one of the coldest winters of the century.

The Châteauroux operation was largely run by American doctors including a group of Quakers, remarkable people who gave us invaluable advice and promised help should we need it. However, we hadn't been at Châteauroux for much more than a week when Mrs Crawshay arrived with fresh instructions. Ambulances and cars were urgently needed elsewhere; Elena and I were to go to Angoulême², whilst Joan and Ronnie were assigned to Limoges. Yvonne was to remain based in Châteauroux, but decided to travel with us so that she could assess the situation in Angoulême for herself.

When we first arrived in Angoulême, we were in a state of euphoria. Capital of the Département of the Charente, the town was renowned for its brandy, truffles and butter, and steeped in history. Our hotel, Les Trois Piliers, was both clean and agreeable though a little old-fashioned. The ambulance could be safely parked in their yard and we found a hosepipe and a tap for washing it. Unfortunately, they were short of accommodation, so the three of us had to share one room. What happened next was rather well described by Yvonne as I made a bee-line for the en suite bathroom.

> Elizabeth immediately took possession of this, and seemed to be under the illusion that her maidenly modesty was amply protected from our vulgar gaze, quite oblivious to the fact that the glass door was all-revealing. She proceeded to make the most tremendous splashings and gurglings, interspersed by a running commentary on refugees and the awful things one could catch from them. The immediate cause for her anxiety seemed to be a flea, which she was convinced had concealed itself somewhere on her person, and in the pursuit of this elusive insect she managed so to inundate the bathroom, and to cover it with *Keatings*,³ as to make it pretty-nigh uninhabitable for any other living creature.

Once Elena and I had both washed, we went down for dinner, leaving Yvonne to sleep. That evening, and every one that followed, we were delighted to find a bottle of claret placed on each table – what luxury! Elena and I both regarded ourselves as gastronomes, and proceeded to indulge in a most delicious meal, finished off with some of the Grand Marnier for which the region was famous.

The following morning, we paid two duty visits, first to the *Préfecture* and then to the local hospital. Used to scrupulously clean English hospital wards, we were appalled at what we found, and feared for any of our Alsace-Lorraine patients we might have to bring there. However, the hospital authorities were extremely co-operative and helpful, supplying us

Alsatian refugees in Angoulême

with all we needed, including gallons of that ubiquitous but disagreeable French disinfectant, *Eau de Javel,* which we used to disinfect our vehicles every evening.

My first call was an urgent summons to a remote farm. This entailed a twenty mile drive through beautiful country, where tall cypresses stood guard by ancient Gothic ruins and historic place names looked down from the signposts. On arrival, however, our euphoria quickly disappeared. The farm was the dirtiest and most primitive I had ever seen and the refugees were housed in stinking damp and filthy barns. They all came from a village called Forbach and the local population regarded them with hostility, mainly because their local *patois,* similar to that spoken in Switzerland, sounded like German. They were reluctant to visit the local village as they were taunted with cries of *"Boches! A bas les Boches!"* Neither the local authorities nor those in Paris seemed interested in them. They had to sleep on damp straw, dig latrines in the nearest field and collect their water from a dripping tap in the farmyard. Refugees in their own country, these people were in a state of shock, completely demoralised and deeply resentful.

My patient was a young man with an advanced case of tuberculosis. He emerged from the barn supported by his elderly parents and wearing his best blue suit. The two old people were in tears, realising how ill their son

A mobile dispensary in Angoulême, with the MTC in attendance

was. It was a harrowing scene, but he managed to climb into the ambulance and lie down on the stretcher. I think we all knew that he would never come back. This was the first time I was to recognise the importance of being in uniform, for it gave me authority and instilled calm and confidence in those I dealt with.

This first case was not untypical of what these people were falling victim to. Here, typhoid, diphtheria, dysentery, tuberculosis, pneumonia and bronchitis were the real enemies we would have to fight. We soon realised that our Girl Guide first aid was useless, and deplored our lack of real nursing capability. We were also in constant danger of infection from our patients, as the only protection we had been given in London was the tourist TAB jab.

We headed back to Angoulême and for about ten minutes I presumed my patient was asleep. Then I heard muffled coughing and choking noises, and glancing through the window behind me saw the wretched youth in the throes of a major haemorrhage. As my first aid training had not provided for such emergencies, I had no idea what I should do. All I knew about TB had been gleaned from Thomas Mann's *The Magic Mountain* and the history of the Brontë sisters. I had to rely on my instinct and common sense. I sat him up, tried to calm him and attempted to mop up the blood before driving on. When they lifted him onto a stretcher at the hospital, he looked very ill indeed and he died the very next day. I felt terribly for his family, but my overwhelming emotion was rage that whilst we were struggling to help these wretched people, their own countrymen didn't want to know.

Although Elena had brought her own car, we sometimes worked together. I particularly remember a mysterious telephone call which came though as we were drinking our coffee one Sunday morning. It was from an outlying district requesting urgent help; we supposed the caller had failed to contact the hospital and in desperation had appealed to us. The ground was sparkling with frost and the cypresses had never looked so impressive, silhouetted against a hard, cold blue sky. Our destination proved to be a small stone peasant house which we had some difficulty in finding. When we finally arrived we found the family around a table eating their mid-day meal.

After a warm welcome accompanied by expressions of gratitude, we were invited to sit down at the table and share their simple but excellent lunch. After a few minutes of general conversation, we found it odd that no-one had referred to the purpose of our visit. The sun was streaming through the windows of the room where we were seated, but we noticed that the back portion of the room was curtained off. We both sensed that something was wrong, but could not define it. After Sunday lunch had been cleared away we decided to enquire about our patient, but our enquiries were met with an icy silence.

Then Elena, straightforward as usual, asked to see the patient. Still no-one spoke. Then one of the younger men indicated that we should follow him. He led us into the curtained-off portion of the room, where we saw the patient lying motionless on a bed. We took one look at him, a very old man, and knew immediately that he was dead, very dead. The signs of rapidly advancing decomposition were staining his face and hands, and there was already a horrible smell. The young man explained that his grandfather had died well over a week ago, but they hadn't called a doctor – what would have been the use? He was old, they insisted, very old, "pauvre grand-père". The ground was frozen so hard that even the curé couldn't have got him buried, but when the smell got so bad they knew they had to do something, so they called that ambulance unit from

Two of the MTC's vehicles in Angoulême: a Standard Twelve car and Ford V-8 1.5T van

England they had read about in the papers. "You will help, won't you?" They wanted us to take away the body and arrange for a Christian funeral.

Elena and I had considerable difficulty in explaining why we could not do this, but eventually managed to convince them that we would get help to them, which we did on our return. As we left, we could hardly bear to see their distress but marvelled at their dignity; as we headed for home, the sparkle on the ground no longer seemed so bright and never had the cypresses looked so black.

We were learning fast the hard way. But soon there was quite a different lesson to be learned, namely how to play politics. We were constantly dealing with one authority or another, and had to be careful not to get embroiled in local intrigues. The 'phoney war' had failed to produce anything good or noble in the French and when I uncovered a glaring example of corruption, I strongly suspected the *Préfecture*, or even the *Préfet* himself. It had begun when a large consignment of blankets and stoves had been dispatched from Paris and had allegedly arrived, but then subsequently disappeared. I was so angry with this that I leapt onto a train to Paris to give the story to the press. I first approached *Le Matin* who asked one of their most distinguished contributors, Jules Saerwein, to

HOTEL LES TROIS PILIERS, ANGOULÊME — 27th December 1939

I am still in my room with the flu — I still have a bit of a
temperature with it, but I do not feel at all ill. Fortunately I have
had to work — because our boss, Mrs Crawshay, from our Embassy in
Paris came to see me to discuss the various problems of the region.
She seems to be very capable and very kind. She explained a bit about
the conditions here — the most urgent needs, and informed me about the
delicate matters of protocol! In any case I'm very happy to be here,
and I was very impressed with the welcome we have been given, one
couldn't imagine a better one. That which we find totally natural, to
help out allies with all our means, they seem to regard as something
extraordinary and they keep complimenting us about it. It's very
touching and makes us want to work like dogs for them! I have been
very impressed by the excellent morale found in this country.

So Mrs Crawshay has decided that I must go to see the authorities in
Paris — in order to arrange the means of transporting equipment and
to put into place the transport necessary to the region…

We eat too well here — it's frightful how I see myself fattening, but
after four months in England we were ready for anything that wasn't
bacon and eggs. I've read a lot since I've been bedridden: Thérese
Desqueyroux by Mauriac, Les enfants gâtés by Philippe Hériat, a book
about Angoulême and Gide's diary. It's funny how I almost haven't
missed my family for Christmas — I am still under the shadow of those
black weeks that I have just spent in London…

I've left my country with no regrets. Here the work empassions me;
it's such wonderful work, and one is accepted on one's own merit. Here
we mix daily in the lives of unknown people — we see all the joys, the
sufferings which can touch human kind. We see brave people, sullen and
disagreeable people, indifferent people, all life types … I try to
understand all these mysteries, all these sufferings and these joys…
It feels each moment that these people are giving me a precious gift.

interview me. The result was a splendid piece of journalism which attracted a great deal of attention. Of course, when I returned to Angoulême, the *Préfet* was no longer on speaking terms with me, and the blankets never did appear.

It was a tough life, always exhausting and usually depressing. It seemed odd that in this exceptionally beautiful part of France we had to encounter so much misery. However, there were a few good moments; most notably when we were invited to Cognac to eat a gourmet Sunday lunch with the Martells. The euphoria we felt after a glass of the *Réserve Spéciale*, their family brandy, made these red letter days. We also felt a certain glow when our efforts were finally recognised in the local press[4]:

> At the request of Lady Crawshay, a car and an ambulance have been freely offered to the medical service for the evacuees of Meurthe-et-Moselle en Charente. Two young English woman – Helen German Ribon and Elizabeth Scott-Montagu, have come to Angoulême to drive these vehicles, and have been placed at the disposal of the medical service. Having abandoned everything in England and taking on all the expenses of the stay and of the job, they have come, driven with one desire, that of voluntarily joining the struggle, as their British brothers, for better conditions amongst the populations tried by war.

Christmas in Angoulême came and went, cold and lacklustre, but in early January we had an unexpected drama. One of the girls under my command, who was quartered in a neighbouring town, announced that she was pregnant. I telephoned Mrs Cook for instructions. She was most upset and tried to blame me for this untoward event – she was so angry that I wondered whether I would be cashiered. I survived my dressing down but my health was in decline and I was confined to bed with bouts of high fever. Poor Elena was struggling on alone and I implored Mrs Cook for help. My request was granted, and another untrained innocent in uniform arrived from London. Meanwhile as I lay in bed in my very small room, I struck up a special friendship – with a mouse! He was a glossy little fellow with fine twitchy whiskers and the brightest eyes imaginable. Even during the day he would creep out of the wainscoting to keep me company, and, being very brave, would take cheese from my hand.

With very little care and few drugs to help me, I got worse by the day. At last a khaki-clad English doctor appeared, sent by the MTC. She quickly diagnosed my condition as pneumonia and decided to take me to a good hospital in Paris. Dr Richards warned me that a long journey in an unheated train was not ideal, but fearing the alternative might be the hospital in Angoulême, I agreed to take the risk. Having made the necessary back-up arrangements for Elena, I was taken to the station and found myself being helped into a compartment labelled *Réservé Ambassade d'Angleterre*. Thoughtfully, Lady Crawshay had arranged this through our Ambassador, Sir Roland Campbell, whose sister Mabel lived at Beaulieu. Such regal treatment in wartime caused quite a stir in provincial Angoulême.[5]

La belle France was not looking her best as the Bordeaux-Paris Express trailed across the wintry countryside, but I was hardly aware of anything as I dozed uneasily in the stuffy crowded compartment. Feeling ill and defeated, I realised it might be weeks before I would return to my post in Angoulême. Dr Richards cared for me very well during the journey – she had even phoned ahead for an ambulance to meet me at the Gare d'Orléans and transport me to the prestigious American Hospital at Neuilly on the outskirts of the city. When the train came to its final halt, I was carefully helped from the coach and stood rather feebly on the platform. What then occurred could have been an incident out of an Ealing comedy.

Standing smartly to attention on the platform were not one but two groups of stretcher-bearers, one in French uniforms, the other British. Perhaps it had something to do with a mad rumour, which only came to my attention much later, that I was a member of the Royal Family! Even in my dazed and feverish state, it was immediately obvious that something had gone awry, and that it was up to me to decide which stretcher party it should be, a difficult decision for someone with a temperature of 102°. Mindful that the MTC was working closely with the French Army, I had a few words with my British compatriots and then lay down on the French stretcher to be efficiently wrapped in blankets and surrounded by stone hot water bottles. The party then set off across the rails towards the station exit. Possibly unnerved by their onlooking British colleagues, one of them slipped on the frozen rails and fell headlong, so down crashed the stretcher, hot water bottles and all. I was not hurt, and luckily conscious enough to be vastly amused by this ridiculous incident. The British contingent could hardly conceal their smug smiles of superiority.

The American Hospital had the reputation of being the best in Paris, and had been loaned to the French Army for the care and treatment of their officers. At this stage in the war the hospital was not too full, so although no provision had been made for female officers, I was accepted and given a most luxurious room to myself. There now followed a hazy period when I was only semi-conscious and largely unaware of the passage of time. Beaulieu had been duly informed of my condition as it was thought I was unlikely to survive. I was dimly aware of this but determined to fight. The process of clawing my way back to life was far more unpleasant than the sensations I had experienced when I was 'sinking'. Indeed it was tempting, and seemed far easier, to give up and die.

Gradually I emerged, and realised that spring must be well on its way as people were bringing me blossom, tulips and daffodils. Best of all, my elegant Schiaparelli friend, Bianca Mosca, recently appointed head of Paquin, London[6], brought me a huge bottle of my favourite scent. Then one day without any warning, Roland turned up looking very smart and trim in his uniform. I hardly recognised him. Following several cold and miserable months in a dugout near Forbach, he had been promoted to *Capitaine* and was enjoying a few days' leave before joining General Gamelin's staff. Although he could not tell me anything about his role, I sensed that he was not at all happy about the state of affairs.

On leaving hospital I spent a few days with my friend Anne Tyrrell, whose father had been British Ambassador to France. Her house in the Rue de la Faisanderie was a great improvement on the hospital, but my lungs were still in a poor condition, and the doctors advised a few weeks convalescence in the mountains. I ended up, of course, at Schloss Berg[7]. Since it was 2,000 feet above sea level, I knew that the air would do me good and that I would receive the best possible care, but withdrawing to the safety of Switzerland filled me with conflicting emotions. On the one hand, I hated being separated from my comrades in No 3 Company of the MTC, but I knew that if I was to be any use to them in the future, I had to get better first.

In the uniform of the Mechanised Transport Corps

17

'Aux Armes Citoyens'

Despite the idyllic surroundings of Schloss Berg, my recovery was slow and when the devastating news of 10th May 1940 arrived, I was still under doctor's orders. It was on the radio that we first heard that the German army had steamrollered into Holland and then Belgium; it seemed inevitable that France would be next. No one who was alive at that time will ever forget the appalling impact Hitler's rape of north-western Europe had on the world. Each day brought news of further disasters, and I knew I had to go back to Paris and to the MTC, and that I should act quickly before the German advance closed the frontiers. The local doctors opposed this idea, but Renata was wonderfully understanding and helpful, even accompanying me to Zurich to put me on the Paris train[1]. In fact, there was no direct train anymore, so it took many weary hours to arrive at the Gare de Lyon and a very subdued Paris.

I had changed into my uniform on the train (I could not wear it in neutral Switzerland) and went straight to join my comrades staying in a small hotel on the Left Bank. I was given an attic room where the floor was covered with bright red linoleum which gave off a not unpleasant but extremely pungent smell. The weather was beautiful, the windows were open and every radio in Paris blared out *"Aux armes citoyens"*. Morale in France was very low, and this borrowed line from the *Marseillaise* was intended to improve it – strangely, it had the opposite effect.

The MTC now had several units operating in France, co-ordinated from its headquarters in Neuilly on the north-west side of Paris. 47 Rue Perronet was a convent which Yvonne had previously attended as a pupil, and perhaps because of this, the sisters were very keen to help and support us. Catching up with other members of the unit, I began to realise just how close we were to the front line. Unless the German advance were halted, they would be in Paris within a week! The MTC units which had gone to support the French army were now embroiled in a chaotic retreat: Ronnie had only narrowly escaped capture when her field hospital was evacuated, and Yvonne had a harrowing tale of a failed mission to rescue the children of a Jewish orphanage near Boulogne. On the brighter side, Yvonne had replaced her 'Gutter Bug' (the Fiat) with a splendid Bugatti sports coupé. This and all our vehicles were now fully employed on mercy missions, evacuating children, the old and the sick, and the MTC began to win the respect of the French. Since my superiors knew I was still a convalescent, I was allotted light duties such as supervising or driving on short trips.

The weather in the early summer of 1940 was quite exceptional, but a sad bewilderment hovered over France. Louis Aragon expressed it perfectly in his evocative poem *Le temps des lilas et le temps des roses*. I was now able to see Roland every day. He had recently been appointed *Chef de Cabinet* to the Prime Minister, Paul Reynaud, but with the German army nearing the gates of Paris, he could hardly conceal his despair. However, he quietly worked on, and every day around midday I would walk to the Elysée Palace, show the guards my pass, and wait for him in the beautiful courtyard before snatching a quick lunch at a neighbouring bistro. One morning while on my way there, the air raid sirens wailed into the sky and I hurried to the first available shelter, the cellar of a vast house on the Boulevard St Germain. I was the last to stumble underground and found that I was the only woman among a large group of French sailors. We laughed and joked, wondering whether we would get out alive, but I was struck that despite the ceaseless advance of the German army, their morale remained stoically high.

My lunches with Roland were brief affairs, so we tried to meet again in the evening for dinner when we could be more relaxed. I was able to gauge how badly things were going by Roland's ever-increasing depression and the sadness and strain that blurred his features. One evening in the first week of June he took me to a very special restaurant, the Tour d'Argent, high above the Seine, overlooking Notre Dame. It was very crowded that night and some high-ranking generals could be spotted among other distinguished guests – hadn't they more important things to attend to than savouring the renowned canard pressé? That night our dinner was a sad and silent affair, and afterwards we strolled along the *quais* watching the last rays of the setting sun illuminate the towers of Notre Dame. It was a perfect evening, warm and calm, but glancing at Roland, I noticed he was weeping. It was then that I realised it was all over – France was lost. I gently took his hand and wiped away his tears.

For Roland to show such emotion demonstrated his intense agony of mind and spirit, but he must have decided that this was to be the moment of truth, and I was to hear it all. What I heard was pretty grim. Prime Minister Reynaud, his ministers and the heads of the armed forces had agreed that the time had come for the Government to leave the capital and move to a chateau south-west of Paris. The British, Roland told me, had been briefed so that our Ambassador and his staff would also relocate. Despite desperate efforts by the French Army, the *Blitzkrieg* was now at its height and the *Wehrmacht* were advancing very rapidly. To complicate matters still further, all the highways into the capital were clogged with people fleeing from the north whilst low flying *Stukas* attacked from above. It was a hopeless situation.

Roland was to accompany the Prime Minister to a chateau 20 miles east of Tours in Montrichard which would now be the seat of Government, with the Allied missions taking up residence in various chateaux along the Loire valley. However, one ministry, the *Ministère des Armaments*, would be sent far away to Mont d'Or in the Auvergne. Paris itself would be left undefended, and hopefully granted the status of an open city, thereby saving its beautiful buildings from air attack. Roland told me this while we stood in the shadow of the great cathedral. The depth of the unfolding tragedy was becoming clear, a tragedy not only for France, but for the entire free world. Today I can still recapture the extraordinary impression that half-hour by the river made on me. I sensed then that if we survived we would find ourselves living in a very different world.

Next day, the information I had gleaned from Roland was confirmed when Yvonne and I visited the British Embassy. Here we met my step-father, Ned Pleydell-Bouverie, who was Naval Attaché. He listened politely to our story – all very calm and 'senior service' – and then told us rather tersely to leave Paris immediately and head for the south-west. After that he handed us over to a colleague, the Assistant Military Attaché, Major Christen de Linde, who turned out to be very well-informed with up-to-the-minute news. He confirmed that the MTC should evacuate its Neuilly headquarters before the roads became completely blocked. We should head for Saumur on the banks of the Loire, where we would have the use of a chateau. After a short session with this likable man, it was decided we should stay in touch as he said we could be of considerable help to him, although he didn't specify what sort of help this would be.

Back at the convent, we relayed the advice from the embassy. After some hesitation it was agreed that evacuation was our only option, but we couldn't possibly leave the nuns behind, most of whom were British. Yvonne decided that we should take them with us, but not before she and Joan had inspected the chateau we had been promised. This would mean the rest of us waiting for 24 hours until she returned. However, events were moving fast and that evening we received new advice from the embassy: we should be out of Paris by 4am! There was no hope of Yvonne being back by then; the consensus was that the remaining Corps members should take the nuns and leave without her. I could hardly disagree with the logic of the decision, but it seemed disloyal to our Commanding Officer. I quickly resolved to stay until Yvonne had returned; she had seen me through some tricky situations, and the least I could now do would be to wait for her.

Unexpectedly, our Australian Quartermaster then spoke up: "Please, I'll stay here with Ensign Montagu – she shouldn't be left here all alone…" Permission was granted, and I accepted this offer from dear, ample-bosomed Mrs Sherington with enormous gratitude, for it was certainly no time to be alone and unarmed. I suppose we found something to eat for our supper, but I remember a very long, hot, sleepless night, spent mainly gazing out of an attic window watching the searchlights and listening to the sound of the guns. Before I had left Berg, Renata had given me a small leather-bound copy of *The Thoughts of Marcus Aurelius* in which she had carefully marked certain passages. I had always kept this book within reach, and now pulled it out of my uniform pocket to gain comfort. Reflecting on the gravity of the situation, I made a special note on the flyleaf: 'Paris June 9th 1940. Read while waiting to evacuate – to the sound of guns and German aeroplanes, and German bombs'.

Mrs Olive Sherington alongside our Peugeot truck

Yvonne arrived back with Joan at about 4.30am looking tired and dispirited, but very pleased to see me. She had passed the outward-bound MTC convoy whilst driving back to Paris, but they didn't notice her and she was left wondering if there was anyone left at the convent. However, her journey had served a purpose; she had found the chateau but it was being used as a refuge for German Jews. They had kindly agreed to store her luggage, but there wasn't much hope that it could be used as a replacement HQ for the MTC.

Utterly exhausted, Yvonne was desperate for a hot bath and some food – in fact we all were – but everything at the convent had been packed away. We therefore decided to take a room at the Ritz and luxuriate in comfort, whilst Joan volunteered to stay behind to 'man the fort'. The rumours that had bedevilled Paris for the last three or four days had now crystallised into solid facts. The change of attitude among most Parisians was clearly illustrated when we drove up the Champs Elysées where, only a few days ago, the pavements had been crowded and cafés doing a roaring trade. Now the place was empty, the cafés deserted and the city strangely quiet. Parking in the Place Vendôme, we checked into the Ritz, the concierge happily oblivious to our crumpled and shapeless uniforms and flat-heeled shoes. It was as if we had stepped into another world, since except for the striking absence of other guests, everything seemed so normal and beautifully regulated. We got a splendid room, indulged ourselves in the bathroom and, after a couple of glasses of champagne, felt as fresh as daisies.

But before we had the chance of a nap, Joan came bursting in with an urgent message from our Military Attaché: he wanted some wounded British soldiers rescued from a hospital somewhere. Arriving at the embassy, we found Major de Linde busy packing up papers and stuffing torn documents into large wastepaper baskets, ready for burning. He gave Yvonne the details of her eleventh-hour mission whilst I stayed behind to assist with the packing. Incinerating such papers evidently required a special technique which none of us possessed, especially as the elegant fireplace was far from suited to the task. Without enough matches or lighter fuel, our first efforts simply produced an evil-smelling acrid smoke, but with streaming eyes and much spluttering we eventually managed to reduce the documents to a pulpy, black mass. Baden-Powell taught scouts and guides many useful things, but he forgot to tell us how to burn secret papers.

At lunch time, I returned to meet the others at the Ritz with the latest news. The Germans were expected to be in Paris by dawn the next day; the Ambassador, Sir Ronald Campbell, was about to depart and Major de Linde planned to leave by 7pm. He wanted two of us to follow him, carrying some important documents; this could be useful, as he would have all the necessary passes and an armed guard. In the event, the Major wasn't ready to leave the embassy until 9pm. We walked down the elegant staircase and looked into empty rooms where there were nothing but echoes for company; the air of unreality made me wonder if this was all a dream. Major de Linde closed the front door firmly behind us and locked it. The embassy was now empty and silent and the Union Jack no longer fluttered from the flagpole.[2]

We now had two cars at our disposal; I cannot remember much about Major de Linde's except that it was rather uncomfortable with so many papers packed into it. He and I led the way, with Yvonne, Joan and Mrs Sherington following closely behind in the Bugatti. Progress through the centre of the city was straightforward, but when we reached the Lion de Belfort, one of the gateways of Paris, we found ourselves engulfed in a solid traffic jam, with everyone heading the same way and straining to escape. We eventually reached the suburbs, but progress was appallingly slow. All around us were cars weighed down to the axles with escaping Parisians, their pets and as many household goods as they could transport. Some even had mattresses tied to their roofs as a precaution against *Stuka* machine-gun attacks. Nevertheless, the general air was of dazed resignation rather than panic, probably because everyone found it hard to believe what was happening.

The evening was hot and still, and because the traffic was so slow moving, exhaust fumes presented a real hazard, making everyone sleepy and slow to react. It was after some minor incident that I first sensed a certain hostility towards us as we sat in our foreign cars and British uniforms. This was particularly noticeable among the refugees from northern France, squeezed into their trucks and assorted vehicles. As the dark closed in, navigating became virtually impossible, but Joan's knowledge of the local roads was better than mine, so we swapped places. Convoy driving in heavy traffic under blackout conditions was a gruelling experience. One was constantly straining to see the car ahead, only sometimes one didn't, so when the Major had a slight accident, the ensuing disorder caused us to lose sight of him. At around midnight, we decided to get out of this mayhem by leaving the *Route Nationale* and heading down a quiet side road. Finding refuge in a field, we shared out our evening meal of biscuits and mineral water, and then got a few hours' uneasy rest on the hard ground.

We awoke, stiff and rather disoriented, and in the light of a crystalline dawn, forced our way back onto the highway. Going against the traffic flow, we back-tracked to the spot where de Linde and Joan had their accident, but there was no sign of them so we joined the throng heading south. The exodus had now become a flood; the traffic included farm carts loaded not just with furniture but also with hen-coops, complete with clucking hens. Many were horse-drawn, while behind them, carefully haltered, walked cattle, horses, pigs and sheep. Most of the refugees seemed bowed down by the catastrophe that had overtaken them, their faces wooden and expressionless, and the children white-faced and silent.

None of us had got much sleep, but Yvonne opted to drive whilst I navigated and Mrs Sherington travelled in the back. But as the sun rose and the engine purred, the temptation to sleep was too great to resist. Suddenly, something made me wake up: it wasn't the road I saw but the verge and a very large tree getting ever closer. Firmly, but without wishing to jolt her into a panic reaction, I placed my hand on Yvonne's knee. She opened her eyes just in time to swerve back onto the road. We had all been seconds from a fatal collision. After that, we all stayed awake and eventually arrived at Orléans where we had a reviving hot coffee and croissants. Finishing our breakfast, we wondered what our next move should be. We were low on fuel and no longer had Major de Linde to lead us to the British Embassy. Then we noticed a major entering the café, and appealed to him for help. As luck would have it, he was heading for the embassy himself, and had access to the French military fuel depot. With our tank re-filled, Major Golding gave us directions to the chateau some 20 miles south of Tours, and drove on ahead.

Before the war, Tours had been a most elegant but rather sleepy provincial town. It was now in total pandemonium with its streets blocked and the pavements thick with people. Even the Hotel de l'Univers, which we had enjoyed shortly after our arrival in France, resembled an untidy gypsy encampment with escaped hens clucking desperately about its entrance. But there was one very welcome sight: Joan waiting on the steps, smiling and obviously delighted to see us. She explained that de Linde's accident had only been minor, but they had been unable to find us, so had pressed on to Tours. Inside the hotel, it was impossible to move; the impeccably attired concierge had never before had to deal with such a curious collection of guests. The reason for this soon became obvious. The l'Univers had been chosen to house those senators who had fled from Paris and were now seeking accommodation. Most of them were elderly, confused and distressed as they pushed their way through the throng in the foyer. However, there was also an element of French farce as some of them were accompanied by ladies in skirts too tight, heels too high and hair too blonde – these were surely not their legal wedded wives! A visit to the hotel bar soon dispelled such frivolous thoughts, for here were many of the international foreign correspondents usually based in Paris. In the bar that night were Philip Cadet of *The Times*, Alex Werth of the *Manchester*

Guardian and some leading American foreign correspondents. Alcohol flowed freely and the sense of unreality increased.

From Tours, we proceeded with Joan to the relocated British Embassy. The chateau in question was quite impressive, but our eyes were glazed with fatigue and our senses dulled. Yvonne went inside to report to Major de Linde while I dozed in the uncomfortable Bugatti awaiting instructions. Suddenly de Linde appeared and told us that we were being given an important mission, to be undertaken without delay. We would be entrusted with vital dispatches which we were to deliver to the *Ministère des Armaments* in the Auvergne. We agreed, but wondered whether we would get through with the Germans advancing so rapidly. Supposing we were taken prisoner; what should we do with the dispatches? Major de Linde looked puzzled and left to discuss these details with his superiors. After some time he reappeared carrying two large service revolvers, one for each of us – we were appalled. "Of course," he said, "if you could burn the papers before they fell into German hands that would be best, as we did in Paris." Yvonne laughed: "But the papers didn't burn, remember?" Major de Linde smiled. "Oh well," he said cheerfully, "I'm sure you girls will find some solution to the problem," and gave us a map.

We were still very tired, extremely hungry and totally bemused. Once we were out of sight of the chateau, we stopped and took stock. We decided to take the route via Tours where we would 'touch base' with our friends at the hotel. Contemplating those awful service revolvers, I remembered some excellent advice once given to me by John Buchan. I had been fascinated by *The Thirty-Nine Steps*, and once asked him if he had ever carried a gun. He paused for a while before replying: "I never carry a gun; that's one of my principles. And I'll tell you why. If you're going to shoot, you've got to be certain that you are the better shot, and how can you know? Without a gun, you stand a better chance…" So, looking dubiously at the heavy firearms, Yvonne and I decided to hide the beastly things in the boot. I still wonder why we didn't throw them into the Loire.

Back in Tours, rumour was rife and all of it bad: the word was that Paris had fallen and that the Germans were advancing on Orléans. Our journalist friends at the hotel seemed reasonably well-informed, but their news was no better. I contacted the embassy back at the chateau to receive further instructions, whereupon we were told that our daring dispatch ride was a non-starter and we should hand the secret papers to a designated British officer in Tours. We were also pleased to return those service revolvers!

It was clear that accommodation in Tours was at a premium, but de Linde had given us a letter requesting the authorities to help us. We tried every available hotel, guest house and hostel, but none of them had room. Yvonne and Major Golding then spent some time at the police station telephoning around, but even the hospitals, prisons and barracks were full. Eventually, we re-grouped at the Hotel l'Univers; the restaurant had virtually run out of food but still had plenty of champagne. Major Golding ordered a bottle for our party, but before we had time to consider our next move, the Chief of Police walked in – he had failed to find us a hotel but offered us a couple of beds in his own house. Touched by this gesture, we passed him a glass of champagne. Then one of the newspaper correspondents came forward and said he had some empty beds in his house. So Joan and Mrs Sherington went with him whilst Yvonne and I gratefully accepted the policeman's invitation.

The following morning, we found the wife of the Police Chief in a very distressed state, packing her belongings. She had decided that Tours was no longer safe and proceeded to blame the British for failing to hold back the German advance. There was little point in arguing with her, but then we had an idea. If the house was to be left empty, it would make an ideal base for us. Yvonne approached the Police Chief and they agreed terms, after which Mrs Sherington and I were left in charge. To begin with, we were thrilled with our new base, but as time went by we started to realise that it wasn't just the Police Chief's family who considered Tours unsafe; a general evacuation was taking place all around us. Meanwhile, Yvonne and Joan were on the road to Limoges. Joan was urgently needed to assist other members of the Corps, whilst Yvonne wanted to check on the nuns who were temporarily staying at the nearby Château de Bonneval. To our huge relief, Yvonne returned by midnight of the second day, but the following morning we received word from the embassy that they were relocating again, this time to Bordeaux.

It seemed that we had no choice but to follow them, but first Yvonne had to contact the MTC units in other parts of France. We found Major de Linde at the hotel, but he couldn't help and simply told us we should leave at once. Undeterred, we went round to the headquarters of the Neuvième Region, where the General was already aware of our work. Mercifully, Yvonne was able to use the telephone to speak to Joan in Limoges, who in turn would relay the evacuation message to our units in Périgeaux and Clairvivre. On returning to the hotel, we were approached by a heavily pregnant British woman who appealed to us for help. Her story was almost too incredible to believe: that morning, she had left England on an Imperial Airways flight for Paris with the intention of carrying on by train to Switzerland. The airline was evidently unaware that German forces had entered the French capital some two days before, and assured her that the journey could still be made. In reality, the plane had been forced to land in Tours, leaving this lady and her maid, stranded. We were just wondering how we could fit them into the car with everything else when, to our immense relief, Elena arrived from Angoulême in our Peugeot lorry with the Austin van following behind.

We bundled the pregnant lady, her maid and another English woman into the Austin with Mrs Sherington and told her to drive straight to Angoulême. The rest of us headed for Saumur where we hoped to find our luggage stored in the chateau that was to have been our new HQ. The sun was already low when the convoy took the road heading west, following the great Loire. We were now joined by a French ambulance unit, so the convoy was a long one. All I knew about Saumur was that it was a small town with a deal of history attached, and the seat of the prestigious military academy. Presuming it would be another elegant and pleasant town, I quite relished the chance to see it, but thoughts of sightseeing soon gave way to the difficulties of driving the Peugeot lorry. I could hardly reach the pedals and had to stand up to exert pressure on either the brake or the clutch. I began to wonder whether I was up to the job.

It was after sunset when the convoy ground to a halt in Saumur. Thankfully, our luggage was still at the chateau, but no one had thought of bringing any food or drink. Since leaving Tours, I had been carrying a young passenger called Anderson who turned out to be a war correspondent from the *Daily Sketch*. His reluctance to attempt any lorry driving had made me wonder if he was going to be any use to us, but he now took the initiative and went to see if there was any food to be had in the town. He returned bearing some bread and garlic sausage plus a bottle of Perrier water. I blessed him!

Then another problem emerged. There is seldom any difficulty in France should a man wish to relieve himself – *pissoirs partout* – but we girls were less well provided for – although this became easier after dark!

We now had to gird ourselves for a long night-time drive to Angoulême, but our route had to be carefully planned, as it was reported that the Germans had already advanced well into the heart of France. I was ordered to bring up the rear of the convoy, a position of considerable responsibility. But as we trundled along the dark roads, I soon realised that I had been landed with one of the worst jobs, as we were all at the end of our tether. We hadn't eaten a proper meal for days, were deprived of sleep, and I was still convalescing from a serious illness. I remember shouting furiously at the young journalist: "Sing, damn you, sing! Pummel me, pinch me – just keep me awake and driving!" But the worst handicap of all was driving in the blackout; the roads were full of fleeing people, their animals and broken down vehicles, none of which were easy to see without headlights.

By midnight everything was slipping into something of a dream-like sequence; people, places and events were all dissolving into a grey blur. All I could concentrate on was keeping my eyes open and remaining the mandatory distance from the vehicle ahead. One thing was paramount, and that was to keep going. I cannot remember if we stopped for food and drink – I suppose we did – but when we approached Angoulême in the early dawn, it meant nothing to me. It was now June 1940, some five months since I had left the town with a high fever; it seemed extraordinary that I should be returning in such circumstances.

We halted the convoy outside the house which had become the MTC base in Angoulême. Everyone from Tours seemed to have congregated there, but I managed to find a spare divan which I shared with Yvonne. I slept briefly, waking up to find intense activity all around me. Someone told us that the German tanks were advancing on the town. I tried to get to my feet, but found to my alarm that my legs just buckled. So I had to lie down again and watch while the others filed out to rejoin the convoy. No-one seemed interested in helping me, with the exception of Yvonne and Mrs Sherington, but eventually even they had to leave me. Someone unkindly told me that I'd be alright when the *Wehrmacht* arrived as I spoke German. How could they abandon me like this, my friends, my comrades! I wept.

Then I remembered Renata telling me to be wary of self-pity – man's worst enemy – and that it would kill me unless I did something about it. I managed to get to my feet, and although still wobbly, walked out of the house. Feeling stronger every moment, I walked across to the Peugeot, climbed into the driver's seat and ordered my replacement to get out and find another vehicle. This entire incident probably lasted less than half an hour, but it had a crucial influence on my life, for it was then I learned to fight self-pity tooth and nail, and to encourage everyone else affected by it to do the same. The result of this decision was truly astonishing, for as I drove down the road on that beautiful June morning, I felt as fit as a fiddle. The rest of the journey to Bordeaux was uneventful and we arrived at our destination early in the afternoon.

We made our way into the beleaguered city, heading for the British Consulate where we quickly found Major de Linde. He advised us that the Military Attaché's staff had taken over a chateau in the village of Sauternes, about 25 miles south-east of Bordeaux, and we were welcome to part of it. There was no news of the other units, but Joan had arrived from Limoges with the nuns who were temporarily staying at the local convent. The Château Filhot was a charming house standing in a large park where, among its ancient trees, we could station our vehicles safely for the night. We soon discovered that the personnel quartered in the chateau were not just diplomatic staff, but high-ranking army officers. A major appeared and brusquely informed us that there was no question of us sleeping in the chateau, nor should we expect any food, cooking facilities or baths, as these were reserved for service personnel! For a group of dead tired women whose last baths had been over a week ago, and worst of all, who hadn't been able to do their hair or make-up in days, this was a bitter blow. The refusal of cooking facilities worried us less as we could either buy provisions or eat in the local *auberge*. Having fired this broadside, the major turned on his heel and strode back to his creature comforts inside.

For a few moments, we sat disconsolately round our vehicles, but soon pulled ourselves together, thought 'damn them', and merely gnashed our teeth. However, we felt that Yvonne, who despite fatigue and travel stains still looked attractive, should deliver a formal protest. She was duly dispatched but returned half an hour later looking distinctly annoyed. Our Commanding Officer had been politely received but told that the only place free was a bothy in the grounds. She was furious and felt that this rebuff had been based on what we now call the 'male chauvinist pig' syndrome. Quite simply, these men did not want to be lumbered with a lot of females in uniform, using 'reasons of security' as an excuse. We decided to send the younger and more energetic among us to the village to forage for food and they soon returned laden with bread, cold meats and some bottles of Sauternes. This much-needed nourishment made us feel human again, but the bothy was so damp that many of us opted to doss down in our vehicles or under the trees. That evening, the male sex was highly unpopular.

Early next morning, Yvonne and I left for Bordeaux, confident that a visit to the British Consulate there might produce some news. I also hoped to find my step-father and discover how to contact Roland, who was somewhere in Bordeaux with the Prime Minister. But as we tried to enter the city, we could hardly believe our eyes. Bordeaux had once been a well laid out city but it now looked like a vast ant heap, the wide boulevards and streets being impassable with people, livestock and vehicles, all crowded together in a swarming mass. The chaos was indescribable, and one saw fear and despair on nearly every face. It was estimated that 600,000 refugees had flooded into the city which clearly could not cope: facilities were running out and law and order was close to collapse. There was an ugly mood and *sauve qui peut* seemed to be the motto of the crowd.

After an immense effort, we were eventually able to locate Roland. The seat of government was now in an unremarkable house, certainly no chateau, and I was fortunate in being able to see Roland for a few minutes. He was practically unrecognisable, his face unshaven, grey with fatigue and deeply lined with distress. I saw him alone, and he was guardedly frank about the situation. It appeared that Prime Minister Reynaud was still in charge and Pétain was hardly mentioned. Roland was adamant that France would fight on – there would be no surrender. Should the worst come to the worst, the French Cabinet might be forced to cross the Pyrenees to regroup in Spain, but at the present moment, he insisted, there was absolutely no question of that. Then I asked him a question of great personal importance – should the MTC remain in France? Without the slightest hesitation he said yes. He then said we should 'keep in touch', and that I should return early the next morning to check. In fact I was not to see Roland again until after the war, when both of us were older, wiser and sadder.

Not long after this meeting, Yvonne and I succeeded in finding Ned Pleydell-Bouverie at the British Consulate, and eagerly awaited his opinion about the situation. I was shocked to hear a completely different story from that of Roland less than an hour before. Ned, usually the immaculately turned out Naval Officer, was looking distinctly frayed at the edges. Apparently he had only just escaped from the port at Nantes before the German forces arrived. Wearily he told us that it was 'all up' with the French, predicting that the government would flee and the army would then surrender. He advised us to 'keep in touch' – that phrase again – as it was highly likely we would all have to be evacuated. This operation would be organised by the Navy, probably sooner rather than later, and he suggested that it might be wise to go down to the quay and wait.

Yvonne and I were now convinced of the gravity of the situation, but we were running out of petrol and the quay was some distance out of town. So far we had been able to use our French Army coupons, but all the city pumps had now run dry. We took local advice, and tracked down the enormous Shell depot some distance from the city. The staff there were friendly and co-operative, and we were able to fill our tank and several jerry cans. But just as we were about to leave, air raid sirens wailed into the sky. Standing in the shadow of the great oil containers, we realised that it would only need a small bomb to start an inferno. We questioned the engineers about air raid shelters but their answer froze us to silence. What would be the good of air raid shelters among millions of gallons of highly inflammable liquid? So we waited and prayed, and when the 'all clear' sounded, tried to depart with a haste we hoped was not too indecent.

Considerably shaken by this episode, I decided we deserved a good lunch to restore our spirits. I recalled that Bordeaux had one of the best restaurants in France and we managed to locate it; the chefs served us a real gourmet meal, quite marvellous under the circumstances. Back at the Consulate, things were getting increasingly chaotic with information and the corresponding orders changing by the minute. In the end, we decided our best option was to re-group at the Château Filhot, but despite being in an ambulance, our journey was fraught with difficulties and delays. When we eventually rejoined our bivouac, we found our comrades in a state of some distress. They had seen some army and RAF personnel leaving the chateau in considerable haste, but no-one had bothered to tell

the MTC what was happening. Yvonne went up to the chateau to find out
what was going on, but somewhat to our surprise, we were told to stay put.
Perhaps there simply wasn't going to be room on the ship for us.

Two long days later, on 18th June, we were finally ordered to make our way
to the quay for evacuation by the British Navy. Wearily, we packed up our
meagre possessions, leaving our camp site clean and tidy. Even at this late
stage we had jobs to do: Mrs Sherington was summoned to collect four
wounded soldiers from the hospital, Joan and another girl had to collect
the Neuilly nuns from the local convent, whilst Yvonne raced ahead to
make final arrangements. This left me to organise the convoy into the city,
in the pouring rain. It was early evening by the time we arrived in Bordeaux
and it was obvious that things were moving very fast indeed. Wild rumours
were circulating and there was panic in the air so we decided to go straight
to the quayside, where we presumed any evacuation by sea would take
place. When we first arrived, the quay was more or less deserted; there were
a few ships at anchor, but the waters of the Gironde were calm and
unruffled. We stood by our neatly parked vehicles, confused and unhappy.
Even Yvonne, whose authority we all respected, was at a loss, although she
made brave efforts to maintain the morale of her 'dog-eared' troops.

I am certain that at that moment, I was the only one among us who still
believed in the French, convinced that they would fight on and never
surrender. This made me sad. We, the MTC, had come to France full of
high hopes and fired by a kind of idealism. We had invested so much
effort, endured such hardship and taken so many risks, and now it seemed
we had been defeated. It was very depressing. Suddenly, I noticed quite a
large crowd gathered along the quay, including some of the journalists I
had met in Tours. We chatted but in a very minor key as they saw not a
glimmer of hope. All around the quayside were parked dozens of
presumably abandoned cars, most of which had GB plates.

When one of the ships moved purposefully towards the quay, our spirits
rose immediately; this manoeuvre was clearly the precursor of the promised
evacuation and no one regretted having to leave. The crowd was getting
impatient, and there were loud cheers and cries of "Let's go!" When the
gangplank was dropped, there was a strange silence and then more cheers.
It was with a sense of shock that I realised that what had seemed impossible

had now come to pass. It seemed like a bad dream. I loved France, I loved Roland, and I still wanted to believe what he had told me. So while everyone pushed and struggled to get on board, I merely stood back and watched them. Then Philip Cadet of *The Times* ran back to me. "Aren't you coming?" he asked desperately. "No," I replied flatly. But he persevered. "Don't you realise what could happen to you in German hands? You're quite mad, you know!" I took his hand but just shook my head. He wished me luck and ran back up the gangplank.

As I watched the ship pull away from the quay I had very mixed feelings. I continued to wave to Yvonne and my MTC friends until they faded into the distance. Suddenly I couldn't bear it any more and turned away from the water. It was then with a pang that I realised that what I had done was irrevocable. Here I was, completely on my own in a foreign city threatened with annihilation, without any means of getting back to England. And there was the painful realisation that Roland, whom I had considered infallible, had been wrong.

The disbelief was no less back at Beaulieu, where Ned would have relayed the news that I had failed to board the boat provided for my evacuation. Pearl's diary entry for 23rd June 1940 summed it up.[3]

> It is just beyond one's understanding – the French people have surrendered completely to the Hun – through their despicable government! I felt very anxious for Elizabeth who is with the Mechanical Transport Corps – I rang up and talked to Miss Hawkness – she said 80 of the Corps sailed from Bordeaux and arrived yesterday, but at the last minute Elizabeth refused to leave and said she would motor to Switzerland! Quite, quite mad. She will probably be taken prisoner or find herself in a French Revolution. One feels so furious that her father's daughter should behave like this – dishonouring the uniform and her Corps!

I now asked myself why had I refused to leave. There were the profound ties I had to the Continent, both human and ideological, and I suppose these then seemed more important than those I had in England. However, all these years later, I realise it was a crazy decision brought about by poor health and my inability to think rationally. But I have never regretted it, for that decision proved to be another turning point and the beginning of a new and extraordinary phase of my life.

Cherbourg

Flers

Le Mans

PARIS

Orléans

Tours

Saumur

Châteauroux

GENEVA

Limoges

Angoulême

Bordeaux

Mende

Sauternes

Agen

Tarascon

Nice

Albi

Bramafam

Toulouse

Carcassonne

——— MTC expedition to Angoulême

═══ MTC evacuation from Paris to Bordeaux

– – – Journey from Bordeaux to Bramafam

18

EAST TO BRAMAFAM

Alone on the quay, I had to pull myself together and quickly find a practical solution to my problems. To contact Roland I would need transport and, looking round at all the abandoned vehicles, I felt that this should not prove too difficult. But I had to try over twenty cars before I discovered a maroon-coloured Fiat Balilla saloon with its key still in the ignition. It had French number-plates, petrol in its tank, and, like most Fiats of that period, was a right-hand drive. Gratefully I climbed into the driver's seat and started her up – perfect! As I was crossing the quay, I was stopped by a dishevelled youth in civilian clothes with a wild look on his face; nearly in tears, he stammered that he wanted to join the British Army or Navy and would I help him. I explained that I was not a recruiting officer, nor even a soldier, but if he wanted a lift back to the city, he should jump in.

As we ploughed our way back to the centre of the city, he told me something about himself. His name was Robert Dormont, a refugee from Paris, where he had been studying law at the Sorbonne. Born into a well-to-do Jewish family, he was finding it very hard to come to terms with what was happening in France. Eventually we managed to park the car at a point not too far from Roland's office. Leaving Robert to guard the Fiat, I began to force my way through the dense crowds. Eventually, quite exhausted, I reached the house where I had last met Roland but found the door firmly locked and the guards gone. There was no doubt as to what had happened – Reynaud and his Cabinet had left[1]. Where they had gone was anyone's guess, and there was no-one to ask. My heart sank and for a moment I considered returning to the quay, and, if I were lucky, boarding another ship for England. But I quickly discarded this idea as unrealistic and made my way back to the car.

I found Robert half-asleep and looked at the little Fiat with new eyes. It was now my most precious possession – it could provide us with a means of escape! While I had been away, Robert had picked up some important news. The Reynaud government had resigned and Pétain was now Prime Minister – it was only a matter of time before France capitulated. With the German offensive drawing ever closer, I knew that we should leave Bordeaux as soon as possible. It was now getting late, and as we drove south-east through the suburbs and into the wine-growing countryside, I thought that France had never looked more beautiful. I could have wept, so profoundly was I moved by the tragedy that was unfolding.

As we approached Sauternes, I was struck by a good idea. We should visit the chateau to see if anything useful had been left behind. I vividly recalled a pile of abandoned jerry cans; we would certainly need all the petrol we could get. When eventually we reached the chateau, all was peaceful and long shadows streaked across the smooth parkland. The deserted house looked haughty and remote, discreetly veiled in a greyish haze. But we were concerned with practical matters and very soon the little Fiat was heavily loaded with as many of the jerry cans as we could fit in. I still had a couple of army coupons, but I feared that all petrol pumps would now be empty.

We managed to gain entry to the chateau by forcing a flimsy door into the kitchen. The building was as elegant inside as it was outside, and we started searching through the rooms for anything useful. We found nothing on the ground floor, but hoped for better luck upstairs. Looking over the luxurious bedrooms and bathrooms, it was difficult not to think about the nights of discomfort we had spent in the grounds, and I felt a huge surge of irritation. But there wasn't anything much to be found here either; some soap, some rolls of lavatory paper and some towels. Then in a small room which had clearly belonged to an RAF officer, we found a current Michelin guide, some maps and two excellent torches – invaluable stuff!

Finally we explored the kitchen area and located the storerooms, which were a veritable treasure-trove. Tins of fruit, pâté, bags of flour, sugar and salt, and also some mineral water, all of which we packed into cardboard boxes; it looked as though we'd been shopping at Fortnum & Mason!

With remarkable forethought, we included some knives, spoons and a couple of tin openers. The car was so loaded to the gunwales that there was hardly room for us to squeeze in, but we knew we might have to be self-sufficient, perhaps living rough for some considerable time.

By the time we left the chateau, the light was fading fast but our morale was relatively high and it all seemed like a wild adventure. Our instinct was to put as many miles as possible between us and Bordeaux which, we feared, might already have fallen. But at that moment we had no specific destination in mind and simply continued driving eastwards. We were now just two human beings, our names and nationalities irrelevant, our past lives forgotten, starting off on an unknown journey.

With the help of the maps we had found in the chateau, we decided to make Agen our first stop. As the town was close to a French air force base, the blackout was well-maintained, but we managed to find a small hotel with garage facilities and the added bonus of a *brasserie*. When we approached the reception desk, the concierge told us flatly that the hotel was fully booked, but seeing my uniform, suggested that we sleep on the benches in the restaurant when all the customers had gone. And the car? That presented no difficulty, and soon the Fiat with all our important supplies was securely locked away.

This seemed to be a most satisfactory arrangement. First, we could enjoy a good dinner and afterwards stretch out on the reasonably soft benches. But we had hardly finished our meal when the concierge arrived at our table to tell us that a room had become vacant. "But we want two rooms," I said. "One room or nothing," he replied and clearly meant it. Soon we were following him up a dimly lit staircase to the top floor, where he ushered us into a small, starkly furnished room with a small double bed, one chair, a table and two hooks on the door. We decided that Robert should have the mattress and sleep on the floor, while I would have most of the bedclothes and sleep on the springs. Robert promised to wake me well before dawn, as we knew we should leave very early.

As I lay between the sheets, I found them unusually stiff and unyielding but put it down to heavily over-starched coarse linen, and in less than a minute we were both fast asleep. At first light Robert, now fully dressed, gently woke me. Now in the half-light I could look around this room which I had shared with a strange young man. Glancing at the sheets on my bed I had difficulty in stifling a scream of horror; the 'over-starched' sheets were in reality stiff with dried blood. Appalled, we left the room as soon as we could. We demanded an explanation from the concierge, who was very apologetic, explaining he hadn't known of it himself, or he would have changed the sheets. It appeared that the hotel had been partly commandeered by the armed forces because the hospitals were full. Earlier that evening a seriously wounded officer had been brought to the hotel but he had died soon after. The military had quickly removed the body, but no-one had checked the room. The concierge offered his most humble apologies and deducted a considerable amount from our bill. I recall, though, that despite a good but hasty breakfast we were still shaking when we climbed back into the car.

Driving along the banks of the Tarn is an exquisite experience at any time of year, but on that June day it was unforgettable. The dew lay heavy on the meadows by the river and the wild flowers seemed like vast herbaceous borders. Above us, the hills, the trees and the tawny rocks were like echoes of a Cézanne painting. For a time the doubts, despair and horror of the previous night were forgotten.

In Agen they had little news of the German advance, but we took it for granted that the whole of the south-west was now in Nazi hands. Anxious to avoid a confrontation with a German patrol, we made enquiries in every village or town we passed. Should we be warned of enemy patrols, we planned to drive into the wild, hilly country to the north, where we would hide the car and find a cave to live in. Whilst such caves did exist, it was a hare-brained scheme; however, we were very tired and reality had left us long ago.

We both longed for coffee and a croissant, but Robert was adamant that our first stop should be Toulouse. As the sun climbed high into the sky, an overwhelming desire for sleep crept over me, and driving became more and more hazardous. Robert had never driven a car in his life, so I struggled to keep awake, but after some alarming swerves, I drew into the side of the road, telling Robert I had to have at least half an hour's sleep. He agreed, promising to wake me in exactly thirty minutes. Meanwhile he would stroll down to the river and have a wash.

In a few seconds I was asleep. Then, as if I was resurfacing from the depths of the ocean, I awoke to feel someone gently shaking my shoulder. I opened my eyes to see one of the most exquisite bouquets I have ever received; wild flowers and elegant grasses, all still covered with dew. Robert stood beside the car smiling, with his hair wet and spiky from his swim in the river. I felt a great wave of happiness and gratitude, jumped out and hugged him. "Robert," I exclaimed, "they're beautiful!" I saw from his expression that he too was happy, and for the first time since we had met. "Don't thank me please, it's me who should thank you for saving my life! I thought the flowers were a way I could tell you how grateful I am. They're just wild flowers, but I loved picking them for you."

By the time we had reached Toulouse, people were crowding the shops and cafés. Before searching out reliable information, we would indulge ourselves in a croissant and a café-au-lait. Cafés all over the Continent are renowned for being centres of gossip and the one we selected was no exception – it was bursting with rumours and up-to-date 'reports'. My clothes excited considerable curiosity; no-one there had seen a woman in uniform before, and certainly not an English one. We were soon the centre of friendly attention, with people crowding around our table. We learnt that Bordeaux had fallen and that the city was in flames. Moreover, we were 'reliably' told that the French Cabinet had been taken prisoners, the entire French fleet had been sunk in Toulon, the British were about to surrender, and Mussolini's troops had occupied Nice and the Côte d'Azur.

Fortified by our coffee, we did not take these rumours too seriously. By this time I had spent many hours with Robert and had learned quite a lot about him. He came from a respectable Jewish family who lived in one of the most elegant districts of Paris. As the Germans approached the city, his family had implored their only son to go south to Nice where he would find refuge with his uncle, a rabbi. But he had ended up mistakenly in Bordeaux, where he knew no-one. Worst of all, his briefcase containing his papers, student's identification card and most of his money had been stolen. So he had been really desperate when he had hailed me on the quay. Fortunately, before we left Paris, I had drawn quite a large sum from an English bank, so I had enough money for both of us provided we were careful. This situation embarrassed Robert considerably, but I told him he could pay me back after the war. He was an agreeable and resourceful travelling companion and I had grown to like and respect him.

Once outside Toulouse, we stopped and consulted our maps, carefully re-planning our route. After what we had just heard, it seemed too much of a risk to go south so we decided to head north-eastwards, cross the Rhône and make for the Haute Savoie and the Alps. Now that we had settled our route, we decided to relax and enjoy the drive. The road we chose took us past Carcassonne and Albi up to Mende on the fringes of the great Massif Central – some of the most beautiful countryside in Europe. In our haste we had to leave Carcassonne unvisited, but we did manage to pause for a short time at Albi to visit its strange and spectacular cathedral.

Happily the small town of Mende proved a pleasant surprise, as we quickly found a small and delightful hotel offering all we needed at a reasonable price. After a night in comfortable beds with clean sheets, we both felt enormously refreshed. At breakfast, the owner of the hotel was most helpful, even telephoning the local gendarmerie and some of his friends to get the latest news. What he told us though was far from encouraging. It appeared that the German advance down the Rhône valley had speeded up; one report spoke of the fall of Lyons, even Mâcon was threatened. But we wanted to stick to our plan to cross the Rhône and make our way into the comparative safety of the Alps. By this time we had heard so many unsubstantiated rumours that we discounted the last one about German motorcycle patrols near Mende and followed our intended route, hoping to be safe and sound in Geneva, or some secluded mountain valley, by sunset.

We cannot have been on the road for more than an hour when I became aware of something happening ahead of us and wondered what the crowd indicated – a French control post perhaps? As we drew nearer I could see men in German uniform with motorcycles and side-cars parked on the verge. Without doubt this was a German patrol now engaged in questioning the locals. Robert had not registered any of this through his thick glasses, but we agreed that to turn round might arouse suspicion. We therefore drove steadily on, searching desperately for some side road or track leading off the highway. As our old and dusty car had French number-plates, we felt we could be mistaken for local peasants or farmers, at least we hoped so. As it happened, luck was with us, and we found a rough farm track, very bumpy but for us a lifeline. When we had distanced ourselves from the main road and were well out of sight, we breathed a sigh of relief. If we had been captured I might have got away with it, but as a Jew, Robert wouldn't have stood a chance.

We now found ourselves floundering about on agricultural land with not a decent road in sight. Then I spotted what seemed to be a farmhouse and knew that it must have an access road, and I was right. We made our way along a network of small roads until we reached a *Route Nationale* leading south. We felt exhilarated, for we were heading in the direction we had originally favoured. But there was still a nagging worry about those rumours that the Italians had already occupied the south. Well, we had to be fatalistic about that; our most pressing problem was to get some more petrol. We were down to our last jerry can, and the moment had come to use the coupons. The first filling station we tried said their tanks were empty but we should try further down the road. The next station was quite large and everything seemed normal. I showed the smiling *garagiste* my coupons and asked him to fill up the car. His expression changed immediately, and he too pleaded empty tanks. I was convinced he was lying but there was nothing to do but move on.

Eventually we found a rusty, dusty petrol pump standing alone by the side of the road. When the owner eventually emerged to our shouts, he looked as if he had been mucking out the cows but was friendly enough. I now decided on a different approach, and simply asked him to fill up the car and only when he had completed this operation did I produce the flimsy coupon. Handing it over, I told him that it entitled the bearer to free petrol. He looked at it, horrified. "Free petrol? I can't do that!" No assurances on my part that the Army would reimburse him had any effect. So I suggested he take the petrol out again. "But how would I do that?" he growled. Now I felt sorry for him, for as things were, would anybody ever repay him? The answer was to pay him using my own cash. He immediately brightened and took the money with one hand while handing me back the coupon with the other. I tucked it back carefully into my wallet – one never knew.

As we neared the Rhône, the countryside changed dramatically. The soil appeared more fertile and the people more affluent. There was no sign here of the panic and distress I had witnessed everywhere since leaving Paris. We were now aiming for the ancient town of Tarascon with its great bridge over the Rhône, where we hoped to cross to safety. As we approached the western end of the bridge, we noticed that it was guarded by a strong military presence, but this time the uniforms were French and there was a tricolour flying in the wind, so we confidently drove on. However, we were soon stopped by a young officer. I saluted and smiled, but in return got a cool, hostile look and a curt order to leave our vehicle. He then instructed some of his men to examine the car very carefully. I found all this rather strange, but then in June 1940 nothing was normal. I thought there must be some misunderstanding, and that as I spoke fluent French, we would soon be on our way.

What then occurred can only be explained by the climate of those days and the over-stretched nerves of all concerned. The young officer, far from the front line, was evidently desperate to strike a blow for France. He started by declaring that our papers for the car were not in order. Of course, there were no papers when I had taken possession of it as the previous owner had removed everything except the ignition keys. Worst of all, the absence of the all-important *Carte Grise* indicated that there must be something seriously wrong. Now I had to show my own documents, including my British passport with its photograph of the bearer in uniform. He regarded it as false.

Then it was Robert's turn. What papers he still possessed also seemed to be unsatisfactory. Poor Robert now seemed to be going to pieces and was nearly in tears. The lieutenant asked me to explain what an alleged female British officer and Jewish student from the Sorbonne were doing here on this vital bridge. He was sure that we were carrying forged personal documents and seized on this trifling incident as one which would enable him to demonstrate his patriotism and desire to defend *La Patrie*. By now, he had worked himself up into a considerable rage, and I realised that it was essential I should act quickly to defuse this ludicrous but potentially dangerous situation. Because I managed to remain apparently calm when I intervened, they listened. Deciding to ignore the matter of the car papers, I went straight to the heart of the matter. I told the young lieutenant that despite being a female officer, I had been entrusted with an urgent message from the British Ambassador for our Consul-General in Nice.

He listened intently but I could see that he was far from convinced. "Can you show me any written proof of this 'mission' of yours? I'd like to see it." I looked suitably shocked. *"See* it? Surely you're not suggesting I would carry such a message on my person?" He considered this, and I pressed the point. "So as this message is both urgent and top secret, please let me continue my journey immediately." Then, for good measure, I added, "And where is your commanding officer? I'd like a word with him." He was now persuaded, and waved to his men to step back; this suggested that I had won the day, but he still wanted the last word. "But who is your companion – what's he supposed to be doing in all this?" I lowered my voice. "He's a Jew," I explained. "A student from Paris and he's trying to get to his uncle who is a rabbi in Nice. He asked me for a lift, and I couldn't refuse him, could I?" The young officer turned away and waved us through the barrier and onto the bridge. Never had the Rhône looked more beautiful.

The rest of the journey was uneventful. We feared that petrol would prove a problem again, but stopped at a small filling station near Fréjus which surprisingly accepted our last coupon. We were now less than an hour away from Bramafam where I had stayed several times before the war. Situated 15 km north of Cannes, I remembered the old farmhouse standing on the side of a hill among vines and olive trees, but wondered how welcome we would now be at this critical moment in history. My friends, both of them middle-aged women from Paris, were highly cultured people: Het Kwiatkowska, a Pole, was a quite well-known painter, while Marcelle Chailliol, a great-niece of the poet Stéphane Mallarmé, was less distinguished with her brush but was an excellent cook. I hoped for the best.

I assured Robert that after a night's rest I would either take him to Nice myself or at least make sure that he got there. I also remembered that there was a telephone at Bramafam so he could contact his uncle right away. Finally, about an hour before sunset, the roads started to look familiar and I recognised some of the old landmarks. At last we could relax, our journey into nowhere was over. The old farmhouse, guarded by two tall cypresses among the vines and the olive trees, looked very good indeed.

Part of a painting of Bramafam by my hostess, Het Kwiatkowska

19

LIFE AS A SUBMARINE

When we drove up the last hundred yards of rough road to the house, we could see no sign of life. Then a stout, middle-aged lady[1] with peroxide hair appeared; perhaps she thought we were Italian soldiers or even Germans, or maybe it was the sight of my uniform that upset her as she quickly scuttled back indoors. Getting out of the car, we stretched our legs but there was still no sign of Het or Marcelle. I wondered whether they had left the farm and had themselves become refugees; after all, Het was a Pole and an enemy alien in German eyes. Fortunately we didn't have to wait long before the stout lady reappeared, this time with Marcelle and Het. They seemed delighted to see me but were somewhat puzzled by Robert; however, they asked us to join them on the terrace, where we were soon drinking tea and laughing.

It had been a long, hot, exhausting day and we were both totally drained. When I stood up to follow them into the house, my knees buckled and I fainted – Het and Marcelle were most concerned. Rousing myself, I confessed that it had been quite some time since our last meal, but despite my hunger there was something I wanted far more than food, and that was a bath! The last one had been at the Ritz in those far-off days in Paris. While Het led Robert away to the back of the house to hose himself down, Marcelle suggested that I should undress among the olive trees. "Just leave your clothes," she told me. "I'll deal with them later." I could have a bathrobe while she found me something to wear. Only later did they tell us that we both stank like badgers! They also feared that we might be 'lousy', and, considering the rough way we had been living, they could have been right.

257

I left my uniform as instructed and made for the bathroom. Never have I enjoyed a bath more. Later, wrapped in a bathrobe and smelling of Roger et Gallet, I joined an equally spruced up Robert on the terrace, where Marcelle handed us great glasses of their own rough but delicious wine. We sat peacefully watching the sun set behind the campanile of Plascassier to the chirruping of the cicadas. The following day was spent sleeping, eating and generally recovering from our ordeal. Het and Marcelle had tactfully refrained from asking us about the war, but on that first night at supper we told them all that we knew. It soon became clear that they had little idea of what was going on, despite having a wireless.

During the course of the next day, Robert managed to telephone his uncle and we agreed that I should drive him to Cannes the following morning to find some transport to Nice. I was most reluctant to pack him off so abruptly, but was becoming aware of an unpleasant undercurrent of anti-Semitism in the house, so it was obvious he should leave before something hurtful was said. He was looking forward to seeing his family and was quite cheerful when I put him on a bus in Cannes. I warned him about control posts and the need to keep a low profile, and was sad to see him go. We had been fellow survivors, and I fervently hoped that his luck would hold. I often wondered whether he did survive, for I never heard from him again.

After Robert's departure, the next move was to get rid of the Fiat. There was no room for it in my friends' garage and to leave it standing outside the house might attract the attention of the authorities or an informer. Then I had an idea. Rather than abandon it, I contacted a well-known hospital in the city and told them I would like to donate a car. I explained that I was a British subject returning to England by sea, and therefore had no further use for the car; the documents were missing because they had been stolen. This did not seem to concern them overmuch, so I said an affectionate goodbye to the faithful little car which had carried me to safety.

Dressed in Marcelle's cast-offs, I was now indistinguishable from any other local. On my return, however, I decided to leave the bus well before Bramafam, making certain I was not followed. I soon realised that my new situation was fraught with problems; with my faithful companion Robert and the car gone, I had lost all my independence. I wondered how much I could count on Marcelle and Het, realising that I might prove too great a liability, both politically and financially. I made it clear that I could just about pay my way until my slender finances ran out but I would help in any way I could in the house and in the garden. Their reaction was heart-warming; they accepted the situation in a way that made me feel both welcome and secure, however I would have to observe certain rules to avoid attracting attention. I should never appear outside the house during daylight hours, and above all, never go into the village.

So early that July, I embarked on a new way of life, that of becoming a 'submarine', the slang for someone in hiding who only surfaced after dark. I knew this would be no hardship, as in the extreme heat of the summer months few people wished to be out of doors, and the deliciously cool rooms of the little stone-built house would prove more of a pleasure than a prison. But as the weeks wore on I felt a growing sense of frustration and something approaching claustrophobia.

Two things preserved my sanity. One was an ancient upright piano which I would play for hours each day, practising Chopin *Etudes* as if I were preparing for a concert tour. This was the only sheet music I could find but it gave me infinite pleasure, presenting me with a daily challenge, especially as I selected the more difficult ones. The other saving grace was the garden, where I was allowed to work or wander as long as dusk was well advanced. It was wonderful to step out into the balmy, sweet-smelling air and turn my eyes northwards to the distant mountains. In those magical evening hours as the cicadas erupted into song and the bats swooped overhead, I could still see the village on the opposite hillside, its slender campanile silhouetted against the western sky. Sometimes I would climb the hill among the silvery, shadowy olive trees up to the point where I imagined I could see the Mediterranean.

In Provence, some farms and peasant smallholdings have serious problems obtaining enough water, but we were lucky to possess large circular cement storage tanks which were fed from a spring. So watering was a relatively carefree task, and I loved the smell of freshly watered earth. The hose may have been awkward, and water cans practically impossible to lift when full, but I got a strange exhilaration from being a benefactor to all these thirsty living things. Priority of course was given to the vegetables; the flowers had to wait their turn!

Bramafam Farm House – my hiding place for two months

Supper was always the best moment of the day. The two painters were usually at their easels during the daylight hours, but Marcelle, the 'Martha' of the house, produced excellent, simple meals. Dining by candlelight and avoiding any talk of the war, we enjoyed some extremely harmonious meals eating home-grown vegetables, coarse peasant bread and local cheese. We were all pretty hard up but Het continued to paint, her atelier now stacked with paintings which were impossible to sell in wartime. Her compatriot, the peroxide blond, had a less robust attitude to events and used to potter about muttering darkly and doing nothing, all of it very Slav.

Before leaving Paris I had cashed all my remaining traveller's cheques, stuffing the notes into a belt I wore around my middle. The bulge was reassuring, but as it reduced, I would wonder gloomily what would happen when it disappeared altogether. Happily, that awful moment never came while I was at Bramafam, so I could accept a second helping of haricot beans with diced bacon and another glass of wine without a sense of guilt. I think I posed more of a political threat than a financial one. For as we witnessed the collapse of France, the emergence of the Vichy government and the mounting stranglehold of the Nazi forces, the situation for refugees

The terraced garden on the south side of the farmhouse

became more and more difficult. This was no less the case in areas under Pétain rule, such as Provence.

Aware that I was becoming increasingly frustrated at Bramafam, Marcelle contacted some acquaintances of hers, the Hansards, an Anglo-American family who lived close by. Gillian, the daughter of the house, became an enchanting and lively friend, and for the short time we spent together, my morale heightened considerably. Being an American, her movements were completely unrestricted, so no-one asked any questions when she roared around the countryside on a recently acquired *motocyclette*, even with me perched on the pillion. It was great fun, and fun was a scarce commodity in those days. She also helped me out with a few articles of clothing, including a pair of terracotta workmen's trousers, two blue shirts, some sturdy leather sandals and a splendid peasant straw hat. I felt thoroughly at home in this gear and, most significantly, I knew I could blend in with the locals without attracting any attention.

The Hansard family urged me to plan an escape from France, but could offer no advice as to how. There were the Pyrenees to the west and Switzerland to the north, but how to get there? These questions remained unanswered, but we agreed that I should at least try to get some official information about what was going on. They had heard that the US Consulate in Nice was being most helpful to allied nationals and suggested that I should go there to enquire. It was now late August, and the situation was becoming more confused by the day. It was rumoured that two coal boats carrying British and other allied nationals had left Marseilles for England. Perhaps there might be others – I should find out.

I was unwilling to risk my reasonably secure existence by plunging into uncertain fact-finding missions but carefully followed the radio news so as to choose the best moment for moving on. Then one day, Gillian, sensing my mood, presented me with a marvellously helpful gift, a bicycle. This rather ancient bike restored to me that most precious thing, freedom and independence.

Back at Bramafam, Het suggested that she should paint my portrait wearing my peasant outfit. It took weeks but turned out to be one of her best works. For security reasons, she titled it simply '1940'.[2] Once the portrait was finished, I could start making plans to leave. I had no luggage apart from my khaki knapsack, which would hold my uniform and basics such as my toothbrush and make-up – I would travel light. Het and I checked the bike, making sure that the rusty little luggage rack would safely carry my bag and trench-coat. I had no puncture repair kit although I insisted on taking a ball of string. I knew I would have to rely largely on St Christopher to get me to Nice.

The last evening at Bramafam was a nostalgic affair as we recalled those last months, certainly the strangest summer of all our lives. My companions were sad to see me depart, and knew full well the risk I was taking, but I had to go. For years I had bitterly opposed Hitler and Mussolini, and now, hearing daily radio reports of the tragic events to the north, I couldn't just sit quietly under an olive tree in Provence. Somehow I had to get back into the thick of it and do something. That night, we drank our fill of the rough Bramafam wine. But before going up to my bare little room under the roof, I stood for a few minutes on the terrace looking at the darkened landscape, the mountains and the winking lights of Plascassier. I vowed that if I survived, I would return.

Lady Hadfield

20

LADY HADFIELD'S SHANGRI-LA

Nice was a long way off, and in September the sun could still be uncomfortably hot, so I departed Bramafam soon after dawn. As a parting present Marcelle gave me a cardigan which would both protect me against the chilly Provence evenings, and make me look more respectable. Then, just as I was about to leave, she ran back inside, reappearing with her own blue beret which I gratefully accepted, swapping it for my straw hat, which wasn't the best headgear for a cyclist. I left my tin hat and gas mask for my friends to bury or destroy – dangerous evidence if they were ever discovered. After an emotional goodbye I set off down the road and did not look back.

I knew that before I could join the main road leading to the flatlands, I would have to push the bike up many steep inclines, allowing myself the minimum of rests so as not to lose time. I was also well aware that from the moment I reached the *Route Nationale*, I would have to keep a sharp lookout for the Axis Armistice Commission control points which were likely to be positioned on the main roads leading to the Riviera. I had not the least idea of what I should do if I were stopped by such a control, but I would try not to show my passport and somehow bluff my way through, trusting to luck. I just hoped my local disguise would serve me well.

Bowling along the road in the fresh morning air, I felt well and strong. The knowledge of the daunting problems that might be ahead presented a challenge and gave me a wonderful sense of adventure. Once on the *Route Nationale*, the gentle down-hill gradient eliminated all effort. The brakes on this bike were of the back-pedal type, but I soon discovered that if pressure was exerted for too long, the brake pads tended to burn out. As I rounded a sharp bend, the gradient unexpectedly increased; I was forced to apply the brakes quite violently, but found to my horror that they didn't work. I hurtled downhill at a breakneck speed, clinging to the machine and trying to keep calm but when at last on the level I looked up, I saw uniformed men and a control post. I shouted and swore, madly waving my arms and legs, showing every sign of panic. Fortunately the soldiers welcomed such a comical diversion. As I flashed past them, they merely roared with laughter and made no attempt to stop me. Weak at the knees, I glanced back as the bike slowed down, but the soldiers had apparently lost interest in me and were standing chatting.

After my close encounter, I rode cautiously along the tree-lined road that led into the city of Nice. It was late afternoon and my first task was to find somewhere to stay for the night, but I knew I had to be careful in my choice of hotel. It had to be the kind of place where few questions were asked and my passport would not arouse suspicion. I was lucky, and soon found a very small hotel where there was no concierge, just a scruffy woman at the desk who didn't bother at all with my papers, only telling me I should pay in advance.

Next morning, I rode into the centre of the town, arriving at the American Consulate well before it was due to open. The office was on the seafront, and what with the sunshine and the sea breeze, it was no hardship to stand in the long queue outside. It seemed to be made up of all kinds of refugees, people who like myself had probably run out of money or people with the wrong kind of passport. Even when the Consulate doors opened, it took a long time before I found myself inside the building awaiting my turn to see the Consular official. Then as I queued again in a rather bleak passageway, I heard two men talking in English a little distance behind me. To my surprise, I recognised one of the voices. I swung round, and saw two rough-looking characters talking earnestly to each other. One of them was easily recognisable, an old friend in the Welsh Guards whom I had first met as a dancing partner at a 'deb' party way back in the Twenties.

I relinquished my place in the queue and slipped back to where they were standing. But they took no notice of me until I spoke. "Jim!" A pale, stubbly face turned to me, and there was a quick smile of recognition before his urgent growl: "For Christ's sake, not Jim, it's Paddy! Paddy O'Brien!" He fumbled in his pocket and brought out an Irish passport and held it up. "See, O'Brien from County Cork, Irish citizen! You remember me?" Then with another smile, "See you outside after all this." I regained my place in the queue and, as I waited, I tried to figure out what Major James Windsor-Lewis, Welsh Guards, could be doing in the American Consulate in Nice. He had last been seen months ago in Northern France when the Guards fought a desperate rearguard action, and it was presumed that he, like many of my old friends, had been killed. I wondered whether he was an escaped prisoner of war, or whether he had somehow evaded capture and made his way south.

Then came my turn to see the Consul. I showed him my passport and gave a brief explanation of my predicament. He was friendly, but told me firmly that he was unable to recommend how I could get back to England, for as far as he knew there was no transport of any kind available now that the coal boats had left. However, he was empowered to provide me with the weekly payment of £10 in French francs. I thanked him profusely and left. Ten pounds! Untold riches! I blessed Uncle Sam. Half an hour later, Jim, his brother officer and I were sitting in the bar of the Hotel Negresco sipping double dry Martinis – we were all so rich! It had been Jim's idea to go to the Negresco, but whilst it might be excellent for our morale, it was highly dangerous for us, sounding and looking the way we did. A smart bar of this kind would be patronised by the Germans and Italians and I suggested that we should continue our conversation on the beach, where Jim told me his story.

In the early summer, he had been involved in the desperate battles around Calais and Boulogne. The Major had been seriously wounded, taken prisoner and sent to a hospital in Liège. Perhaps because he was regarded as a cripple, he wasn't closely guarded and managed to slip out, but that was only the start. Equipped with only basic schoolboy French, he adopted the identity of an American refugee without papers and first headed for Brussels. Here, he chanced upon the English wife of a café proprietor who seemed to be sympathetic until she handed him over to the local police. Mercifully, the gendarmes were friendly and put him into a hospital for the night, after which he quickly discharged himself. Assisted by local people who gave him food, shelter and money, he crossed Belgium and the French frontier by using the local tram network, and then completed his journey to Paris as a hitch-hiker in the back of a German military truck!

He was aware that the British authorities had left Paris, but thought the United States Embassy might be worth approaching. On arrival he was delighted to receive the most friendly welcome at their elegant embassy in the heart of Paris. The Americans did a remarkable job on Major Windsor-Lewis, transforming him overnight into an Irish national, one Patrick O'Brien, a medical volunteer. He was then assigned as a co-driver to a US ambulance travelling south to a town in unoccupied France. When they eventually arrived at their destination, he was ready with a plausible excuse to leave his travelling companion, and they parted the best of friends. Now Jim had to start his long journey to Nice, but his leg was still very painful and he was seriously concerned that he might develop gangrene, because his dressings had not been changed for far too long. 'Thumbing' lifts, he reached Nice, where he went straight to a hospital casualty station to get his leg dressed. That night he had slept rough and in the morning went to the American Consulate, where he met a brother officer, and later myself.

As we sat on that pebbly beach, a most scruffy looking trio, we started hatching plans to make a getaway. Most of these were absurd fantasy, and probably only Jim believed in them. There was his idea for a 'Great Pyrenean Escape', but I said this was out of the question as this route was closely watched and dangerous. Then there was the 'Mediterranean Odyssey', Jim maintaining that it would be child's play after dark to steal one of the large fishing boats berthed nearby. "And then?" I asked. "Easy," he said, "we'll just sail or row out to sea and head for the Balearic Islands and then on to Gibraltar." He was confident we should soon be sighted and picked up by a British ship. After listening to this crazy idea we sat in silence for quite a few minutes. I did not know what I should say; it was all totally insane, especially as Jim had no experience of boats or the sea. I suggested we drop the subject until we had eaten something, so we sought out a small, cheap restaurant.

Over a large plate of pasta, I remembered something which might be of use. The name of the MTC's No.1 unit, 'Hadfield-Spears', suddenly rang a bell. I remembered being told that the wife of Sir Robert Hadfield was an American who lived on the Riviera. If Lady Hadfield was a US citizen, she might, I reasoned, still be living in France. I tried to dredge up more details from my memory, such as where she lived. Then I had an idea. The bistro where we were sitting had a telephone, and next to it a pile of directories. I went over to it, picked out the local directory and scanned the list of names under the letter H. Miraculously, there it was: Lady Hadfield, Villa La Sounjarello, Cap Ferrat. I rushed back to my two companions. We decided that I should telephone her straightaway to explain our predicament and ask if we might visit her.

A man's voice answered the telephone; I took it to be the butler, and he suavely agreed to refer me to 'Her Ladyship'. It seemed an eternity until Lady Hadfield picked up the receiver, long enough to make me wonder if we had drawn a blank. She was most friendly and was clearly interested in our plight. In a typically American way, she spontaneously invited me to 'come right over'. I then had to explain that I had two companions, escaped Guards officers, whom I could not possibly leave, particularly as one of them was still suffering from a serious leg wound. A very slight pause, was followed by a warm, bright reply: "Of course, bring them along with you. I look forward to seeing you all in time for tea." I returned to our table to be met with anxious looks. Jim was the first to speak. "Any luck?" It felt as if I was telling condemned men they had been reprieved, but I merely said: "Lady Hadfield has invited us to tea."

Neither man said a word as we rose from the table, paid our bill and walked into the street. Now all we had to do was find a bus stop and board the next bus for Cap Ferrat. Jim was in favour of taking a taxi until I pointed out that we should save our money; one never knew. We managed to find the right bus stop and were soon speeding along the road to Cap Ferrat. For a moment I wondered about my bicycle left outside the American Consulate, and hoped that whoever took it would avoid steep gradients. The bus dropped us in Cap Ferrat and we made cautious enquiries about the whereabouts of Lady Hadfield's residence. Fortunately for Jim we did not have to walk far, and soon found ourselves in the large and beautiful grounds of La Sounjarello. It was incredible. Here all was order and peace, so very unlike what we had grown used to. As we walked up the drive, we felt a sense of unreality, which intensified with every minute we spent there.

We rang the bell and the butler ushered us into a cool, beautifully furnished drawing room where Lady Hadfield was seated behind a table laid for tea. She rose immediately to greet us, obviously doing her best to put us at her ease. We were well aware of how awful we looked: more like a bunch of down and outs than two Guards Officers and a former west end actress. But Lady Hadfield chose to ignore this, and quickly rid us of all embarrassment by indicating that tea was ready, complete with cucumber sandwiches and delicious-looking cakes. As we sipped our tea, we tried to tell her what had happened to us. She listened intently, then, rising to her feet, left the room, telling us to relax and help ourselves to more tea and cakes.

On her return we felt we should soon be making our apologies to leave, but she forestalled us with a motherly command: "Now into the pool with you! There are plenty of bathing things down there. I'll join you later." We obeyed, feeling we had been granted a temporary reprieve and were soon splashing about. But what did all this mean – that we should stay for dinner? We were bemused. After a while, Lady Hadfield appeared, followed by the butler carrying a tray of drinks. Soft bathrobes were distributed and as we sat by the pool sipping our dry martinis we wondered what on earth we should do now.

Lady Hadfield then explained we could stay for a few days, and when we feebly protested, she told us everything was provided for. She then led us back into the house and showed us our bedrooms. We had serious doubts about our clothes, but on entering my room I had a delightful shock: everything I could want for had been laid out, a silk evening dress, a choice of shoes and even a maid adding undies and silk stockings to complete the outfit. On the dressing table there was even an array of Elizabeth Arden make-up and a bottle of Chanel No 5. Lady Hadfield had forgotten nothing.

As I closed the door, I was becoming more and more convinced I was dreaming. Then came a sharp knock, it was Jim. "Elizabeth, quick! Come and have a look!" He took my hand and led me to his room. On his bed were a crisp evening shirt, black tie and socks, while hanging nearby were a dinner jacket and trousers. "And there's shaving tackle and a sponge and…" words failed him.

We duly appeared for dinner. Jim and his companion looked very smart, and I felt confident in my elegant dress, wafting Chanel No 5 around the log fire. There was an atmosphere of complete normality as we all met in the drawing room that evening. After drinks we moved into the dining room – never had I seen silver and glass gleam and sparkle so prettily. It was a gourmet dinner, but the two men could not do it justice; they had been living at semi-starvation level for too long.

After coffee and liqueurs in the drawing room Lady Hadfield suggested a game of bridge, but when we pleaded extreme fatigue, she agreed we should make it an early night. Before saying a final goodnight we tried to express our gratitude, but she dismissed this with a shrug and a happy smile. "It's wonderful to be of some help… and it's breakfast in bed for all of you! You need rest, so sleep well!" I remember sitting at the dressing table, holding a pot of Elizabeth Arden Orange Skin Food and staring at my face in the mirror; it was as if someone had put the clock back. I got into bed in the most expensive nightdress I had ever worn; I tried to think calmly and rationally, but my thoughts were careering wildly around my head, and I realised nothing would make much sense until I got a good night's sleep.

Late next morning we gathered around the pool, and after a leisurely swim, reviewed our position, wondering what we should do next. Both men looked infinitely more rested and relaxed than on the previous evening, but they were still dazed and talking a lot of nonsense. Meanwhile I had been able to gather a few valuable facts from the ladies' maid who looked after me. Although well into middle age, our hostess, 'Bunny' Hadfield, was a handsome and elegant woman of considerable charm. Born American, she still held a US passport as well as the British one she had acquired on marrying Sir Robert. Endowed with a large fortune, she had chosen to live in the South of France but was eager to support worthy causes, one of these being the Mechanised Transport Corps.

So on that first peaceful morning by the pool, I explained all this to the two men, and we decided that as long as Lady Hadfield was willing, we should stay put until we had come up with a realistic plan, and had regained something of our health and strength. We thought this might take around a week, and at La Sounjarello, such a week would clearly be no hardship. There now followed a period of total make-believe. Lady Hadfield was infinitely kind and provided every creature comfort. We swam, played tennis and bridge, and every night there was champagne at dinner. Furthermore, the contents of our wardrobes expanded as if by magic. It all began to seem like a pre-war holiday on the Riviera, but we had to admit that this couldn't last. The two men longed above all to get back to England and rejoin their regiments, and in Jim's case there was also a romantic reason; he had been about to get engaged.

So at last we decided that, whatever the risk, we must re-enter the real world. We were unsure of how we should tell Lady Hadfield in case she might think we were unhappy under her roof. Instead she immediately understood, and as warmly and generously as she had welcomed us in, she now set about devising ways of getting us out.

There were of course problems. The two men had their American-issued Irish passports, but were really serving British officers. My passport was no deception, but the photograph portrayed me in uniform, which would make it impossible to obtain a visa to leave France. Indeed at this date, it had been decreed that all foreigners should be arrested, questioned and interned, and that all applications for exit visas would be referred to the Gestapo. Exit visas were obligatory, and as Allied personnel were being rounded up, there seemed little chance of getting out of France legally.

When we discussed these problems with Lady Hadfield, she concluded that it was imperative that we should split up. I should be the first to leave and try to get into Switzerland, although it was common knowledge that the Swiss were refusing to accept any more refugees. Fortunately I remembered that one of my father's best friends, Charles Paravicini, the former Swiss Ambassador in London, had now retired and was living in Bern. Would he remember his friend John Montagu's red-haired daughter? Although we had not met for years, we decided that I should try to contact him; it was at least worth a try. Lady Hadfield instructed her butler to drive me to the Swiss Consulate in Nice where I should first apply for a visa, and while there, try to send a message to Charles Paravicini. I pointed out that even if I succeeded in getting a Swiss entry visa, I would still need a French exit visa. Lady Hadfield considered this for a moment, then smiled rather enigmatically. "Leave that to me!"

When I entered the Swiss Consulate I was optimistic, but my confidence soon evaporated when I saw the endless queue of desperate-looking people, their quest probably identical to my own, and I realised it would need quite exceptional luck to obtain that visa. I filled in the application form and settled down to a long wait. When my turn eventually came, my worst fears were confirmed. I was informed that since the Consulate had received thousands of visa applications, Switzerland had now called a halt to their issue: in other words, the answer was 'no'.

It was now time to play that other card. I explained that there was another matter on which I needed advice. My family in England did not know whether I was alive or dead, and it so happened that an old and dear friend of my father's lived in Bern. Could the Consulate inform him that I was alive and well in Nice? As soon as I mentioned his name, Monsieur Charles Paravicini, the Consular official's demeanour changed, and I quickly responded with another request. Would it be possible to telephone him? The official requested me to wait while he consulted a colleague. I now scented success, and soon he returned to tell me this might be possible, but as Bern would have to be consulted, I should return the next day. I also learned that Switzerland was one of the very few countries where official telephone communication was permitted. When I left the Swiss Consulate, I was in a buoyant mood, confident that when Monsieur Paravicini heard of my plight he would do his best to help.

When I walked into the Consulate the following day, an official led me past the weary queue and into a much more impressive office than that of the previous day, I had evidently gone up in the world! It may have been the Consul himself who gave me the good news; I would be granted a visa to enter Switzerland. Monsieur Paravicini had been contacted and would pass on the message to my family. I handed over my passport, which was duly stamped, and noted that this visa was valid for entry into Switzerland at Annemasse, a town near Geneva. This presented no problems as the train from Lyons to Geneva usually took that route. We shook hands, and as I was leaving he added as an afterthought, "You do realise you have to have a French exit visa?" I realised this only too well; this is what now stood between me and freedom like a gigantic question mark.

When I got back to Cap Ferrat the others were jubilant on hearing my news. Then Lady Hadfield spoke. "And now we must set about getting that other visa. I'm afraid that may be a little more difficult, but leave it to me...". She then changed the subject and suggested a swim before tea. Next day, she asked me for my passport, promising she would take great care of it. Waiting for its return became a great strain, and I began to visualise every kind of disaster. Before dinner on the second day, she drew me aside and asked me to go with her to her boudoir. I could see by her expression that she had something important to tell me. She took my passport out of her bag, and turning to the relevant page, pointed to the French exit visa, duly stamped and signed. She offered no explanation, no clue except for one cryptic reference to her butler. Such a good, kind loyal man, she said. But the whole matter should now be forgotten, and I should never refer to it again, ever.

As I ran back onto the terrace to tell the others, I knew we now faced a completely new situation, and one that would need careful thought. We quickly decided that I should leave as soon as possible in case the situation in France deteriorated further. When I reached Switzerland, I would immediately contact the British authorities and urge them to work on getting Jim and his brother officer out of France and back to England. Also their families should be informed of their whereabouts, as they had both been listed as missing.

I now began to realise the full implication of what lay ahead of me. This journey to Switzerland was full of uncertainties. Even the basic travel details, trains and so on, were unknown to me, but it would be folly to go to the station to enquire. We had been warned that we should not go back to the US Consulate as it was probably being watched, but I was confident that as long as I kept a cool head and used every ounce of intelligence I possessed, there was a fair chance I would get through. In Nice there was little information on the general situation in the north of unoccupied France: Lyon was still 'free', but how 'free'? The trains still ran, but were there controls in place? And didn't that French exit visa in my passport look a little bit too good to be true? The others were concerned about me undertaking this journey alone, but I reassured them. I only spent a few more hours in Lady Hadfield's 'Shangri-La' and was well aware that I would soon be back in the real world.

As a parting gift, Lady Hadfield suggested that I take a suitcase packed with the beautiful clothes I had been wearing at La Sounjarella. This I politely refused, pointing out that I must travel light, carrying only my old knapsack as before. However, I did accept some warm clothing for the journey, asking that it should be as unobtrusive as possible.

When I bade her that final goodnight it was difficult to find the right words to express my gratitude. I gave her a hug, and silently we looked at each other for a moment, then I went to my room. I had tears in my eyes, wondering when and where we would meet again. Meanwhile the ever-efficient butler had made enquiries, and it was decided that the best course would be to get to the station early and jump onto the first train bound for Lyons. It was essential that I should take a slow train as there were no corridors on these and the danger of controls en route was considerably less. Lady Hadfield instructed him to buy me a through ticket to Geneva, changing at Lyon. I found it difficult to sleep on my last night at Villa La Sounjarello. It had indeed been a strange interlude.

My passport with French exit visa and Swiss entry visa

My route out of France:
Nice to Aix-les-Bains by train, and the final part of the journey by road

21

FRIDAY 13TH – LUCKY FOR SOME

The weather was still quite hot, and although it was early when we arrived at Nice station, the waiting rooms and platform were stifling and airless. It was impossible to get any information about the trains, and with every minute the platform became more crowded. When the first train pulled in, destination Lyon, I boarded it. I soon discovered that I was on a corridor train but considering the incredible overcrowding, it seemed unlikely to attract a control. Furthermore this was a 'local' that crawled from station to station. The journey took all day, so I had plenty of time to review the extraordinary turn my life had taken since I had left England in December 1939. I tried not to speculate on what could happen before I reached Switzerland. I also wondered what the Swiss would do with me; would I be interned? There was always the threat that the Germans might invade this small neutral country as they had Norway, Denmark, Holland and Belgium. Where would I hide then? I comforted myself with thoughts of the Alps and the story of William Tell. It was already dark when at last the train drew into Lyon. I was very tired, but content that at least the first hurdle had been surmounted.

I had already considered how and where to spend the night in Lyon, as it seemed more sensible to take a train to Geneva in the early morning. It would be too dangerous to remain in the station sleeping on a bench, for there would certainly be a police presence there, perhaps even military patrols, so I decided on a nearby hotel, the Terminus. I recollected staying there with my father and Pearl during a tour of the French Alps. As I emerged into the dark street, it was raining and rather chilly after the warm *Midi*, but I found the hotel, and once inside it was just as I remembered.

I asked for a room, but the concierge politely regretted there were no rooms free that night. But pleading that I was a woman alone and a foreigner, he relented, informing me that as long as I didn't mind sleeping on the floor of the lounge, I was welcome to stay. He added that a lot of people slept there every night, and seemed to like it.

Could I get some dinner? "Of course," he replied. "Dinner will be served at seven o'clock in the *salle à manger*, but I'm afraid we cannot offer the usual choice; there is only a set menu." Now that we were on friendly terms, I told him that many years ago I had stayed here with my family. He shook his head ruefully, "Hélas, madame, we can no longer look after our guests as we used to…". I handed him my passport and filled in the obligatory *fiche*, by which time it was already past seven o'clock. Being very hungry, I went straight to the dining room.

The set menu provided one small stale roll without butter, watery soup followed by some vegetables, and a minute piece of cheese. I glanced round the dining room, which was fairly crowded, and saw what must have been a stage for a small orchestra and a table laid for a large party. I wondered who these guests might be and was horrified when, after a few minutes, a group of uniformed German officers trooped in. Without a glance at the rest of us, they settled down to their evening meal. Every available waiter now rushed over to their table, and it was obvious that they were about to enjoy a menu very different from ours. Bottles of wine appeared, and soon the only laughter in the room came from the German party while the rest of us sat in resentful silence.

Instinct told me I should leave the dining room without delay, and ask the concierge what was going on. He confirmed what I now suspected, that there were German officers staying in the hotel, including some members of the Gestapo. He then drew me aside and whispered that it might after all be wiser not to remain in the hotel. "Your overcoat, Madame, they recognised it. It is a British military one, n'est-ce pas?" I had carefully removed all badges of rank and insignia some time ago, but was horrified to realise that it was still identifiable as a British Army trench-coat. "And the German officer, madame, said he wanted to inspect your passport." I felt myself go cold inside, realising that the refuge I had chosen also hosted a bunch of Nazis! This was indeed bad luck. One thing was clear though; I must leave as soon as possible. However, on making enquiries about trains, I learned there were none to Annemasse (the border station) until the morning. It was still raining, so I decided to take a calculated risk and booked a place on the lounge floor. I would take the first train out in the morning.

The lounge had a very hard parquet floor, and, with my knapsack for a pillow and coat for a blanket, discomfort and anxiety banished any idea of sleep. But all around me people snored; perhaps they were used to sleeping on parquet floors! I rose long before dawn, realising it would be better to leave before it was light, with only a few people about to observe my movements. Since leaving Paris I had quite often met with anti-British feeling, and sometimes with downright hostility. Being a confirmed francophile, I found this particularly distressing, so the incident that occurred in the ladies' room that morning touched me deeply.

I was doing what I could to my face and hair when I noticed a shabby middle-aged woman approaching me. We were alone but she spoke in a whisper. "There is something I must tell you," she said. "You English must go on fighting! You must defeat the Boches! We French know you can do it!" She then wished me good luck and left. I remained for a moment staring into the mirror. How, I wondered, had this splendid lady known I was English, for she had been the first to speak. However, this was a good omen and a wonderful send-off for the last lap of my journey. When I walked back to the reception area, the concierge was already on duty, so I was able to pay for my 'bed' and to thank him warmly for his help. It was then that I noticed the date, Friday 13th September. I had never been over-superstitious, but one way or another, I thought the date ought to prove something! Then, buttoning up my trench-coat against the rain, I walked out into the street.

There were only a few people in the station, so I didn't have to queue to get on the platform. When the train for Annemasse pulled in, it was easy to find a corner seat in a reasonably comfortable compartment. However, I was rather concerned that it had corridors throughout. So far no-one had mentioned any controls on this route, but I feared that when the Gestapo discovered I had left the hotel, they might try to follow me, knowing they could arrest me at the frontier. There seemed to be very few passengers on that train so I was surprised when, only minutes before we were due to leave, two men burst into the compartment and settled down on the seats opposite. One was young and good-looking, the other slightly older; both of them were well dressed and clearly well-to-do. I recognised the *Suisse Romande* accent, and it soon emerged from their conversation that they were travelling representatives returning to their home base in Geneva. The older man, sitting in a corner next to the corridor, was a 'traveller in hats', most superior ones judging from the elegant hat box in the rack above him. The younger man sitting opposite me apparently had no samples with him, but I soon learnt he was in watches and had just concluded a highly successful business trip. They both seemed happy and relaxed; these good, solid, Swiss citizens seemed to be without a care in the world.

As the train dawdled through the countryside, the beauty of it all entranced me, and I spent most of the time gazing out of the window. Then something made me turn round, and I saw a stranger standing outside in the corridor, similarly gazing at the landscape. But as the train was half empty, why was he standing there? Was this a Gestapo man detailed to pull me off the train at the frontier and put me under arrest? I tried to remain calm. I told myself it couldn't be – what use could I possibly be to them? This was pure paranoia and I should pull myself together. Then I decided to put it to the test.

It was a simple plan. I would leave my seat and walk down the train to find a WC. However, I would select one several coaches away, so if the stranger still followed me, I would have my suspicions confirmed. I walked down the train and having reached my objective, deliberately took an unusually long time to 'freshen up'. When I emerged, I was shocked to find the rather unpleasant-looking, burly stranger still waiting outside, gazing at the countryside. Now I knew I was faced with a very real threat and, sure enough, when I returned to my compartment the stranger resumed his post in the corridor. I sat down and stared out of the window wondering what I should do. When the first moment of panic had passed, I started to think clearly again. Those two Swiss businessmen, still chatting happily away – I must appeal to them.

The compartment door was closed, so it would be impossible for the stranger waiting outside to eavesdrop. So as quickly and clearly as I could I addressed the younger man opposite me. I told him who I was, explained my present predicament, and then asked him outright for his help. He was silent for a moment, obviously considering the matter. Then Monsieur Pierre Dubois, for that was his name, reacted swiftly. He told me to look out of the window and that as we talked, he would pretend to be pointing out interesting features in the landscape. I should listen carefully and memorise every instruction he gave me. I was quite taken aback by this quick reaction, but as I listened, Monsieur Montand ('in hats'), seemed as interested as I was.

I have rarely concentrated more intensely, memorising carefully each detail, for I realised that my life might depend on my ability to remember all he told me. The train would stop at Aix-les-Bains, where anyone wishing to continue their journey would have to change. There was usually quite a long wait between trains, so the moment I stepped onto the platform, I should start audibly asking questions such as, "What is happening?" and, "When does the train for Annemasse leave?" Then I should proceed to the station restaurant where one could normally have some kind of snack – there would be enough time between trains for that. And I knew that the word 'time' was all important, for it was essential to Pierre's plan that the timing for all this should be as accurate as possible. I should then sit down at a table and place an order. At the appointed time, I should ask for the Ladies' Room, and walk through a door which led not only to the WCs but also to the station yard. All this should be done in a relaxed manner, but fast. I should then take the door leading into the yard, where I would find a small black Lancia saloon waiting for me. All I had to do then was to jump into the back of the car and in seconds we would be on our way.

As we sat in the train, Pierre Dubois gave me these instructions in instalments, thus making our conversation appear more natural. I tried to fix every detail in my memory although as we approached Aix I was getting very tense. The presence of the burly stranger outside made it clear that I had to get it right, or else. Soon enough, the suburbs of Aix came into sight and we pulled into the station. The two Swiss retrieved their luggage from the rack and helped me with my modest bag. Then, with strictly formal courtesy, they took their leave and left the train. The stranger outside made no move, and I realised that he was waiting for me to alight.

Once on the platform, I started asking about the trains and then enquired where I could get something to eat. Walking towards the restaurant, I noticed the stranger was not far behind and wondered whether he would follow me inside. Mercifully, he remained on the platform, sitting down on a seat near the door. Presumably he thought that as I had no choice but to catch the next train to Annemasse, he only had to wait for me outside.

The station buffet at Aix-les-Bains was half empty and I chose a table near the door which led to the street. There was no waiter, so I went to the bar and asked for something to eat, explaining that I had to catch the next train to Annemasse. Meanwhile I was busy consulting my watch, and it was now time to ask for the *Toilette pour Dames*, but what on earth should I do with my haversack? People don't usually take their luggage with them. Fortunately, as I puzzled over this, a group of noisy children entered the restaurant from the platform, and I took advantage of the momentary confusion to slip out to the ladies, my bag slung over my shoulder.

Quickly opening the door into the station yard, I looked anxiously for the black Lancia saloon with Swiss number plates, and there it was! I ran quickly towards it, threw my bag in and leaped onto the back seat. I couldn't believe it; the plan had worked down to the last detail, and we were off! For a few moments I was speechless; it all seemed like a dream. I stammered out a few words of thanks, and then sat in stunned silence while the car made its way through the traffic.

After a few minutes, and having recovered my wits, I asked if we were on our way to Geneva, but to my consternation, got a firm negative. "We have to eat first," said Dubois. "Why, aren't you happy?" He explained that they had arranged to have lunch with an old friend on the outskirts of town, and he assured me I would be most welcome. I had to accept this, however reluctantly, for the two Swiss 'reps' were clearly in no hurry. I was in their hands, and as everything had worked like clockwork so far, I felt there was every reason to trust them. But still I worried about the steps the Gestapo might take when they discovered they had lost me. There would be questions asked at Aix and the frontier guards would be alerted. For one crazy moment, I imagined we were being followed and that we were already under surveillance. I looked nervously out of the rear window, but there was nothing suspicious, and it was then that I realised how hungry I was.

I did suggest that after lunch we should make our way to Geneva as quickly as possible. This suggestion was casually brushed aside and I was told firmly not to worry; my troubles were over. Then I remembered that the French exit visa was only valid for the frontier at Annemasse. "No problem," said Dubois, "just leave it to me."

We drove through the elegant spa town until we reached a bourgeois residential area with rather ugly little houses. Stopping outside a particularly unattractive villa, Dubois rang the front door bell which was answered immediately by a pleasant middle-aged lady who ushered us all into the house. She led us into her dining room, and I saw that the table was set for nearly a dozen people. She evidently knew both my companions well, and Pierre introduced me, merely explaining I was *une Anglaise* and an old friend. The other guests now appeared. I was not introduced to any of them. They were a motley lot but seemed pleasant and friendly. As we took our places at the table, delicious smells drifted in from the kitchen, and this had a wonderfully calming effect on my nerves, food now seeming immeasurably more important than safety. The lunch was excellent, demonstrating once more the high quality of the French *cuisine bourgeoise*. It was not until we had reached the last course, a splendid array of local cheeses, that I began to wonder what this was all about and who these people were. However, despite listening intently to their conversations, I was none the wiser.

When we eventually left the table, Dubois ushered me into the front parlour, but I noticed with considerable irritation that our fellow guests disappeared into another part of the house. I must have appeared rather upset but he pacified me, explaining that this was only a temporary delay; there was important business to be discussed but it wouldn't take long. At last we took our leave, thanking our hostess profusely for her hospitality. As we drove out of town, I could see by the signposts that we were on the *Route Nationale* to Geneva, but we hadn't been on the road for long when we branched off westwards along a minor road to the Lac du Bourget. Dubois explained that they must pay a short call on some friends; their house was by the lake and in any case, it was on our way. It wouldn't take long, he promised, and we were in no particular hurry. No particular hurry!

It was a beautiful evening and the Lac du Bourget glowed in almost lyrical beauty. Soon we turned off the road down a well-kept drive that led to an impressive villa surrounded by parkland. It looked deserted and very different from that small house in a back street of Aix. Before the two men entered the house, I was told that I should get a breath of fresh air, but should be careful not to stray too far from the car as we would soon be off again. The door was opened by a liveried servant who ushered the men inside. Walking around the well-kept garden, I began to wonder what these respectable 'reps' might be up to. I was not unduly alarmed, but the pieces somehow didn't fit. The idea of some kind of criminal activity entered my head, but I dismissed such suspicions as nonsense. My friends kept their promise and within half an hour they reappeared, both in a very good mood, and we were soon on the road again. This time the signposts unmistakably read Genève.

It was already dark when Dubois indicated we were not far from the frontier. Soon afterwards he abruptly turned off the main highway and headed down a very minor road. He told me this detour was essential so we could cross the frontier at a little-frequented frontier post, and one he knew well. It was clear that my safety was his primary concern. After only a few miles, he pulled the car off the road and switched off both the lights and the engine. For a moment I was afraid something untoward had happened until Dubois calmly gave me my final instructions. This frontier, he explained, was at the village of St Julien, and most of the people who passed this way were locals. As this post was of minor importance, it was usually manned by two customs officers at the most, on both the French and Swiss sides of the frontier. However, there was one unusual feature, and that was about one hundred yards of 'no-man's land' between the two customs houses. I was to lie on the floor of the car and he would cover me with a rug and then their entire luggage, coats and even the hatbox! I was doubtful.

"But what if they search the car?" I asked. He laughed "They won't, not at St Julien! I know them all too well; I always cross here, it's near to where I live. All you have to do is keep still. And don't worry! We're nearly there!" So I lay on the floor of the Lancia and waited as I was covered over. It was uncomfortable, stuffy and dusty but I knew I wouldn't have to endure it for long. As we drove on, he added that I should neither move nor speak until we were safely over both frontiers and into Switzerland; only then could I emerge. Ten minutes later the car began to slow down, so I knew we must be approaching the French frontier. I prayed that this small customs office had not been warned of a fugitive, an English woman wanted by the Gestapo.

Of course I was unable to see what was going on, but able to hear what was said. The situation was exactly as Pierre Dubois had described it, with the French officials being on the friendliest terms. There were mutual enquiries about the well-being of their families, and about how the watch trade was doing. Monsieur Montand was teased about his hats – what good Frenchman would wear a hat when he could wear his beret, etc – all good harmless stuff. To my great relief there were no enquiries about the contents of the car. Curled up under the rug and luggage, I kept as quiet as a mouse, telling myself that please God I mustn't sneeze. After what seemed an eternity, the two men got back into the car and drove off at a leisurely pace. Still I didn't move a muscle, realising that we were now crossing that area of 'no-man's land'. Then, when I heard voices and the engine was switched off, Dubois told me to emerge, and I stepped out onto Swiss soil and safety.

Dubois was clearly equally well-known to the Swiss customs officers and they were very jovial and friendly until they noticed me. I was calm and confident, and with a flourish presented my passport. There were two *douaniers* on duty, and the senior officer, an older man with grizzled hair, took it and examined it carefully. Then, giving me a frosty look said, "This visa isn't valid for St Julien. You have to go back to Annemasse."

I protested, "But there's nothing wrong with the visa!" He agreed, but pointed out that the visa stated clearly that it was only valid for Annemasse. I quickly explained that I was English and in real danger from the Gestapo, who had been following me since I had left Lyon that morning. To re-enter France would be suicide. He listened carefully but remained adamant. "You must go back to Annemasse." I pleaded with him, "But how do I get there? I have no transport of my own!" He hardly listened and walked away. However I followed him, insisting that he listen to me. I explained the difficulty I had had to obtain the visa in the first place, then told him about Monsieur Paravicini, demonstrating that perhaps my case was a rather a special one. By now I was nearly in tears; it seemed an incredible irony to have got this far only to be turned back for what seemed to be a purely bureaucratic reason. Gradually his manner changed and he became more friendly, eventually agreeing to contact Monsieur Paravicini through official channels in Bern. Meanwhile I had to wait outside. I joined my two friends as they stood by their car, apologising for holding them up.

The call to Bern only took a few minutes, yet those minutes seemed like hours. When the officer reappeared, I could see by his expression that it was good news. Beckoning me inside, he stamped my passport and shortly afterwards the barrier was lifted. We were on our way. Arriving in Geneva, we went straight to the Hotel Cornavin near the station. My friends tactfully quizzed me about my finances and were clearly prepared to advance me any money I might need. Luckily though, I still had some Swiss francs left over from the previous spring at Schloss Berg, so declined their generosity. Before we parted, I tried to find words to thank them both. I realised only too well what they had done for me, and that I very probably owed my life to them, particularly to the ingenious and courageous Pierre Dubois. When we shook hands for the last time and they drove off, I felt really sad saying goodbye.

I walked forlornly into the bleak modern hotel, booked a room and went straight to the restaurant. I sat down at a table and looked round the room. It was just as I remembered Switzerland, everything clean, well ordered and unmenacing. At that moment, and throughout the war years, Switzerland seemed like a museum, showing the rest of Europe what life had been like before 1939. I ordered a modest dinner and it was good, but the best part was the dish of beautiful Swiss butter, great luscious curls of it. I helped myself liberally to it. I hadn't seen so much butter for a long, long time. Then, having finished my meal, I telephoned both the Paravicinis and Schloss Berg to announce my safe arrival in Geneva, and to explain that I would be taking a train to Bern the next morning.

When I climbed into bed that night and lay listening to the muffled roar of the traffic and the trains, I reflected on the events of the day. So many strange and inexplicable things had happened, but I was too tired to be able to make sense of it all. However one thing was clear; throughout the whole day I had been 'dogged by good luck', and it had all happened on Friday 13th.

Although the Germans were unused to the idea of women in military uniform, this passport picture was something of a liability as it gave the impression that I was a member of the armed services

Charles Paravicini (Swiss Ambassador in London 1920-39) with his wife Lilian.
Without his help, I would probably never have got to the safety of Switzerland

22

PERMIS DE SÉJOUR

Despite a good ten hours' sleep, I awoke next morning tense and confused, a feeling that would persist for many days. I think it was a kind of aftershock; ever since those terrible days in May, the nerves of most people in Western Europe had been as taut as piano strings. The world as we knew it had crashed about us; the change had been abrupt and violent, and the shock appalling. One simply had to come to terms with this new and frightening world, adjust to different values, and learn how to survive. Coming to terms with what had happened to me, not to mention Western Europe, would take time, but I was sure that Switzerland with its slower tempo and ordered way of life would soon restore my equilibrium. The train journey to Bern was a tonic in itself. Watching the countryside progress past my window, I saw the peasants lifting their potato crop, working slowly and methodically in the time-honoured way, and it was all very reassuring.

At Bern, the Paravicinis seemed to have retained all the standards of pre-war embassy life. They proceeded to spoil me in every way, and even kitted me out in warm and elegant clothes. Feeling rather more presentable by now, I went across to the British Legation to call on the Minister, the rather bluff Sir David Kelly, and his elegant Belgian wife, Marie-Noële. Here, too, the welcome was most friendly but the telegram I sent to England confirming my safe arrival – and survival – might have contributed to the view that I was having an easy time:

HAVING LOVELY BIRTHDAY THINKING OF YOU ALL EVERYTHING ALRIGHT PARAVICINIS TOO SWEET GOD BLESS YOU AND KEEP YOU ALL LOVE ELIZABETH MONTAGU

I could now elaborate on the reasons for my hazardous journey from Nice to Geneva, and the Minister listened intently as I described the plight of the two Guards officers stranded in the South of France. Kelly acted swiftly. The Military Attaché was summoned and immediate action was assured; not long afterwards I heard that the two men had reached Portugal and had then flown on to England. So for me, the outcome of that crazy scheme hatched at Cap Ferrat was enormously rewarding and a seemingly hopeless situation had ended happily.

It was vital that I should regularise my position; although I had entered Switzerland legally, a *permis de séjour* was now urgently needed. My passport photograph showed me in uniform; whilst I tried to explain that the MTC was not part of the British Army, the Swiss authorities still thought I belonged to a military organisation. While the officials were puzzling this out, they recommended that I leave Bern and take up residence somewhere deep in the countryside. I suggested Schloss Berg, which was immediately accepted, although I was told I would have to report to the local authorities at regular intervals. After thanking the kind and generous Paravicinis, I left Bern and made my way north to Berg.

It was strange to travel through a landscape I knew so well, and when I finally arrived at the Schloss it was as if all the clocks had stood still, especially as I was given the room I had left only four months previously. But the cast had changed; many of the pupils I had seen in May had left for home, including all the Germans and most of the Anglo-Saxons. The pupils who were still pursuing their studies were mainly Scandinavian, together with a few anti-Fascist Italians and some Swiss. As usual, the house and garden rang with music, but the place seemed dull and lifeless without Renata's ebullient personality.

At the time, Renata was staying near Lugano with our friends Walter and Michele Baumann-Kienast, but before I could join them it was essential for me to register my domicile in Berg, or risk internment. I impatiently awaited the moment when I could leave for Lugano, and as soon the formalities had been completed, I took the train south for Italian Switzerland via the St Gotthard Tunnel. To Italians, Lugano seems a very Swiss town, but to northerners it is redolent of Italy and those famous Italian Lakes. My reunion with Renata was an extraordinary moment;

Relaxing with Michele Baumann-Kienast in her garden

there had been times when I had thought I would never escape from France alive, but seeing her again confirmed that I really had made it to the safety of Switzerland. The Baumann-Kienasts' ochre-coloured house was built into a hill overlooking Lake Lugano; set among vineyards, olive trees and tall cypresses just outside Castagnola, it commanded one of the most beautiful views in Europe. From the outside, the house looked typically Italian, but on entering the front door, you stepped into another world. Although the hall was dark after the brilliant sunlight outside, one's eyes soon adjusted to see the oriental brass and exotic artefacts hanging on the walls. As one advanced room by room, it was evident that everything was a reflection on the years which the Baumanns had spent in Java: the Buddhas, the strange erotic carvings and wall paintings, even the furniture was as far from European culture as it could be.

Michele, a painter, was so deeply drawn to oriental thought and philosophy that she sometimes seemed to exist, though quite unaffectedly, on another plane. When she and Walter changed for dinner, they would wear the same exotic clothes they would have worn years before under quite another sun. Sitting in the shade of the cypresses that guarded the ruined chapel on the hill, it was difficult to believe that most of Europe was at war. Unfortunately, these halcyon days were numbered as the promised *permis de séjour* had still not materialised. I was well aware that I should do something about it, so Renata and I reluctantly crossed the Alps back to the grey north. But my stay in Castagnola did much to dissipate the traumas of recent months and the memory of that week with the Baumanns still glows today like a precious jewel.

My return to Schloss Berg was not before time, as an official letter awaited me containing specific and urgent instructions: I was to report immediately to the cantonal authorities in Frauenfeld, the capital of Thurgau canton. This I did the very next day, and was told by a friendly official that for the time being it would be in order for me to stay at Berg as long as I remained strictly within a radius of five kilometres. This news was both good and bad. Good, as this was infinitely preferable to internment, yet bad because it would preclude any visits to my friends in Bern or Zurich. I soon discovered that I was not the only 'allied national' in the region with permit problems, as there were also several groups of French officers scattered around the area. Inevitably we got together,

Back on familliar ground: Schloss Berg

meeting at the village inn for a meal of sausage and hunks of bread. Aided by the local wine, our meetings were always great fun and considerably raised our morale.

One day, these officers decided to give me a surprise. I had gone to the inn for our weekly get-together, but on entering the bar found myself faced by the whole group, all in smartly pressed uniforms and wearing unusually silly expressions on their faces. Then the senior officer among them stepped forward and made a touching little speech. The gist of it was how delighted they were to have such charming female company, and that quite remarkably the lady in question turned out to be *une officier anglaise*, a species they had never encountered before. The *capitaine* explained that they wished to show their affection and respect by presenting me with a little gift of their own making. Then, with a grand gesture, he drew from under the table a beautifully carved walking stick with an inscription running in a double spiral along its length:

TO LIEUTENANT SCOTT MONTAGU FROM THREE FRENCH OFFICERS WITH BEST REGARDS 1940 - 1941

Renata working in the greenhouse at Schloss Berg

Quite incredibly, this splendid object even included the Montagu coat of arms on its handle. They must have spent hours carving the stick and I was deeply moved. It is still in my possession today, and I am very proud of it.

Another delightful gesture came in the form of a letter from François de Rose, an old colleague of Roland's from London. Writing from France, de Rose explained that Roland had declined to serve under de Gaulle and had instead opted for a posting as French Consul-General in Shanghai. This was a strange decision since Roland had initially helped de Gaulle, but he found the leader of the Free French impossible to work with. Having reached London before the capitulation, he was reluctant to return to France and took the opportunity to be posted far away. Somehow, news of my escape to Switzerland had reached him, and, fearing that I was in financial difficulty, he asked de Rose to send me a cheque on the *Crédit Lyonnais*. It was signed by Roland but indicated no specific amount – it was a blank cheque! Had I wished to, I could have made it out for a million, but I took it as a most wonderful gesture and sign of affection, and kept it carefully throughout the war in my Swiss bank.

Now confined to the remote rural area around Berg, I returned to study the piano under Frau Anna Hirzel-Langenhan, practising ten hours a day like all the other pupils. Life at Schloss Berg was now rather odd, though in fact it always had been. There were too many nationalities and age groups, and too many temperamental outbursts and tensions for it to be in any way normal. However, I managed to avoid most of the emotional turbulence by helping Renata in the kitchen garden where we endeavoured to grow enough vegetables for the whole school. We even managed to get some ancient glasshouses back into use, triumphantly producing fine crops of tomatoes and peppers to supplement the very tight Swiss rations.

Such work was hardly recommended for hands dedicated to the keyboard, and few pupils volunteered their help, but despite being an international concert pianist, this was Renata's caprice. She would work indefatigably with spade and hoe, just as her peasant forefathers had done on their farm near Bologna. One of the few remaining Anglo-Saxon pupils at Berg was Beth Tregaskis, who had returned to Switzerland before the occupation of France. Beth possessed a radio, and every evening we would crowd round it to hear the BBC news, which always seemed to be bad. It was difficult

Beth Tregaskis

not to be depressed, not to worry about friends and relations, and not to feel frustrated and angry for being unable to participate in the struggle. In early 1941 however, that frustration diminished when a letter marked urgent arrived, offering me a part-time job at the British Legation. They knew I spoke French, German and Italian, and the fact that I did not pose a security risk made me an ideal candidate. I replied immediately, telling them I would love to work at the Legation but doubted whether the Swiss authorities would permit me to go to Bern. Soon afterwards, I mysteriously received official permission to visit Bern on condition that I limited my visits to two nights a week. Berg, they said, must remain my official residence.

When I left for Bern to discuss my prospective job, I was determined to remain an unpaid volunteer. This was a half-baked idea as I was in desperate need of cash, but I attached some kind of moral and ethical value to being a volunteer and that mattered a lot to me. After a series of interviews, I was informed that I had been accepted as a part-time member of the Legation staff, attached to a high-security department. Despite my volunteer status, I was given an *abonnement général* on the Swiss Railways and reimbursed for any expenses incurred. Actually, the free railway pass turned out to be the most wonderful perk. I returned to Berg delighted with my new job and the fact that I was back in the fight against Hitler.

I wondered what this job would involve, but my uncertainty was soon dispelled. Before the war, I had met the distinguished Swiss publisher Emil Oprecht and his wife Emmie, and through them I had got to know the great Italian writer Ignazio Silone. It was not long before I became aware that the Oprechts, who were fiercely and openly pro-Ally, were in contact with the United States and British governments. I was therefore not surprised when Emmie invited me to lunch at their Zurich flat to meet a special friend from the British Legation in Bern. This turned out to be my future boss, Elizabeth Wiskemann. Although much of her work was concerned with the analysis of the German press, her 'Assistant Press Attaché' title was purely a cover. Her real job was collecting political intelligence from Nazi Europe and relaying it to the PWE (Political Warfare Executive) in London. Elizabeth was working entirely on her own and desperately needed an assistant to sort out and translate the mass of information she received.

So in Zurich that day I was given a confidential report to translate, this time from German, a language Elizabeth spoke perfectly. After a good lunch – Emmie's lunches were always good – I was taken to a small guest room where I found a typewriter and a sheaf of papers. I was then told to get on with it; the door was closed firmly behind me and I nervously tackled my first intelligence job. The translation apparently met with approval, for not long afterwards I was told I had been appointed Assistant to Elizabeth Wiskemann. This was marvellous news and I was sure that in

Above:
Dr Emil Oprecht

Far Left:
Emmie Oprecht
in later life

Left:
Elizabeth Wiskemann

such a job I could do more towards the war effort than anything I had done in the MTC. I realised that I owed all this to the Oprechts; as publishers, their 'list' included writers publicly banned in both Germany and Italy. The Nazis had even offered a DM 100,000 reward for his arrest, but unintimidated, he continued to display the banned books in his Zurich book shop window – a courageous stand in those days.

When I first arrived in Switzerland, anti-Nazi feeling had been subdued, but it was growing stronger each day, both among the people and in the press. It was common knowledge in Zurich that the Oprechts were anti-Nazi but I had not realised how deeply they were involved in working against the Axis powers. Had the Nazis invaded Switzerland, the Oprechts would certainly have been high on the list for arrest, and they wouldn't have been difficult to find as their apartment was opposite the German Consulate on the Hirschengraben. I too would have been in difficulty, but a former landlady from a *pension* in Engadin had thought of that and offered to hide me in her mountain retreat for as long as was necessary. Such gestures, which tended to come out of the blue, were tremendously touching, and really gave me confidence that the silent majority in Switzerland were on our side.

Emmie Oprecht was similarly courageous. The daughter of one of Switzerland's leading trade union pioneers, she always stuck to her principles and would never deviate from what she considered to be right. Refugees could always rely on the Oprechts' compassion but they never referred to these things, and I only heard of their generosity through the grapevine. They were to become my most loyal friends and central to my life during those war years in Switzerland. It was through Emmie that I learned so much about the Swiss and Switzerland, for during those war years, the spirit of William Tell was still very much alive.

A portrait of me by Michele Baumann-Kienast

23

THE RITUALS OF ESPIONAGE

My new job cheered me greatly; I was now a part of the war effort and it felt as if a great weight had been lifted from me. When I set out for Bern, I realised I knew little about Elizabeth Wiskemann except that before the war I had read her book *Czechs and Germans*. A Cambridge scholar, she had spent much of the 1930s living in, and writing about, Central Europe and was now a highly regarded political analyst. Few people could have been better equipped to do the job, as her contacts ranged far and wide, and the information she received was both accurate and reliable. However, she was a committed anti-Nazi, and like her friends the Oprechts, would certainly have been arrested had the Germans invaded Switzerland.

My new way of life turned out to be rather schizophrenic, one half of it spent in an idyllic rural setting and the other in a town seething with intrigue and suspicion. Whilst I never really got used to my weekly train journeys on hard wooden seats, my work with Elizabeth was always stimulating and I soon came to appreciate the value of what she was doing; her reports to London were remarkable, influencing British policy on many subjects. Perhaps because she lacked charm and had very little sense of humour, Elizabeth was not generally popular with the Legation staff, who afforded her little co-operation. However, her work was paramount to her and woe betide anyone who impinged on this – they soon found themselves at the receiving end of her cutting sarcastic wit. Fortunately, we got on famously, but it was not long before I discovered that one of my most important tasks would be to smooth the feathers which she constantly ruffled; these ranged from the Minister down to Junior Attachés.

When I was in Bern, I would either stay at the rather basic YWCA or with Elizabeth at her flat on the outskirts of the town. She was a generous hostess, and after one of her excellent meals, we would forget the war and talk books. She also loved chatting about men and her ex-lovers, transforming herself into an extremely sexy, almost nymphomaniac, character. Occasionally my own translations had more to do with sex than politics, a report from Berlin about Hitler's kinky sexual behaviour with his mistress, Eva Braun, being a notable example. When I took the report to Mr MacKillop, the rather staid Councillor at the Legation, to be coded, he gave me a horrified look. "My dear Miss Montagu, you should not be concerned with this kind of filth." Despite his alarm, I imagine that the information eventually reached Britain via the *Atlantiksender*, adding a little spice to the usual grim round of war reports.

Some of the missions entrusted to me could have come straight out of John le Carré's *Smiley* chronicles. There was one particularly important contact who endangered his life each time he passed a report to us. Every detail that concerned him had to be treated as top secret and only Elizabeth and I knew who he was: a German national working at the German embassy. To do this I had to learn the basic rituals of espionage, including the use of dead letter boxes, where secret messages could be dropped and picked up. Most importantly, I was taught how to avoid being followed: this could involve complicated, circuitous journeys around the city which were always very time-consuming. For instance, I would first take a taxi, then unexpectedly pay it off and jump onto a tram, sometimes repeating this operation several times if I were suspicious. To be absolutely certain I was not being tailed, I would then complete the journey on foot. It was certainly good exercise and occasionally good fun too.

Throughout the war, the atmosphere in the big cities of Switzerland, and particularly in the capital, Bern, was very tense. During the early years of the war, the radio reported disaster after disaster and there was little to comfort those of us on the Allied side. However, those Swiss who had hitherto concealed their pro-Nazi sympathies under the cloak of neutrality now came out into the open and could easily be identified and watched. Happily for us, we discovered that the vast majority of the Swiss people, and particularly those in German-speaking Switzerland, were fiercely opposed to Hitler. In fact, this antipathy to their northern neighbour was so intense that it was better not to speak German in public but English, or, if one could manage it, their own language, *Schweizerdeutsch.*

At Berg, things were becoming more and more strained. The pro-Nazi element at the school had grown highly suspicious of my activities and I now realised that I was being watched. I had been in the habit of bringing work back to Berg, but wearing the pouch I had been given for confidential papers made it impossible to practise the piano or hoe the potatoes. I therefore took to concealing the documents in my room, but one day I found that my ingeniously hidden papers had been disturbed, proving that someone in the house was spying on me. I had also noticed a woman shadowing me when I took the train to and from Zurich. From then on I brought back only dull reports, such as those on ecumenical conferences.

Mercifully, the war failed to detract from the wonder of spring in Thurgau. In April, the whole countryside foamed with blossom and the grass around the trees was studded with wild flowers. Unfortunately, this was also the time of year when the peasants sprayed their pastures with liquid manure. The incredible stench was dubbed by my French officer friends as *le parfum fédéral.* Living in this rather simple rural community, it was most interesting to see how little those who worked on the land were affected by world events, however catastrophic. There were admittedly some grumbles about rationing, and the peasants would be gleeful if they managed to sell eggs or poultry to the townies at exorbitant black market prices, but otherwise life seemed to take its leisurely seasonal course.

My work in Bern had its hair-raising moments, but at other times it was fairly dull. The legation seemed to operate in tight compartments and only mixed on social occasions, usually at other diplomatic missions. There was an unwritten convention that Allied and Axis guests should never mix, even at neutral venues, but this didn't prevent us from going to the Swedish mission, which threw the best parties. These were presided over by Their Excellencies Mr and Mrs Prybyzewski-Westrup, who always dispensed lashings of *Akvavit* and butter imported from far-off Scandinavia.

One day my routine was interrupted by an unexpected call from the office of a colleague, John McCaffery, who was head of the Special Operations Executive (SOE) in Switzerland. Knowing that this was a top secret organisation, I was most surprised to get an invitation to join him for lunch. McCaffery was a slight and wiry Irishman with a rather red face, who always appeared to be in a hurry. I supposed it was routine for him to choose a rather dingy restaurant, where we engaged in mainly superficial small talk. Afterwards he drove us away from the city until we reached the stretch of parkland that ran along the side of the river. Suggesting we take a brief walk, he explained that I had been suggested as a suitable recruit for the SOE. Apparently, I had all the right qualifications, and with a wry smile he admitted that they were desperately short of the right people for the unusual work demanded by the organisation.

He briefly described something of this work, giving me a rough idea of the kind of activities in which I would be engaged. He did not attempt to play down the very real dangers involved, and perhaps to emphasise them, he patted his chest, where he concealed two guns. "I am never without them, not for one minute!" he insisted. He confided that he regarded his office as unsafe for confidential meetings, even though the walls, floor and ceiling had been specially treated. I understood his fear, as Sir David Kelly had recently discovered a bug in his drawing room fireplace.

McCaffery explained that he had a specific job in mind for me. Since my Italian was good, I could work in Tessin, the Italian part of Switzerland. Here, at the border town of Chiasso, detonators and other vital objects were handed over to the *Partigiani*, the Italian partisans. He assured me that such transfers would be quite simple. There would be a carefully arranged plan, and all I would need to do was proceed to the busy frontier railway station and hand over the goods. I couldn't believe my ears; it sounded just like *Boys' Own* stuff and so very dangerous. Sensing my lack of enthusiasm, he decided to play his trump card, an act which was extraordinary considering the great secrecy involved.

"Do you know where I was trained, where so many of us in the SOE learn our trade? Well, I warn you, for when I tell you, you won't be able to wait to join us!" He was now quite agitated, but I looked blankly at him; I had no idea what he was talking about. "Well, take a deep breath, and I'll tell you! We train at *Beaulieu*, your own home – think about that!" With that we walked on. I was truly speechless. Later, I did think about it – a lot – for his job offer came as a considerable shock. When we returned to the legation, I was still undecided, although my instinct was to say a definite 'no'. McCaffery must have sensed this, as when we parked the car he said rather sadly, "Ah, well, think about it, and take your time."

I desperately needed someone to talk to about this unexpected proposal, someone moreover who was already on the inside. McCaffery had mentioned the name of Ignazio Silone, and since he was already a friend of the Oprechts, I felt he could give me impartial advice. Silone, now a political leader in exile, was a key figure in the anti-Fascist partisan movement in Switzerland, the *Partigiani* being very active all along the Swiss-Italian border. Despite ill-health arising from serious respiratory problems, he was still prepared to devote all his time and energy to the fight against Mussolini.

When I told Silone about the SOE proposition, he was horrified. "What! Send you of all people, so typically Anglo-Saxon, to hang about on the platform at Chiasso! You'd be spotted in a matter of seconds. Doesn't McCaffery realise that the station is swarming with Fascist spies, and anyone seen talking to you there would be shot the moment he crossed back into Italy!" He was very shaken that an organisation as serious as the SOE should contemplate doing something so irresponsible and potentially dangerous to his dedicated partisans. However, when I told him that I would refuse to work for McCaffery he became calmer, but I fear this incident may have dented his confidence in the British. It had similarly dented my confidence in the SOE. Through talking to Silone, I realised how little suited I was to undertake this kind of work, so telling McCaffery I had decided against joining the SOE was less painful than I had expected. I constantly questioned my motives; was it loyalty to Elizabeth Wiskemann, my unsuitability for the job or perhaps just fear? Fortunately my contact with Silone did allow me to help Renata, who was anxious to do her own bit towards the war effort. Having effected an introduction between them, I saw her grow visibly happier, and realised later that she had become a recruit.

Having declined McCaffery, I was relieved to get back to my work with Elizabeth, even if it was dull at times. Then one day, as I was running up the stairs to our office at the top of the Chancellery, I collided with a young man who apologised profusely. When I looked up I saw it was Pierre Dubois. We were both speechless. When we recovered, we both laughed and decided that this strange meeting had to be celebrated and duly went off to lunch together. This lunch was the first of several we were to have during the following weeks, but not once did we refer to our odd meeting on the stairs at the Chancellery. I had always felt that there was something about Pierre Dubois I couldn't explain, but now all the pieces of the puzzle started to fall into place. He never betrayed his interest in anything but the watch trade, although one or two clues did emerge.

Since Elizabeth Wiskemann had built up excellent relations with the Free French representatives in Bern, I was now reasonably well-informed about the *Maquis* – the French Resistance. In the light of this knowledge, I began to interpret the events of that extraordinary day, Friday 13th September 1940, and the part that Pierre Dubois had played in the chain of events. These had started with our chance meeting in the train out of Lyons, followed by his careful and efficient planning of my escape. Then there had been that odd lunch party in the suburban house in Aix-les-Bains, and the mysterious visit to the shadowy villa by the lake. And, most significant of all, the practised and skilful manner in which he had smuggled me out of France. I recalled too how he had not once dropped his cover, even to the point of inveighing against the British for continuing a useless struggle against Hitler and calling Churchill a warmonger. When we parted that night in Geneva, I was convinced that we would never meet again.

I found myself enjoying his company, his sense of humour and his optimism, and we were rapidly becoming good friends. Then one day, over lunch, he asked me if I had ever seen the famous Bern Bears in their special pit on the outskirts of the city. I admitted I hadn't, so he immediately suggested a visit. It was a lovely afternoon and it was fun watching these heraldic animals (they are the emblem of the Canton of Bern) as they played in the sunshine. Suddenly, to my surprise, Pierre took my hand. He said he had something very important to say to me. I thought he was about to tell me the truth about himself, that he was working for the British and was deeply involved in top secret matters. But it turned out to be quite different, and something he found difficult to put into words; he loved me and wanted to marry me.

Coming like this and completely out of the blue would have been something of a shock anyway, but it was worse than that, for he had previously told me he was married and had a family in Geneva. So for a few tense moments I remained silent, for I liked him and didn't want to hurt him. Eventually I gently told him that it would be best to forget what he had just said. Now it was his turn to be silent as we stood watching those silly bears playing in the sun. When we both came to our senses, we agreed we should not meet again for some time, and when we got back to the city, we said a solemn and sad farewell, knowing that we should very probably never meet again, and we never did.

At first I missed him, for I had liked him a lot. This prompted me to find out more about him; a difficult but interesting task. Pierre Dubois was a rich young *Genevois* of good family, passionately devoted to the allied cause and prepared to risk his life for it; there was no doubt that he was a very brave man. Being genuinely involved in the Swiss watch industry, he was able to obtain those highly technical, delicate and much-prized components which were badly needed by the aircraft industry for the RAF. So, in the guise of an eager, hard-working watch 'rep', he would take these devices to the Pyrenees where he handed them to other agents and thus, via Lisbon, they would reach England.

Looking back on the events of that day in September 1940 and seeing them in the context of the recently-formed *Maquis*, everything made sense. For instance, the two houses we visited were probably *Maquis* safe houses, the motley collection of guests at Aix were most likely members of the Resistance, while the man with the hats was another committed anti-Nazi Swiss. But I still regret that I never discovered the precise facts, so the happenings of that Friday 13th remain, to this day, one of the unsolved mysteries of my life.

The Bern Bears who witnessed
Pierre Dubois' strange proposal

Therese Giehse playing Mrs Alving in 'Gespenster' by Henrik Ibsen

24

'THE MAGIC MOUNTAIN'

By the middle of 1942, things had become easier for British subjects in Switzerland, and thanks to the intervention of my friends with the Swiss authorities, I was now permitted to move freely around the country. The restrictions on my *permis de séjour* still held, and I had to report to the local police monthly; however, I could now make full use of that fabulous *abonnement général* and travel freely around Switzerland. I particularly liked to visit Zurich where I could stay with friends for as long as I liked, and very soon became a regular theatre-goer at the Schauspielhaus. This, the principal theatre in Zurich, had managed to assemble the most distinguished ensemble in the German-speaking world. Here were the leading players, directors, scenic designers and composers, both 'Aryan' and Jewish, who had come to escape the Nazis. I was fascinated by it all, and, seeing such superb performances, my old love for the theatre came flooding back.

In addition to his publishing work, 'Opi' (Dr Oprecht) was the Administrator of the Schauspielhaus, and I soon got to know the leading members of the company. Some of them were already established stars, such as Therese Giehse from Munich, whilst others were destined for brilliant careers, notably the leading actress, Maria Becker. What united them was their dedication, enthusiasm and team spirit; the Schauspielhaus could not afford star salaries, so they literally lived for their work. Zurich was in the forefront of those Swiss cities opposed to Hitler and this was reflected in the repertoire of the Schauspielhaus. Their productions included many plays by British and American writers, as well as dissident playwrights such as Brecht, and it was this policy that led one day to an amusing incident.

John Steinbeck's *The Moon is Down* had been translated into German and dramatised. As an outright condemnation of the German occupation of Norway, it seemed perfect for the Schauspielhaus. Set in Nazi-occupied territory, it portrayed the German army in a very unpleasant light. News of this forthcoming production leaked out and the German Consul-General in Zurich lodged an energetic protest in Berne, claiming that it contravened Swiss neutrality laws. The theatre management denied any such intention and, to prove it, invited the German authorities to attend the dress rehearsal. If they produced any reasonable objections, the production would be cancelled forthwith.

As the German delegation trooped into the auditorium, the atmosphere became electric, but the performance went without a hitch and after the final curtain, the Germans, looking rather sheepish, rose to their feet and left the theatre. What had happened? Not a single line of the play had been altered, and as the portrayal of the occupying force was just as unpleasant as Steinbeck had intended, this was distinctly odd. But there had been one vital alteration: the uniforms. All the invaders wore British uniforms, so if anyone had any reason to protest it was the British, yet they did no such thing, leaving the Germans to fume. Happily, when the play opened, the Swiss quickly got the message, and vastly enjoyed both the show and the joke played on the Nazis. *The Moon is Down* played to full houses for many months.

Despite my two years in Switzerland, I had still not completely recovered from that bout of pneumonia caught in Angoulême and was still prone to coughs and sore throats. I realised that if I was to cope with all the hard work ahead of me, I had to shake it off once and for all. So, on my doctor's advice, Renata and I decided to spend two or three weeks somewhere in the mountains, where we hoped the dry, pure air would clear up my complaint. It was just before Christmas, and we chose Davos, high up in the Southern Alps, and long renowned as a *Kurort* for chest and TB sufferers. We chose a reasonably priced *pension* and arranged to hire a piano, so that while I skied on the slopes, Renata could practise. In the evenings we could enjoy the company of Ignazio Silone, who was living there while in exile from Zurich. So we set off, Renata with her music and I with my skis. Silone was delighted to see us and sometimes while Renata was sitting at the piano, he and I would walk in the sun along the Hohe

Ignazzio Silone

Promenade. The setting might have been good for his lungs, but it was most inconvenient for his work, just as the Swiss authorities intended it to be. Silone was a strange and remarkable man and despite his health difficulties was pouring all his energies into the fight against Mussolini.

Ironically enough, soon after I arrived I was struck down by an attack of pneumonia! Fortunately there were plenty of lung specialists in Davos, and Renata proved herself a devoted nurse. Confined to bed, coughing into a classic TB spittoon, I vividly recall Renata practising as I read Thomas Mann's masterpiece *The Magic Mountain*, which was set in Davos.

Her music really lifted my spirits and I was soon on the mend. I was then visited by a local TB specialist, Maria Walter, who insisted I should have a chest x-ray, and shortly after this had been done she invited us both to a party. When we arrived at her house, I had hardly taken off my coat when she led me into a side room to show me the x-ray results. Dr Walter pointed out what she suspected to be a patch on my lung which could be tubercular. She told me that this shadow was a real threat, and that I would need to stay in Davos for anything up to a year – returning to Zurich was out of the question until I was completely better.

This came as a great shock, and I thought of Keats, the Brontës, Chopin and, of course, Thomas Mann. When I returned to the party, I tried to behave normally but gradually discovered that most of my fellow guests were TB sufferers of many years and were forced to live in Davos – it was an eerie feeling. On our way home, Renata suddenly said that she needed some fresh air, and, getting out of the sleigh, let me finish the journey on my own. Directly I arrived at the *pension*, I rushed to the telephone, eager to contact Emmie to ask her advice. She listened intently, then replied firmly that we must leave Davos the very next day. She would meet us at the station and we could stay at her flat that night; explanations would come later. I had hardly put down the receiver before Renata appeared. Not wishing to alarm me, she had phoned Emmie too and concurred that we should cut short our visit and leave the very next morning.

Back in Zurich, we met the Oprechts for supper and received the long awaited explanation. Not long after they had been married, Opi had been taken ill in Davos, and what followed matched my experience in practically every detail. But Emmie was unconvinced by the diagnosis and took him back to Zurich. Away from the sinister lure of the 'Magic Mountain', Opi resumed his busy life and work, and never had any more trouble with his lungs. "You see," she told us, "all those sick people up there belong to a kind of freemasonry, and they're always trying to recruit new 'cases' into their magic circle. Understandable though, isn't it, when you are not only under a death sentence but dreadfully bored as well…" she smiled. "Of course our friend Silone would have been delighted to go for daily walks with you, a charming, blonde English woman…" In hindsight, I can see that Emmie took a huge risk, but it paid off handsomely and neither of us was plagued with serious chest troubles again.

Because many of my friends were involved with the theatre, I became increasingly anxious to return to the stage myself. My German wasn't good enough to compete with the local professionals, so I decided to form my own company of English-speaking players. To get my new venture off to a good start, I knew that the choice of play would be paramount. Swiss audiences loved plays by Bernard Shaw and Somerset Maugham, so I eventually decided on Maugham's delightful comedy *The Constant Wife*, which had the advantage of a small cast and only one set. Next, I set about finding my cast. First I tried recruiting through the British and US Consulates and then advertising in the press. The response was disappointing but I interviewed everyone who applied and eventually had just enough players. Among those who wrote to me was a young man who signed himself George Joyce; this led to a meeting with his mother, James Joyce's redoubtable widow, Nora. Another contact made whilst searching for players was altogether more important, and would radically alter the course of my life during the last years of the war.

Mary Rufenacht-Bancroft was a good-looking and witty American. I took an instant liking to her; she seemed highly intelligent, warm-hearted and possessed of a wonderful sense of humour. Born in 1903 of Irish-American stock, she grew up in Boston, Massachusetts, and must have been the kind of girl maiden aunts would describe as 'wild'. She had worked as a journalist but was now living in Zurich with her banker husband, Jean Rufenacht, and a teenage daughter from her previous marriage. Whilst she didn't have any stage experience and I wasn't able to give her a part, our meeting was a great success. As Mary recalled in her memoir, *Autobiography of a Spy*, we particularly laughed over some of the absurdities in our respective legations and their attempts at oblique propaganda. At the time, I thought I was merely interviewing a pleasant would-be actress from the Zurich society round, but within a few months, Mary would become my employer, enabling me to do more for the war effort than I had ever imagined.

Dr Hans-Bernd Gisevius

25

THE GISEVIUS AFFAIR

The beginning of 1943 found me busy with rehearsals for *The Constant Wife*. These took place in a cheerless and chilly community hall, and were hopelessly chaotic. Inevitably I came to the conclusion that for me to direct the production and play the lead was far too demanding. Taking my courage in both hands, I appealed to Therese Giehse and Maria Becker for help; they were both leading members of Schauspielhaus company, and to my relief, Therese took over the direction of the play. Her instructions were very helpful, but as a director, she was quite ruthless. I found myself working harder than I ever did in the West End, but her creativity, with bursts of impatience and irritability, really freshened things up. Three weeks later, after a lot of gruelling work, the Anglo-American Players were able to present quite a polished production to a packed house in Basle. The audience were wildly appreciative, but we all realised that this rapturous and heart-warming acclaim was directed more at the allied war effort than at the performance of the Anglo-American Players. We went on to perform in Bern, Geneva, Lausanne and at the Schauspielhaus in Zurich.

Therese's somewhat rotund figure made her an unlikely-looking star, but she was a dramatic genius and, fortunately for the cast, spoke very good English. Through working together, Therese and I became close friends; she was a remarkable human being and I owe her a great deal. Being Jewish and uncompromisingly left-wing, she left Hitler's Germany in favour of Switzerland where she became one of the most renowned stage personalities of the German-speaking theatre. She certainly enriched my life during those war years in Zurich. Because *The Constant Wife* had been given such excellent reviews, I began to receive all kinds of offers to give lectures and appear on the radio, and was asked to do a series of recitals of English poetry with Maria Becker. There was also public interest in my MTC experiences in France, and I travelled around the country giving lectures to quite large audiences. These would earn me up to 50 Swiss Francs per lecture, although on one occasion a textile factory preferred to reward me with a night-gown from their product range!

Since the time when I auditioned her for *The Constant Wife*, Mary Bancroft and I had become good friends. I would often visit her at her Zurich flat to have a good laugh, discuss politics and speak English once more. On one occasion in the autumn of 1943, however, I arrived to find Mary in an unusually serious mood. She smiled when she saw my expression, and explained that this evening would be different; we had important and serious matters to discuss. Having fortified me with a drink, Mary revealed that she secretly worked for Allen Dulles, Head of the American Office of Strategic Services in Bern (the OSS was the forerunner to the CIA). Her role was to analyse the German press, gather information on the German Resistance and establish contact with refugees entering Switzerland who might be sympathetic to the allied cause. I was listening with growing fascination as Mary then outlined a work proposition, by far the strangest I have ever had. She wanted me to join the OSS and work for American Intelligence!

Any sensible person would have asked for time to reflect, but I accepted her offer without hesitation. Thankfully, I have never really been a sensible person! Mary made her work sound so easy, but I knew in my bones that it would not be like that at all. As I walked back to the Oprechts that evening, it dawned on me that this new and challenging job would revolutionise my life and present me at the same time with some thorny problems. To begin with, I would have to tell Elizabeth Wiskemann that I couldn't continue to work for her and explain why. Secondly, I would have to leave Berg and move to Zurich, and come up with a plausible reason for doing so. A few days later, Mary confirmed that the job offer was official, and I would soon have to go to Bern to meet with Allen Dulles and learn what would be expected of me. From the way Mary insisted how very agreeable he was and how much I would like him, I suspected she might have a weakness for him.

The first thing I did was to ask for an interview with Sir David Kelly, our Minister, to tell him of my decision to quit the British Legation and work for Allen Dulles and the Americans. To my surprise, his reaction was entirely favourable; he affirmed that the Americans were doing a very fine job and "good luck to them". But Elizabeth was very upset. She obviously felt betrayed and deeply hurt, and it would be more than twenty years before we could meet again as friends. Having dealt with Bern, I was now faced with what promised to be a difficult situation at Berg. This was all the more traumatic as I had come to regard the Schloss as a second home. I had lived there on and off since 1936, enjoying the music, the pleasant country life and, above all, Renata's company. Plainly I was unable to give the real reason for my relocation and Renata was both mystified and hurt. Happily though, this estrangement was to be comparatively brief and we were soon able to resume our friendship.

My next priority was to find somewhere in Zurich to live. I was helped by the Oprechts who suggested the Pension Wachs in the Plattenstrasse, an inexpensive bed and breakfast lodging used by theatre folk. Run by two respectable spinsters, it was only a stone's throw from the theatre. Moreover, several members of the company had rooms there, including Therese Giehse and her sister. It was clean, well-run and very reasonable, the latter being vital since the £30 a month I received from my bank in London did not go very far in Switzerland. If the food there was a trifle dull, there was at least always plenty of it, despite rationing. I duly settled happily into my rather dark little ground floor room, which would give me the privacy I needed for working in espionage.

My time with Elizabeth Wiskemann had taught me that as the Swiss were sternly opposed to intelligence activities one had to be extremely circumspect and, if possible, establish some kind of cover. I therefore enrolled myself in the Faculties of Sociology and National Economy at the University of Zurich. Unfortunately, as a foreigner without proof of any academic qualifications, I became a kind of second-class citizen at the university; I could attend all the lectures but was precluded from the students' social activities. I soon discovered that a number of my fellow students had similar problems, especially those who had escaped from the Nazis. Realising I was not alone, I took it all in my stride, for it was wonderful to be able to study at a university.

Then came the day for my interview with Allen Dulles in Bern; rather than meeting at the American Embassy, he asked me to come to his house in the old part of the city. Bern is not only the Federal Capital and seat of Government, but also a beautiful medieval town commanding a superb view of the distant Alps and the River Aare below. The Dulles' house was of a later date, but its spacious 18th century elegance far exceeded the kind of accommodation usually allocated to foreign diplomats. Dulles was a man with a tremendous personality and a commanding presence but he also radiated a curious aloofness, a kind of chill. On the surface he was friendly, even affable, but he had a hollow, mirthless laugh. Later I came to regard this as a kind of warning signal, since when he was genuinely amused, he could laugh as heartily as any man.

Tall, fresh-complexioned and with a small, neat, greying moustache, Dulles always wore thick rimless spectacles, through which he would peer at one with his piercing blue eyes. He was an excellent host, and after a lunch that bore little trace of rationing, we got down to business. Dulles explained that when he had first arrived in Switzerland, he had been highly sceptical about the existence of a resistance movement within Germany, being convinced that such activities could not possibly exist under the Nazis. So when he was offered proof that it did exist, he tracked down every available scrap of evidence. And when incontrovertible proof did reach him, it came in a somewhat singular manner.

Among the members of the German Consulate in Zurich was the Vice-Consul, Dr Hans-Bernd Gisevius. Through what must have been the most clandestine of channels, Gisevius had managed to contact Dulles and reveal that his diplomatic posting was merely a cover; he was really a member of the *Abwehr*, the intelligence division of the *Wehrmacht*. Headed by Admiral Canaris in Berlin, the *Abwehr* was more clandestine than the Gestapo and often in conflict with it. This friction went deeper than the usual rivalry between different Nazi organisations; several of the *Abwehr's* senior members were actively planning to overthrow Hitler. Gisevius' role was to establish high-level contact with the Allies, but in doing so, he was also helping to protect his own future in the event of a German defeat. Despite his initial suspicions that Gisevius might be a double agent, Dulles felt he could not afford to ignore this man, especially as he was offering highly sensitive information.

Much of this information was contained in a lengthy manuscript, which Gisevius wanted translated and ready for publication at the end of the war. There were no less than 1,415 pages of typed manuscript bound into four weighty volumes. Like the volumes of an historical epic, each had a dramatic title: *The Burning of the Reichstag, The Thirteenth of June, The Fritsch Blomberg Crisis* and *Reinhard Heydrich: The Story of a Futile Terror*. It was clear that Gisevius knew a great deal about the innermost workings of the Third Reich, the private lives of prominent Nazis, and even of Hitler himself. Dulles must have been fascinated. Here at last were the facts behind events which up to that time had only reached us piecemeal from underground sources. Gisevius' account presented the whole horror of the Third Reich, and the background to the hierarchy in Berlin, related in a manner so punctilious that no gory detail was omitted.

Dulles knew that from the moment he had taken possession of this manuscript, he had Gisevius totally in his control. Then he came to my part in this extraordinary affair; I was to help Mary Bancroft with the ongoing debriefing of Gisevius and undertake the translation of his manuscripts. Emphasising that some of the information might not be really important, Dulles stressed that it should nevertheless all be treated as top secret. I responded to his trust by assuring him of my unfailing loyalty and discretion. Then, as I was about to leave, he mentioned rather as an afterthought that I would receive 300 Swiss francs monthly plus any expenses incurred while on the job. I was stunned; it seemed a fortune, especially as I had worked for the British as an unpaid volunteer since 1939, with money always being a nagging worry. Returning on the train to Zurich, I carefully considered the events of that day. I realised that I was now an agent working for the OSS and no longer my own master. I reflected too on the veiled, remote and mysterious figure who was my boss. However, the fact that I would be working closely with Mary Bancroft was a reassuring and delightful prospect.

After a couple of months spent on fairly routine work, I was finally asked to meet Gisevius at Mary's flat. My first impression of Dr Hans-Bernd Gisevius was neither favourable nor reassuring. What I saw that first evening was a tall, powerfully built and reasonably handsome man who radiated an ice-cold ruthlessness and something indefinably sinister. Mary had already been working with him for some months and later told me she found him rather attractive, but to me he always remained positively repellent. That first afternoon started more as a social occasion, but then we turned to more serious matters: recent events in Germany and the translation of his manuscript. The relaxed atmosphere was not at all what I had expected from my first encounter with a high-ranking enemy official but it seemed to go well and further meetings were planned.

Mary and I decided that we should do as much translation as possible away from Gisevius, so that our time with him could be devoted to his story-telling. He relished having an attentive female audience and clearly wanted to impress us, so my addition to the 'interrogation team' was all that was needed for him to make some new revelations. We soon discovered that Gisevius had a taste for whisky and that a couple of double Scotches would keep him chatting late into the night. He even took delight in telling me about my aristocratic ancestry. As he did not like to drink alone, we had to devise a system for one of us to remain sober and memorise any extra information he gave us. Mary would fill one bottle of Haig with cold tea, leaving the other in all its pure Scottish glory. There can be few drinks more depressing than cold tea and soda, so Mary had to be careful not to mix up the bottles, but I don't think Gisevius ever suspected anything.

These late night sessions in Mary's flat continued for many months until the major part of Gisevius' bulky manuscript could be read in English. Of the many translations I had undertaken, there were few to rival Gisevius' chronicles; strange, sometimes sinister and horrific, but always fascinating. There were some lighter, even gossipy passages, which could be amusing, but the unpleasantly salacious sections left little to the imagination. The Nazi hierarchy were indeed a nasty lot. There was, however, rarely an evening when Gisevius did not produce something of value, and Dulles was rightly pleased with our work.

Meanwhile, other very important things were afoot. Through Gisevius and his contacts[1], Dulles had come into possession of one of the Nazis' most jealously-guarded war secrets; the development of the V2. Hitler believed that once his rockets were unleashed on London, they would bring the British to their knees. Gisevius' report was very precise, and pinpointed the factory at Peenemünde, a small town on the Baltic, where it was being assembled. Construction was now so far advanced that it would not be

*Mary Bancroft and myself in a spoof photograph, taken to illustrate
the effects of working long hours on the Gisevius manuscript!*

long before this weapon could be in full operation. This, combined with
other sources of information, persuaded the Allies to launch bombing raids
on Peenemünde which delayed production of the V2 by several months.

After an evening at Mary's flat, I would feel distinctly uneasy walking back
in the darkness with Gisevius by my side. I had heard that the Germans
snatched people off the streets of Zurich and bundled them into a car,
knowing that within less than an hour they could be in Germany. After a
while, however, I became aware of a different kind of danger which became
more apparent every time we met; Gisevius was paying me far too much
attention and was obviously attracted to me. At first I tried to ignore it, but
when Mary started teasing me about it, I had to face up to the unpleasant
reality. One morning, Fraulein Wachs called me to the telephone. "It's a
gentleman," she said, "and he says it's urgent." It was Gisevius. I was
horrified that he, of all people, should call when we knew that the Swiss

frequently monitored the telephones of suspect foreign nationals. Gisevius did not waste time: he wanted me to spend the weekend with him at a hotel at Vitznau on Lake Lucerne. Trying to sound casual, I replied that I had already promised to spend that weekend with some friends in Thurgau, but thanked him all the same.

When I eventually spoke to Allen and told him of Gisevius' suggestion he listened carefully, then, after a short pause, gave one of his hollow laughs. "Well, my dear Elizabeth, you must do what your conscience tells you…" and rang off. My conscience told me clearly that it was neither right nor my duty to spend an illicit weekend with an *Abwehr* agent who was also physically repulsive to me. When I saw Gisevius the next evening, I told him the Vitznau idea was far too dangerous and therefore out of the question. I think he read between the lines but took the rebuff very well. Fortunately, he was soon to meet his future wife, so the problem never occurred again.

Early in July 1944, Gisevius told us that our sessions would have to cease for a while as there were a few things he had to do in Berlin. He had previously told us that he wouldn't be returning to Germany until a conspiracy to kill Hitler was ready to be put into effect: his visit appeared to signal that the plan was due to commence. Later, when the news did start to trickle out of Germany, we realised that the '20th July plot' had ended in disaster for the conspirators. Reading of the terrible retribution that Hitler meted out to his would-be assassins, we took it for granted that we would never see Gisevius again. However, six months later, in January 1945, he reappeared in Zurich, very much alive and eager to tell us about the whole affair.

After the failed assassination, Dulles found him a safe house in Berlin, but when this became too dangerous, Gisevius was furnished with false papers so that he could escape to Zurich by train. When we all met again, Gisevius tried hard to be his old self, but he looked pale and haunted – his old ebullience was sadly lacking. After a period of recuperation, he moved to a house on the Lake of Geneva from where he worked on his account of the 20th July plot, later published in *To The Bitter End*. From time to time he would visit us in Zurich to go over the translation of his latest work, but he was nervous, fearing that the Nazis were out to get him. No longer able to serve as a 'mole' for Dulles, his purpose in life had gone and any information he might have held was becoming less relevant as the war drew to an end. Eventually Gisevius was able to leave for the United States, where he lived for some time after the war before returning to his native country.

I thought I had seen the last of Hans-Bernd Gisevius at the end of the war, but one day, in 1961, I saw him at a hotel in Düsseldorf. I had gone down for an early breakfast and there was only one other guest in the dining room. After giving him a long look I realised, with something of a shock, that this was Gisevius, so I walked over to his table and spoke his name. He turned, recognised me immediately, and in the most easy and friendly manner invited me to join him for breakfast. I was amazed at the change in him. Now white-haired and slightly stooping, his vitality had gone and he seemed weary, sad and very much older. He explained that he had gone back to Germany because he had wanted to return to his original profession, the law. He told me nothing of his private life or his years in America, but kept the conversation as light-hearted and trivial as possible, and, as in the past, he never dropped his mask. Since I had to keep an early appointment, I had to leave him still sitting at the breakfast table. When we said goodbye, we were both well aware that we would probably never meet again, and we never did. But that chance meeting stirred up many memories of a chapter in my life as unreal as a paperback spy story.

Myself as Candida in the show of the same name, staged by the Anglo-American Players

26

CANDIDA

From the end of what I still think of as the 'Gisevius Affair', I was to continue my work for Dulles, although what followed was an anticlimax. My duties included research into the background and activities of people suspected of being Nazi sympathisers, or perhaps even double agents. This research was mostly conducted on a social level, and I found this a difficult and eventually a hateful task. I knew some of these people quite well and they considered me a trusted friend; fortunately most of those under suspicion turned out to be totally innocent. There was also a great deal of translation to be done, including a report on some very grubby paper smuggled out of Treblinka in Nazi-occupied Poland. As I translated the scribbled message, the full horror of the concentration camp's purpose became clear to me. Hitherto unknown to the Allies, the name Treblinka was soon to become synonymous with the Nazis' extermination of the Jews – a realisation so terrible, so nightmarish, that it haunts me to this day.

1944 heralded distinctly better news of the war and now, full of energy and enthusiasm, I decided to embark on another stage production. Whilst this was an excellent cover for my OSS activities, I knew that I would need help if the production was to continue the standards set by *The Constant Wife*. Fortunately, Therese agreed to direct the play and Dr Hans Curjel, a refugee theatre manager from Holland, offered to handle the administration.

The play we chose was Shaw's *Candida,* since it only needed one set and a very small cast. This time I knew that finding actors should not be too difficult, as hundreds of British 'escapers' had flooded over the Alps into

Myself and John Hoy

Switzerland after the collapse of Italy. The Swiss, of course, had promptly interned them, some in camps close to Zurich. So I went from camp to camp, talent-spotting and hoping that I might stumble on some professional actors. The first to come to my attention was a Lieutenant John Hoy of the East Yorkshires, who had made a dramatic escape from a prisoner of war camp in Italy. A young actor with West End experience, he was tall, slim, good-looking and a natural to play the poet Marchbanks; he was overjoyed at the prospect. Then I found another young actor, Henry Rayner, for the part of the nervous young curate. Initially, Ivor Murillo played the parson, but the part was later taken over by an experienced

Gordon Dickens and Max van Embden

amateur, Gordon Dickens. Needless to say, the detention camps didn't
have any women to offer me, but Therese introduced me to a talented
young actress whose émigré status had prevented the Schauspielhaus from
giving her a contract. Susan Lehmann was a German refugee who spoke
good English; initially we thought she was too young to take the part of
the secretary Prossy, but with the help of make-up she did a splendid job.
To top our list, Max van Embden, formerly the stooge to Grock, the
famous clown, took the role of Ernie. As for Candida, I had the rare
opportunity of casting myself in the role. No part has ever given me so
much pleasure, and I treasure the memory of those performances.

Susan Lehmann

Shortly before our first night at the Casino Theatre in Wintertur on 15th February, the production was the subject of a feature article in *Die Weltwoche*.

> Candida is Shaw's finest comedy and the enchanting, slim, blonde creature with the shining aquamarine eyes... half child, half woman, totally English, full of charm is Miss Montagu... Is it unthinkable that this enchanting being, working as a volunteer ambulance driver, sped through a hail of bombs ... heading south as the Germans were coming.

I think that the writer took a bit of a liking to me – in any event, his lavish praise ensured that we played to full houses. We also took the show to the British and American camps in the mountains, which went down well, as Susan Lehmann recalled to me recently in a letter:

Susan Lehmann, hairdresser Maria Magnani and myself in the dressing room mirror

It was really very rewarding to play for the interned soldiers, who must have had a very dull life. They were grateful and their spontaneous reactions motivated us of course. Max and I – or more correctly put, Mr Burgess and Miss Prossy – aroused fits of laughter and much applause thanks to the character of their parts. And of course we appreciated it very much that we were allowed to perform for these evacuees, hoping to give them at least a tiny bit of pleasure and entertainment. In a way it seemed to us more satisfying and significant as well as rewarding than playing to a Swiss bourgeois audience for whom (of course only partly) it was just *à la mode* to go to an English performance to prove on whose side one stood during the war.

Our tour, which took in Zurich, Basel, Bern, Lausanne, Genf, Luzern and St Gallen, proved to be an even greater success than the previous one, prompting most encouraging reviews such as this one in *Tages Amzeiger* on 3rd March.

> Guest plays in a foreign language don't usually make for full houses in Zurich as happened recently on the occasion of the first appearance in the Playhouse of the Anglo-American Players with Shaw's *Candida*. But the rare opportunity to be host to a troupe of Anglo-American professional actors produced this astonishing drawing power, and the applause which greeted the performance was undoubtedly richly deserved.

> In Elizabeth Montagu we had a sharp, fresh and – may one say – Shawesque Candida, in Max van Embden a typical Ernie with his wild Cockney, in John Hoy a subtle Marchbanks and in Gordon Dickens… a deeply English Victorian Pastor Morell. The likeable Henry Rayner must also be mentioned – and a special plaudit is due to Susan Lehmann's 'Prossie' – all in all a really talented group of players who under Gordon Dickens' direction and Therese Giehse's supervision[1] delivered a very amusing and above all thoroughly English performance of *Candida*.

> If this was not a 'theatrical landmark', it was certainly a keen pleasure to be able to enjoy such a smooth, fresh and competent production in the English language in the middle of a war.

Despite such praise, our director kept us on our toes. Whilst we were performing at the Schauspielhaus, Therese was on the stage in Winterthur but arrived back in time to see the last act. As I came off to rapturous applause, she tore me off a strip for going too fast! Fortunately, not all our backstage callers were so critical. After one of our performances in Geneva, the leading producer of Swiss films, Lazar Wechsler, came to my dressing room and offered me a film contract, to be discussed on my return to Zurich. Wechsler was undoubtedly a phenomenon. Born in Poland of very poor parents, he was now a naturalised Swiss, despite having arrived as a penniless Jewish immigrant, unable to speak the language. I believe he started by selling goods from a street stall but, obsessed with films, he was determined to become a big-time film producer. Switzerland had little tradition in film-making and no film industry of its own, but in a remarkably short time, Wechsler was engaging top directors and making high quality films. Despite this remarkable progress, he was still looking for a subject which would capture world interest, and in 1944 he thought he had found it.

Not long before, there had been considerable public indignation over an incident on the German-Swiss frontier. A group of refugees had managed to reach the border, only to be turned back by the Swiss authorities and brutally treated by the Germans, all in full view of the townspeople of Schaffhausen. Similar things were happening all along the Swiss frontier, and, it was rumoured, many Allied 'escapers' were being refused entry and being handed back to their captors. Wechsler sensed that here was a story waiting to be translated into a movie. The film would be set in Italian Switzerland, and as by that date the Italians were hardly in a position to raise any objections, he knew he could find the perfect location for it.

When it came to the question of engaging a writer to produce the script, the choice presented no problem; it had to be Ignazio Silone. His close links with the *Partigiani* meant that the Italian could put first-hand knowledge into the project and Wechsler felt it was a real coup when he accepted. Despite this, Silone had little experience of script writing and moreover, commercial considerations required that British and Americans should play the leading roles. Knowing Silone's spoken English to be poor, Wechsler stipulated that he should seek Anglo-Saxon help; my role was therefore to collaborate on the script, and then to assist the director with the English-speaking actors.

Once the *Candida* tour was over, I returned to Zurich to pursue Wechsler's offer, but first I had to seek permission for extended leave from the OSS. Fortunately Dulles supported me, and by the late summer I had signed a contract with Wechsler's production company, Praesens Films. I was absolutely delighted; this was my entry into an industry which I had been observing with interest ever since I had arrived in Switzerland. After the war, I was asked to give a radio talk on European films[2] and some of what I said then still provides a useful insight:

> When I escaped into Switzerland a film battle was in full swing... As they were neutral, the Swiss were able to exhibit films from all the belligerent countries and remain, in theory, completely dispassionate. You must remember that the three principal languages spoken in Switzerland were German, French – Vichy French – and Italian. So Nazi and Fascist films could be shown to Swiss audiences without any alteration, and distribution from studio to screen was only a matter of weeks. The Nazi newsreel service was even more rapid. On the other hand, British and American newsreels were nearly always so old by

the time they reached Switzerland that they'd lost all their interest. I can't tell you how exasperating this was!

The Allied feature films suffered from another great disadvantage. They had to be dubbed, or alternatively sub-titled, in two languages at once – in fact you could hardly see the picture at all! ... For three whole years, no Allied film could be sent into Switzerland in the ordinary way. They had to be smuggled in in the most adventurous manner possible, and people risked their lives to get them there. The most important propaganda film of the war – Noel Coward's *In Which We Serve* – arrived in a crate of bananas. After the fall of France (when our fortunes were at their lowest), the Swiss were unhappy and confused. It seemed inevitable that German Victory films such as *Feuertaufe* and *Sieg im Westen* would persuade the Swiss that their admiration and confidence in the British were sadly misplaced. But their style did not appeal to the descendants of William Tell, though they were technically perfect and terrifyingly well-made.

And that brings me to one of the most curious phenomena of the war. The Germans saw the success of our war feature films and must have been well aware of their effect. They were a serious challenge to them, and with the huge resources of the Axis film production you would think this challenge could be easily met ... Well, it wasn't! The combined efforts of the studios in Germany, Austria, Italy and all the occupied countries failed to produce one single film to stand up to ours. In fact, there's no great feature film about the German war effort... the Nazi ideology didn't encourage those very simple human reactions that largely contributed to the success of films like Coward's *In Which We Serve* and Asquith's *The Way to the Stars*. The German race had to be taught that it was a race of supermen. To attain the millennium of the Thousand Year Reich they had to learn to be hard and ruthless. It was obvious, therefore, that as little publicity as possible must be given to any negative human emotions. Under these conditions it was obviously impossible to make a film about real men and women in wartime.

My first assignment at Praesens was the translation of a couple of German language films for subtitling in English. One of these, *Marie Louise,* won an Oscar in 1945 for Best Original Screenplay. Before long however, I was able to get to work on Silone's project, and we soon produced a first treatment consisting of the basic story line and the bare bones of the shooting script. But neither Wechsler nor Silone were easy people and they soon fell out; Silone felt that he had more important matters to deal with

Lazar Wechsler   *Richard Schweizer*   *Leopold Lindtberg*

than fighting a Swiss film producer and quit. Realising that I had not the experience to write a film script on my own, I asked Wechsler to bring in one of his own scriptwriters. This turned out to be Richard Schweizer, writer of *Marie Louise*, but he too spoke little English, so it was plain from the very start that I would be responsible for the English dialogue. As this accounted for over half the film, I sometimes had to write whole scenes.

Once the script was nearly complete, we started looking around for the cast, technicians and crew. Wechsler engaged the very fine stage director Leopold Lindtberg to direct and there was no difficulty with the German-speaking actors as the Schauspielhaus could supply them. There were three main English-speaking parts, so I was able to suggest the good-looking John Hoy for the lead, supported by two amateur actors from the internment camps; Ewart Morrison, a major in the British Army, and Ray Reagan, a young American airman whose plane had made an emergency landing at Dubendorf, just outside Zurich. As for the refugees who were to be the subject of the film, a lead role was given to Therese whilst other parts were given to genuine internees from camps all over Switzerland. Dutch, Italians, Yugoslavs and Poles, each spoke his or her own language, a technique that gave *The Last Chance* its distinctive character.

By the late autumn of 1944, the cast and film unit had been assembled, the locations had been chosen and we were able to start shooting[3]. I remember how tremendously excited we all were, especially as most of us had never worked on a film before. There was always an element of doubt about the whole venture, as an objection from the Axis powers could have persuaded the Swiss authorities to call a halt at a moment's notice. For this

Myself talking with Robert Schwarz who played Bernard Wittels.
Therese, who played his mother, is sitting on the right

reason, we deliberately kept a low profile. We did take some amazing risks
though, one of which was when we were on location in Gandria on Lake
Lugano. The scene we were shooting was a harmless 'boy meets girl'
romantic episode, but our director was planning ahead. At around midday,
as we sat in the lakeside inn munching our sandwiches, we were surprised
to see our props man staggering in with two large sacks, which he carefully
dumped in a dark corner of the room. We wondered what was in them, but
attached no particular importance to the incident. However, a short time
afterwards our Italian-Swiss Assistant Director appeared, accompanied by

Refugees in the 'The Last Chance' trudging their way to Switzerland and freedom

some rather villainous-looking characters, all of them young, but scruffy, unshaven and clearly ill at ease. To our surprise, the props man led them straight to the mysterious sacks, which they slung over their shoulders before disappearing again, wreathed in smiles. It was only a few days later that we got the explanation, and it was indeed a strange one.

The script contained a dramatic scene near a small, primitive bridge in the mountains, supposedly on the Italian side of the lake. There was to be an ambush as the bridge was held by Italian partisans, all armed to the teeth.

But where in neutral Switzerland could a film company obtain real sub-machine guns? It was doubtful whether the authorities would even permit us to use fake ones, so we had a real problem on our hands. Lindtberg then had an idea. He sent our *Produktionsleiter*, Urs Planta, on an undercover mission to contact a group of Italian partisans operating on the other side of the lake. A deal was done, but the partisans wanted payment up front in an unusual currency – beans! Our props man was duly dispatched to buy two huge sacks of coffee beans on the black market in Lugano and – hey-presto! – our problem was solved. The *Partigiani*, delighted with their sacks of what was a near-unobtainable commodity in Italy, now declared themselves more than willing to take part in our film. So Lindtberg had the bridge guarded by real partisans, armed with real sub-machine guns and looking fiercer than any make-up could possibly have made them. I vividly remember how blissfully happy they were, play-acting for the day and eating fat sandwiches washed down with red wine and coffee, all of it so far removed from their usual hazardous existence[4]. Fortunately, we managed to get all our 'Italian' location work into the can before the weather broke, so we could return to Zurich to complete the film at the Bellerive and Rosenhof Studios.

By the spring of 1945, we knew that the Third Reich was going through its final death throes and events of historical importance were imminent. So much happened in the world during those weeks that it was hard to keep abreast of the news; but when the free world celebrated VE Day on 8th May, our lives seemed to be transformed overnight. We celebrated in a fitting way and woke up with monumental 'victory hangovers!' But however elated we were, however happy that the Allies had won the war, we could never forget the misery and devastation all around us in Europe. We felt compassion too for the ordinary people of Germany, who were not only suffering from the moral defeat of the unconditional surrender, but also from the terrible physical misery of everyday life in their devastated country. There seemed to be little purpose in continuing my intelligence work for the OSS. However, both Elizabeth Wiskemann and Allen Dulles had offered me a unique experience when they introduced me into their strange, shadowy worlds. But now I looked forward to other things, working on something as 'open' as the other had been 'secret' – a career in films.

German language poster for 'The Last Chance' featuring John Hoy and Luisa Rossi in the foreground, with Maurice Sakhnowsky, Therese Giehse, and Ewart Morrison inset clockwise

The success of 'The Last Chance' made everyone associated with the film a celebrity

27

Return To England

The première of *The Last Chance* was finally held in Zurich in September 1945. Its release had been delayed for over six months as the Swiss Federal Council feared it would reflect badly on their country, but they need not have worried – the press were ecstatic. Whilst the film accurately portrayed the reluctance of the Swiss authorities to admit further refugees, the overriding impression was of Switzerland as a land of hope. In fact, *The Last Chance* did a lot to restore the post-war image of the Swiss. There now came an unexpected development. Through my American contacts, I heard that Hollywood was looking to Europe, and that MGM was sending one of their top executives to Switzerland on the lookout for interesting films and talent. The US Press Attaché arranged for us to meet and I was able to convince him that he should see our recently completed film. He agreed to attend a special screening and, having seen it, admitted to being so impressed that he would contact MGM in Hollywood straightaway.

From that day on, there was no stopping the progress of *The Last Chance*. Encouraging noises came from England too. It happened that the head of the Swiss Desk at the Ministry of Information in London, the Princesse de Rohan, was on an official visit to Switzerland. Her reaction to the film was similar to that of the US press attaché, and she insisted that it should be shown to the Ministry. Jack Beddington, previously of Shell, was in charge of the films division and largely responsible for the renowned Crown Film Unit. At his suggestion the film was taken to London together with the director and scriptwriters. These developments delighted Wechsler, who immediately offered to fund our journey. Such money, he must have felt, would be well spent, especially since the picture had been made on a shoestring budget. With half-a-dozen languages spoken and not a single 'name' in the cast, no one could have guessed it would be an international success.

Having spent nearly seven years on the Continent, I was now fast developing an expatriate mentality. Although I had kept up a correspondence with friends and family back home throughout the war, my image of England had become a little blurred – only Beaulieu remained sharp and poignant. So when I climbed into the primitive-looking Dakota that was to fly us to London, I was nervous. How, I wondered, would it all turn out, this reunion with my country, family and friends? Such thoughts were temporarily banished by awful air sickness as Dakotas were unable to fly above the weather, and when we touched down at Northolt, I was simply grateful to be alive.

Lindtberg and Schweizer were to stay at a hotel, while I was to be the guest of the Princesse de Rohan at her Bloomsbury flat. Dilkusha de Rohan had been married to the late Prince de Rohan, a French aristocrat, and it was obvious that she greatly relished her title. She shared the flat with her friend Katusha, an eccentric Russian ex-prima ballerina. The flat was lined with books and pictures by contemporary painters and had a delightfully bohemian atmosphere. Occasionally people such as Cyril Connolly, whose *Horizon* office was next door, would drop in for drinks. Dilkusha and her Russian friend proved most hospitable, and in their way helped me to readjust to England and English life. They took me to pubs and shops and introduced me to English rationing and the five-bob-a-meal, so different to the rigid Swiss coupon system.

Dilkusha would drive me around London in her rackety old car, and I soon realised that the great metropolis I remembered was now so disfigured as to be hardly recognisable; large areas seemed to have disappeared altogether. When I asked to go to St Paul's, I was hardly prepared for the shock of seeing the great cathedral standing alone, bleak but magnificent, amidst acres of rubble. And the beautiful Wren churches – where were they? Just piles of shattered and blackened stone, with the odd tower still standing as if to mark the spot. Further on, where the docks had once been, there was more desolation. The great spice warehouses now stood like skeletons, silent and deserted except for the huge rats scuttling over twisted girders. However, there was one miraculous thing that softened this bleak and cruel landscape – an unbelievable profusion of wild flowers pushing up through the rubble and broken glass. These had sprung up out of nowhere, especially the pink feathery fireweed waving gently above a host of smaller flowers. The seeds of these flowers must have lain dormant since Shakespeare walked in the fields beside the river Thames. Generally it was all so sad and depressing, but it seemed appropriate to call in at The Prospect of Whitby, one of the few old river pubs still left standing after the Blitz. Amazingly, it seemed quite unchanged; even the cheeky parrot had survived to squawk obscenities from its cage.

Within a few days of our arrival, we heard that the business side of our visit had advanced better than expected. The Ministry of Information had screened the film, considered it "remarkable" and assured us of its wholehearted support. It was clear that we had a winner on our hands. Lindtberg and Schweizer decided to return to Zurich bearing the good news, while I was given a week's leave to visit my family.

Sadly, this long dreamt-of return home turned out to be the opposite of what I had expected. In fact, it was one of the most traumatic experiences of my life. The trouble started with the Beaulieu taxi driver who met me at the station; greeting me in a surly manner, he became downright rude as he fired barbed questions at me. Wasn't I fed up with all that chocolate and cheese I had been eating all the past years? With difficulty, I managed to keep my temper, but when I arrived at Palace House, my stepfather was equally hostile. I started to explain that Swiss rationing had been quite severe, and tried to give details, but it was no use. Then he sarcastically asked whether I had done anything to help the war effort, or had I been too busy sipping cocktails in the Palace Hotel in St Moritz? I found it difficult to explain anything as I was still bound by secrecy, so I simply kept my mouth shut. Feeling sad and hurt, I was only too happy to return to Switzerland. In the years that followed the war, Ned never made me feel welcome at Palace House, and even told Pearl to charge me 5/- for every night that I stayed there; I had become a paying guest in my own home! It was very upsetting, but when my Aunt Rachel found out, she was outraged and immediately gave me a room at Lepe so that I could go there to stay whenever I wanted.

Late autumn in Zurich can be raw and distinctly unattractive, with fog and sleet preceding the winter snows and fierce frost. But when I stepped out of the plane and saw my friends Therese and Emmie waving, I felt a great surge of happiness and a real sense of returning home. When I turned up at Praesens Films the next day, there was more good news. During my absence, Lazar Wechsler had clinched a deal with MGM, who had undertaken to distribute the film worldwide. This was followed by even better news – the film would be premiered in England at the Empire, Leicester Square early in 1946. No such multilingual film had ever been shown in a West End main cinema before, and it fell to me to organise the subtitles.

Christmas in Switzerland promised well; Zurich was completely transformed from its wartime sobriety, with lights erupting all over the city and shop windows crammed with tempting goods. A walk along the famous Bahnhofstrasse had for the last few years been a limited pleasure, confined mainly to window shopping as clothes and shoes were severely rationed. But now one could goggle at the gorgeous display of watches, silks and fine leather shoes, and actually buy them as well! However, walking in the city was still not an entirely pleasurable experience because of the acrid stench emitted by cars and taxis. Such vehicles were fitted with *gasogène* contraptions for producing fuel from charcoal, but we blessed them for they provided mobility. Once again, I spent my Christmas as a guest of the Oprechts but there was a poignancy to our festive gathering. The war may have been over, and that was a great relief to us all, but we wondered what it had all been for. Any sense of triumph over the Nazis was overshadowed by an enormous feeling of waste and sadness at the loss of dear friends.

In January 1946, we took off for London. The Praesens Films delegation was much the same as it had been before but the circumstances of our arrival this time were totally different. From the moment we landed, we found ourselves treated as VIPs, driven around in luxury cars and lodged in the Dorchester which, miraculously, the Blitz had left unscathed. Our VIP treatment had all been laid on by MGM, who seemed prepared to foot the bill for more or less everything we needed or desired. As we settled uneasily into this unaccustomed luxury, the press was already hovering around us. MGM sensed a winner and the powerful Hollywood publicity

My presentation to HM Queen Mary at the Empire Theatre, Leicester Square.
John Hoy and Ewart Morrison are behind me chatting to the
Princess Royal (Countess of Harewood, daughter of King George V)

machine went into top gear. There were interviews, photographic sessions, and press cocktail parties, and I made an appearance on the well-known radio show *In Town Tonight*.[1]

With MGM's blessing, I had approached Lady Cynthia Colville, Queen Mary's Lady-in-Waiting, to ask whether Her Majesty might be interested in attending a special screening of the film. As the day of the première approached we were beginning to wilt, but were elated to learn that Her Majesty had agreed to the idea. This special charity performance was arranged to take place on the night preceding the main première and when the night came, a packed house gave both Her Majesty and the film a tremendous ovation. Looking around, I noticed a number of my own family sitting in the front row of the Dress Circle, including my brother Edward, looking rather young and vulnerable in his Grenadier Guards uniform.

Then, on 1st February, came the real première at the Empire, Leicester Square which was a resounding triumph. None of us had anticipated that our low budget and distinctly unorthodox film would become an international success – the experience was quite unnerving. "Talk about suspense. This has it," Hitchcock was reputed to have said after he first saw the film[2]. Overnight, most of the principals on both sides of the camera had become objects of considerable interest. When I signed that first contract with Praesens Films, I had been happy to accept an extremely modest salary. After all, I had been a beginner, and the whole project had appeared decidedly risky. Sensibly though, I had suggested that should the film prove a success and obtain general world-wide distribution, I should get a small percentage of the gross. When I put this to Wechsler, he smiled enigmatically and replied, "In principle I agree, but for various reasons, I won't write it into your contract. But my dear Miss Montagu, I give you my word as a gentleman that, should this happen, you will get your two and a half per cent." Once the success of *The Last Chance* was assured, it dawned on me that a small slice of the gross which I had been promised could give me financial security for life! So one morning, I went to see Mr Wechsler and raised the subject with him. He gave me a sad and puzzled look. "Two and a half per cent of the gross? Oh no, I couldn't possibly have said that. Anyway, have you got it in writing?" I was flabbergasted. "No, of course not – you gave me your word as a gentleman!" Mr Wechsler smiled broadly. "My dear Miss Montagu, whoever told you I was a gentleman?"

Fortunately, I found myself bombarded with offers, including some from Hollywood. But as I disliked the idea of having to leave my native country again, the only one I welcomed was from Sir Alexander Korda's London Film Productions. Being completely overwhelmed by all these developments and not having an agent to guide me, I turned to Dilkusha de Rohan for advice. Although she was little more than an acquaintance, I knew she was highly intelligent and had some knowledge of the business side of the entertainment world. When I approached her she seemed surprisingly keen on the idea, but stipulated that it should be a completely professional arrangement where she, as my agent, would receive the usual 10% commission. So when I was summoned to an interview with Korda himself, Dilkusha insisted on accompanying me to see that I got a good deal.

This interview with the redoubtable Sir Alex was to take place at London Film's office just off Belgrave Square. I was understandably nervous, since Korda was greatly admired and respected; he knew everybody, including

Sir Alexander Korda – mogul of the British film industry

Churchill, to whom he sent a new film every week for viewing at Chartwell. The Kordas were an extraordinary family who had emigrated to England from Hungary at the end of World War I. A combination of talent and capacity for hard work meant that success had come remarkably quickly, and Alexander was now the King of British films. Always impeccably dressed, he had charm, a natural authority and charisma, and was undeniably attractive.

Sir Alex had seen *The Last Chance* and read the reviews, but because the distribution rights had already been captured by MGM, he probably decided to target someone associated with the success of the picture. I had hardly sat down in his elegant Canaletto-hung office when he made me the offer of a three-year contract. I couldn't believe my ears. But when he rather tersely asked me in his heavy Hungarian accent, "How much do you want?" Dilkusha de Rohan gave me a sharp kick on the shins in case I forgot her instructions. Swallowing hard I replied, "Fifty pounds a week."

A long pause ensued. His thick grey hair brushed back from his imposing forehead, Sir Alex peered at me through his heavy glasses, then gave me one of his most captivating smiles and replied, "Far too much!" At this point I was prepared to accept anything, but Dilkusha now intervened, explaining that as my agent she must insist on £50 a week or we would have to consider other possibilities. Korda knew this was no empty threat and quickly and elegantly agreed to my terms. We shook hands and agreed I would join London Film Productions the following July. I still remember with affectionate amusement his parting remark: "But my dear Miss Montagu, what on earth will you do with all that money?" Perhaps he had a point: £50 was a large sum indeed and I had never before earned so much. We left Belgrave Place with Dilkusha jubilant while I sat silent and preoccupied. I was appreciating the enormous impact this contract would have on my life. Soon afterwards I signed on the dotted line, but far from having a feeling of achievement, I had considerable misgivings about the whole affair. I had to face up to the fact that I would find myself living in a world that bore little relation to the one I knew. I had an uneasy feeling about my own competence; after all, I was still a mere beginner in the world of film-making. So at this moment when I should have been happy, I was the very opposite.

After the unrelenting pressure and razzamatazz of launching *The Last Chance* I was exhausted, and delighted to return to Zurich, albeit to pack my bags. It was a lovely spring that year, but the thought of leaving Switzerland and all my Swiss friends filled with me with great sadness; they had played such a vital part in my life during the war years, and without them my world would have seemed a bleak and hostile place. In London, most of my old friends had either moved away or been killed in the war, so there would be an awful vacuum. Indeed, the war, and the seven years that had passed since 1939, had separated me from many in my circle of friends.

A case in point was Ezra Pound, whose fate was related to me by TS Eliot at a dinner party. Soon after the US forces had entered Italy, he had been branded a traitor, arrested and imprisoned. His crime: broadcasting Fascist propaganda to American troops. Having heard his political ramblings, I felt sure that this was more foolishness on his part than any serious treacherous intent. Sent for trial in the United States, he was declared unfit to plead on the grounds of insanity and duly incarcerated in a mental hospital. Devoted friends such as Eliot and WH Auden appealed for his release, but it was a long campaign. He was not set free until 1958. I was also sorry, if not ashamed, to learn that Count and Countess Mongelas, whose dinner party I went to just before the war, had been detained as enemy aliens and sent to the Isle of Man for the duration. This seemed a poor way to treat Germans who had remained in London precisely because of their anti-Nazi views.

And as for Roland de Margerie, a man so very central to my life in those pre-war years, he briefly reappeared in London in early 1946. We arranged to have dinner at one of our old haunts; the restaurant was now very run-down and the food lousy, but it didn't matter. For us, the occasion was pure nostalgia and it was wonderful to be able to sit together again at our usual table. He told me how his posting to Shanghai was the Pétain government's method of keeping an anti-Nazi diplomat out of the way. It might have suited Roland too, as he had planned to leave his post as soon as the French Resistance established themselves in North Africa, but this never came about and he remained in China until after the end of the war[3]. I took the opportunity to return the blank cheque which he had sent me in Switzerland during the war, and which we ritually tore in half over a glass of wine. It was a strange, emotional moment; we were not destined to meet often during the post-war decades but our story had a happy ending and I will always remember Roland with gratitude and deep affection.

The portion of Roland's blank cheque which I kept after we ritually tore it in half

30 South Street – the top floor became my post-war London home

28

LONDON FILMS

On my return to Zurich, I went straight to Mr Wechsler and told him that I would be leaving Praesens Films as I had signed a contract with London Film Productions. He was very nice about it and appeared genuinely sorry that I would be leaving. To show his good will, he gave me several small jobs, all reasonably well paid, as a parting gift.

The summer of 1946 was remarkable for its rediscovered sense of gaiety and optimism. At last the clouds of war had rolled away, the sun appeared to be shining as never before and the world seemed a marvellous place. The British Consul was also full of optimism, busily preparing all kinds of delights for a Swiss public who, he felt, were hungry to see leading English personalities once more, especially artists and writers. The first among these *prominenti* were Benjamin Britten, Peter Pears and Yehudi Menuhin, all of whom received a rapturous welcome. The crowded concerts and receptions, whether official or private, showed a measure of the affection and gratitude felt by the Swiss for the British.

The Britten-Pears visit was to prove very important for me as it marked the beginning of what would be a lasting friendship. Their visit to Zurich entirely changed my attitude to life in England, which I now saw in a new light, and, like so many people at that time, my imagination was fired by the idea of an England vibrant with creative talent. It was through Ben and Peter that I was to form a new circle of friends, among them Iris Holland Rogers and Ben's sister, Beth Welford. I could not have had a better re-introduction to the British musical scene.

More immediately, there were some practical matters to sort out. For instance, where was I going to live in London? I realised that because of the extensive bomb damage, accommodation would be very difficult to find. Then I had a stroke of good luck. My good friends and fellow refugees, Walter and Marianne Feilchenfeldt, were now running the world famous art dealership Paul Cassirer of Berlin from their house in Zurich. He was an internationally respected art dealer and she, then Marianne Breslauer, had been an exceptionally talented photographer trained in Paris by Man Ray. Originally there had been two other branches of this firm, one in Holland and one in London, but Hitler had eliminated the former. However, the latter still functioned and was run by the distinguished art historian Dr Grete Ring, an ex-Berliner turned British subject. The house, at 30 South Street, was apparently undamaged apart from some holes in the roof and the Feilchenfeldts assured me I could have the top floor all to myself as Dr Ring never used it. When they quoted a rent that seemed very modest for Mayfair, I quickly accepted their offer and thanked my lucky stars.

My good and loyal friend Therese Giehse had been very concerned about my reluctance to up sticks and go to London, and was puzzled to see me so depressed when I surely had so much to look forward to. I was therefore delighted when she suggested coming to London with me to spend her annual holiday in England instead of in the Swiss mountains. According to her passport, Therese was Mrs Hampson-Simpson and a British subject, something of which she was inordinately proud. Her husband, John Hampson-Simpson, was a writer, and as a friend of Auden, Isherwood and Graham Greene, was one of that élite group of English writers and poets who dominated the literary scene at the time. But when John took Therese to be his lawful wedded wife, the circumstances surrounding their wedding were rather unusual. There was no doubt that this was an arranged marriage, a deliberate parallel to that of Thomas Mann's eldest daughter Erika, who was a great friend and colleague of Therese's and had recently become Mrs WH Auden. So as a British subject, Therese could now travel without hindrance and was very happy to go to England and see her husband again. The Feilchenfeldts arranged that she too could stay at South Street, thus eliminating our accommodation problems.

Therese and I left for London in July, but as I had every intention of visiting Zurich on a regular basis, there was no need for elaborate goodbyes. I even decided to keep my flat as a bolt hole. This definitive return journey to my native land should have been charged with positive emotions, but I still had a disturbing sense of insecurity. I suppose the basic reason for this was that I had begun to question my ability to cope with the unknown and strange world of movie-making that lay ahead. Such thoughts were soon banished, as our arrival in Mayfair was to provide both an anti-climax and some comic relief.

I knew little about my future landlady, Dr Grete Ring, apart from the fact that she was highly regarded in international art circles and was an old and valued friend and colleague of the Feilchenfeldts. This had naturally led Therese and me to expect a friendly welcome when we rang the front doorbell. It was late afternoon when we arrived and the sun was slanting across the façade of this exquisite, small Georgian house, making it look most attractive. But the welcome we had expected was not forthcoming. Indeed, we had to knock several times before Dr Ring decided to open the door. Then, with a pale smile, she ushered us into a house that seemed very dark and gloomy and had a strange, musty smell. Without a word, she led us up the worn, carpetless stairs to our top floor apartment which consisted of two rooms, the first being extremely small. Then, with a flourish, Dr Ring opened the door of the larger room and in her inimitable Berlin-English announced, "This is the sitting room." We stood there for a moment in the doorway, not sure whether to laugh or cry: the furniture was shabby, the carpet worn and dirty and there was a large heap of rubbish dumped right in the centre of the room. We stood there speechless until Therese, with admirable presence of mind, announced with a brilliant smile that it didn't matter a bit, we would soon tidy things up, and what a nice room, thank you. Now it was Grete Ring's turn to be speechless.

Later that evening, Therese and I discussed the incident, and it was not long before we discovered what lay behind our landlady's hostility. We knew that the house was the property of the firm Paul Cassirer and that Grete Ring lived there as head of the London branch. When she had been told that I would be her lodger for an indefinite period, she was probably appalled, for Dr Ring was basically a reclusive scholar. Clearly she could not refuse to take me in, but she could try to put me off. The top floor already had small, dirty windows, peeling wallpaper, and ugly stains on the

Grete Ring in a sale room with the famous art historian Max Friedländer

ceiling from bomb damage. All she had to do was to make it look a little worse, whereupon she assumed I would politely decline her hospitality and go elsewhere. But seeing Therese's reaction, she knew this plan had failed and, to do her justice, she accepted defeat with humour and good grace.

Next morning, with all hostility forgotten, Grete Ring showed us around the house and we discovered that she was not only an art historian and dealer but also a collector of drawings. These took up nearly all the available wall space and were packed like postage stamps throughout the length of the house. I soon learnt that while Dr Ring was regarded as an eccentric, she was a world authority in her field. It did not take long for the three of us to become the best of friends, for Grete was wise, detached and loyal. Even on that first day, as Therese and I humped our luggage up those three flights of stairs, I knew that I would be happy in this house.

It was clear that if I intended to make this top floor flat my home, I would have to find some decent furniture and make it comfortable. So Therese and I decided on a visit to Beaulieu, where I hoped to wheedle the necessary pieces out of my family. I knew that several of the larger houses on the estate had been requisitioned during the war by the SOE, and presumed that there must be a quantity of furniture still in them. Our Resident Agent, Captain Widnell, proved most helpful and directed us to Sowley House which proved to be a treasure-trove; crammed with furniture, pictures, china, and even valuable Persian rugs, it soon gave us all we needed. Some of the pieces had received very rough treatment during the war years; there were delicate 17th century tables with holes in them, Sheraton chairs with legs half off and rings on every polished surface. We were just about to leave when we discovered a pile of dusty pictures lying jumbled on the floor, some with broken frames, others with great gashes in their canvasses. I dimly remembered these Italian landscapes from my childhood but had no idea who had painted them. Therese suggested that we should take half a dozen back to London where Grete identified them as the work of Antonio Joli, a contemporary of Canaletto. They now rate as some of the most important paintings hanging in Palace House.

The top floor of 30 South Street began to look more like a home, but I now had to turn my mind to the matter of reporting for work at London Films. It was a brilliant summer morning when I first made my way to the imposing town house at 146 Piccadilly which had recently become Korda's head office. I was understandably nervous, but was immediately put at my ease by the friendly and completely informal atmosphere there.

If I had expected clear instructions regarding my work, I was to be disappointed. My initial job was to act as a Story Editor, which meant reading books, scripts or treatments sent in by hopeful writers and recommending the promising ones to Sir Alex. I was shown to my office by Korda himself; mine was a very tiny room next door to his own. But this room had one great asset – it smelled absolutely delicious. This was not surprising as it was panelled with cedar wood and had been the previous owner's Cigar Room. I settled in that afternoon, spread a few papers on my empty desk and waited impatiently for something to happen. How little I knew about the movie business, for waiting is part of life in films

I was, however, co-opted into Korda's inner cabinet. We met every week for what seemed to be a wasted hour or two as nothing important ever emerged. To make matters worse, my fellow committee members deeply resented my presence because I appeared to have Korda's ear. I wondered how long I would survive on that committee; not long, I thought, and in the new year I was told that my presence was no longer required. However, the scripts continued to arrive on my desk together with various notes and memos from Sir Alex. I read them all carefully and wrote a full report on each one. I am sure no-one ever read those reports, and anyway, how could I evaluate them in film terms when I knew so little myself? Then one day I was overjoyed to hear I was to be assigned a real job.

Nicholas Davenport was a well-known and respected journalist specialising in financial matters and married to the painter Olga Edwardes. Despite being a landowner and having a distinct liking for the good life, Davenport was very interested in left wing politics and had several prominent Labour politicians among his friends. These were the years of Attlee, Morrison and Bevan, and since Korda understood the importance of having close links with the Government of the day, Davenport appeared to be the right man to forge such links. The prospect of joining the film world greatly appealed to this jovial and highly intelligent man, who responded just as Korda had intended: before long he brought Harold Wilson, the President of the Board of Trade, to meet Sir Alex in his penthouse flat at Claridges. To ensure that Davenport remained in his magic circle, Korda had agreed to sponsor a project close to his heart, the making of *Maria Chapdelaine,* a Canadian classic novel, into a film. Nicholas had produced a script by Rodney Ackland, but despite the fact that shooting had already started in Canada, Korda wanted it re-written. Davenport and I therefore spent several weeks on a new story treatment, but it didn't meet with anyone's approval, and, as I had expected, the whole project was then cancelled[1].

Feeling more settled in London, I finally decided to give up my flat in Zurich. I therefore arranged to spend my Christmas holidays in Switzerland so that I could pack up my remaining possessions and see something of my sorely-missed friends. This was a happy interlude and I dreaded my return to 146 Piccadilly with all its boredom and intrigues. I was of course learning fast, mainly that vitally important lesson 'always stand with your back to the wall so that no one can stick a knife in it'.

Korda directing 'An Ideal Husband' at Shepperton Studios

I was still doing little apart from reading scripts; several projects were floating around but most of them came to nothing. Then, one day, I was summoned by Sir Alex who told me in his most charming way that I would be working on his next picture, which he would be directing himself. This would be Oscar Wilde's drawing room comedy *An Ideal Husband*, and would feature an all-star cast. Shooting was to start at Shepperton Studios within a matter of weeks, and I was to be Dialogue Director. I wondered why this vastly experienced director should want my help, but, reading my thoughts, he added, "My dear Elizabeth, we can't have our stars speaking with a Hungarian accent, can we?"

In fact, I had little idea of what was expected of a Dialogue Director, so after thanking Sir Alex profusely, I made haste to discreetly find out exactly what this would entail. The explanation was really quite simple: I would help the players with their lines, regardless of whether they were stars or just bit players. Since English was not Korda's first language, I realised that help of this kind was vital. I was delighted to be given the job, little

Korda waits for the sun with cameraman Georges Périnal on one of the outside sets of
'An Ideal Husband'

realising that this would be the first of a long line of similar postings, and that the credit title of Dialogue Director would define my niche in the movie world for some years to come. However, there was one thing that still puzzled me. Although I had been engaged by Korda as a screen writer, I had never been asked to write a single word! I soon learnt that such anomalies were accepted as normal in the crazy movie world in which I now lived. Notwithstanding my doubts over becoming a Dialogue Director, there was another matter to be settled before I could set foot in the studio: I had to become a member of the film union, the ACT. This might have been a problem, as British studios were very much 'closed shops', except that my application was sponsored by Anthony Asquith. Since he was a leading director with strong links to the Labour party, his name ensured that my membership was approved without a hitch.

The shooting of *An Ideal Husband* turned out to be a delightful experience. I had never worked in a major film studio before and my first days on the set were very exciting. However, after a few weeks I reluctantly decided that

*Paulette Goddard as Mrs Cheveley and Hugh Williams as Sir Robert Chiltern in
'An Ideal Husband'*

movie-making is one of the most tedious ways of earning a living known
to man. Most of our working day seemed to be spent just sitting around
waiting. In reality of course, a great deal was going on, but for those not
directly involved in all the technical problems, there seemed to be endless
hours spent in the half-darkness with nothing to do. But at first I was quite
happy to wait, sitting in my own chair with my name on it – an important
status symbol. I was fascinated by the complicated work going on around
me; the set being lit by the sparks (electricians), the chippies (carpenters)
making adjustments, the gardeners seeing to the potted plants and the
props man checking every item on the set. I loved working amongst 'the
boys', as their simplicity, warmth and direct approach to everything
seemed so refreshing. Off-stage, but always at the ready, were the
hairdressers and make-up squad waiting for the principals to appear.
Meanwhile, the stand-ins would be doing their boring duties on stage for
the benefit of the Lighting Cameraman.

The starring role in *An Ideal Husband* went to Paulette Goddard, who was to play the villainess Mrs Cheveley, the other major roles going to Diana Wynyard, Michael Wilding and Hugh Williams. Most of the unit only knew Miss Goddard from her films, so when she appeared on the set that first morning she was still an unknown quantity. Resplendent in an extremely low-cut emerald green dress and dripping with jewels, she swept majestically onto the set and took up her position. Now it was the turn of the sparks, who, under the eagle eye of their gaffer, proceeded to make the final lighting adjustments. This was a simple process as each of the powerful lights had a number, so it was just a matter of calling out the relevant number: "Hey Bill, bring down 42, and you, Ted, 24 needs to go up a little…" and so it went on. Then came the final instruction. "Now you, Walt, bring down 39 a bit more onto her bristols…" Miss Goddard, who hadn't moved a muscle during these routine exchanges, suddenly came alive.

"Hey, what's this about my bristols? What the heck are my bristols?" There was dead silence, but Miss Goddard insisted. So, clearing his throat, the First Assistant Director discreetly explained that 'bristols' were part of Cockney rhyming slang. Miss Goddard was not satisfied. "But these bristols, what *are* they?" she persisted. Hugely embarrassed, the Assistant Director explained. There was a football club named Bristol City and the word 'city' rhymed with… but Miss Goddard was quick on the uptake and roared with laughter "You mean my 'titties' – is that right?" She roared with laughter again, and everyone loved her for it. But that wasn't the end of the incidents centred around Paulette Goddard, for the next day we were threatened with an all-out strike. The trouble was that Miss Goddard had brought her personal hairdresser over from Hollywood, and the union insisted that in a British studio a British hairdresser should have the job. Understandably, Paulette Goddard refused to surrender her hairdresser, so Shepperton Studio came to a dead standstill for several days. Eventually a compromise was found and we started work again. It was quite simple: a British hairdresser would sit in Miss Goddard's dressing room whilst the American did the work.

Apart from this strange incident, I found my work on *An Ideal Husband* enthralling. Everything about Shepperton Studios was agreeable; the house

Korda and Vivien Leigh

with its elegant green lawns and the excellent restaurant run by a Hungarian with access to the black market. Everything I recollect about that early spring in 1947 was positive, for this was to be my honeymoon period in the dream factory. Unfortunately, it was comparatively brief. I felt terribly sad when Sir Alex told me that he was transferring me to another production: I was to work on a new version of Tolstoy's *Anna Karenina,* starring Vivien Leigh and Ralph Richardson. Korda's charming younger brother Vincent would help with the set design and Cecil Beaton was to design the costumes.

Apparently, Korda had already signed up a number of stars for this production and had appointed Julien Duvivier as its director. Realising that the highly successful Greta Garbo version might still be fresh in many people's minds, he knew that this new version presented a considerable challenge, and therefore set about assembling all the talent and star quality he could. Jean Anouilh and Duvivier would write the script, but, since neither of them spoke English, I was to be the 'link man'. At the time, Sir

Ralph Richardson as Alexei Karenin and Vivien Leigh as Anna Karenina

Alex was still busy with *An Ideal Husband*, so we were to work in his own palatial London office. It was an odd feeling.

I had admired Julien Duvivier for years, so it seemed a remarkable privilege to be working with him. I enjoyed every minute, but he proved a hard taskmaster. Small of stature and unimpressive looking, he seemed to compensate for this by adopting an aggressive manner, part arrogance, part melancholy. On the rare occasions that he was amused, his thin lips would part in a bitter smile, for there seemed to be no real mirth in him.

Eventually there came the morning when we had completed our work and he shut the script with a bang. "Now all there is to be done is to shoot it, and that is the part I dread; it is always so tedious!" I suppose I must have looked rather taken aback. "You see, when I have finished a script, in my mind I have already shot it and edited it too. So what goes on afterwards is purely technical and I find the actual shooting process really a great bore."

I thought a lot about that statement, but when the actual shooting started in the early summer, the extent of Julien's boredom became evident to us all and did little to help the film. Everyone at Shepperton from the stars down began to resent his attitude, and an atmosphere of hostility towards our director started to build up. This latent animosity was soon to surface, particularly in Vivien Leigh, who was playing the demanding role of Anna. It was clear from the very beginning that Vivien and Duvivier heartily disliked one another. It was later suggested that she had been the wrong choice to play Anna, seeming cold and hard compared with Garbo's portrayal of the character, but Duvivier himself was at least partly to blame, for he gave her very little support.

I hadn't seen Vivien since our time together at RADA, but now she was really famous, having recently triumphed as Scarlett O'Hara in *Gone With the Wind*. Knowing the difficulties she was having with Duvivier and sensing that she was suffering from bouts of depression, I dropped in to see her one morning. Seeing her staring gloomily into the mirror of her orchid-filled dressing room, I decided I would cheer her up. Looking at the many floral tributes around her, I pointed out how things had changed since those far-off days at the RADA. "And to think, Vivien," I said with a laugh, "that you once played Celia to my Rosalind!" Vivien wheeled round and glared at me – she was not amused. In fact, she was livid and would hardly speak to me for days. But it was during this marathon of a production that I realised what a splendid trouper Vivien was; always on time and never complaining, she was the complete professional. This was particularly apparent when she had to endure endless takes on the final suicide scene. Soaking wet, and cold enough to be threatened with pneumonia, she did not flinch even when Duvivier demanded further re-takes.

Shortly before *Anna Karenina* went into production, Korda had asked me if I knew anyone who could act as Russian Advisor on the film. I was delighted to assure him that I knew of the perfect person for the job, the remarkable Baroness Budberg. In the years since the outbreak of war, she had changed a great deal, the Dietrich look now being superseded by a 'Mother Russia' persona. She may have grown a little stout but her eyes were as beautiful as ever and she moved with astonishing grace. Moura had been a central figure in Korda's life, especially since the death of HG Wells in 1946, and he was therefore delighted at the idea.

As Moura and I both lived in central London, I would give her a lift to Shepperton Studios each morning. I think she quite enjoyed this strange world of films, but her non-comprehension of union procedures presented certain problems. She could never understand why she, as Russian Advisor, could not walk onto the set and correct something wrong with the samovar. "Is that not my job?" she would ask. I tried to explain to her that although of course it was her job, such things had to go through channels. She would watch with amazement as I ran around trying to pacify the shop stewards of the various unions she had offended. Duvivier was no better, as his lack of patience and poor English got everyone agitated. His abrupt manner was probably made worse by back pains, which prevented him from standing for long. Sitting on top of a tall stool, he often ended up insulting the cast because he didn't really understand the meaning of the words he used. As a result, we regularly teetered on the edge of all-out strikes, with frequent Work's Committee meetings convened to discuss the situation. One such meeting was held on the set of the Moscow Railway Station, but our director, not wishing to miss out, eavesdropped by hiding in the locomotive!

Fortunately, I could round off the working day in a slightly more relaxed way. Whilst Moura would get a ride home in a Rolls with Korda or Laurence Olivier, I would give a lift to some of my other colleagues, usually three jolly sparks from the unit. Keen to unwind, we would head for a pub in Mortlake, order a few drinks, and a chat about our respective difficulties on the set. My principal gripe concerned Clarissa Churchill[2], who had been given a job by Korda, who probably wanted to score points with her Uncle Winston. As she hung about the studio, it soon became clear that her 'publicity' role was an invented one, and that she had no real interest in film-making. To make matters worse, she adopted a very superior attitude and made no effort to get on with the members of the crew.

Moura Budburg

*The country station where 'Anna Karenina' reached its dramatic climax,
with Anna walking under a locomotive. A remarkable studio creation*

Perhaps the niece of the Conservative leader felt uncomfortable
surrounded by so many committed socialists and union activists. My own
political credentials would have seemed especially unfavourable to her as I
had recently joined an Anglo-Soviet friendship society; however, this was
entirely due to a new-found passion for Russian culture rather than to any
interest in communism!

By the autumn, the film was already several weeks over schedule, and it
wasn't until the following February that the final shot was 'in the can'. In
all, *Anna Karenina* took nearly a year to complete and cost an astronomical
£750,000. A good bit of this was due to Vivien Leigh, who, after her
contract had expired, was able to demand £500 for each extra day spent on
the set. Despite the valiant efforts of the publicity men, it was a
disappointing film, earning indifferent reviews and little support from the
public. This was sad, as so much talent had been poured into it. It was
certainly wrong to lay all the blame on Duvivier, who himself had much to
complain about. Korda had inflicted great plaster palace sets on his

Left to right: Henri Alekan, Lighting Cameraman; Maisie Kelly, Continuity; Mickey Delamar, 1st Assistant Director and Julien Duvivier (seated), Director of 'Anna Karenina'

director, who must have felt utterly lost, accustomed as he was to atmosphere, subtle sets and locations. The film he had directed was evidently very different from the one he had made in his head with the completion of the script.

For me, *Anna Karenina* had many positive aspects, as I learned a great deal about my job and about films in general. I had also been able to get work for several of my friends: my cousin Ray[3], Martita Hunt[4], and Therese Giehse[5] all had small parts in the film, whilst behind the scenes, Moura Budberg remained on Korda's payroll for some time. When, on New Year's Day 1948 I looked back on the events of the past year, I felt sure that this had been one of the best years of my life. Having worked on two major films, I hoped to have gained the experience necessary to make me into a true 'pro' and give me the confidence I lacked. I had made friends with some interesting, indeed outstanding, personalities, and it was a comforting thought that I no longer had to worry about money.

Etienne Amyot, apparently more interested in smiling
for the camera than acknowledging the lady on his arm

29

MUSICAL RENAISSANCE

Despite the long days spent working for Korda at Shepperton, the workload did not eliminate my social life; in fact 1947, turned out to be exceptionally rich in new friends and interesting activities, most of them totally unconnected with films. Shortly after returning to England, I had contacted Benjamin Britten, Peter Pears and their friend Iris Holland Rogers; it was not long before I received an invitation from them to join the committee of the recently formed English Opera Group Association. This entailed attending as many of Ben's operas as possible, something that filled me with delight. Most of these works were performed at Glyndebourne, where there were wonderful performances by Kathleen Ferrier, Peter Pears and Joan Cross. At that date, the Aldeburgh Festival and the Maltings were merely a project which, though uppermost in Ben and Peter's minds, was still to be realised. But music had come back into my life, and with it a group of friends I came to love dearly.

Meanwhile, my oldest and dearest musical friend, Etienne Amyot, had been working for the BBC as Assistant Head (Planning) of the Third Programme. As an international concert pianist with an encyclopaedic knowledge of music, he was ideally placed to plan the output of the new network, which first broadcast on 29th September 1946. Working with George Barnes (Head of Third Programme) and Leslie Stokes (Assistant, Presentation & Publicity), Etienne played a central role in creating a great cultural institution. Although he didn't wish to remain in the job after the network's first year 'on the air', he did record a number of piano duets with Renata which the Third Programme used as interlude 'fillers' for many years after.

Another musical opening arose when I was introduced to Walter Legge, head of the classical section of HMV-Columbia. Legge's office was at the Abbey Road studios, where he was very much in command and the guiding spirit of classical recording. Sensing a new public interest in serious music, he entered into this revival with the enthusiasm and dedication of a crusader. At the time, first class concerts were thin on the ground, as were first class concert halls; the Queen's Hall, destroyed in the Blitz, was a particular loss. Fortunately, the creative side of English music was now burgeoning, led by Benjamin Britten, Michael Tippett and Lennox Berkeley. I soon learned that Legge nurtured dreams of founding his own orchestra, devising his own concert programmes and selecting his own artists. But before he could achieve this, there were many obstacles to surmount: first, disapproval from HMV-Columbia, and secondly, the question of money which was not very forthcoming in those post-war years. He also knew there would be fierce opposition from the established English orchestras, such as the Royal Philharmonic and the BBC Symphony Orchestras. But Legge, determined to make his dream come true, now looked around the world for finance and found it from a wealthy Indian patron.

The Maharajah of Mysore was an ardent collector of gramophone records, and Walter Legge had previously visited him in India to advise him on his monumental collection. The Maharajah was intensely interested in music, and so when Legge broached the idea of founding a new orchestra, he found him highly enthusiastic. The outcome was a commitment to provide £20,000 annually for the foundation of a new orchestra, and then a series of first class concerts which would take place over the coming years. The orchestra would be called The Philharmonia and behind it would be an administrative body, The Philharmonia Concert Society, both run by Walter Legge from his office at HMV. There would be a carefully selected committee which would include the Maharajah's representative, Captain Binstead, and there would be regular meetings which would take place at Abbey Road, under the very noses of HMV-Columbia!

Walter first revealed all this to me over dinner in a dingy Soho restaurant, an evening which ended up with an invitation for me to join the committee, as well as a smaller group which would advise on purely musical matters. I could not help being both pleased and flattered, although I sensed that such an undertaking might prove a considerable responsibility. Walter knew I had a serious musical background, and of my friendship with the Toscaninis, Horowitz and Renata, so I obviously appeared to be someone with good contacts. However, Legge had one great advantage: he could lure famous artists and great orchestras to perform for him by tempting them with attractive recording contracts.

It wasn't long before he had assembled a first class orchestra with a programme of engagements: these included not only orchestral performances but also chamber music and recitals performed at such august venues as the Albert, Kingsway and Wigmore Halls. With my daylight hours taken up with film work and Walter busy at Abbey Road, we usually met in the evening. We would start with a quiet meal, then go to his office, where we would plan and talk music into the small hours. Sometimes, though, Walter would interrupt our Philharmonia business and we would spend an hour or two listening to his favourite recordings.

The advent of this new orchestra and the promise of concerts featuring some of the best artists in the world aroused enormous interest among English music lovers. Not only would there be old favourites such as Alfred Cortot and Wilhem Furtwängler, but also an opportunity to see new stars such as the brilliant young Austrian conductor, Herbert von Karajan. There were first performances too, notably of Richard Strauss' *Four Last Songs* sung superbly by Kirsten Flagstad at the Albert Hall.

Although Walter engaged a most efficient secretary to help him with the Philharmonia administration, I became a kind of Girl Friday, ready to take over at a concert should he be called away on HMV business. As such a summons usually occurred at the last minute, this became a fearful responsibility. One evening at the Albert Hall, Cortot was performing Chopin's E minor concerto for piano; he must have performed the piece countless times, but on this occasion he had a lapse of memory, and the orchestra ground to a complete halt. I sat agonised and immobile – what on earth should I do? Fortunately Manoug Parikian, the leader of the orchestra, had greater presence of mind and hastened off-stage to find the music. The audience waited in a clenched silence until Parikian calmly returned to the platform, placed the pages before the white-faced pianist and quietly walked back to his desk. The performance was resumed as if

Edwin Fischer

nothing had happened. It was an awful moment, but when I told Walter about it, he merely laughed. It was not long before the Philharmonia Orchestra and the Philharmonia Choir had established themselves, with the orchestra now rated as one of the finest in the world – Legge's dream had come true.

One of the musicians I had met at Schloss Berg was the great pianist Edwin Fischer, so I was delighted when I heard that he was coming to London at the behest of Walter Legge to make a series of recordings for HMV. The filming of *Anna Karenina* was drawing to a close, so whenever I could, I would slip away from Shepperton Studios and attend Edwin's recordings, after which we would have a meal together. He would also visit 30 South

Street where I had recently installed a splendid Bechstein concert grand in Grete Ring's dining room. Here Edwin would practise to his heart's content; at other times we would simply talk. I was soon seeing a great deal of Edwin Fischer; he was old enough to be my uncle, but had an amazing vitality and was totally dedicated to his music. Without being handsome in the conventional sense, he was the epitome of the great artist, with flowing white hair, beetling eyebrows and a noble profile. He was a curious mixture of worldly wisdom and complete naïvety, cautious and crafty as a Swiss peasant, yet sometimes as exuberant and enthusiastic as a child. I found him fascinating.

One evening, while returning from the studios in my little car, I realised with something of a shock that I was in love with Edwin. Even today, I can still recall the moment when this dawned on me. Within days it became clear that Edwin felt the same way, but despite being attractive to women, he was uneasy with them and I foresaw problems. Edwin had been married many years before to the glamorous and physically alluring Eleanora Mendelssohn, whom I knew from Salzburg. She once confided to me that it had been a *mariage blanc* – never consummated – and that the relationship had quickly ended in divorce. She admitted to still being very fond of Edwin, but blamed his mother for his strange attitude to sex. "If you sleep with a woman, Edwin, you will never be able to play Bach again..." Poor Edwin, to whom Bach meant so much!

Edwin and I travelled all over Europe together, but the routine for his concerts was always the same; Edwin would occupy a suite, while I had more modest accommodation nearby. He poured enormous energy into his performances, and after the concert we would have a simple supper together in his sitting room, rarely accompanied by any wine. Edwin always showed me great tenderness and affection and to the outside world we must have appeared as lovers, but in reality it was an *amitié amoureuse*. I valiantly tried and even succeeded in sublimating my natural feelings, but felt extremely frustrated. I am sure that Edwin felt the same way, but the ghost of his mother was still whispering 'Bach' in his ear. Despite the unhappiness and disruption that my relationship with Edwin brought, I never regretted a single moment that I spent in his company. I was never closer to music than I was at that time and seemed to walk not only with Edwin, but also with Bach, Mozart, Schubert and Beethoven.

Ready to make a good impression on Korda's behalf

30

KORDA'S EMISSARY

Once the shooting of *Anna Karenina* was complete, I returned to the London office. To begin with, there was nothing for me to do, so I spent most of my days kicking my heels either in Piccadilly or at home in South Street. During this waiting period I was more or less free, so I was able to meet many of Grete Ring's friends. They were an extraordinary assortment of people, ranging from down-at-heel refugees to world-famous artists. One of her regular guests was the sculptor Henry Moore, whom I grew accustomed to meeting as he ran up the stairs; another was the painter Oscar Kokoschka, whom I would regularly find in the kitchen drinking coffee. I might also meet Ludwig Goldscheider, founder of the Phaidon Press, or Oscar Hafenrichter, the distinguished film editor. From the art world there were David Carritt, the well known critic, Peter Wilson and Anthony Hobson, the leading lights of Sothebys, and Anthony Blunt who, as Keeper of the Queen's Paintings, often required Grete's expertise. All were intimate friends of the *Hexe* (the witch) as she was known to her friends. It was through two of the *Hexe's* friends, Ben and Nigel Nicolson, that I first met George Weidenfeld. Despite being a refugee from Vienna, he was clearly already making his way in the world. He immediately struck me as an exceptionally bright young man, bursting with vitality and enthusiasm which centred mainly around his passion for books and publishing.

Then, one day in early February 1948, I was summoned to Sir Alex's office to be told that he had a new and most interesting assignment for me. Korda, with his central European background, knew the Continent well, and felt the time had come for him to reactivate his interests there.

Before the war, London Films had possessed a considerable distribution network across the Continent but that was now dormant or had been destroyed. He knew that copies of some of his most successful films, such as *The Private Life of Henry VIII*, were still lying around somewhere in the former Axis territories, and he wanted to get hold of them and re-establish European distribution for his current pictures. To set this in motion, he decided to send a trusted emissary to visit these areas to assess the situation and ferret out the facts. Old contacts would have to be renewed and new ones established. He was also interested in new writers, directors and artists in the shattered but previously considerable film industry of central Europe. It was of course essential that this emissary be something of a linguist, possess good judgement and a sense of quality. Yet even today I find it astonishing that he should have elected to send a woman, especially one with absolutely no experience of the labyrinthine ways of film distribution. However, when Korda told me that I was to be that emissary, I was thrilled; it was just the challenge I needed.

Korda always did things handsomely, so before I left, I was given a sheaf of introductions, copious terms of reference and a great deal of cash. It was extremely difficult to get money for foreign travel and I imagine that Korda pulled some powerful strings. The firm's doctor, advising me to take warm clothing and stout shoes, gave me a protective jab and an alarming briefing about conditions in most of the countries I would visit. These would be Switzerland, Czechoslovakia, Austria, West and East Germany and Holland, in that order. Then, with a briefcase stuffed with papers and a suitcase full of woollies, I took the plane to my first port of call – Zurich.

Once there, I was determined to contact Bertolt Brecht, who was staying in the city. Before leaving London I had spoken to Korda about Brecht but he had shown little interest in what was undeniably a blazing talent, perhaps because Brecht was a leading communist, and film moguls are cautious animals. Knowing that Brecht and Therese Giehse were great friends, I was confident it would not prove too difficult to arrange a meeting, and meet we did at the Schauspielhaus. I had often seen him in photographs, but the person facing me now was not at all what I had expected. Sitting bolt upright at the theatre manager's desk was a shortish, clean-shaven man, with a severe crew cut. He wore a typical German workman's suit, although this one was clearly made of the most expensive cloth and tailored to perfection. As we sat down to discuss things I wondered how this High Priest of the Left would react to me, representing a High Priest of the Right. But I soon discovered that Brecht was genuinely interested in Korda and felt instinctively that as long as the money was right, he might be open to an offer. Accordingly, I wrote to Korda, but to my chagrin, nothing came of it.

My next port of call was Prague, where I arrived shaking and airsick after a particularly horrible flight through a blizzard. I was understandably apprehensive about this leg as I did not speak a word of Czech or have any friends there, only letters of introduction. I therefore decided to enlist the help of the British Embassy, which provided me with all I needed, together with some excellent advice. Within days I had secured appointments with government departments and film distributors, and with the assistance of my pocket Czech-English dictionary, I seemed to be making some progress. Then I made a *faux pas* whilst visiting St Vitus' Cathedral: unable to make myself understood in English or French, I tried asking a question in German and got a very disapproving reaction. I later made the same mistake in Holland. Such was the Nazi legacy that one simply didn't speak German in the countries previously occupied by Hitler.

Although Czechoslovakia was then the most westernised of the Slav bloc, there were disquieting stories of unrest and political intrigue. When I first arrived at the Esplanade Hotel, everything seemed remarkably calm and ordered, but I quickly detected a widespread unease, as if something momentous was about to happen. Then, two or three days into my trip, I awoke to learn from my breakfast waiter that there had been an overnight revolution and that the whole country was in a state of turmoil. I was genuinely alarmed and ran downstairs to find out more, only to be warned by the hall porter that I should not venture out of the hotel under any circumstances as there were armed troops on the streets.

In 1945, when the Nazis finally pulled out of Czechoslovakia, an apparently stable government had been installed, but the country was merely an enclave of Western influence, and it seemed inevitable that the Soviet Union would try to impose itself sooner or later. However, the speed of its coming was astonishing and took many of the best-informed Czechs by surprise. Mindful of the far-reaching consequences of what had happened overnight, I had to consider the people I had met over dinner just the evening before. I knew they all feared Soviet intervention and soon discovered that I was the only one still walking free, the others being either under house arrest or in prison.

On that morning I wanted to see things for myself, so heedless of the hall porter's warnings, I went out into the snow-covered street and made for Wenceslas Square. This usually busy thoroughfare was now strangely quiet, and every intersection was guarded by sullen-looking soldiers standing by their machine-gun posts. In the Europe of 1948, this was a most unusual sight; my breakfast waiter's tales had not been just wild rumours – this was indeed the real thing: the revolution. Although nothing seemed to be happening, there was a distinct feeling of fear in the air. I was fascinated by it all, and continued my walk until I reached a point where I had a splendid panoramic view of the Karlovy Most (the Charles Bridge) and the River Moldau. Beyond it lay the magnificent baroque Old City, St Vitus' Cathedral and the towering medieval Hradchin Castle. It was a still, dark and bitterly cold day; the black and sinister-looking river was full of jagged lumps of ice, the sky was a uniform iron grey and the whole scene was completely colourless, unreal and chilling. The Karlovy Most, with its massive towers and parapets lined with swirling baroque statues, is impressive at any time, but on that day something very unusual and dramatic was taking place – an event unique in the history of Czechoslovakia.

I watched an apparently endless column of men marching across the bridge in the direction of the Old City, the only splash of colour being the occasional scarlet banner unfurling in the breeze. It was odd that I couldn't hear a single sound as these stocky marchers tramped slowly across the Moldau and into the heart of the city. Profoundly moved and not a little disturbed, I made a rapid but cautious return to the safety of my hotel. I took it for granted that the city's working life would stop and wondered when things would return to normal. I was therefore surprised to discover that my appointment with a government official, due to take place the next day, still held. Early that morning, though, I had telephoned the British Embassy for advice, to be told briskly that I should leave the country as soon as possible. When I insisted that I still had work to do and needed a few more days, I was sharply admonished and told how foolish this would be. Actually, the decision was made for me by an acute attack of flu, but I was determined to keep the appointment with the government official responsible for the Czech Film Industry.

On arriving at the Ministry, I was told that I would be seeing Comrade Linhart. Greeting me in a cold and aggressive manner, Ingénieur Linhart was a sallow, gaunt and unpleasant-looking man. However, to my surprise, he showed a genuine interest in what I had to say, in Korda and in his films. He was also curious to hear about what Britain was like under a Socialist government, and as I was then a keen supporter of the Labour Government and a member of an Anglo-Soviet friendship society, there was some common ground between us. I must have made a favourable impression, as Comrade Linhart then asked me to join him and a few friends for supper that evening, the rendezvous being an expensive restaurant of international repute.

That evening my temperature had risen alarmingly, but I was determined to keep that supper date. So, high on aspirin and linctus-codeine, I climbed resolutely into a taxi. Linhart and his friends gave me a warm welcome and I discovered that most of them spoke English. It was clear that Linhart was a fanatical Communist and that his party credentials had secured his appointment at the time of the coup. The food looked very good but I hardly ate anything, and then when I should have returned to the hotel, Linhart persuaded me to join him for a nightcap at his flat. His apartment was as grey and colourless as its owner, but after a few glasses of *Slivowitz*, the atmosphere became warm and friendly, and as the other guests departed, I remained there, eagerly talking films, theatre and eventually politics. All the time, the comrade was re-filling my glass, trying to get me to the point of passing out; was this his idea of fun or was there another motive? In any event, my high fever and the large quantities of aspirin I had taken neutralised the *Slivowitz* and so, instead of getting hopelessly intoxicated, I merely felt light-headed. With my head still clear, I finally left my bleary-eyed host in the early hours.

The *Slivowitz* proved to be an excellent medicine and when I woke up the next day, I was much improved. I telephoned Linhart to thank him for his hospitality, and he suggested that we should meet that afternoon at his office to discuss things. I was delighted to find him in a most affable mood and he assured me that he would cooperate in every way possible to help straighten out Korda's interests in Czechoslovakia. He would also arrange for me to meet the most important Czech film producers and directors. But the political crisis was becoming more acute, intruding into every facet of daily life. I was convinced that it was time to go, but soon discovered that this would not be easy, since under the latest decrees, an exit visa was obligatory. When I visited the Government visa office, I was told that every case had to be carefully reviewed and that I should return in a few days. Realising I might be regarded with suspicion, I began to feel alarmed. On the eve of the revolution, had I not been in the company of people now branded as 'enemies of the people'? Might I not now be considered a counter-revolutionary, or even worse, an enemy agent?

With this in mind, I went back to the British Embassy and saw our Ambassador, Sir Piers Dixon. When he heard my story he agreed I might very well be at risk and should therefore leave the country without delay. But how, I asked, could I leave without an exit visa? With an enigmatic smile, Sir Piers told me not to worry about that, but rather to hurry back to my hotel, pack my bags and return to the embassy as quickly as possible. I threw my belongings into a suitcase, paid my bill and left the hotel in a flurry. On the way back to the embassy I realised that my taxi was being followed, and wondered if they would stop the car and arrest me in the street. Thankfully, nothing happened, and once I was inside the embassy grounds, I knew I was safe. The embassy staff could not have been more helpful, although I sensed they considered me a little eccentric.

It was just after dark when, well muffled up, I was piled into the ambassadorial car with some other passengers. We headed for a US military air base just outside the city, where we were to board an American military aircraft bound for Vienna. The embassy was confident that the Czechs would not stop a car bearing Diplomatic Corps number plates, but I was less certain. As we sped through the streets of Prague and out into the wintry countryside, I had time to reflect on this strange Bohemian interlude. From a professional standpoint, I had managed better than anyone had expected. But all the rest of it, those remarkable people I had met so briefly, would I ever see them again? Would they even survive? And would I see this strange, beautiful city again in happier times? The aircraft looked very basic and was clearly intended for the transport of military personnel. We sat around the sides of the plane in bucket seats and for the first and last time in my life, I wore a parachute. The whole Prague episode seemed like one of those dream sequences in a film, but I was glad I was seeing the real post-war Europe, and learning to expect anything and everything, and how to survive.

Having completed my flight to freedom, I now had to adjust to post-war conditions in Austria. After the war, Vienna had been divided into four sectors, administered by each of the occupying powers. An exception had been made for the inner city, which was under joint control, with each of the four powers taking it in turn to command the units who patrolled the streets in Jeeps. Miraculously, some of Vienna's best hotels had survived, including the legendary Hotel Sacher, now reserved for British officers and visiting British VIPs. I was to be quartered there; despite being far removed from its former glory, it still remained a most agreeable place to stay. I was given a very grand room with an equally elaborate bathroom, but the effect was somewhat diminished when I found that only one cold tap worked. I had another shock the next morning when I found that the pre-war *cordon bleu* chefs had been replaced by NAAFI cooks and the best you could hope for was tinned 'bangers' and powdered eggs. But this mattered little compared with the relief of being able to speak freely once more. There were also the Viennese opera, theatre and music to enjoy; despite the fact that performances were taking place in battered and unheated buildings, it was typical of the Viennese to attach such importance to this side of their lives. Music and wine were still priorities, and although the performances themselves were often patchy, with orchestras and artists working at near-starvation level, there was rarely an empty seat and audiences were as enthusiastic as ever.

Where film matters were concerned, Vienna was to prove complex. The J Arthur Rank organisation was already well established in many parts of Europe and this was certainly the case in Vienna. Furthermore, they had formed a 'special relationship' with several British officials who were distinctly antagonistic to me. Fortunately, the Head of the Foreign Office Films Section, Captain Braydon, was above all this and gave me much useful information. I also found that Korda's letters of introduction, or even the mere mention of his name, opened a lot of doors. As usual, Vienna was bursting with talent, and I was soon meeting Austria's leading

Graham Greene

film directors and writers. Among these was Karl Hartl, the head of the country's foremost production company, who was an old friend and colleague of Korda's. Hartl had just completed *Der Engel mit der Posaune* (*The Angel with the Trumpet*) about a wealthy family in Vienna and their changing fortunes as the Austrian Empire gave way to the Nazis and war. The film had impressed me greatly and would, I was sure, appeal to Korda. At my suggestion, Hartl telephoned London and Korda invited his old friend to England, telling him to bring *Der Engel mit der Posaune* with him[1]. Among the people I met in Vienna was *The Times* correspondent Peter Smollett, a Czech refugee who was confined to a wheelchair. He was wonderfully well-informed about the city and had written some very unusual and gripping tales, which he hoped to get published in London.

Shortly before I was due to leave Vienna, I received a telegram from Korda announcing the imminent arrival of Graham Greene. I was to meet him at the airport and look after him. Korda had evidently decided that a story centred around post-war Vienna would prove interesting, and, wanting the best, must have persuaded Graham Greene to work on the project. I had admired Greene's work for many years and had previously met him at Shepperton studios, so I awaited his arrival in happy anticipation. Accordingly, I reserved the best available room for him at the Hotel Sacher, then sat back awaiting the telegram announcing his time of arrival. In due course a telegram arrived, but it was far from being the one I expected. Sent from Brighton and signed Graham, it stated that as he had been delayed, I should wire his wife with the message, 'Arrived safely, love Graham'. I did this immediately but the telegram gave me considerable food for thought; when Graham did arrive several days later on the 11th February, he made no reference to it.

Greene proved to be the most delightful and stimulating of companions. He showed a passionate interest in every aspect of the city, its architecture, its life and its citizens. His comments and wry humour made every minute we spent together a real pleasure. He explained that Korda had asked him for a 'no holds barred' story dealing with post-war Europe, either set in Vienna or possibly in Rome where he was due to go next. Consequently, Graham was not interested in the romantic Vienna of the past, but in the run-down, seedy, devastated city of the present. He would talk to anyone he met, constantly searching for a theme on which to build his story.

Here again the British Information authorities were most helpful and he interviewed every journalist they could produce. I also told him about Peter Smollett and his highly topical stories concerning the shady aspects of post-war Vienna. Greene was very interested, so I contacted Smollett who invited us to tea at his villa in a suburb of Vienna. This meeting was very successful and the two men talked for almost two hours; when we left, I noticed Graham had Smollett's manuscript tucked under his arm. "Please don't lose it, will you, I've only got one copy," pleaded Peter, full of hope that Graham might help him find a publisher.

Later I handed the stories safely back to their author. I had the impression that Graham had only glanced through them, for he made no comment to me and Peter's longed for introduction to a publisher was not forthcoming. However, there was one tale which I found particularly interesting, about a shadowy man who peddled diluted penicillin. Later I realised that this bore a striking similarity to Greene's Vienna-based story which became *The Third Man*; however, Graham could have heard about this trade from several of the people he met in Vienna during his visit.

Meanwhile, Graham had decided that my daytime guided tours should be complemented with some extra forays after dark. These would centre around the uniformly dismal and squalid night spots in the city. There was one in particular that aroused his interest; a dive that was built to look like a small theatre, with boxes instead of seats. I was sure it was really a brothel and an inordinately expensive one, aimed at the occupying soldiers. We sat together in one of the boxes while we watched nudes of all shapes and sizes writhing and cavorting on a grubby, ill-lit stage. Graham took one sip of the wine we had ordered, pronounced it lethal and ordered *Slivowitz* instead. Watching his reaction to this awful place, I saw he was clearly fascinated by it all. I asked him how he could equate his religious principles with sitting in a brothel getting drunk. He equivocated brilliantly on every point until he nearly succeeded in convincing me, but by that time, we were probably both a little tipsy. It seemed all too soon when Graham had to depart for Italy and I to move on to Munich. He had collected a considerable amount of material, some of it anecdotal, some based on hearsay, but the seeds of *The Third Man* had been sown.

Munich came as a far worse shock than Vienna, for this beautiful city

Actor Joe Cotten sits at the base of Vienna's Big Wheel in the Prater.
The wheel, a miraculous survivor of the war, was soon to become a major
feature of Greene's Vienna-based film, in which Cotten played Holly Martins

which had once been the capital of Bavaria had now been reduced into one huge heap of rubble. Curiously, the Nazi propaganda notices proclaiming *Stadt der Bewegung* (City of Movement) were still a common sight, but Munich was now part of the American Zone and I was able to stay at the Hotel Vierjahreszeiten which had been commandeered as the US officers' quarters. I could recall this splendid hotel in all its glory, but now it reeked of decay, as did all of Munich. The building had been severely damaged and only part of it was habitable; even the kitchens had been bombed, so there were no meals served, nor was there any proper heating. I was allocated a room with a bath, but of course the plumbing didn't work. The hotel guests were given special instructions about how to find food and drink at an improvised canteen about five minutes' walk through the ruined streets. This was housed in the nearby Modern Pictures Gallery, which had become the US officers' mess. The dangers of walking along the ruined Wurzerstrasse at night were such that guests usually opted to make their way to dinner in groups, but this brief nightly sortie was well worth the effort. The American officers were treated to much better food than their British counterparts, and I was left wondering why our NAAFI cooking had to be so uninspired.

To my disappointment, I was unable to contact any of my old friends around the city, and wondered whether they were still alive; but amidst the awful devastation, I did have one unforgettable experience. It was nearing Eastertide and on a cold, clear morning I went to an inspired performance of Bach's *St John Passion* in a ruined church, its roof open to the sky. Because the pews had been destroyed, the audience stood huddled close together, grateful for the warmth of each other's bodies. Never have I been so moved by Bach's masterpiece. As for my brief, the US authorities were extremely helpful, but I soon found there was little I could achieve in Munich and decided to move on again, this time to Berlin.

I had planned to be in Berlin by the end of March, but to make the trip by train rather than by air. This was a mistake, as the journey turned out to be most disagreeable, with every kind of discomfort and delay. It was also most depressing as everything I saw was either devastated or moribund; the towns, villages, and even the once beautiful countryside. However, my first sight of Berlin was to prove the greatest shock of all. Here the devastation seemed complete, the city was unrecognisable, just a hell of twisted girders, mountains of rubble and huge bomb craters. But I still had work to do and was hopeful that my visit might prove rewarding, for it was known that a great deal of talent was emerging from the ruins.

Before arriving in Berlin, I had written to my old friend, Stephen Laird, now CBS correspondent in Berlin. My memories of the Vienna and Munich hotels not being too happy, I was delighted when he asked me to stay with him, promising all the help he could give. Laird lived in Zehlendorf, a once smart residential suburb now reserved for the US forces. Here he occupied an ugly but comfortable villa together with his typewriter and two enormous Dobermans. Steve's villa was ideal, peaceful, undamaged and not too remote from the centre of the city. However, there was one disadvantage – the dogs failed to understand that I was a guest of their master!

My first step was to contact the British Military Authorities who once again proved extremely helpful, even providing me with a car and a driver for as long as I needed them. The car was a VW Beetle with a German driver in a dark blue uniform provided by the British. He proved to be a friendly man and was touchingly grateful that I spoke fluent German. Conscious that my food supplies were rather better than his, I regularly sneaked him the packs of sandwiches allotted to me by the NAAFI. On that first day as we drove through the city, I looked in vain for old landmarks. But the mountains of rubble betrayed no identity and even that lovely park, the Tiergarten, was now a desert pitted with bomb craters and without a tree in sight. I had to face up to the fact that the Berlin I knew had ceased to exist; it had been replaced by a moonscape which was as horrifying as it was frightening. On a human level, there was grief and despair everywhere, as well as desperate hunger. I twice saw people collapse and die on the pavement, but when my driver and I tried to help, the more fortunate passers-by merely shrugged their shoulders, casually muttered *"Hungertod"*,[2] and walked on.

I soon discovered that Berlin functioned reasonably well on the barter system. A packet, or better still a carton, of American cigarettes was valued above rubies. With such currency, you could get bread and black market tinned food, and stave off your *Hungertod* for a few more weeks. Unfortunately, after a few days, my relationship with Steve Laird became tense and difficult, our first clash being over the dogs. Being very large and hungry animals, they had to be supplied with huge quantities of food. He insisted on feeding them in his garden which, although securely fenced in, was in full view of the road. Steve managed to get great sacks of meat and bones from the American PX[3], and I was horrified to see pale and emaciated people gathering to watch the Dobermans as they tore at their hunks of meat. I protested, accusing my host of extreme insensitivity, and he became very angry. One row led to another, ending up with Steve calling me a "damn Commie" – the ultimate insult of the time.

It was clearly time to move on, and I relocated to the British Officers' hotel in the Fasanenstrasse just off the Kurfuerstendamm. I had a comfortable room with a bath and full board for just 1/6d a day. As the hotel was so central, I was able to operate on all fronts much more easily and even look up the few surviving friends I had in Berlin. First among these was Dolly, Countess von Roedern, one of my old friends from those pre-war days at Schloss Berg. Dolly had been bombed out and was now living in a wooden shack near Lake Tegel in the French sector, a modest home that she shared with her new love, Vladimir Lindenberg, a doctor working tirelessly at one of Berlin's remaining hospitals. Dolly's husband had died before the war and their two daughters were now living abroad.

When I visited her attractively arranged but desperately cold shack, I was given what appeared to be a cup of tea, but I soon realised that the ingredients were herbs of some kind. Both Dolly and Vladimir looked pale and desperately thin and were evidently very hungry. Learning that there was no food in the house and little prospect of getting any until the end of the week, I invited her to lunch with me the next day at the British Officers' Club. It was strictly forbidden to bring Germans to the Club, but Dolly spoke perfect Roedean English, and so I felt it was a risk worth taking. Touchingly, she put on her remaining good clothes and we set off full of happy anticipation. But we had both forgotten something vitally important; a person suffering from severe malnutrition should only eat more gradually, starting with only very small quantities. Dolly began splendidly on the first of the three rich courses, then precipitately left the restaurant looking rather ill; she collapsed in the Ladies' Room and I had to help her to the car. I had learnt my lesson and thereafter stuck to the barter system, giving her a carton of cigarettes.

On my last day in Berlin I decided to visit the ruins of Hitler's State Chancellery and the notorious bunker nearby. It was a haunted and sinister place, with a horrible smell of decomposition hanging over it. What I had last seen as a monument to the Fuehrer's majesty was now reduced to rubble and dust. The peeling masonry and weather-streaked walls betrayed nothing of the former glory of the *Reichskanzlerei* that had been intended to last for a thousand years. I stepped from the car and walked across to the bunker where Hitler and Goebbels had met their end only three years before. Then, with my faithful driver standing close behind me, I ventured to the top of the steps leading down into the interior of the bunker. Foul water and black slime prevented me from descending these steps, but that didn't extinguish the palpable aura of evil coming from the ruins. I remained there for quite a while, contemplating the final awesome drama which had been played out here, and was suddenly gripped by a feeling of terror. I turned and ran panic-stricken across the once neatly kept lawns and through the debris-strewn *Reichskanzlerei* until I reached the safety of the car.

It was now time to move on. I would never forget the dreadful moonscape of Berlin in 1948, nor the fact that here was a city where the rats were fat while people were dying of starvation. Of course, London had been devastated, but miraculously our morale had always remained intact. Tragically this was not so in Berlin, where bitterness and despair prevailed, fuelled by the knowledge of defeat and national humiliation. Sitting in the plane heading west, I reviewed the situation as regards my work. I had managed to meet many interesting personalities in the film and theatre world and also to establish contact with the surviving distributors, but the general chaos in the city had prevented me from doing anything more. Munich had produced somewhat similar results, so I now pinned my hopes on Hamburg where I had heard that a lot was going on in the film and theatre worlds.

I knew that Hamburg was yet one more devastated city and recalled that it was here that the RAF had dropped those apocalyptic phosphor bombs which had inflicted the most terrible suffering on the civilian population. In common with many people in Britain, I felt a deep sense of shame and wondered how this formerly anglophile and basically Nazi-sceptic city now felt about their erstwhile friends. However, I was soon to discover that, unlike Berlin, morale in Hamburg was remarkably high, and although it had largely been flattened by air raids, there was an astonishing optimism and vitality in the city. I was shown great kindness and was able to meet a number of up and coming young film directors and producers, together with some leading publishers.

Hamburg proved fertile territory, but the time soon came for me to leave the Atlantic Hotel with its NAAFI catering and heavy drinking sessions, and move on to Holland. Once again, I chose to travel by train, and again it proved a bad choice as the journey to Amsterdam was long and wearisome. Fortuitously, I shared my compartment with the documentary producer, Sir Arthur Elton, in whose company no-one could be bored. He had a happy knack of tracking down food and drink, so we didn't do too badly. Up to the Dutch frontier, the landscape still bore the scars of recent warfare, but once we were across the border we entered a world that had not changed for centuries; quiet villages, neat houses, browsing cattle and lush green fields. Amsterdam was similarly unchanged; the canals still flowed serenely and the streets were full of orderly people going about their business, all of it a balm to jangled nerves.

My hotel conformed to the best pre-war standards, but the excellent food was served in such huge quantities that I could not cope. Spring in Holland is traditionally something special, and the spring of 1948 was no exception. Everywhere there were great mountains of daffodils, tulips and blossom – it was intoxicating – but despite the optimism which this brought, my contacts in film and publishing had nothing of interest for Korda. On a personal level however, my visit was not wasted as it coincided with a visit to Amsterdam by my friend Klaus Mann. Klaus had grown up in the shadow of his famous father, Thomas, but was a gifted writer in his own right, his best-known work being *Die Wendepunkt* (*The Turning Point*). He was a charming and modest man, and his arrival in Amsterdam was a godsend. We saw quite a lot of each other in those early spring days, but apart from some lighter, even hilarious, moments, I sensed a profound melancholy in him. Klaus was battling against internal psychological conflicts and was becoming increasingly depressed. Later I heard that he had killed himself.

Returning to London, I found the great city transformed; all the rubble had miraculously disappeared, gleaming new buildings had arisen, and the parks were remarkable more for their spring flowers than for the bomb craters of the war years. But settling back into everyday life was quite difficult: I had only been away for three months but after that traumatic scramble around Europe, it felt like three years. When I had completed my report, I took it to Head Office and gave it to Korda in person. A few days later I was summoned to his office to receive a real accolade. Alex was delighted, both with the report's facts and figures and with what I had actually achieved. I was to be rewarded with an assignment to work with director Carol Reed on a film written by Graham Greene which would be shot mainly on location in Vienna. This was, of course, wonderful news, but a few days later I was summoned back to Korda's office to discuss matters less pleasant.

Korda told me rather sternly that, in the opinion of his fellow directors, my otherwise excellent report touched on too many sensitive matters and threatened to get us all into serious trouble. What concerned him most was the section that dealt with Vienna, where I implied the existence of corruption, devious practices and downright dishonesty; I had even mentioned names. The firm's lawyer pointed out that should my report get into the wrong hands, it might result in a lawsuit with huge damages. I would be in the dock! Fortunately, it emerged that, because I had headed the report 'highly confidential' and specified the directors to whom it was addressed, I should be safe from legal action. I breathed a sigh of relief, determined not to fall into such a trap again.

Orson Welles as Harry Lime in 'The Third Man'

31

The Third Man

Graham Greene spent the summer of 1948 producing treatments and scripts for his Vienna-based story, and it was not long before he decided on another visit to the city, this time with Carol Reed. Graham would do more research while Carol soaked up the atmosphere and looked for suitable locations. This was the first of several such trips during which I had to be on hand to assist in any way I could. Those days spent with these two completely contrasting but fascinating personalities were most stimulating and quite delightful.

Apart from exploring the city each day with Carol Reed, I started to make lists of Austrian actors and actresses who might play local characters in the story. There was so much talent in the Viennese theatre at that time that the final choice might have been difficult, but Carol always knew exactly what he wanted, and was later able to cast these parts to perfection. By late summer, the shooting script on which we had all been working was finished. Its title: *The Third Man*. Since most of the film would be shot on location, a large unit had to be assembled and flown out to Vienna together with a considerable amount of equipment. I was to go out with the advance guard in the early autumn, with the rest to follow when all the arrangements had been completed. There were many practical matters to be dealt with but we soon managed to find acceptable living quarters for everybody, with the director, top technicians and cast staying at the Astoria, a hotel conveniently located in the centre of the city. This establishment offered reasonable comfort, with a central heating system that worked and a restaurant that actually served food! Though hardly a luxury hotel, it was excellent for our purposes, as we would have two units

391

working night and day shifts. Even the pampered, demanding Hollywood stars such as Orson Welles appeared happy at the Astoria, run-down though it was.

I was still uneasy about the matter of Peter Smollett and his story. Surely sooner or later he would spot the similarity between his tale and *The Third Man*. Although I had spoken to Korda about the problem, I got no reaction, but felt it was still not too late to warn the Associate Producer, Hugh Percival. I was relieved to find that he took me seriously, and delighted when, a few days later, he told me the matter had been settled. However, I was horrified when he explained how. "We've given Smollett a contract to assist with the writing of the script and the handling of the local press, that sort of thing. There's just one condition in it though; he can never make any claim against the company or its associates." I was speechless. "And he signed that?" I asked. "Of course," Percival smiled. "He hasn't read the script…" Even if he had, his 200 guinea fee was generous and left him with little to complain about.

The advance guard included Carol Reed, the production staff, ace lighting cameraman Robert Krasker and a few other senior technicians, so that the task of setting up the picture could begin immediately. I noticed how much Vienna had already changed for the better since my last visit six months before. Much of the rubble had been cleared away, taxis had reappeared on the streets and many of the well-known cafés were now doing a roaring trade. The improvement, though, was only patchy, as many of the streets were still impassable and the condition of the average Viennese truly pitiable. There was hardly any food available and little or nothing to be bought in the few shops still operating. So, like people all over Europe, the people of Vienna were forced to resort to the black market with its exorbitant prices and questionable suppliers.

During those first days in Vienna I found myself fully occupied, tramping around the city with Carol and Krasker as they selected various locations. This was a period of intense activity; permits had to be obtained from both the military and civilian authorities to shoot in the city, we needed the consent of individuals whose houses were earmarked for certain scenes, and we had to find restaurants willing to provide us with hot meals day and night.

Vienna's sewer police with Art Director Joseph Bato (centre)

One of the first things I undertook was to contact the Sewer Police as the film included several scenes in the notorious sewers, which might also be used as a 'cover set' should the weather deteriorate. Vienna's Sewer Police were remarkable men. Clad in their smart white uniforms, they were always helpful and friendly, and the stories they told us about sewer life were both fascinating and frightening. Having listened carefully to what we had in mind, they gave us a rough idea of how the sewer system worked. First, there was the River Wien, a small river that ran under the city to join the Danube. Running into this were all the local sewers, which sub-divided again. At one point near the Stadtpark, the River Wien was accessible, its huge tunnel opening being clearly visible, but the real sewers could only be reached through gratings in the streets, where one would climb down a metal ladder to reach the noisome depths below.

So one afternoon, we were taken to explore this mysterious underground maze. We were accompanied by three stalwart Sewer Police officers carrying torches and axes, and all heavily armed. This was essential, for the sewers were now home to large numbers of homeless people and some very nasty criminals. Carol Reed planned to build a sewer set at Shepperton and so our nervous Hungarian Art Director, Joseph Bato, had to be one of the party. He clearly hated every minute of it. I too was apprehensive, but was assured that the bustle and the noise we created would scare away the rats, and as for the smell – well, one got used to it.

The Sewer Police explained that there had been a big increase in the rat population at the end of the war, when the inhabitants of many rat farms escaped. These Bisam rats were bred for overcoat manufacturers, but whilst their fur made a warm, soft coat lining, the animals themselves were unusually large and aggressive. However, as we walked awkwardly along the egg-shaped tunnels, there wasn't a rodent in sight. The Art Director was quite surprised. "But where are all these rats?" The senior police officer laughed. "Do you really want to see them?" Resolutely we replied that of course we did. "Alright," he said, "but be prepared for a shock." Wheeling around, he shone his powerful torch down the sewer behind us where, to our horror, we saw a squirming mass of rats, some of them quite huge, their eyes glittering as they slowly crawled towards us. Terrified, we yelled to the police officer to stop them, but he merely laughed. "It's alright, it's the light that attracts them, just walk on and don't worry…" But from then on I found it difficult to forget the horde of hungry rodents hard on our heels. Needless to say, when at last we emerged into the street, we ran to the nearest café to down a couple of stiff glasses of *Schnapps*.

Red tape was rife in the Vienna of 1948, and of the four occupying nations, the Russians were the most prickly and difficult to deal with. This meant that whenever we wandered into the Soviet sector without their express permission, we were inviting trouble. The first incident arose when Carol decided to use the Sudbahnhof railway station for an important sequence. As it was only yards inside the Russian sector, Carol must have felt we could get away with it, so did not bother about the permit. Within minutes of us arriving to set up our gear, a heavily armed and hostile Russian patrol appeared. We were lucky to escape with nothing worse than a severe reprimand, as at one moment the Russians threatened to arrest the entire unit and confiscate all our gear. Later, when we needed to shoot the Great Wheel in the Prater, which was well inside the Russian sector, we took great care to obtain every possible permission.

Although some members of the unit were still rather confused by Vienna, they gradually settled down to the strange life we were leading and to the unfamiliar food and drink. Few of them had ever been abroad before and this was brought home to me on their very first night in the city. Carol had decreed that the unit members should be offered a special meal and asked me to find a restaurant which could lay on a really good spread. Such places were hard to find, but by good fortune I discovered a black market restaurant willing to serve 'the best' – but only to foreigners who paid in dollars or pounds sterling. I went to see the owner of this back street restaurant, but the choice on the menu was very limited. I just hoped the food I chose would please the boys from London: an egg dish as a starter, then Wiener schnitzel and chips, followed by chocolate gâteau and cream.

The cuisine in Vienna was generally very good and I was confident that the evening would be a huge success. But alas, I soon found I had got it dreadfully wrong. In fact, the evening proved a near disaster, with food left uneaten on plates, wine rejected and only the chocolate gâteau a winner. Next day I asked the gaffer what on earth had gone wrong, and he told me. "The lads didn't think much of the starter but they were hungry. But my dear Miss Montagu, the meat done up like fish! We couldn't eat that!" Meat done up like fish? Then the penny dropped. They saw the chips, so expected fish and were horrified to find it was veal! After that initial experience, I monitored the menu with the greatest of care. With time, however, the crew discovered the delights of the famous wine garden pubs near Vienna, where fried chicken and *Heurige* were a speciality. *Heurige* is a very young local wine, served in beer glasses. It appears light, refreshing and perfectly harmless but in reality is highly potent: drunk in excess it can fell the strongest man. The first time our boys tried it, they passed out in droves.

Everyone concerned with the picture had now arrived: Trevor Howard, George Baker and Bernard Lee from London, Orson Welles from Hollywood and Alida Valli from Italy. Whilst everyone else had flown, Joseph Cotten and his wife had chosen to travel from Rome by train. This proved an unfortunate choice, as the Russians, for no particular reason, had turned them out of their sleeping car while they were still in their nightclothes and forced them onto the snow-covered line. They arrived understandably disgruntled, but soon forgot the incident and got on with

Joseph Cotten and Alida Valli in the Josefsplatz

the job. As the year advanced, snow and impenetrable fog made shooting in the streets impossible. Fortunately we could retire to our cover set in the sewers; the air may have been a trifle smelly but at least it was warm, dry and clear. What's more, there wasn't a sign of the rats.

Meanwhile, Korda had heard that Joe Cotten's wife, Lenore, was an accomplished pianist, so he ordered a superb Boesendorfer grand to be installed in the Cottens' suite at the Astoria – a typical Korda gesture. An intelligent and attractive personality, Lenore was an excellent pianist, and we spent many pleasant hours listening to her play. Generally the cast seemed

Paul Hörbiger and me rehearsing some lines

happy enough, although some of them preferred large quantities of alcohol to thermal underwear. I was happy too, for it was my responsibility to coach the Austrian actors such as Paul Hörbiger who played the porter. In some cases, I had to teach them to repeat their lines parrot-fashion, as they spoke not a word of English, but Carol was delighted with their performances.

Work on *The Third Man* hardly ever ceased and some members of the unit, including Carol Reed and myself, found themselves working day and night. Unsurprisingly, we became weary and somewhat frayed, with frictions erupting between cast members. More often than not, these could be traced back to Orson Welles: in the company of those he considered his equals, the maverick was usually his charming, witty self, but woe betide anyone of lower status who annoyed him, even over some insignificant detail. Orson would pick on people he disliked and try to destroy them – a most unpleasant aspect of his character.

As the film progressed, a certain amount of tension built up between Carol and Orson, both of them being world famous directors. This came to a head just before we were due to shoot the scene where Harry Lime was cornered in the sewers. Orson just couldn't resist offering his advice. This was clearly neither wise nor tactful and we all watched anxiously to see how Carol would take it. Fortunately, there was no explosion, since Carol knew exactly how to handle the situation. Listening intently to every word Orson uttered, he seemed to consider it all carefully and then, with a most disarming smile, replied, "Brilliant, Orson, really brilliant! I wish I had thought of that!" He then paused and looked around. "But as everything is set up to shoot it my way, we'll go ahead. But then, Orson, we'll do it again, your way…" However, after many, many exhausting takes, 'Harry Lime' had had enough and conceded defeat. There were several other similar incidents until Orson realised he could never win and gave up trying.

Before we had left London in the autumn, Korda told me that following my advice, he was considering making an English version of *Der Engel mit der Posaune* and asked me to contact the author, a Colonel Ernst Lothar who was now serving with the American Forces in Vienna. I contacted the Colonel through the US administration and found that he was involved in 'de-nazification' of the cultural sphere – a difficult and delicate task. Lothar was an ex-Viennese with a distinguished record as a lawyer, theatre manager and writer, but, being Jewish, had been forced to flee to the United States just before Hitler marched into Austria.

We agreed to meet at the official US hotel, The Bristol, and discuss matters over a drink. Lothar turned out to be a pleasant man and proved most amenable to the idea of an English remake of his book. I had arrived at the meeting after a long day's work and was feeling rather tired, but we got down to business and soon agreed that he should come to London in the New Year. He invited me to dine with him but I still had some work to do and therefore suggested we should meet again another time. Ernst, not being a man to let the grass grow under his feet, made sure that this was so.

The crew assembled in one of the larger sewer tunnels

Harry Lime attempts to evade arrest in the sewers

From the first moment I had found him attractive. He was good-looking, witty and attentive. I was now in my late thirties and had come across many such attractive men over the years, so I didn't give him a lot of thought. At that time I knew little about Ernst except that he was married to a famous Austrian actress; I certainly knew nothing of his reputation as a *homme-à-femmes*. His charm was undeniable and I was soon totally captivated by him. Before long we became lovers, then one day and with a shock, I realised that I had fallen hopelessly and helplessly in love with him. By now I was incapable of thinking straight, and I am sure that my work suffered as I could only think of one thing – my next rendezvous with Ernst. Confused and unhappy, I confided in Lenore Cotten but there was nothing she could do to help, although she and Joe made valiant efforts to cheer me up. I looked forward with dread to the day that I would have to leave for London.

Despite various delays in the shooting schedule, it became clear that we should all be home for Christmas, although the date was somewhat later than planned. The change of timing was awkward for me as I had previously promised Edwin Fischer to accompany him to Belfast, where he had an important concert. I was now in a dilemma, which I solved by giving some plausible reason for leaving several days ahead of the rest of the unit. However, I suspect that Korda saw my early departure as a kind of defection, and from then on held it against me. On the evening before I left, I dined with the Cottens and Orson Welles at the Schwarzenberg Palais, which now housed an expensive restaurant for Allied VIPs. I recall looking gloomily out into the swirling fog as a pianist played *La Vie en Rose*, wondering into what deep and treacherous waters I was venturing. Nevertheless, I left Vienna with at least one cheerful thought: I would be spending Christmas with the Cottens and Orson in Paris.

As arranged, I met Edwin in London and we made our way by train and boat to Belfast. We arrived tired and dispirited, having endured an uncomfortable night in an unheated train and a very rough crossing. Adding to the chapter of mishaps, he mislaid the address of the concert hall where he was due to appear. When we eventually found it, the audience, who had been waiting, were palpably irritated and impatient. He sensed this, became more tense and agitated, and played rather badly, even having a memory lapse in the middle of Beethoven's *Moonlight Sonata*. We returned to London the next day. I could see he was not well but it was only later I discovered that he was suffering from severe diabetes. I made a tremendous effort to appear affectionate, but I am sure that Edwin, sensitive as he was, realised that things had changed between us.

Christmas was approaching and Edwin had to get back to Zurich, so he only stayed in London for a couple of days. I was glad when he left for I was feeling very guilty. I could hardly bear the thought of the pain I would have to inflict on him sooner or later; it seemed too cruel. When I had told Ernst about Edwin, he made some flippant remark which I really resented; Fischer had an outstandingly noble nature, while Lothar, I already had to admit, did not.

I was to see Edwin briefly only once or twice before the summer, when we were to meet at the 1949 Salzburg Festival. Then, although I hated doing it, I told him the truth. He took it very badly. Most of us have had moments in our lives of which we are deeply ashamed and would prefer to forget, and that *adieu* to Edwin in Salzburg must count as one of mine. But in December of 1948 there were only two thoughts in my mind, Ernst in Vienna and Christmas in Paris with the Cottens.

Lenore and Joe Cotten

32

CHRISTMAS IN PARIS

Christmas in Paris! For days these magic words rang through my head and when I boarded the *Golden Arrow* at Victoria I was as excited as a child. Arriving at the Gare du Nord, I had dreaded all the hassle of getting a porter and a taxi, so I was agreeably surprised to see the Cottens standing on the platform with Joe clutching an enormous bouquet of holly. We were not popular as we made our way through the crowds with this prickly bundle! Outside the station, I climbed into the Cotten's sleek limousine and we sped off to the fashionable Hotel Lancaster just off the Champs Elysées. It was a favourite haunt of top film stars, notably Marlene Dietrich, and I was very amused by it all. Such hotels were quite different from the more modest ones I knew on the left bank, although after a few days I had to admit that the Lancaster was rather nice!

The two days left to us before Christmas were to be devoted to buying presents for the rest of the party. This gave us considerable problems – what on earth could one give the likes of Orson Welles, Noel Coward and his faithful companion, Coley? My difficulties were compounded when I discovered that my hosts, Joe and Lenore, only seemed to know four shops in Paris, all of which began with a 'C' and all of which were horribly expensive. Having nearly fainted at Cartier's, I just about managed to afford some elegant ties and handkerchiefs at Charvet's nearby, thereby practically bankrupting myself. Eventually all the parcels were wrapped and neatly stacked under the Cottens' special and very expensive Christmas tree; no familiar dark green conifer, but a beautiful, slender beech sapling. Leafless, delicate and painted white, it was elaborately decorated with dozens of little scarlet bows.

On Christmas Day we assembled in the Cottens' beautifully decorated penthouse suite at around midday. Here we were served caviar and Dom Perignon champagne, followed by a very special Christmas lunch. Predictably, Noel Coward was the most articulate of us all, keeping up a flow of witty and amusing anecdotes all day. Lenore sat at a grand piano, entertaining us with Christmas music, and only Orson seemed unusually subdued. I suspect he disliked playing second fiddle to the irrepressible Coward, but in all other respects it was an exceptionally happy occasion and one of the best Christmas Days I can remember.

The next couple of days were not so radiant. These were either spent in gourmet restaurants, after which I felt decidedly liverish, or wandering around deserted parks. Only the evenings approached the original euphoria, when Orson, who had been bad-tempered and surly by day, would recover and regale us with some truly wonderful stories. Indeed, there was one story it would be difficult to forget.

Just before he had arrived in Vienna to film *The Third Man*, Orson had been pursuing a nubile and attractive Italian film starlet in Rome. She was then living with her parents, and as parental control was very strict, poor Orson was getting nowhere. When it became clear that he would never prise her out of the family circle, he decided that the next best thing would be to invite the entire family to be his guests at a luxury hotel on the Italian Riviera. His offer was gratefully accepted and soon afterwards Orson found himself paying the hotel bills, not only of his lady-love, but also of her parents, two sisters and a brother. As Orson was very much in love, he took the family group in his stride, except for the brother, whom he found rather obnoxious. However, the weather was still good, the sun shone brightly and long walks along the seashore with his love soon led to a tender relationship. When he proposed to her, she agreed to become secretly engaged to him.

Orson rushed off to a jeweller and the next morning, as they stood by the sea, he produced a magnificent ring set with a huge diamond that sparkled and glittered in the sunlight. His fiancée tried it on and admired it, but then took it off her finger, replaced it in its box and put it in her handbag. Orson objected: "But why? Why can't you wear it?" She smiled. "Because I want to be absolutely sure. So, Orson, when you see me wearing it, you'll know that I truly love you." Several days were to pass but the lady's left hand remained unadorned. Then, one moonlit evening as they walked by the sea, came a dramatic development. They had perched themselves high up on a rock to contemplate the idyllic scene. There was not a sound to be heard except for the sighing of the waves, until suddenly the silence was shattered by a hoarse cry from Orson: "The ring, the ring! You're wearing my ring!" And indeed, there it was, his ring – and on the correct finger – sparkling in the moonlight. Orson was speechless with happiness. What a girl! And what a lovely, sensitive and romantic way to accept his proposal! He fell on his knees, covering her hands with kisses.

But she recoiled. "Not so fast, Orson, not so fast. You've got it all wrong, this doesn't mean what you think it means. No, not that at all!" Orson fell back, stunned. "Then what does it mean?" She seemed embarrassed. "Well, I caught my brother in my room today, he was going through my things…" Orson remained silent. "Perhaps I didn't tell you, he's a habitual thief and I knew he was after the ring." Orson didn't utter a word. "So I felt the only thing to do was to wear it – to be on the safe side, so to speak." Orson smiled wryly as he told us this, but we were silent, for it was all rather sad. But, I thought, anyone who can tell such a story against himself must have stature, and I soon found myself revising my opinion of Orson Welles.

In the New Year of 1949, we returned to work on *The Third Man*, now in its final weeks of production at Shepperton Studios. Here, a series of elaborate sets had been constructed, including whole sections of the Viennese sewers and the cabin on the Prater Great Wheel where Harry Lime meets Holly Martins – a shot in which back projection was used to magnificent effect. A curious incident took place while we were shooting that scene. As the Great Wheel slowly revolved, we saw Harry Lime and Holly Martins confront each other just inside the door of the cabin. This was a highly dramatic moment but one with a minimum of dialogue, yet Orson couldn't get it right, fluffing his few lines for take after take. I think there must have been twenty-five to thirty before Carol was satisfied. It was very embarrassing for all concerned and even Carol seemed unable to help him. Afterwards, Orson looked completely drained and left the studio without a word.

Holly Martins (Joe Cotten) and Harry Lime (Orson Welles) come face to face

The Cottens were quartered at the Savoy, and after work I would often return with them to their suite with its imposing view over the River Thames. Later that evening, Joe tried to explain the incident. "There's no doubt that Orson is one of the greatest directors of all time, but the trouble is he's unsure of himself as an actor. And he knows that I know that." I was fascinated. "It all goes back to our days together at the Mercury Theatre, when he had a kind of an inferiority complex about acting, especially with me." Then Joe fell silent and it was never mentioned again, for Joe was a very loyal friend.

In May, zither player Anton Karas arrived in London and it was left to Oswald Hafenrichter, the editor of *The Third Man*, and myself to take charge of him. Karas had been discovered by Carol Reed at a party given for the crew in Vienna by Karl Hartl. He had a somewhat limited repertoire, consisting mainly of sentimental Viennese songs, but Carol was entranced by it all, particularly one piece which stuck in his head after the party. This was the music which became the world famous 'Harry Lime'

Anton Karas recording the Harry Lime theme. Carol Reed listens from the sofa (right)

theme tune. Carol wasted no time and soon afterwards Karas was signed up and told he would be leaving for London to make a recording. The poor fellow, then a mere run-of-the-mill zither player, was totally bemused, but as the money offered was beyond his wildest dreams, he agreed.

Karas was very excited about his visit and was amazed by everything he saw; the fine rooms in his luxury hotel, the amount of food available and the goods on sale at the department stores. So we were not unduly surprised when he announced his intention to buy a multitude of household goods, including china and a suite of furniture, all of which he wanted dispatched to his wife in Vienna. We pointed out that there might be difficulties, not least the matter of money. He implored Hafenrichter and myself to advance him a considerable amount of cash, and when we hesitated he made us an extraordinary offer. He would give us the rights to any monies accruing from his recordings of *The Third Man* in return for two thousand pounds. Naturally we refused this offer; we had great confidence in the film and felt that Karas stood a fair chance of making

Ernst Lothar

good money out of it. He eventually got the money he needed from another source, perhaps a record company.

The Third Man had hardly been completed when I was summoned to Korda's office to be told that Ernst Lothar would be arriving shortly and that I should look after him while he was in London. I assured my boss I would be delighted to do this, but just how delighted I was Sir Alex could not know. Ernst had been given a luxury suite at the Dorchester and, apart from his sessions with Korda and London Films, we were able to spend most of that week together. I remember this as an ecstatically happy time with both of us deeply in love, without the smallest cloud on the horizon. It was then that Ernst told me something of his background. Born in Moravia, in Brunn (now Brno), he was the second son of comfortably off parents, and after his university years, chose the law as his profession. He soon rose to become a State Attorney but, being an artist by nature, was inevitably drawn into those extraordinary intellectual and artistic circles that distinguished Vienna at that time.

This was the age of men such as Mahler, Freud and Max Reinhardt. Recognising an unusual talent, Reinhardt made him manager of Vienna's famous Josefstaedter theatre, a prestigious post he held until Hitler marched into Austria. However, once he had reached the other side of the Atlantic, Lothar managed to build another career as a professor at Colorado University. He also became an award-winning novelist, one of his books being *The Angel with the Trumpet*. This was no mean achievement considering that Lothar had landed in New York in 1938 hardly able to speak a word of English.

Ernst managed to conclude a most satisfactory deal with Korda, with the assurance that *The Angel with the Trumpet* would go into production no later than the spring with its original director, Karl Hartl, at the helm. The appointment of Hartl was a bonus for me. He spoke very little English so I was to be his Dialogue Director. The future now seemed bathed in a rosy glow. However, I was faced with a problem to which I could see no solution. Although hopelessly in love with Ernst, I knew there was little chance that he would leave his wife. Despite being of Jewish descent, he was raised as a Catholic, so there could be no question of divorce. This was a hopeless situation but I was undeterred. As a result, everything in my life became confused, I lost any ability to make a common sense judgement and my career seemed completely irrelevant.

The Third Man was at last in the can and due to be premiered in the late spring of 1949. Those of us who had worked on the picture were convinced it was exceptional and even dared to prophesy that it would be a big hit. Meanwhile, back in my Piccadilly office, I was hard at work on the preliminary stages of *The Angel with the Trumpet* and the translation of the script. For Ernst's sake, I was determined that this production should be given the best possible chance, but some indifferent casting soon led me to have doubts. Most notably, the choice of Eileen Herlie to play Henrietta Stein (a part played brilliantly by Paula Wessely in *Der Engel mit der Posaune*) seemed misjudged.

When the film was completed in the early summer, it was clear to all of us that *The Angel with the Trumpet* faced a doubtful future. Even our director, Karl Hartl, appeared to share this view: he was used to working in the small studios of Vienna and seemed like a fish out of water on the vast sound stages of Shepperton. At first I tried to keep Ernst well-informed of our progress, but he showed little interest, so I dropped the subject. In fact, he never saw the English version of the film, which was perhaps a good thing, as the finished product was as near to being a flop as anything that ever appeared under Korda's name.

The first week in July 1949 signalled the end of my three-year contract with London Film Productions and I was not too surprised when it was not renewed. Whilst I had been very committed to Korda at the start, my affair with Ernst had increasingly distracted me, to the point that it must have been obvious that my mind was not 'on the job'. Of course, I fully appreciated the implications: I could soon find myself as hard up as I had been in the old days, but at least I had now learned my trade and could reasonably expect work to come my way.

I still had my delightful eyrie at 30 South Street with Grete Ring, but my life had changed a great deal during the Korda years. Film work had gradually consumed more and more of my time and as a result, my ties with the Philharmonia had diminished to practically nothing, as had my work with the English Opera Group Association Committee. However, I still managed to hear as much of Britten's then prodigious output as possible, and I remember some historic first performances at Glyndebourne, such as *The Rape of Lucretia* with Kathleen Ferrier. And there was one other passion I could always find time for – a daily letter to Ernst.

The summer of 1949 saw the première of *The Third Man*, which became an overnight smash hit and won praise the world over. It was around this time that an incident occurred linking back to my wartime work in Switzerland. I had made several good friends among the staff of the British Legation in Bern and kept in touch with some of them. One of these was Nicholas Elliott, son of a famous Headmaster and later Provost of Eton, who was now working in Whitehall. From time to time he would invite me to dinner at his club, Bucks. We usually dined alone but on one occasion a friend of his turned up to join us. His name was Brooman-White and I found him a most likeable chap. This *diner à trois* was repeated a few times; it was always pleasant and I thought no more about it.

Then one day I received a mysterious telephone call. It was from a man whose name I remembered from my Bern British Legation years; one of Elizabeth Wiskemann's most helpful colleagues, whom she greatly respected. What on earth could he want of me now? His message was strange, but having had some experience of such things I could read between the lines. I was not in the least alarmed, only mystified and curious. He gave me careful instructions, which were both terse and to the point. I was to meet him on a specified date at a specified place in Hyde Park, and he urged me to make a careful mental note of this. Accordingly I turned up in the right place at the right time. At first, we seemed to walk aimlessly around the park, saying little. Then he suddenly seized two park chairs, placing them on the grass well out of earshot of any strollers. As we sat down I was reminded of the meeting with John McCaffery in that icy park overlooking the river in Bern.

When 'Mr X' explained the reason for our meeting and put forward a proposition, the whole conversation took on a sense of *déjà vu*. I recall how he elaborated on practical matters, such as my salary and eventual pension rights. He made it all sound very prosaic and harmless, but I was not deceived. For in the strange, shadowy world I had known during the war years, I had learned my trade and I knew it was not one I wanted to return to. So I calmly and politely explained to 'Mr X' that I must refuse his offer, although of course I was honoured to be asked. After 'Mr X' had walked me back to my front door, I was in a state of considerable agitation, and desperately needed to talk to someone. In retrospect it seems extremely odd that of all the friends I could have turned to, I chose Moura Budberg, as Roland had always claimed that she was a Soviet agent.

For me, however, Moura was a trusted friend and the ultimate mother figure – someone I could always turn to for wise counsel and impartial advice. When I told her the nature of my problem, the strength of her reaction took me by surprise. She became quite vehement in her rejection of the whole idea. Moreover, she urged me to refuse to have anything to do with these people and not to become embroiled in such matters, either now or ever. Her arguments were so convincing that when 'Mr X' telephoned again, I told him firmly that my decision not to accept his offer stood. The conversation was short but polite, and I was never to hear of him or his department again.

Moura's reaction to my job offer was very revealing. That she had an extraordinary range of influential connections in Britain, Russia and Germany was not in doubt, indeed she clearly knew more about the world of espionage than she let on, but I never believed Moura to be a spy. With forty year's hindsight, however, I can believe that she was operating as an 'agent of influence', trading information between these countries on her own account¹. If this was the case, her 'Tuesdays', which continued after the war, were certainly an excellent way of bringing her contacts together. The *Dramatis Personae* might change from week to week, but among my fellow guests I remember Laurence Olivier, Peter Ustinov, Robert Bolt and John Julius Norwich. She was also reputed to be a friend of Guy Burgess and Donald Maclean.

Despite its ugly exterior, Moura's flat in Ennismore Gardens was a friendly and welcoming place which, in times of tribulation, became a refuge for me. Only a stone's throw from the Russian Orthodox Church, it was filled with old-fashioned shabby furniture, worn rugs, and row upon row of books. Guarding the fireplace and dominating the sitting room was a large and crudely embroidered picture of the Russian Imperial family. On the walls were several faded watercolours of her home in the Ukraine and an old photograph of herself with Gorki and Wells, the Baroness looking like a young Marlene Dietrich. In times of difficulty – usually some disastrous love affair – Moura would 'take me in' and I would stay overnight on a lumpy but comfortable divan. Being the perfect listener, she was always ready to minister comfort to distressed friends, some of whom were very much in the public eye. What we only learned many years later was that Moura was under surveillance by MI5, who were convinced she worked for the KGB. Nothing was ever proved, but as a guest at her flat, I might have put myself under suspicion – and all within a few days of declining a job with the organisation now watching me!

Moura Budberg:
under surveillance

With Edward in Salzburg, 1949

33

DIALOGUE DIRECTING

In August 1949 I departed for Salzburg, the first time I had been there since 1937, when the last of the great pre-war Salzburg Festivals had been held. The festival was now under the aegis of its new director, Baron Puthon, and every effort was being made to restore the event to its former glory. The festival owed its existence mainly to the great pre-war impresario and director, Max Reinhardt. As Ernst had worked closely with Reinhardt during that period, it was accepted that he should now play an important role in the post-Hitler festivals. One of his main tasks was to direct that pillar of the Salzburg Festival, the morality play *Jedermann* (*Everyman*). This was performed in the open air every Sunday with the impressive west façade of the cathedral as a backdrop, and Ernst's production was hailed as a great success.

I very soon realised that my involvement in the 1949 Salzburg Festival would be far closer than anything I had experienced during the pre-war years; through Ernst, I would now be seeing it from the inside. Ernst suggested that I stay at his small chalet just outside the city, as he and his wife preferred to stay at a hotel nearby. His wife Adrienne was not at all happy with this arrangement, and when we met she made no effort to disguise her hostility. However, I was soon to suffer similar anguish when I discovered that Ernst was often seen in the company of Anita, the attractive wife of the conductor Herbert von Karajan. Up to that date, I had never suffered unduly from jealousy, but now I was really sick with it. Fortunately, my preoccupation with Ernst was interrupted by a visit from my brother Edward and an old school friend of his, Mark Chinnery. Having completed his National Service in Palestine, my brother was now

Left to right: Etienne Amyot, myself, Mark Chinnery, Robin Amyot,
Georg Fröscher and Renata photographed by Edward in Salzburg

at Oxford, where he seemed totally carefree and relaxed. He had long been
my companion at the Philharmonia concerts and was now becoming
passionate about opera, so a visit to Salzburg was a 'must' for him. Edward
was always interested in famous people, and at the end of a concert, he would
often ask me to introduce him to the *prominente* I knew – I had my uses!

Those post-war Salzburg Festivals were unforgettable. You could see the
Vienna Philharmonic under the baton of Furtwängler and von Karajan
and hear world-famous opera singers in superb productions. But as the
festival was drawing to its close, I became aware that my funds were getting
alarmingly low and there was not the whisker of a job in sight. Then, just
as panic was setting in, I had a stroke of luck.

Karl Hartl was to direct a picture for Korda called *The Wonder Kid*, the story
of a musically talented child prodigy and his greedy manager, and he
wanted me as his Dialogue Director. As the film was to be shot in Austria I
happily accepted his offer and started work almost immediately. The first
stage of production took place on location, partly in Thiersee, close to a

Bobby Henrey as the Wonder Kid

delightful lake. Here I spent many a happy evening fishing for large freshwater prawns, called *écrevisses*, which we would take back to the hotel and feast on for supper. Unfortunately, the film was less promising. The lead was played by Bobby Henrey, child star of Carol Reed's remarkable picture *The Fallen Idol*, but without the support given by Ralph Richardson (who had played opposite Henrey in *The Fallen Idol*) and the near-genius of Carol Reed, the film's prospects were not good. Moreover, Hartl's grasp of the actors' performances was not helped by his limited English, as Bobby Henrey's mother recalled in her book *A Journey to Vienna*[1]:

> Karl Hartl, seated on his canvas chair, prepared his next scene. Elizabeth Montagu, in navy blue trousers, a coloured scarf round her neck, was holding a script. She had, amongst other duties, the strange task of listening on behalf of Kart Hartl, that the actors spoke the sort of English that an English audience might be expected to understand... When Oskar Werner repeated the lines he had learnt like a parrot, Karl Hartl turned his large face enquiringly to Elizabeth Montagu, as much as to say: 'It sounds all right to me but of course I don't understand a word.'

The next stage of production was planned to take place in Hartl's studio in Vienna, and it was decided that I should go there one week ahead of the unit to rehearse the Austrian actors, as I had done on *The Third Man*. This was good news for me as it meant I should see Ernst again, and much earlier than I had expected. But when I arrived in Vienna, I hardly recognised it. The city was now tidy and organised, with life almost back to normal, and it was hard to imagine a character like Harry Lime roaming the streets. Ernst had booked me into a really good hotel where he had filled my room with flowers, each bouquet or pot plant bearing its own enticing little message – he was an expert in such trifles. I now had a few days before Hartl and the unit were due to arrive, but I remembered from *The Third Man* how difficult the work of rehearsing and schooling non-English-speaking artists could be. I was therefore determined to start on the job immediately, until Ernst revealed he had other plans for me. We were to go to Paris and it would be 'a week I would never forget.' I am sure he added phrases like 'romantic', 'unique experience' and so on, and for one heady moment I was caught up in words, and wildly, ecstatically happy.

Then, sobering up a little, I began to come to my senses and face facts. I had a contract to fulfil and urgent work to do. Hartl was relying on me and after all those years as a pro, on the stage, in films and in journalism, how could I now walk out on a job? It was unthinkable, and I was amazed too, that Ernst, himself a pro, could expect this of me. But he merely laughed at my objections, using every argument and wile to convince me. He was an expert at that kind of thing, for not only was he an acclaimed romantic novelist but he was also a man who had started life as a successful State Attorney. So inevitably I agreed to go to Paris. But when he left me that evening I was less than happy; indeed I felt miserable and ashamed about the whole thing. It was then that my first doubts about Ernst crept in, for I was beginning to understand what emotional blackmail could mean.

When I telephoned Hartl about this change of plan, he was justifiably very angry, and as I put down the receiver, I detected the acrid reek of burnt boats. In fact, Ernst had wanted me to resign and hoped this act of desertion would trigger my dismissal, which it did. To make things worse, this romantic 'experience of a lifetime', was plagued with bad weather, unheated trains, bad hotels, and, worst of all, a guilty conscience. Ernst

Michael Hordern and Alastair Sim in 'Scrooge'

had insisted on going to the elegant-sounding Hotel Claridges in the Champs Elysées, but this bore little resemblance to its namesake in London, being as bleak and unromantic as French hotels can sometimes be. Absolutely nothing in Paris that week seemed to work out, and to make it worse it rained continuously, was unseasonably chilly and I developed a horrible cold. The whole thing was a fiasco. Ernst seemed like a fish out of water in Paris and was far from his charming best.

Inevitably I began to recall other visits to Paris, with Roland, Renata and my Pitt-Rivers cousins – the comparisons were truly odious. Sitting in the train taking us back to Zurich, I was appalled that because of this moment of madness, I had probably wrecked my promising career. Furthermore, the role of mistress didn't suit me, for I hated the lies and the furtiveness of it all. In short, I was badly miscast. Nevertheless, when the moment came for Ernst to board the train for Vienna, my face was streaming with tears and I had to admit that I was as much in love with him as ever. He now had a serious hold over me.

I spent Christmas with the Oprechts in the company of old friends, so this

'Four in a Jeep': Leopold Lindtberg directs from the right-hand side of the jeep while I look on from my dialogue director's chair

was a happy, carefree time. But instead of returning to London to look for the work I so desperately needed, I headed back to Vienna and Ernst. After a particularly depressing few weeks, I was forced to return to England as my money had, quite simply, run out. I first went home to Beaulieu, but I had hardly been there a week before I received the offer of work from the producer-director Brian Desmond Hurst; he wanted me to be the Dialogue Director on his new film, *Scrooge*. Based on Dickens' *A Christmas Carol*, the film would star Alastair Sim as Scrooge and was just about to go into production at Nettleford Studios in Walton-on-Thames. For me, the picture is memorable because Bette Davis was working on a neighbouring stage, and I had the privilege of meeting her several times. Contrary to all the gossip, I found her totally charming and utterly courteous.

Towards the end of *Scrooge*, I was most encouraged to get the offer of a contract from my first employer, Praesens Films in Zurich. Lazar Wechsler planned to build on the success of his previous multilingual films with another called *Four in a Jeep (Die Vier im Jeep)*. Directed by Leopold

Left to right: Leopold Lindtberg (his back to us) Albert Dinan, Paulette Dubost, Ralph Meeker, Viveca Lindfors and myself during the filming of 'Four in a Jeep'

Lindtberg, the story centred around four military policemen, one from each of the occupying powers, patrolling post-war Vienna. The lead role went to the Swedish star Viveca Lindfors who played the wife of an escaped prisoner of war, wanted by the Russians. It would have been impossible to shoot the picture in Vienna itself, as the Russians were still an occupying force and would certainly have blocked it, so Graz, the capital of Styria, was chosen instead for the location work as it was architecturally similar to Vienna. The film was very well received and deservedly won the Golden Berlin Bear award, Best Drama category. But at this stage, my heart was more with Ernst in Vienna than in my work. I could hardly wait for weekends, when I would drive at breakneck speed over the Semmering Pass to Vienna to be with him again, if only for a few hours.

Work on *Four in a Jeep* started late in 1950 and was completed the following year. Wondering where on earth the next job would come from, I did not make it any easier for myself by deciding to live in Vienna, for however delightful life there might have been, there were few jobs for an

English Dialogue Director. It was a crazy decision, but at that time I *was* a little crazy. I could not bear to be away from Ernst for any length of time, and even while working that summer in Zurich I made frequent dashes to Salzburg, where he was busy with the festival. My emotions had taken over my whole life, and I seemed powerless to shake off what had now become a veritable obsession.

I settled down in Vienna, where I was to live, on and off, for nearly seven years – perhaps my wasted years. There were moments of intense happiness, but these were offset by periods of acute depression; to my friends it must have seemed that I had abandoned all the things I most valued to wander about central Europe in a haze of emotion. But this was a period during which I was able to experience many wonderful things, nearly all of them connected with music. In Vienna, then as now, there is hardly an evening when one is not given the choice of a first class concert, a superb performance at the opera or a visit to one of the many excellent theatres.

Through Ernst, I was introduced to a number of remarkable people, including the great conductor, Wilhem Furtwängler. When we first met he was undergoing a traumatic experience at the hands of the musical establishment. Herbert von Karajan was in the ascendant and, being fiercely ambitious, was now bidding strongly to supplant Furtwängler. This battle raged for months and only ended when the older man decided to resign from his Vienna music posts, return to Berlin and rejoin his beloved Berliner Philharmoniker. But the great German conductor was deeply wounded by the whole sad episode, which was surrounded by the usual Viennese intrigues. Tense and profoundly depressed, he was very grateful when I accompanied him on long afternoon walks in the beautiful Vienna woods, but it was not long before he was to leave Vienna for Berlin, never to return.

Despite the fact that I was living very modestly indeed, my funds were always alarmingly low. Then, at a critical moment, I had one of those lucky breaks: an offer of work from Morjay, a Hollywood film company. *No Time for Flowers* was directed by Don Siegel and would feature his wife, Viveca Lindfors. A low-budget reworking of *Ninotchka*, the picture was a romantic comedy drama with a strong anti-communist message. It may not have amounted to much, but it saved my life.

Ralph Meeker, Michael Medwin, Albert Dinan and Joseph Yadin in 'Four in a Jeep'

Viveca Lindfors going through the script

By this stage I had found a reasonably comfortable flat, and was able to see Ernst almost every day. On one level, the summer of 1951 seemed perfect, but those financial worries would not go away and Coutts, my bank in London, were writing the kind of letters one prefers to push under the carpet. However, such problems seemed unimportant compared with my state of mind. Caught up in a turmoil of emotion varying between great happiness and profound depression, I felt rudderless and lost. There was no denying the facts: I was out of work, involved in a liaison which could only end badly, and gradually losing touch with my friends, family and profession. Worst of all, there was no-one I could talk to. Ernst seemed unaware of my feelings; indeed he wouldn't even acknowledge there was a problem. Although I was learning to live with such difficulties, it was a very wearing business, so one day I decided to take temporary leave of Vienna and return to England to sort things out.

It was good to be back at Beaulieu, where there was a feeling of change in the air. My stepfather Ned had died in May 1951, and now Pearl was preparing to move into The Lodge, a large house at the other end of the village. This would leave Palace House free for Edward to take over on his 25th birthday on 20th October 1951. Since he needed a hostess to help him with his weekend guests, he suggested I might fill that role for a time. Edward had been reading history at Oxford, but was offered a job by the well-known advertising firm, Colman, Prentis & Varley. He was very flattered, and stoutly maintained that the job would prove more useful than a degree – for him it was an offer too good to refuse. I violently disagreed and told him that I would not have anything to do with this CPV firm, but I soon had to admit that he was doing very well and was finding the work absorbing. After a while, he was transferred to the CPV subsidiary, Voice & Vision, where his flair for public relations quickly emerged.

An excellent host and gregarious by nature, my brother had a mass of friends. These included film personalities such as John Ford, John Wayne, Jack Hawkins, Lana Turner, Lex 'Tarzan' Barker, and Diana Dors. He also had links with the theatre world through the critic Ken Tynan and his wife, the writer Elaine Dundy. There were girlfriends too, usually very beautiful models. These people would be invited to Palace House with various advertising executives and clients, and the rather staid and stern family home was transformed. At first it was all rather fun, but the combination

Donald Buka as Toni Sponer in 'Stolen Identity'

of guests from sometimes very different backgrounds meant that the atmosphere could be a bit brittle at times. For me, the drinks flowed a little too freely and it all seemed a little superficial and glitzy, but for the first time in years I had the strength of mind to resist Ernst's pleas that I should return to Vienna forthwith. Was the spell broken? Not yet.

Fortunately for me, it was difficult for any film company to work in Vienna without us hearing of each other, and in January 1952 I was hired as the Dialogue Director for *Stolen Identity*, an American production to be made both in English and German. *Stolen Identity* was the story of a Viennese taxi driver who saw his chance to start a new life using the identity of an American businessman who was killed in his cab. The film, which starred Donald Buka, Joan Camden and Francis Lederer, was unmemorable, but the people I met through it left lasting impressions. First among these was the charming and good-looking Donald Buka, who escorted me on many enjoyable evenings out in Vienna. Second was the producer who issued my contract, Liz Dickenson. A shamelessly pushy lesbian with short hair, collar

Donald Buka visits me at Beaulieu

and tie, she never stopped making unwanted passes at me. The third was the screen writer Robert Hill, who spent several months in Vienna soaking up the atmosphere whilst completing the script. He later put his observations and recollections down in writing, an account which is so perceptive and amusing that I have included it in the appendix.

In April 1952, Edward opened Palace House to the public. Working in the public relations business, he was well placed to publicise the event and the family home became the subject of much press attention. Visitor numbers exceeded all expectations, and by Easter Palace House was already the third most popular stately home in the country. In August I returned to Zurich to work on *The Village (Unser Dorf)*, another Praesens Film. This promised to be an exceptionally interesting production, being a story based on that remarkable Swiss post-war project, the Pestalozzi Children's Village. The purpose-built village consisted of a collection of large, attractive chalets for orphans and homeless children from war-torn areas. At Pestalozzi they could live safely in an atmosphere reminding them of home, and speak their own language. There was a Polish House, an Austrian House, a

Ray Pitt-Rivers and John Justin (centre) in 'The Village'

German House, and so on, each presided over by a House Mother of the same nationality. It was a wonderful concept, named after the great eighteenth century Swiss pedagogue, Heinrich Pestalozzi.

Initially I found myself working with Richard Schweizer on the script, and when the film went into production I became the Dialogue Director. This was more complicated than usual as the film was to have an English, French and German version, demanding that each shot was done three times. Although not terribly involved with casting, I did manage to secure a part for Ray Pitt-Rivers, who played Miss Worthington, the British House Mother. There was a great deal of location work in the village itself, where we employed quite a number of the children as extras. Since the village was quite high up in the Canton Appenzell, we had to make certain that our location work was finished before the alpine winter set in, after which we completed the studio work in London. By the end of January the picture was safely in the can: Lazar Wechsler, the head of Praesens Films, had once more sensed a great film subject, and, with an international cast, had produced a remarkable and touching movie.

*Eva Dahlbeck, the leading lady in 'The Village', with some of the children
from the Pestalozzi Children's Village who appeared in the film*

In the spring of 1953, Coronation festivities began to get under way.
Seldom in our history have the muses been more active, whether in music,
art or literature. I recall in particular one brilliant occasion when Edward
and I went to Covent Garden for the gala first performance of Ben Britten's
opera *Gloriana*. The Coronation drew a lot of additional overseas visitors
to Britain, and Edward took the opportunity to put Beaulieu and its owner
well and truly on the map. The combination of his good looks, youth and

title made him a bit of a wonder boy when it came to publicity. Very sociable, he was always in the right place to get Beaulieu publicised and was a gift for anyone who wanted a good press photograph.

During that summer, Edward was entertaining prodigiously, and among the guests invited to Palace House was the famous actress Adrienne Gessner with whom I had worked on *Stolen Identity*. Of course her husband, Colonel Ernst Lothar, was due to come too! Having arranged the visit, I began to doubt my actions, but my brother loved playing host to the rich and famous, and I suppose I was trying to please him. Another guest that summer was Elizabeth Arden, who had come over from New York to attend the Coronation festivities. I was allotted the task of accompanying the great Miss Arden from Claridges Hotel in London to Beaulieu. We travelled in the CPV Rolls-Royce, Elizabeth Arden being one of their most important accounts. This was a memorable journey; immaculate and without a hair out of place, she was impressively beautiful though rather daunting.

In late July I left for Salzburg knowing that the second season of public opening was going well and that the future of Beaulieu was looking rosy. On 30th July I got a message that Edward had become engaged to Anne Gage, a history graduate at Oxford. I had met Anne at Palace House and liked her; she was young, attractive, amusing, vivacious and totally charming. But my mind was now on Ernst, and the following four weeks were devoted to hearing superb music, often in his company. These were very happy, carefree weeks, and when the festival drew to a close, I planned to drive my Ford Pilot to Vienna where I would move into a new flat. On that last evening in Salzburg there was no serious music on offer, so I decided to go to a movie, a brash Hollywood musical which was good fun. Returning to the hotel, I was in the best possible mood and totally unprepared for what was awaiting me – a message to call Palace House as a matter of urgency.

Family solidarity: Walking with Edward beside the mill dam

34

The Montagu Case

The voice at the end of the telephone was familiar, but he spoke with a gravity which immediately signalled that something was horribly wrong. It was Tate, the Butler at Palace House. He said I must come back immediately, something very serious had happened and Lord Montagu was under police investigation. I demanded to know more – what was it all about? He was very reluctant to elaborate but mentioned something about a boy scout. I remember freezing when I heard those two words and knew that I should pack my bags without delay.

By 10 o'clock that same night, I was sitting in a hard-seated railway carriage bound for Zurich. Arriving there the next morning, I went straight to Mary Bancroft's flat, where I could stay until I took the evening plane to London. I telephoned my friend Gérard André, Second Secretary at the French Embassy in London, and arranged for him to meet me at the airport at 6pm. Everything went according to plan and within a few hours he was driving me into London. Gérard was also a good friend of Edward's and during the journey explained exactly what was going on.

During the August Bank Holiday weekend, some three weeks before, a group of boy scouts had been camping on the estate and helping out in Palace House as security guards. Since it was rather hot, Edward decided to go down to his beach house with his guest Kenneth Hume for a swim, and asked the boys if they would like to come along – two said yes. It was a brief visit to the sea, as Edward had to drive some of his guests to the station. Earlier that day, he had noticed that his camera had gone missing from Palace House. The police were called in but, to Edward's amazement,

431

their line of enquiry quickly turned on him, with an accusation of sexual assault on one of the scouts. Film director Kenneth Hume was similarly accused by the second scout.

By the time we arrived at Edward's flat in Mount Street, I was feeling pretty agitated. Climbing the stairs, I could hear voices coming from his flat. The door was ajar so I decided to let myself in; Edward suddenly appeared and flung his arms around me – he was in a highly emotional state. After he had pulled himself together, I followed him into the sitting room where some of his friends were trying to work out how they could help him. The situation was so frightening in all its implications, and Edward had been so shattered by the whole incident, that our advice was that he should get out of England. This was not to escape the police but to re-unite with his fiancée, Anne Gage, who was on the Continent. Arrangements were quickly made and I soon found myself sitting with my brother in an aeroplane bound for Zurich, from where I had left only a few hours before!

Once we were on the plane, Edward relaxed and temporarily turned to lighter matters. "Oh Liza, isn't this exciting! Do you know what we're on? It's one of the new *Viscounts!*" I was amazed that he could think of such things at a moment like this. During the flight, we had the chance to talk. He told me that the boy scouts' allegations were absolutely not true. This fitted with my reading of the situation; he certainly had several gay friends, but homosexuality was hardly the *leitmotif* of his life, especially as he had just become engaged to Anne Gage, with whom he was very much in love. My overriding feeling was that Edward was being attacked, that there was some dirty work about, and that I had to defend him.

In Zurich, Mary Bancroft's flat only had one bedroom so Edward and I spent the night on her sitting room floor. We planned to leave for the South of France via Geneva, but the following morning we discovered there was a railway strike in France and the trains weren't running. Edward was terribly keen to see Anne, so we decided to get to France via Italy. This meant that we had to go by rail to Milan, change, then to Genoa, change, and finally take a train which crawled along the coast until it reached the French border. After a long and arduous journey we were met at the frontier by Anne and her aunt, who took us straight to Vence, where Anne was staying with her grandmother.

Whilst we now had the seclusion of a lovely house in the countryside, Edward still had the awful task of telling Anne what had – or rather hadn't – happened. They would sit alone for hours looking very serious; Edward had obviously confided in Anne, but in doing so he inevitably put their relationship under great strain. She was really too young to deal with it all and I sensed that she might be wavering. Whilst she was completely prepared to come to Beaulieu and take on the role of Lady Montagu, she was somewhat innocent and hadn't been exposed to the full spectrum of Edward's friends. Another innocent was Mrs Crake, Pearl's 'darling mummy', who now lived with her daughter at The Lodge in Beaulieu. My sister Helen told a wonderful story about how, on one awkward occasion, she drew her step-granddaughter aside and asked, "What exactly do these 'homosexuals' do?" Helen was briefly dumbstruck, but eventually explained that they were simply rather effeminate, showing their mutual affection by touching and cuddling. That seemed to satisfy her, and Helen was spared any further questions. Mrs Crake died early the following year, aged 87.

Whilst staying at Vence, I received a telephone call from Martin Stevens[1], Edward's former assistant at CPV, whose mother had rented one of the Needs Ore cottages at Beaulieu. I don't know how he got our number, but he explained that he was with Kenneth Hume in Cannes and that they had something very important to discuss with me. It all seemed very strange. He wouldn't go into any detail but asked me to visit him at the Martinez Hotel, where they were staying.

As I sat with them in the hotel lounge, I remember coming out in a cold sweat as I listened to their nefarious plan. They were convinced that Edward would not want to stand trial and saw an opportunity in this for themselves. Stevens explained that he could look after Beaulieu whilst Edward lived in safety abroad, with a monthly living allowance transferred to him out of estate funds. But to make the arrangement work, Edward would have to sign a power of attorney over to him! My brother would, in effect, have become a remittance man, in exile, with no control over the estate. The strangest part of it was Hume's involvement, as he was as much in the dock as Edward. Stevens had clearly masterminded the scheme, but Hume's presence indicated that he was somehow involved. He was very reticent, but I wondered whether he was planning to turn Queen's

Evidence against Edward if he didn't sign up to their plan. It was so appalling that I kept on thinking I would wake up to find it had all been a bad dream, but I kept calm and said I needed time to think it all over. When I returned to the Gages' house, I told Anne's aunt and her American fiancé what had happened and asked for their advice. I had deliberately not told Edward anything.

It so happened that the American had recently acquired a tape recorder and he suggested that we could put it to good use. I therefore telephoned Stevens and asked him to repeat the proposal so I could get it absolutely straight before putting it to Edward. Whether the recording amounted to proof of attempted blackmail I'm not sure, but once I had the conversation taped, I felt in a much stronger position and told Edward what was going on. I think he later met Stevens and Hume, if only out of curiosity, but as he always intended to return to face justice, the whole pretext of their scheme was invalid, not to mention immoral. The experience made me realise that in just a few days, we had been drawn quite unwittingly into a world of criminality and blackmail in which we had to keep our wits about us.

After about a week I felt I had no further purpose in staying with Edward and Anne, and returned to Vienna. Following his stay with the Gages, Edward travelled to Paris where he was visited by Pearl, who spent a week with him at the Hotel Bellman. Just before she departed on 12th September, I arrived for a few days. Edward was looking pale and thin, and soon developed a temperature which confined him to bed for the weekend. Whilst this was almost certainly brought on by the stress of what he was living through, it wasn't the only worry; the cost of living in Paris, with strict currency restrictions, was crippling. On 25th September, in an attempt to further distance himself from press attention, he flew to the United States. But even there he was hounded by newspaper men milking the 'Montagu Case' for every salacious detail they could. I knew the story had become international when I picked up a paper in Vienna to see a photograph of Edward looking terrified outside a telephone box in New York, his hand raised to cover his face.

On 8th October warrants for the arrest of Edward and Hume were served at Lymington. No longer just on the run from the press, my brother was now a fugitive from justice. His attempted refuge in the US having failed,

Edward returned to Paris on the 21st October to lie low. When I met him at a small hotel off the Champs Elysées, Edward told me that Anne had broken off their engagement, a decision she had cabled to him in the US. At the time it was intended only as a temporary break and they remained very close for some months. It was while I was with Edward that the *Sunday Pictorial's* correspondent, Audrey Whiting, somehow tracked us down. Fortunately Edward already knew her from his CPV days and she was very helpful to him. Postponing the kudos of a scoop, she took us to her friend Virginia Vernon, who looked after us, told us where to have meals without being discovered, and eventually found us a place to stay outside Paris.

Edward had been due to give our youngest sister, Mary Clare, away at her wedding on the 31st, but avoided any disruption to her happy day by staying out of the country until after the event. His return to England on the 7th November was followed by formal arrest, preliminary hearings and the granting of bail at Lymington Magistrates' Court. Hume came before the magistrates at the same time, and was also committed for trial, but separately from Edward. The case was then referred to the Winchester Assizes. Whilst I remained on the Continent when Edward returned to England, I did fly back in time to be with him during his main trial in Winchester.

At 9.30 on Monday 14th December, Johnnie Chichester (who had married my sister Anne) arrived at Palace House to drive Edward to Winchester. Two press photographers were at the gate but this was nothing to what we encountered outside the court at Winchester, which was heaving with photographers, reporters and onlookers. When the prosecution called their prime witnesses, the scouts, they gave a very muddled account. In fact, there was very little that was convincing in the whole story, and I just hoped that the jury felt the same way. It was an exhausting day for all concerned, and because Edward had to meet his QC afterwards, he didn't get back to Palace House until 8.40pm.

On the second day, my sister Anne and I attempted a light diversion for ourselves with a shopping trip in Southampton. When we returned to Beaulieu, Pearl relayed a report from Edward's solicitor, Eric Summer, that Edward was conducting himself very well. He got home at seven looking much less strained than on the first day. After several months of waiting, he had finally had his say in the witness box, and looked rather the better for it. The whole case had always seemed like a conspiracy against Edward, but even the court now had an inkling of this; the judge, no less, had spotted an inconsistency in Edward's passport. It appeared that the police had tampered with it to make it look as if he had visited England during his self-imposed exile, but had failed to give himself up.

On the third and final day, I travelled to Winchester with Pearl and Anne in the Hillman driven by the family chauffeur, Wallis. Eric Summer met us and got us seats at the back of the Court, but it was very difficult to hear the judge's summing up over the noisy coming and going of the press. Waiting outside as the jury made their deliberations was agony. Pearl, Anne and I found somewhere to have lunch, but none of us could eat a thing. Back in court, we got some seats nearer the front so we could see and hear rather better. The foreman of the jury announced that Edward was acquitted on the first major charge but they could not reach a decision on a second minor charge which the prosecution had introduced at the eleventh hour.

There was a further agonising delay as the judge conferred, but he eventually announced that the second charge and Hume's case would have to come up at the next assizes, starting in March! It was a strange outcome which left us somewhat stunned. There was considerable relief that Edward had been acquitted on the major charge, but it was impossible to celebrate when the second charge and the prospect of another trial hung over us. After Edward got back to Beaulieu at 5.30pm I drove with him to London, as he was desperate to see Anne Gage.

Despite the situation not having been satisfactorily resolved, we all felt that we should try to dismiss thoughts of the trial over Christmas. I spent a delightful Christmas in Vienna with the Amyots and Renata, who did their best to heal the shock and distress I had been through over the last few months. In fact, all seemed well until early January, when a new bombshell hit us.

On 9th January 1954, Edward, together with his cousin Michael Pitt-Rivers and a journalist friend, Peter Wildeblood, was arrested and accused of 'conspiring to incite certain male persons to commit serious offences…

' The 'certain persons' concerned were two RAF orderlies, Reynolds and McNally, who had been to Beaulieu when Edward had loaned Wildeblood his beach house for a weekend in August 1952 – a whole year before the alleged boy scout incident. The relationship between Wildeblood and McNally, and his friend Reynolds, would have remained unimportant had it not been for some intimate letters to McNally which the police obtained. One of these, from Peter Wildeblood, made reference to a weekend on Edward Montagu's estate at Beaulieu, a name and place now synonymous with the first case. Despite the semi-failure of that trial, the authorities had scented blood and were evidently prepared to go to any lengths to get a conviction. The discovery of the letters was therefore a godsend to the police, who put huge pressure on the RAF men and persuaded them to turn Queen's Evidence against their friends. This included information about their visit to Michael Pitt-Rivers' estate in Dorset, which followed on from their weekend at Beaulieu.

Once again, the proceedings started with a hearing at the Lymington Magistrates' Court, followed by a trial at Winchester. I flew back from Vienna on Sunday 14th March, in readiness for the first day at the assizes on the Monday. In the evening, Edward gave a big dinner to which Mike Pitt-Rivers, his mother Ray and brother Julian were invited, together with the solicitors. Julian and I attended every single day of the trial at the assizes. It was a strange feeling going through it all again, except that this time I was sure that Edward was the victim of a high level witch-hunt and that the authorities would go to any lengths to bring him down. The timing of the arrests, so soon after the first trial, and the searching of their houses without warrants underlined that.

Edward was much calmer and more composed than in the first trial, but it became apparent that the slant of the case was different this time. In addition to allegations of homosexual acts, it was implied that Edward had committed a terrible social impropriety by entertaining people of an inferior social class. By treating them as his friends, he had supposedly encouraged them to commit immoral acts 'under the seductive influence of lavish hospitality'. In fact, Edward had seen little of his beach house guests as he had spent most of the weekend looking after friends at Palace House.

The routine of driving to Winchester with Edward each day, sitting in court and then returning to Palace House each evening became increasingly gruelling. As we discussed the day's proceedings over dinner, we became progressively more despondent. All the papers were full of the 'Montagu Case', and the floor of the library at Palace House would be scattered with newspapers which Edward pored over. But what could he do? What could we do? Wildeblood admitted his homosexuality, and the police had carefully rehearsed Reynolds and McNally to present the testimony needed for a conviction. There were also conspiracy charges: Edward had loaned these men his beach house knowing that they would commit a serious offence.

In the final three days of the trial, Pearl, Anne, Johnnie and Captain Widnell all came to give Edward support. Sitting in what was a temporary courtroom built within the Great Hall, it wasn't easy for any of us: on the one hand it was very difficult to hear, but the sexually explicit details of the prosecution were also invasive and thoroughly unpleasant. During the lunch breaks, Julian and I would sometimes find ourselves chatting with Fleet Street journalists, whose faces were becoming increasingly familiar. On one occasion we had a beer with the *Daily Mirror* correspondent, Peter Woods. It was just before the end of the trial and Julian and I were trying to be up beat, but Woods took a more cautious view. "I don't think it's going well; there's something going on here and I wouldn't be too optimistic if I was you," he warned. It was true that, despite the evidence being based on the testimony of two self-confessed 'inverts' who had been offered immunity, the prosecution had gone to great lengths to build a case in which Edward would be judged guilty by association.

The trial lasted eight days and on Wednesday 24th March Mr Justice Ormerod completed his summing up. The words he used may not have amounted to a misdirection, but he couldn't disguise his prejudice in the way he delivered them. It was therefore no great surprise when the foreman of the all-male jury delivered a guilty verdict on most of the charges. I shall never forget how wonderfully upright and dignified the three men were as their sentence was pronounced: Wildeblood eighteen months, Pitt-Rivers eighteen months, Montagu twelve months. Edward's sentence was shorter as his offences were considered slightly less serious; the others were guilty of 'felonies' whilst my brother had only committed a 'misdemeanour'.

I went down to the strange small room below the court to collect Edward's personal belongings; his wallet, watch and car keys. The three prisoners looked shattered but Edward was being amazingly brave, holding his head high. As he emptied his pockets the warder asked Edward if he had been in the army.

"Yes, the Grenadiers."

"Where did you train?"

"At Pirbright."

"Well, you'll be alright – anybody who went through that will find prison quite a picnic." Edward had to laugh.

The warders appeared very compassionate, there was no rattling of handcuffs, and the situation seemed amazingly normal. It was only when the awful moment came for me to say goodbye to Edward that I realised the full horror of it all. Every evening we had been driving home together, but now I had to take his car home alone, my pockets full of his valuables. I wouldn't see him again for at least eight months. Julian had the same ordeal driving Mike's car home, but he came over to Palace House and Tate got us something to eat. After dinner we both took refuge in a bottle of whisky and I decided to vent my anger. I knew the telephone at Palace House was being tapped, so I rang up my dear friend Moura Budberg and told her exactly what I thought of the police, the British legal system and the establishment. I used a lot of very obscene words, but knowing that 'they' were listening, I got a load off my chest. It helped, but I still didn't sleep a wink that night.

The following week, when Hume's case finally came to court, the crown offered no evidence, and he was acquitted. By now, of course, the authorities had got their man and further pursuit of the case was clearly pointless. However, information which later came to light concerning Hume's behaviour with the scouts, and the episode I witnessed with Martin Stevens in Cannes, left a serious question mark over the integrity of both men.

On 6th April, Edward returned to court as the minor charge from the first case was still due for a re-trial. As with Hume, the prosecution offered no evidence and so the jury formally returned a verdict of not guilty. It was a great irony that the allegations which started it all had come to nothing, but had set in motion a chain of events which saw my brother, his cousin and a friend put behind bars.

The following months were difficult in Beaulieu, for while most of the estate tenants were loyal to Edward, some of the 'gentry' in their large houses were not. I remember going to church the following Sunday and sitting next to Edward's empty seat. When I left at the end of the service, it felt as if the whole congregation was staring at me with hostility. The most hurtful incident was relayed to me by the housekeeper to Commodore and Mrs Larcombe, who lived at Buckler's Wood on the Beaulieu River. "Do you know, last night, when they heard that Lord Montagu had gone to prison, the two of them opened a bottle of champagne and danced around the table." Edward had really made some enemies, but why and how?

Since inheriting the estate in October 1951, Edward had been using Palace House to entertain a succession of interesting and glamorous people. His house parties were doubtless the talk of the village, but invitations were rarely extended to local people. This probably caused resentment in some circles, but there were few local people who really drew Edward's interest. This was very much the pattern of his father, who was not greatly involved in the social life of Beaulieu and never held cocktail parties at Palace House. Some might also have believed that they had been slighted by Edward. Whilst he would never set out to offend, if his mind was on other things he could easily walk past someone or look straight through them without passing the time of day. I can't help wondering if he did exactly that at a civic reception where the Chief Constable, Colonel Lemon, was expecting some acknowledgement from this well-known local peer. If he had felt insulted, this could have sown the seeds of resentment which later drove the Hampshire Constabulary in their extraordinarily zealous pursuit of Edward.

The person that I felt most sorry for was Pearl. We were having tea outside The Lodge and got to talking about Edward and the effect the trial had had on us. Pearl paused. "You know, one of the things I find so difficult is that where I used to be asked to dinner, I now only get occasional invitations to lunch or tea." I thought she must be joking, but the social circuit was a large part of her life and this was how she gauged the effect of it all. My feelings were rather different. Every time I passed through Winchester, I would glance up to where the prison stood. Even after Edward had been transferred to Wakefield I could not rid myself of a fierce anger. There was a belief in some parts of the establishment that homosexuals posed a threat to the moral fabric of society and that these 'inverts' had to be exposed and driven out. Someone high up had decided that Edward's case should be used as a warning to homosexuals everywhere and he had become the sacrificial lamb. Not a pretty chapter in English history.

Not yet a wife, but a 'sales rep' for Fortnum and Mason!

35

THE SCHOOL FOR WIVES

After the trial was all over, the family was understandably in a state of shock. It was as though we had been struck by a tornado that had left our lives clouded and disrupted. Ever since the sensational publicity which had preceded the first trial, I found that work from the film industry had dried up and I was fast running out of money. Then my brother-in-law, Grainger Weston, suggested a course of action which to me seemed utterly ridiculous. Grainger was married to my sister Caroline, and was the eldest son of millionaire Garfield Weston, who owned Weston's Biscuits, Sunblest Bread and Fortnum & Mason. They needed someone in Central Europe to market their products, and he suggested me. For a moment I remained silent. "But you speak four languages, don't you? And know your way around the Continent better than most people? Why, you're a natural!" A natural at what, I wondered. It all sounded quite awful and was the last thing I wanted to do; but not wishing to hurt his feelings, I asked for time to think it over, changed the subject and hoped the idea would be forgotten.

However, a few days later I was summoned to the impressive Berkeley Square headquarters of the Weston organisation, where I was interviewed by their General Manager. I was offered a position as the Central European 'rep' for Weston's Biscuits, Burton's Biscuits and Fortnum & Mason. I duly signed on the dotted line, gave a pale smile and then walked out into Berkeley Square in a dazed condition.

Before I left for the Continent, it was decided I should learn how Weston's Biscuits were made and so I was dispatched by train to their factory in

Newport. Under the watchful eye of my departmental head, I was initiated into the mysteries of biscuit manufacture. It was fascinating watching the toothsome little objects slowly jogging along the assembly line to be packaged for dispatch all over the world. On my return to London, I was given my final instructions and a comprehensive set of samples, but sitting in the coach on my way to the airport, I felt far from happy. My head was a jumble of uncomfortable thoughts; a few years before, a journey to Vienna would have meant a joyful reunion with Ernst, but this time I hardly gave him a thought. I remember trying to cheer myself up by reviewing the positive aspects of my present predicament; I would be getting a regular £25 a week plus expenses and would be far away from everything concerned with the 'Montagu Case'. I had a real job to do, and would have to do it well, as this might be the start of a new and successful career. But, I told myself sternly, don't bet on it, you are just a bloody amateur in this business and you know what can happen to amateurs!

My samples, which ranged from refined groceries and miniature whisky bottles to smart menswear, had been skilfully packed into two large wicker baskets. Not only were they difficult to carry, but the wicker would catch on everything, including my stockings. As an official 'rep', I had to take my samples to a special customs office where various forms had to be filled in. All went well until the official started writing my name. He was clearly puzzled by a treble-barrelled surname. "Douglas-Scott…" he hesitated, "I'll leave out the 'Montagu' – that name stinks, doesn't it!" I nearly hit him! I learned a lot and I learned fast. For instance, I soon discovered that a judicious mixture of flattery, cajolery and the shameless application of personal charm can sell almost anything. I sold whisky to the Austrians, groceries to the Italians, and menswear to the giant US 'PX' at Nuremberg. But by far the hardest nut to crack was Switzerland, where international competition was fierce and 'reps' were firmly put in their place.

On 11th November I flew back to Beaulieu, arriving in time for dinner. Edward had completed his sentence and was now back at Palace House. Lesser men might have been broken by the ordeal he had been through, but Edward only looked forward and impressed us all by quickly getting back into action at Beaulieu, as well as picking up his busy social life. He told me of his plan to drive out to Vienna in the New Year to spend a few weeks with me. I was absolutely delighted and immediately set about finding a flat for both of us, so that when he arrived I would already be comfortably installed in the centre of the city. However, I explained that as I still had urgent work to do on the libretto, he would have to look after himself most of the time. Fortunately, I was able to introduce him to quite a number of young people in Vienna and he was soon caught up in a social whirl of carnival balls and skiing events.

As the months went by, my confidence as a 'sales rep' grew, and when I landed a massive contract to supply whisky to a North German shipping company, I felt I had really made it. I wired head office with news of the order, but first they ignored me and then sent a telegram to Zurich terminating my employment. What had I done? It was only when Grainger made the necessary enquiries that the truth was revealed, by which time I was in no mood to go back. It appeared that I had unwittingly drawn so heavily on the company's whisky stocks that the 'rep' for the US market would be deprived of his sales and all-important commission. Incensed by this female upstart in Central Europe, he had laid down an ultimatum: it was him or me. Guess who they chose! I had been in the job for about a year, but what I learned would be of immense value in the years ahead and I had no great regrets.

I decided to stay in Zurich for a few days to recover my morale. I would look up old friends and refresh memories of a city where I had once lived so happily. I was puzzled one morning to receive an urgent telephone message from composer Rolf Liebermann asking me to lunch that very day. He said he needed to talk to me about a matter that couldn't wait. Although I had met Rolf several times during the war, I knew little about him. I had heard that he was the son of a well-to-do banker but that he had refused to follow in his father's footsteps, wishing instead to become a composer. His family thought he was mad, but Rolf had genuine talent and an original musical mind. Indeed it was the success of his opera *Penelope* at that year's Salzburg Festival that he became internationally recognised and was hailed as an exciting new name in music.

Over lunch, he explained that he had received a commission to compose an opera for the City of Louisville, Kentucky, where he would be following some of the most distinguished composers of the time. As a subject, he chose Molière's comedy *L'école des femmes*, with his friend Heinrich Strobel due to provide the libretto. Everything augured well until Rolf realised that his Kentucky patrons expected an English text, and Strobel did not speak English. Then Rolf remembered his English friend, the film writer Elizabeth Montagu, who had been responsible for the English dialogue in several successful Swiss films including *The Last Chance*. He made some enquiries, discovered I was staying in Zurich, contacted me by telephone, and there we were.

When I left him that afternoon, I felt as if I had been dreaming. To begin with, I found it amazing that a man as hard-headed and ambitious as Liebermann should entrust such an important task to someone with no experience of the genre. If my writing subsequently proved useless, it would be too late to hire someone else. Louisville had stipulated delivery by the early summer of 1955 and it was already mid-February. I decided to accept the offer, as I found the idea of writing a libretto both fascinating and a real challenge, but there was one matter I had completely forgotten to raise: the financial arrangements. Liebermann somewhat took advantage of my naïvety in this respect, giving me a basic payment of £100 and only a tiny percentage of the royalties.

I decided to return to Vienna immediately, for two very good reasons. First, I was confident of finding a haven where I could work undisturbed, for time was short. Second, and this was still very important to me, I would be near Ernst. My friends Jean-Georges, Count Hoyos and his wife Helga had often invited me to stay in their house near the centre of the city, so it only needed a brief telephone call and I was offered a quiet room under their roof. They seemed delighted to see me and most intrigued by the reason for this precipitate return to Vienna. I started work right away and was soon able to complete two or more pages of the libretto a day. Every evening I would hot-foot it to the nearest post office to mail them to Zurich. This was a wonderful period in my life, and despite the pressure of work, writing the libretto gave me an intense feeling of happiness. It was wonderful to have absolute peace and freedom, the only interruptions being the excellent meals shared with my considerate hosts.

Jean-Georges and Helga were well aware of the disaster that had befallen the Montagu family, and as true and loyal friends they now endeavoured to do all they could to make things as pleasant as possible for me. Their

Re-united with Edward

first step was to re-establish contact with my compatriots at the British Embassy for, like so many people at that time, even our diplomats tended to shun me. However, the Hoyos soon put an end to that by giving a large party in my honour, so that instead of being cold-shouldered, I was warmly welcomed in society once more. Today it is hard to understand such attitudes, but the moral climate of the Fifties was very different. It took real courage for Jean-Georges and his wife to give me such open and unqualified support at that time.

Once the libretto was complete, I decided to go to Zurich to find out whether I had got it right. The door of the lakeside house opened and Rolf pulled me inside and hugged me, exclaiming, "Hello genius!" I was very taken aback – was he being facetious? Then I realised that this really was an appreciation of my work, exaggerated though it was. This was a very happy moment, for I knew then that I had indeed got it right! Soon afterwards Liebermann left for Louisville to attend rehearsals, and I went back to Beaulieu. It was here that I received a lengthy telegram following the opera's opening night on 3rd December 1955. *The School for Wives* was

*Above: The cast of the premiere production of
'The School for Wives' in Louisville, Kentucky:
Charme Riesley, William Pickett, Audrey
Nossaman, Monas Harlan, Richard Dales and
Robert Fischer*

Left: Rolf Liebermann

a great success and the cuttings which followed confirmed that the critics agreed. 'The scurvy wit of the Molière original has been ably captured by Strobel, whose libretto was in German. The English adaptation by Elizabeth Montagu is superbly done,' reported *Musical America,*[1] incorrectly assuming that Strobel had written the libretto in German which I had simply *adapted* into English. Next the opera progressed to New York, then across the Atlantic to the 1957 Salzburg Festival with an all-star cast under the baton of George Szell. Had Strobel's libretto existed it would, no doubt, have been used, but it was actually my English original which was translated into German by Hans Weigel. The opera was subsequently staged in all the great opera houses in Europe to packed houses. I was amazed and very happy. It was finally staged in England by the Cambridge University Opera Group in March 1958: 'Elizabeth Montagu's excellent libretto kept the house in continual laughter,' reported *The Times*, finally giving recognition to my contribution as librettist[2].

There is no doubt in my mind that the libretto for *The School for Wives* is the best work I ever produced and it certainly gave me the greatest satisfaction. I continue to find it odd that this first attempt at a libretto, together with the film script for *The Last Chance*, brought me more success and genuine acclaim than anything else I have ever done. But as these successes did little to further my career, they were perhaps considered to be one-offs and their author not taken seriously. Regrettably, the opportunity to further my work as a libretto writer, rather than a translator, never arose again; perhaps I gave up too easily.

Myself at the wheel of a 1913 Fiat (right) passing through Beaulieu village in a commemorative run prior to the opening of the Montagu Motor Museum in April 1956

36

OH! MY PAPA!

Throughout 1955 I continued to write and translate, dividing my time between Beaulieu and Munich where I would stay at a delightful small hotel, the Pension Biederstein. This was the home of that most aristocratic German family, the von Harrachs, but they had fallen on hard times and were making ends meet by renting out some rooms. I was allotted a tiny attic room, yet despite its size it had a good view over the Englischer Garten, making it an excellent place to work. It was from here in June and July 1955 that I translated Carl Zuckmayer's *Das Kalte Licht (The Cold Light)*, a play based on the real life treachery of the atom spy Klaus Fuchs. At the time, Zuckmayer was considered Germany's foremost playwright and I knew that working for him would bring me great prestige. I also heard that he would drive a hard bargain, but in negotiating my fee I now had the support of Suzanne Check, my literary agent, and Robin Fox who advised me on matters of finance. Money was never my strong point and it was really wonderful to feel that there was someone on hand to advise me. Zuck stipulated that we should meet from time to time so that he could check my progress; knowing that he had spent the war in the United States and spoke faultless English, I wondered if he might be an exacting taskmaster. It was only a matter of weeks before my first summons arrived, requesting that I should go to Hamburg, where we would spend a few days together going through the manuscript.

I took the night train to Hamburg and found myself quartered in a small but excellent hotel overlooking the water. Meeting the Zuckmayers at the -Hotel Vier Jahreszeiten, I was relieved to learn that apart from one or two minor corrections, Zuck was entirely satisfied with my translation. I was so elated with his verdict, or else intoxicated by the North Sea air, that on my way back to the hotel I did something really crazy. There was a specialist music shop in the street near my hotel, and I had been admiring their wind instruments in the window. I went in and twenty minutes later emerged clutching a large parcel. I was the proud possessor of a clarinet, a splendid instrument of the highest quality and price, and one that had a most impressive provenance. Only when I reached the hotel, went up to my room and opened the parcel did the euphoria wear off; I was unable to explain to myself why I had spent nearly my last penny on an instrument which I couldn't play and which I probably never would. The next morning I took it to the shop where, much to my relief, they agreed to take it back, thinking that I must be a little mad! Naturally I lost on the deal, but I later gained considerable satisfaction when Rudolph Cartier produced *The Cold Light* for BBC Television using my translation[1].

Although I still spent a good deal of time in Europe, I liked to be back in England before the onset of winter. When the trees in the Englischer Garten had turned to gold, and autumn was well on its way, I would pack up and head towards the Channel ports, often accompanied by flurries of snow. I count myself lucky never to have suffered a major breakdown on the lonely roads of France, where garages were hard to find. Arriving at the coast, I would board one of the Channel steamers, preferably at Boulogne, and then from either Folkestone or Dover, make my way to Beaulieu, always stopping off at a favourite café where I knew I would find the best bacon and eggs in the world.

In late 1955, Edward offered me life tenure of a small but delightful house in Beaulieu. The Mill Race was a converted timber-frame cart house built of mellow red brick and old abbey stone; then as now, it commands a view that constantly surprises and delights, at any time of day, in any season. Overlooking the mill dam, it is a bird watcher's paradise, while on sunny days the interior of the house positively sparkles with light. I was now in my middle forties and it seemed the right moment to forego my *wanderlust*, return to my roots and settle down. The Mill Race was an ideal place for me to write, make music and offer hospitality to my friends.

Before I could move in and make the place my own, though, Edward decided that I should have a paying guest. Whilst his desire to boost my

Myself outside the Mill Race

income was touching, his real motive was to find somewhere for his new House Administrator to live. My dear brother was so sure of the arrangement that he told Iris Goldsworthy to move into The Mill Race in my absence. When news of his actions reached me, I was well miffed, but I eventually came to realise that she would be a great help to me, looking after the house when I was on the Continent. She and I worked together all hours of the day to decorate the interior of the house and she was equally valuable at Palace House, quickly demonstrating her ability to cope with the quicksilver demands of my brother.

I finally moved into the Mill Race on 29th December, and from the moment I did so my life took on an entirely new aspect. For the first time I had a home of my own, could till my own garden and cite a permanent address; but when I told Ernst about the Mill Race, his response was far from enthusiastic. However, I did not allow his reproachful letters to unnerve me and was soon firmly ensconced in the house and loving every second of it. In time, Ernst came to accept the situation and even consented to be my guest on several occasions.

Films no longer played an important part in my life, but I did get a steady flow of translation and adaptation work, making me free of financial worries. My German was now fluent, and I could even deal with local dialects. At that time there were only a small number of theatrical translators, so work soon started coming my way. One such approach was from the Swiss composer Paul Burkhard, who contacted me about a new project. He had adapted one of Gottfried Keller's tales, as had Delius before him with his opera *A Village Romeo and Juliet*. In Burkhard's case this would not be an opera, but more a play with music, and he had chosen the charming story *Spiegel das Katzchen (Spiegel the Pussycat)*. Burkhard hoped the work would arouse interest in the English-speaking world and so commissioned me to produce an English translation. Sadly, *Spiegel das Katzchen* got a cool reception from the critics and any idea of an English production was soon abandoned; my translation was therefore never used. But Burkhard and I had worked well together and he soon approached me with another project.

In 1936, he had scored a musical comedy entitled *Feuerwerk (Fireworks)* specially for the Zurich Schauspielhaus where he was then Director of Music. The show was written to be performed by actors rather than singers, and told the story of the respectable Oberholzer family about to celebrate their father's 60th birthday. Then, in walks the black sheep of the family – who left home as a boy to join a circus – accompanied by his glamorous wife, a trapeze artist. Their beguiling presence triggers a metamorphosis, with the cast turning into clowns, performing animals and muscle men, their circus characters being a parody of their normal selves. This light-hearted fantasy was successfully re-staged after the war and the show's finale song, *Oh Mein Papa*, had been a number one hit for trumpeter Eddie Calvert in December 1953. Burkhard was now intent on getting his foot in the door of the English-speaking theatre with a new version. He gave me a free hand, and, perhaps to obliterate all traces of the play's Germanic origins, the title was changed to *Oh! My Papa!*

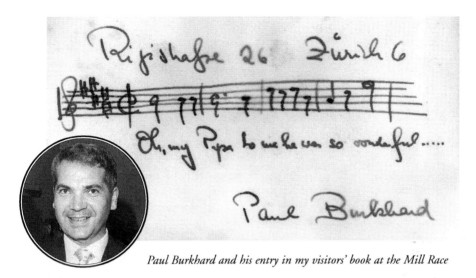

Paul Burkhard and his entry in my visitors' book at the Mill Race

I spent the early part of 1956 on the Continent and then returned to Beaulieu in time for the opening of a major new attraction. The historic cars and motorcycles which had been exhibited around the house since 1952 were now to have their own building: the Montagu Motor Museum. On 22nd April, a veteran and vintage motorcade made its way through Beaulieu to the new museum, north of Palace House, where Lord Brabazon performed the opening ceremony. I was dragooned into driving the museum's 1913 Fiat with Pearl, Anne and her son David as my passengers. Luckily my pre-war training in how to double-declutch held good!

Throughout most of the summer, I sat at my desk at The Mill Race typing the 'book' (the dialogue) and working out the lyrics at my piano. Sometimes I would take the car and charge around the peaceful New Forest trying out some new number at the top of my voice, much to the astonishment of the quietly grazing Forest ponies. After a time, I received some exciting news: *Oh! My Papa!* would be produced by the Bristol Old Vic Company the following spring. 'Burki' was jubilant – a dream come true! He fully realised that Bristol was not Broadway, but the company enjoyed great prestige and its productions at the Theatre Royal attracted the attention of critics on both sides of the Atlantic. Moreover, there would be a talented cast, including Rachel Roberts who was to play the circus queen and a 24-year-old hopeful called Peter O'Toole who was to play Uncle Gustave. *Oh! My Papa!* would be given every chance.

The Oberholzer family in the
Bristol production of 'Oh! My Papa!'

Standing: Phillada Sewell,
Robert Lang, Gwen Nelson,
Jospeph O'Conor & Wendy Williams

Seated: Peter O'Toole &
Ray Pitt-Rivers (Mary Hinton)

Kneeling: Wendy Hutchinson

Under Warren Jenkins' imaginative direction, we were confident of a most polished performance; the dress rehearsal went smoothly and everything seemed to augur well. Nevertheless, we were not expecting the outright triumph that the first night, on 2nd April 1957, proved to be. The applause was deafening, the curtain calls endless, and the final curtain had hardly fallen before offers came flooding in. Even the national press was unanimous in its praise: '..neat though the plot was, it was the music, full of melody and variety, and the well-turned lyrics, cleverly adapted by Elizabeth Montagu, which raised the show well above the ordinary,' reported the *Daily Telegraph.*[2] *Oh! My Papa!* was a smash hit. Being central to this success was heady, intoxicating stuff, and when I drove back to Beaulieu a few days later, I was still in a state of euphoria. For at least a week my feet hardly touched the ground, but then I learned that Jack Hylton had bought the production, and came down to earth with an awful bump.

Hylton, the ex-band leader turned West End manager, was a crude and distinctly vulgar individual. Subtlety was a word unknown to him, and as he was clearly unable to grasp the niceties of Burkhard's work, he set about 'improving' it. He started with some disastrous re-casting, then, taking an intense dislike to the leading lady, Rachel Roberts, tried to replace her. He failed in this but his obvious opposition did little to boost Rachel's morale. Two days before we were due to open at the Theatre Royal, Brighton (a two-week run before moving to London), he conceived a quite devilish idea. Knowing that on Broadway musicals were now appearing in a two-act form, he decided that *Oh! My Papa!* should conform to this new fashion. Burkhard and I were ordered to make the necessary changes over the weekend for the rehearsal on Monday morning. Burkhard, milder and more accommodating than I, merely shook his head gloomily, but I was openly furious with Hylton.

By working flat out throughout the entire weekend, Burki and I managed to complete the two-act version just as Hylton had decreed, but we both disliked the result. Exhausted by our weekend's work, we attended the first night, but soon realised that the alterations had made a nonsense of the play and utterly destroyed its balance. Hylton invited the entire cast to stay at the plush Metropole Hotel, but Rachel, Peter O'Toole and I preferred to find our own accommodation in the form of theatrical digs in a sleazy part of the town.

Predictably, the first night at the London Garrick was a lacklustre affair. Foreseeing that Hylton had a flop on his hands, I refused to take up my free seat in the stalls, stood miserably in the pit and rushed out of the theatre long before the final curtain. Peter O'Toole, on the other hand, was not so affected. He had given a brilliant performance and decided to celebrate in the Irish way. Inevitably this got him into trouble. He was arrested for being drunk and found himself in a cell at Vine Street Police Station. He was so desperate to read his notices that the police took pity on him and despatched a car to collect the early editions, which were flung into his cell. The critics' reaction was less than enthusiastic and the show played to nearly empty houses; after a few weeks Hylton had to admit failure and the play closed. The success I had been so much a part of after that opening night in Bristol had evaporated like a dream.

It was with some relief that I turned to my next job, which involved a return to the Continent to work on another Praesens production, this time at the CCC studios in Berlin. *Es geschah am hellichten Tag (It Happened in Broad Daylight)* was a thriller about a police inspector's hunt for a psychopathic murderer of young girls who terrorised a Swiss forest community. Since the film had already been shot in German, my role would be to assist with its adaptation into English which we did by re-shooting some scenes and dubbing others. The film was later described as one of the more accomplished European 'suspensers' of the period, but its theme was hardly my cup of tea – I was simply grateful for the money! My abiding memory of this production was the smell of gas which permeated the old factory we used as a studio, its only redeeming feature being the studio fruit-machine on which I hit the jackpot!

Zuckmayer and Cartier's satisfaction with my work on *The Cold Light* was demonstrated when, in late 1957, I was asked to translate Zuck's most famous play *Der Hauptmann von Köpenick (The Captain of Koepenick)*. The BBC was about to present a series entitled *World Theatre* and had chosen Zuck's play to represent the best of German contemporary drama. However, this decision must have been made at the last moment, as I was only given seventeen days to complete a translation of this very demanding work. I was immensely pleased to get the commission but was faced with a near-impossible task, especially as I had to deal with a Berlin dialect.

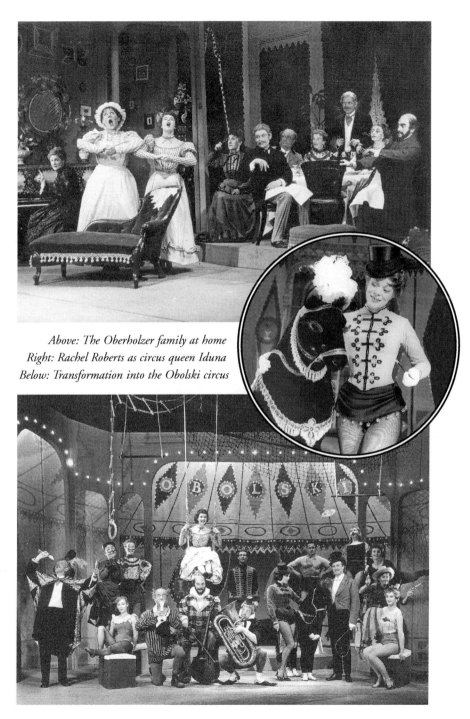

Above: The Oberholzer family at home
Right: Rachel Roberts as circus queen Iduna
Below: Transformation into the Obolski circus

George Pravda, Freddy Mayne and Harold Kasket in the BBC Television production of 'The Captain of Koepenick'

However, with the aid of sleeping pills at night and pep pills in the morning, I managed to deliver the manuscript on time, although it took me weeks to recover from the ordeal. Cartier had insisted I should be present at rehearsals as a dialogue advisor, following which I was able to attend the actual performance at the BBC's Riverside Studios[3]. I found this backstage experience of television a fascinating contrast to film work; whereas feature films were shot with a single camera, take by take, television involved multiple cameras with the entire performance done live.

By now the Zuckmayers had become great personal friends and I was invited to spend the summer with them at Saas Fee, their mountain home in the Swiss Alps. Here, the delightful company, combined with the stimulating effects of the high altitude, acted like champagne; sadly the outlook was less promising in my private life. Ernst resented anything that diverted my attention from him and he showed little interest in my work, so at this crucial moment, I received no comfort at all from him.

Fortunately, our relationship was gradually fading and when we did meet, we seemed to get involved in the kind of quarrels people falling out of love are prone to. I was hurt and resentful, and as a result, my trips to Ernst in Vienna gradually gave way to visits to Renata in Rome and to the Amyots in Switzerland.

During the late 1950s I became seriously involved in the anti-nuclear movement and joined the women's committee of the CND. The president of this committee was the writer Jacquetta Hawkes, wife of JB Priestley. So together with my friend Margaret Lane, Countess of Huntingdon, I attended meetings at Priestley's flat, where we would endlessly discuss ways and means to stop nuclear warfare. Our convictions were deep and our feelings intense, and before long, I found myself marching from Aldermaston to London in one of the great CND protests of the time. But for Margaret and myself this event ended in disappointment; we developed large and painful blisters on our feet and therefore had to fall out, missing the celebrations in Trafalgar Square.

My involvement with CND re-ignited my interest in politics and I seriously considered standing for Parliament. I mentioned this to a friend of the Amyots, Patrick Gordon Walker, then a Government Minister; he appeared interested and suggested he arrange a meeting with Morgan Phillips, then Secretary of the Labour Party. Phillips' interest in my candidature may have been connected with the beautiful young Lady Tweedsmuir, the Conservative MP for Aberdeen South (formerly Priscilla Grant, she had married John Buchan's son). The papers were full of her achievements and perhaps he thought that I could do for the Labour Party what Lady Tweedsmuir had just done for the Tories. But the whole thing was scuppered in five minutes flat when, on my return to Beaulieu, I told my friend Jack Huntingdon about it. He seemed appalled at the idea and pleaded with me to put the whole notion right out of my head. Politics, he told me, was a dirty business and I was completely unsuited to the rough and tumble of it. "Keep your ideals intact," he said, "for if you ever become a professional politician you will risk losing them altogether." Jack was a good and wise man, and, having served in Attlee's government for several years, he knew what he was talking about. Next day, I rang up Gordon Walker to say that I had changed my mind. And that was the end of my political career!

Tony Britton and Nadja Tiller in 'The Rough and The Smooth'

37

FRANCIS-MONTAGU IS BORN

By the end of 1958, the only thing that seemed to be flourishing was my overdraft. Then came an unexpected telephone call. The director Robert Siodmak, best known for his film *The Spiral Staircase*, was looking for a Dialogue Director in his making of *The Rough and The Smooth*, which was adapted from Robin Maugham's book. It was the author's nephew who suggested me for the job, to assist Tony Britton's co-star Nadja Tiller. For reasons which remain unclear, my role as Dialogue Director even merited a report in the *Daily Herald.*[1]

> Down at Elstree from 8.30am to 6.30pm, with weekends thrown in, a sprig of the English aristocracy is teaching film stars to talk proper. And no-one talks properer than Miss Elizabeth Montagu…who has two pupils right now: Austrian Nadja Tiller and American William Bendix, stars of *The Rough and the Smooth*. Bendix, of the sandpaper tonsils, has defied Miss Montagu's best efforts. "Americans," she says sadly, "are often a little touchy if you suggest they don't speak English."

It felt wonderful to be back in a film studio, where the crew included lighting cameraman Freddie Francis, who had recently shot the Oscar-winning film *Room at the Top*. With so much in its favour, the film should have been a good one, but it turned out to be unremarkable in all but one regard. I had always held the curiously named Continuity Girl in the greatest respect, for there were few individuals on the unit who worked harder, and on *The Rough and The Smooth* this was Doreen Francis. Since she was the wife[2] of our star cameraman and also a slightly bossy type, I was careful never to speak to her unless spoken to, and was therefore rather puzzled when Freddie and Doreen invited me to lunch with them.

Rehearsing some lines with William Bendix

They proposed that we should form a company to produce commercials for the new but quickly expanding independent television sector. In 1959 there were already several small production companies engaged in making commercials, but their work was distinctly mediocre. Doreen intended that we would produce advertisements of an altogether higher quality by employing top technicians, predominantly from feature films. That way, she insisted, the sky would be the limit and we would soon be driving our own Rolls-Royces! I listened to all this somewhat sceptically. "It sounds interesting," I said, "but what exactly do you expect me to do?" Doreen had a quick answer to that: "Bring in the work of course!" I knew little about advertising, and nothing at all about how commercials were made, but they were so persuasive that I eventually agreed to join them.

As soon as *The Rough and The Smooth* had been completed, Doreen and I got down to work. The company was to be called Francis-Montagu and we established a small office at Shepperton Studios from where I started to look for work. When I first told Ernst about this development, he was quick to express his displeasure and disapproval, together with dire warnings about getting mixed up in the business world. But by now I could coolly disregard his reproaches and just got on with the job.

Edward marries Belinda Crossley

Meanwhile, on the home front at Beaulieu, the village was agog with excitement. Edward had recently announced his engagement to Belinda Crossley, whose mother was a Drummond, a well-known family from the nearby Cadland Estate.

Belinda was an exceptional young woman: attractive, gifted and intelligent. Above all, she was a very caring person, and was joyfully accepted into the community. I was very moved by everything surrounding their betrothal, particularly as I could see that they were very much in love and that Edward was once again relaxed and looked really happy. I thought that Beaulieu, this traditional village and estate, could count itself lucky to have someone of 'Lindy's' calibre as their new Lady of the Manor. Predictably, such a wedding in a small English village was the event of the year. Everyone celebrated, happily, confident that 11th April 1959 would usher in a new era.

From Shepperton, I dictated letters and telephoned dozens of advertising agencies but no-one was the slightest bit interested in our 'exceptional services'. As the weeks passed by, we began to get seriously worried, but then in late summer we finally got our breakthrough. I had contacted

Jimmie Cleveland-Belle at Colman, Prentis & Varley, where Edward had worked for three years. Over lunch, I tackled him about work and he declared himself interested, promising to contact me should anything crop up. Something did indeed crop up, and very soon. CPV were about to make a commercial for *Ryvita*, and one of their usual production companies had let them down. Grasping the opportunity, we assembled an absolutely first class unit, choosing the famous director, Joseph Losey. We were well aware that this, our first effort, must set the standard of excellence that should always be associated with Francis-Montagu productions. If our charges were slightly higher than those of our competitors, it would soon be seen that this extra expense was justified – and it worked!

We had hardly completed the *Ryvita* assignment when I had to leave for Düsseldorf to fulfil a contract made months before with the German production company UFA. I was to dub *The Adventures of Baron Muenchhausen* into English and although UFA was no longer a household name, they would pay me handsomely. This type of dubbing is exacting work and demands great concentration. The procedure, done at the cutting-table, not only entailed translation but the exact matching of mouth movements to every word of the dialogue. It proved to be one of the most difficult tasks I have ever undertaken, and I was certainly not helped by having to spend long hours in a small, stuffy cutting room in the middle of a heat wave.

While still hard at work in Düsseldorf, I received an excited telephone call from Doreen. It was election year and CPV had asked us to produce a number of political commercials for Conservative Central Office. Doreen realised that the job would be a considerable feather in our cap, but was aware of the great responsibility we would be carrying. She begged me to return as soon as I could, but even working all the hours that God sent, I still only managed to get home when the job was almost complete. Before long, we heard that Harold Macmillan was delighted with this new type of political persuasion and heaped praises on CPV, who shared them with us. We were gradually building a name for quality commercials and it was becoming progressively easier to obtain work. We dealt only with the best and most prestigious agencies, but within a year we had a steady flow of commissions, producing good results for the company.

In our first end-of-year report, dated 23rd August 1960, we listed 25 films made by Francis-Montagu, including commercials for Perkins engines, *Surf* detergent, *Ryvita, Black Magic* and *Dairy Box*. The time seemed right to move our offices to central London, where we took two floors of a house just off Marylebone High Street. We increased our staff, bought a small van with our name on the side of it, and I exchanged my old VW Beetle for a smart new Ford Zodiac. By now we were established in the London advertising world and I began to look around for clients further afield, casting an eye across the Channel. I had been told that no British production company had ever succeeded in getting a foothold in Germany, but I knew that in my case it might be different, as I held several trump cards. First, I spoke fluent German, and second, I had worked there for Westons and had experience of selling to the Germans. Boarding the plane to Munich, I travelled light except for a large and glossy casting directory containing photographs of glamorous models from British advertising. This was the best thing I could have done, as there was nothing like it in Germany.

Having received a welcome from the British Consulate-General, I travelled to a number of German cities, visiting as many of the leading German and US agencies as I could manage. The reception was very favourable and when I opened my model directory, I also opened their eyes; they had never seen such models or been presented with such a choice. By the time I returned to London, I had several offers of work, many of which were soon to materialise and prove highly profitable. One of these commissions required us to fly a large unit with special film equipment, actors and models to Madeira. This was for the launch of a new mentholated cigarette, *Reyno*, already well known in the US as *Salem*. It had to be a top secret operation, hence the choice of Madeira.

In London, I had been living under the roof of an old friend, Anne Rendall, in a beautiful but completely unmodernised house in Park Square East, Regent's Park. Cousin of the theatre director Tyrone Guthrie, she was half-Irish, half-French, and beneath her composed exterior lurked something wild and free, giving her great charm. But Anne's health was failing and it was not long before cancer was diagnosed. I suppose I had not registered the extreme gravity of her condition before I left for Madeira, and was shocked on my return to find her in a truly desperate way, in bed and visibly deteriorating. She died within weeks. Although I could have stayed on in that lovely house, it was too sad, and I decided to move to Edward's new flat at 24 Bryanston Square, where I became his lodger. This was an excellent arrangement for both of us; we were both working all day, but always saw each other at breakfast.

After the shock of Anne's death, the glitzy world of advertising suddenly lost its appeal. I hated all those 'ad men' in their sharp suits and the superficiality of it all. I began to regret the loss of my old life and the absence of the things I really valued, such as music, books and art. Most of my close friends now lived in Italy, Germany or Switzerland, and were unattainable except on brief, snatched visits. And my private life, too, seemed empty and bleak: I would spend many an evening gazing out across Bryanston Square desperately trying to compose a letter to Ernst. At one time, my pen would have flown across the page but now I had to search for words and try to make them ring true. I knew only too well that everything I wrote was simulated, and I despised myself for the deception. All I seemed to have at that moment was work, and I wondered about the purpose of it all. It may have been paying good money, but it wasn't buying me happiness.

As Francis-Montagu was now enjoying considerable success, we engaged a manager recommended to us by J Walter Thompson. Colonel Bill Heald was an efficient and energetic man who took much of the administrative load off Doreen whilst I continued to concentrate on bringing the work in. Now that the company was well-organised and our order book was full, the strain of the work was less, but for me the tedium seemed to increase. I used to think back nostalgically to my years in the theatre and in feature films, feeling that anything would be better than this. Despite these difficulties of morale, there were, of course, good moments: John Schlesinger directed some *Black Magic* chocolate commercials for us and we won a Hollywood award for a Chevrolet commercial. Following the award, I had the idea of opening an office in New York. Everyone thought I was crazy, but it turned out to be a success and continued to operate for many years.

We also moved into the more interesting field of documentaries, our most notable production being shot in the spring of 1960[3]. Released as a short by Columbia, *Wonderful Beaulieu* was made as a semi-promotional film aimed at the American Market. As the commentary writer, I was able to put

Stills from 'Wonderful Beaulieu' and 'The Living Museum'

a little of my own slant on the subject, and couldn't resist including some references to Beaulieu's ghosts. However, whilst on location, two of the crew had strange encounters of their own. First, the cameraman was setting up a high-level shot on top of the north cloister wall when he suddenly descended into the magnolia tree below. Recovering himself, he insisted that something or someone had pushed him, even though there was clearly no-one else up there. Later on, we were doing some night-time shooting in the Upper Drawing Room of Palace House. The electrician, a well-built cockney, went to collect an extra lead and came back in a very distressed state. He said that as he was running down the staircase he heard steps coming after him. Assuming it was one of the sparks, he looked around, but the steps just kept coming and then he felt something brush past him. He came back as white as a sheet, trembling. From then on, he would only use that staircase if someone went with him. Later that year, Beaulieu was featured in another Francis-Montagu production, *The Living Museum*, about the museum's participation in the London to Brighton car run.

In early March 1962, I decided to combine my work in Hamburg and Frankfurt with a brief visit to Zurich, where Ernst was staying with his wife. It rained steadily throughout the two days I spent with the Lothars, and as he and I took gloomy walks around a desolate park beside the lake, Ernst was relentless in his bitter recriminations on every subject. I remember him calling me a 'purple communist' because I expressed disapproval of McCarthy's activities in the States. It was during those days that I finally realised that our fourteen years of deep and passionate love were slipping away into the fog that swirled around us. When my old friend Maria Becker, now a leading Swiss actress, drove me to the airport and I told her something of my feelings, she appeared unmoved. "I never liked him anyway…" she said, and alas, neither did I anymore.

Colonel Arthur Varley of Colman, Prentis and Varley, known to everyone as 'Varley'

38

VARLEY

I arrived back in London with a sore throat and immediately took to my bed. This was a classic example of Freud's 'flight into illness', since I probably preferred the sore throat to my thoughts. However I had to pull myself together as before leaving for the Continent, I had accepted Hardy Amies' invitation to go to the first night of Handel's *Alcina* at Covent Garden. The evening promised to be one of those special Royal Opera House events as Joan Sutherland was to play the leading role, something I was loath to miss. I therefore decided to forget my ailments and take advantage of the invitation. It was indeed a splendid evening, and by the end of the first act my sore throat had miraculously vanished. Then, after the final curtain fell, Hardy invited me to a party given by Sir David Webster in honour of Miss Sutherland, and, feeling much better, I agreed to go. Had I refused that invitation, the subsequent course of my life would have been very different, for on that evening I was to meet my future husband.

Soon after we arrived, Hardy was snatched away by Jimmie Cleveland-Belle to discuss something urgent concerning the London Fashion Group, but before disappearing, he found me a seat on a sofa beside a distinguished-looking silver-haired man. There were no introductions; Jimmie simply told the man to fetch me a glass of champagne and some food. Most of the guests there were eminent in some way or other and so I wondered who he was. When he returned with my supper, we settled into a conversation that was to last the entire evening. I found my companion so fascinating that I was hardly aware of anyone else. Extremely well-informed, he had the kind of mind I liked most; inquisitive, wide-ranging and liberal. He also had a well developed sense of humour, so we laughed a lot. Indeed, he was by far the most interesting person I had met in years and it was most refreshing.

Inevitably, the hours passed and it was soon time for us to take our leave. As we stood up, my companion suggested we should meet again. I had taken quite a liking to him and agreed. A date was fixed then and there, the following Tuesday: "Just a few friends coming for drinks, not a party." I explained that as I rarely left my office before six, I might be late. "Doesn't matter," he said lightly, "just come when you can." Then suddenly I realised there was something missing. "But you must give me your address, and your name too; I don't even know your name!" He smiled. "But I know yours. Elizabeth Montagu, isn't it? Edward Montagu's sister." I was speechless. "Oh, and my name? Varley…"

When I left Weymouth Street that night I was confused and agitated. Hardy Amies had already departed, perhaps in a huff, as I had not exchanged a word with him at the party. Great couturiers can frequently be as vain as their customers, but at last I had met, and whiled away several hours talking to, the great Varley of CPV. This was the same person I had regarded as a kind of bogey-man, responsible for my brother leaving Oxford before his finals. Edward had often asked me to meet him, but I had always refused. Now, however, I realised that there was a great deal more to Varley than I had ever imagined.

Colonel Arthur Noel Claude Varley was an outstanding figure in the international advertising world. Chairman of CPV, he possessed great imaginative powers, a brilliant brain and the kind of charisma that could charm the birds out of the trees. The only son of an impoverished Yorkshire parson, he soon stood out from the crowd both as a personality and for his intellectual ability. After a scholarship to Winchester, he progressed to Worcester College, Oxford, also on a scholarship, where he read history and rowed for his college. For years the Varley family had scraped and saved so that Arthur could study for the Diplomatic Service. His father's dream seemed about to be realised when he passed his Foreign Office exams, but at the oral exam, he was asked about his 'private means'. In those days diplomats were expected to have their own income, and without it, a career in the Foreign Office was a non-starter.

Hard-up and discouraged, Varley decided to take up tutoring, which led to a job in Switzerland, where he taught a tubercular young Englishman in a sanatorium in Leysin. Being quartered in the same hotel as his pupil's parents, he met many of their friends. Among them was Sir William Crawford, then the head of his own advertising agency, Crawford's of Holborn. Sir William was very impressed by the young tutor and moved by the story of his frustrated efforts to get into the Diplomatic Corps. So before Sir William left Leysin, he offered Varley a job. As Varley knew very little about advertising and what he did know, he didn't like, he demurred. However, he desperately needed a job, and so in the end he decided to try it for just a few months. Before long, he was being entrusted with important accounts and found himself travelling all over Europe. By now he had developed a real taste for advertising, and within a comparatively short time he and two of his colleagues at Crawfords, Terence Prentis and Robert Colman, decided to break away and start an agency of their own, Colman, Prentis & Varley.

Even before the outbreak of World War II, CPV had established a reputation for creativity and excellence, and was expanding in a big way. Then, in 1939, Varley volunteered for service in the army, where his abilities were quickly recognised. Starting as a 2nd Lieutenant in the Royal Army Ordnance Corps, he rose to the rank of Colonel, with several mentions in dispatches. His 'qualities of ingenuity and initiative' were later referred to in the written history of the RAOC: 'Colonel Varley – a civilian turned soldier – had a brilliant brain and unlimited restless energy. His speed of thought left lesser mortals standing, but there was nothing slap-dash in his planning and organisation'. A case in point was his analysis of the perils incurred by the convoys carrying vital military supplies from Britain to North Africa. As all the vehicles and tanks were stacked tightly on board, the loss of only one ship could be very serious. Varley proposed that wherever possible, vehicles should be packed part by part into crates for re-assembly in North Africa. This was what we now know as containerisation. In his advertising days, Varley had established close contacts with Austin and Morris, so he was able to further his idea and it worked! Typical of Varley at his most ingenious, his initiative earned him a military CBE. In 1945, he turned down promotion to Major-General and returned to his firm and the job he loved. Soon CPV was once more at the top, staffed mostly by enterprising and ambitious young men, all eager to work under its aegis – my brother being one of them.

Following my evening at Covent Garden, I stayed the night at Edward's flat and saw him the next morning over breakfast. Aware that I had been to the opera the previous evening, Edward enquired whether I had enjoyed the performance and Joan Sutherland's singing; I replied that both had been very good. Then with repressed excitement I asked him, "And guess who I met at David's party?" Without the slightest hesitation and scarcely glancing up from his boiled egg he replied, "Varley." His answer was so unexpected that I remained dumbstruck for a few moments. Then, pulling myself together, I replied, "Yes, you're right. It *was* Varley. But how on earth did you know?" He looked puzzled, even a little embarrassed. "I don't really know why I said Varley – it just came out…"

As usual I spent the weekend at Beaulieu and never gave Varley another thought, but back in London and with Tuesday being an exceptionally busy day, I regretted having accepted his invitation. However, I had promised I would be there, and I was more than a little curious. I arrived at Varley's roof-top flat in Mount Street feeling tired and frayed at the edges, but as I entered I could not detect the usual buzz of party voices. "Oh Lord!" I thought, "It's one of those invitations," and made up my mind to leave as soon as I decently could.

Varley's flat reminded me of a coach on a train, with all the doors opening on one side of a long corridor. My host ushered me into a rather austerely furnished sitting room where I discovered, to my relief, that I was not the only guest. Standing gazing out of the window was Tony Wysard, an old Korda colleague, but after about ten minutes, Tony looked at his watch and left, leaving Varley and me sitting rather awkwardly side by side on a small and uncomfortable sofa. I tried to make some conversation but failed, so we sat there in total silence sipping our drinks. I was really starting to regret this visit, but just as I was about to leave, Varley spoke. "Wait, please, there is something very important I want to say to you." This did not sound like the usual proposition, so I waited. After a few moments of silence, he tried to explain. "You see, I asked you here tonight for a very special reason." Another long pause followed. My host seemed unduly agitated, then suddenly it came tumbling out. "I brought you here tonight to ask you to marry me…"

I had received quite a few proposals in my life, but none of them could remotely compare with this one. I was genuinely amazed, even thunderstruck, so I just sat there staring at him, unable to speak. However, Varley pressed me. "Well, what do you say? Do you accept? Will you marry me?" I tried to collect my wits and then in a shaky voice replied, "I'm afraid I don't know what to say." Varley seized on this: "Ah! But you haven't said 'no', have you!" I tried again, this time with more energy. "I don't understand. Is this a joke? Why, I don't really know you!" Quick as a fox and smiling he replied, "But you still haven't said 'no'!"

I remember thinking that I must be dreaming, as things like this don't happen in real life. But it was abundantly clear that Varley was serious, and that for some mysterious reason this brilliant, highly sophisticated man of over fifty had made up his mind to marry a woman he had met for only a couple of hours at a party. He must be mad, I thought, for what a risk he was taking! However, I was now rather agitated and also distressed for him, for there are few things more disagreeable than having to give such a rebuff, even to a near-stranger. So I quickly rose to my feet, said a perfunctory goodbye, and as I emerged into the street vowed that I would never see him nor cross that threshold again.

Once more over breakfast I had news for Edward. It was now not, "Guess who I met…", but, "Guess who asked me to marry him?" And once more Edward gave the right answer. Very odd. However, if I had thought that I could dismiss this episode as an irrelevance and forget it, I was wrong. From that moment on, hardly a day went by without some communication from Varley. This might take the form of a splendid bouquet of flowers or a touching little nosegay packed lovingly into a small box and sent express from his home in Devon, and many other such gestures. Then there were repeated invitations to lunch or dinner, usually at Claridges or the Connaught, as both were within easy reach of his office and flat. At Claridges, he would get the lunchtime Hungarian quartet to play his favourite music as we enjoyed our drinks in the foyer. Varley, undeterred by my reiterated refusals, plied his suit with undiminished vigour and skill. Nothing that he thought might please me was too much trouble.

Although a little shaken by it all, I remained adamant, and reassured myself that I had good reasons for refusing him. At the age of fifty-two, I was far too old to contemplate such an upheaval. Why, I asked myself, should I take such a step when I had established such an agreeable life? I was now successful in my work, financially secure, and could enjoy the company of my many friends. There was also the Mill Race with my family close by; did I really want to throw all that away? But still Varley didn't give up. He would telephone me from all over the globe, sometimes forgetting the time difference from South America or New York; being woken at three in the morning, even by protestations of love, is rarely agreeable!

In June 1962, Doreen Francis and I departed for Venice to attend the Advertising Film Festival on the Lido. Varley, too, was to leave England on CPV business, this time for New York, so I was confident I could relax for at least a week. That year, in perfect weather, Venice seemed more beautiful than ever: *La Serenissima* at her best. Francis-Montagu was now recognised as one of Britain's top production companies and had entered several commercials in the competition. Following the usual parties and civic receptions, we were awarded a prize for our *4711* eau de cologne commercial, made for one of our German clients. Doreen was delighted – but I remained quiet and monosyllabic. Never before had the superficiality of the world I inhabited seemed so painfully clear. I couldn't help comparing this visit to Venice with those far-off pre-war years when, as a guest of Wally Toscanini, I mixed with great artists and spent my time going to concerts, recitals and elegant parties.

It often happens that memories of very special events remain associated with sharp visual images; the moment when I suddenly decided to marry Varley was one of those. Doreen and I had attended the final official reception and were returning to the Lido by the usual launch. It was already evening and as I looked back across the opalescent waters of the lagoon, I could see Venice at its most exquisite, bathed in a golden light. When we turned into the inlet where we would disembark, that same golden light was falling on the ancient brick walls of the harbour entrance so that they, too, glowed. In a few seconds I made up my mind: I would return to England as soon as possible and tell Varley I would marry him. I went straight to my hotel to telephone to him; I wasn't planning to tell him of my decision, but the fact that it was me calling him would alert him to something – up to this point, all the calls had been placed by him.

I got through immediately. He had just returned from New York and I could hear his amazement and delight at getting my call. Undoubtedly he could read between the lines and during that conversation we both realised there had been a sea change in our relationship; we needed to see each other as soon as possible. I felt a great sense of relief: the decision-making was over, and when I went to my room that night I was light-hearted and happy, certain that I was doing the right thing. Next morning came the realisation that marriage would change my whole existence. I would probably have to give up some things, change old habits and perhaps even have to create a new persona for myself. Marriage would mean the end of my life as a wanderer with complete freedom; being Varley's wife would introduce me to a completely different world. My status as a married woman would feel strange at first, but it would give me security, and this was something that had been conspicuously absent during my wandering years.

We had now reached the day when we were due to quit Venice, leaving the Lido and the great moviedrome to the grand feature film world and their dazzling annual festivities. Doreen left for London by air but I took a train to Rome to see Renata and tell her what had happened. She had been a kind of guru to me for so many years and I needed her advice. I spent two nights under her roof and found to my delight that she was all in favour of my decision, although I do remember her adding, "If he were an Italian I would have said no, but in England divorce is so easy…"

I was met at London Airport by CPV's chauffeur-driven Rolls-Royce, and that evening found myself once more at Mount Street sitting on the same uncomfortable sofa drinking a strong Scotch to steady my nerves. How would I broach the subject? I need not have worried, as Varley came straight to the point and when I told him of my decision he hugged me so tightly that I could hardly breathe. Then he rushed away to telephone Fleet Street to ensure that our engagement would be announced the very next day. However, he was out of luck; the papers had already gone to press and we would have to wait until Friday. "But Friday is the 13th!" Varley was appalled, but I was able to calm him by explaining that for me this was an especially lucky day, for on Friday 13th in September 1940, blessed by good luck, I had eluded the Gestapo and escaped into Switzerland. It was a wonderful omen.

Next morning at breakfast, for the third time, I had interesting news for Edward, but he showed little surprise and said he had been expecting it anyway. He was very happy for us both, but added, "Liza, for Heaven's sake, don't do your old trick and break it off at the last moment. You simply can't do that to Varley." I was surprised at his concern until I remembered how deeply attached he was to Varley, who had become a kind of father figure to him while he was working at CPV. I laughed and replied, "No, Edward, I solemnly promise I won't do that this time!"

So on Friday 13th July our families, colleagues and friends were able to read of the engagement of Colonel ANC Varley CBE and the Honourable Elizabeth Scott-Montagu. We then had to fix a date for the wedding – Varley would have liked it to be 'yesterday', but we eventually settled for the end of August.

Relaxing with Varley at Hewton

Varley and me on our wedding day in London, 29th August 1962

39

HEWTON

Getting married at fifty-two meant that there would be some professional complications for me. Doreen feared that I would abandon Francis-Montagu, but I was able to reassure her that I had no intention of giving up my work, although I would no longer deal with any CPV business that came our way. The worst problem of all was telling Ernst. I was completely at a loss, and had to write that letter nearly a dozen times before I posted it. Despite our mutual awareness that we had reached a point of no return, I feared the news would come as a great shock to him. He knew nothing of what was going on, and was completely unaware of Varley's existence. I knew that his vanity and macho self-image would be hurt most of all. As I feared, he took it badly, and wrote me some sad and bitter letters.

In the run-up to our wedding, I was able to spend two weekends at Varley's Devon home in Bere Alston, and liked everything I saw. Hewton was a large but unpretentious Victorian house overlooking the River Tamar. Admiring the splendid garden and view of Cornwall in the distance, I loved the idea that this would be my home. I had already met, and liked, Varley's eldest son, Jo, at the Venice Festival, where he was representing CPV Italiana, but now had to meet the rest of the family. This was not inconsiderable, consisting of Varley's own children, Jo, Claudia and Martha, three step-children, Sarah Duthie and Jon and Ben Hillier, together with their spouses and six grandchildren! It seemed enormous and I got quite scared, but Varley's youngest daughter Martha was to become a friend for life, as was his sister Enid. It was Martha who 'chaperoned' me on my first weekend in Devon, and we took a great liking to each other immediately. It seems a little eccentric that I insisted on a chaperone, but it amused Varley and was certainly approved of by the household staff. Curiously, I still recall a piece of advice offered to me by Martha. "Dear Elizabeth, as long as you feel that the morning is the best part of the day, marry Daddy, but if you don't – *don't!*"

During the six weeks before we got married, I tried to learn all I could about this man with whom I would presently share my life, for at that time he was little more than an acquaintance. He appeared to have a tremendous zest for life, great sensitivity and a lively sense of humour – that seemed a good start. He had a brilliant mind, was very well-informed and had an insatiable curiosity. Any question that came up during meals had to be answered then and there, so we rarely completed a meal without leaving the table strewn with reference books. History, whether classical or mediaeval, remained a favourite, and once, when we were about to leave for Greece, I suggested getting some guidebooks. "Guidebooks?" he replied tartly, "Nonsense! Just pack a copy of Homer!" At times he could be impatient, touchy, authoritarian, and even quite bitchy. Some people were rather scared of him, but most came to know Varley as the kindest and most generous of men.

A handsome individual, Varley was once described in the *Sunday Telegraph* as looking like a retired Roman Emperor, and when we were in Rome together, I found this description very apt. He abhorred lies and deceit, but as an ad man he sometimes had to equate his principles with a profession where being 'economical with the truth' was part of its stock in trade. However, despite all his experience and sophistication, he was essentially a creative scholar rather than a businessman, and was often deceived or cheated. I was now beginning to know and like him better; love between us was not instant, but when it came it was deep and lasting. He was a fascinating companion, with whom I would share so many interests, and as the day of our wedding drew nearer, I knew that in his company there would never be a dull moment.

Varley and I were married at Marylebone Registry Office on 29th August 1962, with Edward giving me away. After an informal reception given for family and close friends by Ray Pitt-Rivers, we left for Devon. Varley had decided that we should make the journey by car, with CPV's chauffeur John Bambury at the wheel. He had planned that we should have a

In the garden at Hewton

celebratory dinner en route at the well-known hostelry The Old Ship at Mere. He was most eloquent about its special charms and it seemed the perfect place for the newly married Colonel and Mrs Varley to have their first conjugal meal together. Unfortunately, when we got there, we discovered it was closed for repairs! Poor Varley – and after all that build-up! He looked terribly crestfallen, but I hastened to assure him that I wasn't really hungry and would prefer to carry on to get home before midnight. "Get home?" As I uttered those words, their true implication sank in. The house in which I would sleep that night was to be our home, and the realisation brought with it a feeling of great happiness.

As the bare hills of Dartmoor with their grey stone walls loomed ahead, the whole landscape bathed in a strange luminosity, I was overcome by an extraordinary euphoria. I knew I had done the right thing for both of us and suddenly knew that I *was* in love with him. It was a wonderful moment, and even today I can recall the intensity of what I felt that night.

*Varley and me with the Captain on board the RMS Queen Elizabeth
on one of her final voyages in 1968*

Our 23 years together were as varied and fascinating as the *Tales of Hoffmann*. As chairman of an international organisation, Varley's work took him all over the world, and as his partner, I was to visit many of the places I had always longed to see: Scandinavia, Greece, South America, the Caribbean and the United States. New York became a regular destination. I was able to visit these places not as a tourist but as someone on the inside. In the case of South America, sometimes too much so, for in Caracas I was to enter the world of the gun, where the poor lived in cardboard shanties while the rich could hardly count their Cadillacs. I was also reasonably certain that I had recognised some ex-Nazi war criminals – a repellent and depressing scenario. In the Venezuelan jungle, I had an alarming encounter with a python, but still got much pleasure from watching the monkeys and hummingbirds at work. Varley had a wonderful talent for bringing out the best in both places and people, and all our journeys were eventful. He even made Denmark seem exciting!

My half-sister Joan Moorby and me with Edward's son Ralph
at the 'Rosehill', the Moorby's home in Horrabridge, Devon

Whilst my life with Varley is almost entirely another story, there was one extraordinary event which connected me right back to my roots, to a time even before my birth. At Hewton, we had a rather tiresome gardener who I had to tick off for something he had done wrong. He was sitting in the kitchen and suddenly brought his fist down on the table. "You wouldn't speak to me like that if you knew what I knew about you and your family," he threatened. Fortunately, I knew what he was going to say. Nan Spencer, a friend who lived on the other side of the valley, had telephoned me just a few days before to explain everything. She started with an apology for being unintentionally indiscreet in front of the gardener, but the significance of the information she disclosed was far more important than any embarrassment that it might have caused.

Nan explained that an old friend of hers who lived just 4 miles away in Horrabridge, was actually my half-sister! Her name was Joan Moorby; Nan had known the identity of Joan's father since their student days, but it didn't seem important until we all moved to Devon and I met Nan as a

Hewton

near neighbour. Once Nan learned that I was Lord Montagu's sister, she had suggested to Joan that she might effect an introduction, but Joan declined – she didn't want to cause any trouble or awkwardness. Being a very old friend of hers, Nan respected Joan's wishes, but some people noticed the family resemblance, including the jobbing gardener, who mentioned the similarity to Nan. "That's not surprising," replied Nan without thinking, "they're sisters". As soon as she had opened her mouth, she knew she would have to come clean to me before the gardener did.

I had learned long ago that my father and Eleanor Thornton had produced a child, but no-one in the family knew what had happened to her. Finally, 40 years after our father had died, I had found her. Our first meeting was very touching and rather emotional. Joan had the unmistakable Montagu look and even the same strawberry blond hair which I used to have. Her two sons, particularly John, inherited this too. I liked Joan immediately and from that point on, Varley and I saw a lot of her, together with her charming husband, Leslie. Joan was evidently a modest person, but it seemed awful that we had been passing each other in Tavistock for years

Varley and me

without me knowing who she really was. I often asked her why she didn't approach me, but for her it would have been presumptuous and potentially embarrassing. We also got to talk of the distant past. Joan never knew her mother, but she told me how our father would go and visit her at school, masquerading as her uncle. He gave her quite a lot of nice presents, including a lovely new bicycle. That bought a wry smile to my face – mine was a very second-hand model!

Many years later, when Varley and I retired to Beaulieu, people asked me if I missed my old life as a wanderer. I would reply that the new one was just as good, indeed even better. And now, with hindsight, I see how incomplete my life would have been without the 'Varley years'. My usual good luck served me well; we had a very happy marriage. If there was anything in my life that I do not regret, it was the decision I made on that golden evening in Venice.

Back at Beaulieu: Elizabeth in a recreation of the photograph taken
on the south lawn during the First World War (see page 42)

In 1988 Elizabeth returned to Ditton as a guest of the Admiralty who were still using the
property as a research establishment. It was subsequently sold to a software manufacturer

EDITOR'S POST SCRIPT

Elizabeth's decision to marry Varley proved to be the right one and their marriage lasted a happy twenty-three years until his death in 1985. But by concluding her memoir in 1962, the final part of the story, which many of her friends will remember, is missing. As time passes, the memories of those years will fade, and so this post script is included in recognition of what Elizabeth achieved in her 'Varley years'.

Arriving at Hewton, Elizabeth's first task was to make improvements to the house: central heating was installed, corridors were brightened up and a spacious new entrance hall was added. With the house in order, Elizabeth was able to put some fizz into the social life of her husband; as well as welcoming Varley's family and friends, she extended the hand of friendship to their neighbours and cultivated a circle of local friends.

The house had a impressive view down to the River Tamar, which was ideal for dinghy sailing. Investing in their own small boat, Varley and Elizabeth found new pleasures in exploring the estuary, and soon met like-minded people. This lead to the creation of the Weir Quay Sailing Club, of which Elizabeth was founding President. She also became President of the local branch of the St John's Ambulance, an echo of her days with the MTC, from which she parted in rather prematurely in 1940.

At Hewton, Elizabeth was able to re-kindle her love of animals. There was Toby the golden labrador, numerous cats, and two donkeys – Sacha and Dum Dum – who were very popular with the ever-growing brood of nephews, nieces and step-grandchildren. As Elizabeth settled into life in Devon, her interest in film production with Francis-Montagu gradually gave way to an enthusiasm for a home-grown business. Perhaps encouraged by what they had achieved in Hewton's wonderful garden, she and Varley started a project to propagate ericaceous plants such as camellias. The climate in the Tamar Valley was especially suited to the task and they recruited a leading nurseryman who, using their greenhouses, produced large quantities of valuable plants. At its height, the business was despatching plants to destinations as far afield as Holland, but their ambitious expansion plan coincided with the 'Barber Bubble' of the early 1970s and they were forced to sell up.

The resolve which had helped Elizabeth through the difficult parts of her earlier life came, once again, to the fore. Moving to the Mill Race in Beaulieu, she was once again on hand to support Edward, sometimes as a wise, elder sister, and at other times as a co-host at social functions. For Varley, now retired, the move cannot have been so easy, but he found solace in his books and in the cloisters of Beaulieu Abbey ruins, where he could pursue his interest in Medieval history.

Never one to stand idle, Elizabeth joined Beaulieu's marketing department. Taking charge of leaflet distribution to local guest houses and hotels, her endorsement had a special significance coming, as it did, from someone who had actually grown up in Palace House. Her training as an actress and translator were put to good use when she gave guided tours of the house and the abbey, enthralling visitors with her ghost stories. Whether told in English, French or German, her tales were liable to be embellished with each telling! In the late 1970s, she became a founding committee member of a new society called Music at Beaulieu Abbey. Today it continues to present top-quality musical performances in the setting of the splendid Abbey Church, for which it has raised large amounts of money.

Following an unfortunate accident, her last few years were spent in a wheel chair, but she was always bright and optimistic and never lost her passionate interest in life. After the death of Varley, her beloved animals became especially important; there was Sophie the papillon dog, Orlando the canary, and George and Speckley the muscovy ducks. Elizabeth also kept in close touch with her friends around the world; in particular, she never missed her nightly telephone conversations with Etienne Amyot.

Elizabeth died at home after a short illness on 6th May 2002.

ENVOI

This excerpt from one of Elizabeth's letters to Renata was written in 1935 while she was staying at Palace House for Christmas. The passage was read at the Service of Thanksgiving for Elizabeth's life at Beaulieu Abbey Church on 21st May 2002.

I have known what it is to be really unhappy, I have lived a society life, I have a position socially which I am fully equipped to maintain without the help of money or a husband, and I have learnt a great deal about values, and I know what I want out of life, more or less... I want to be moderately self-sufficient – I want to have my own work and make a success of it – and in that lies stability and a promise of content. I want to learn how to conquer laziness and all its companions. I want to be loved – and earn such love by unselfishness, understanding and by helping others. Above all, I want to be freely independent as the winds – and I want to learn all I can of human beings, of art, of science, of nature, of the stars and of philosophy. Then when I die, I will not be reluctant to go, for I shall leave nothing behind me but pleasant memories, I shall not have wasted my span of life and shall take with me to oblivion, or another life, real treasures. If I could have created one really worthwhile thing I should be incredibly happy – and I believe that if I can conquer certain things it is within my power to do so.

MONTAGU & KERR DESCENT

Some marriages and children are omitted

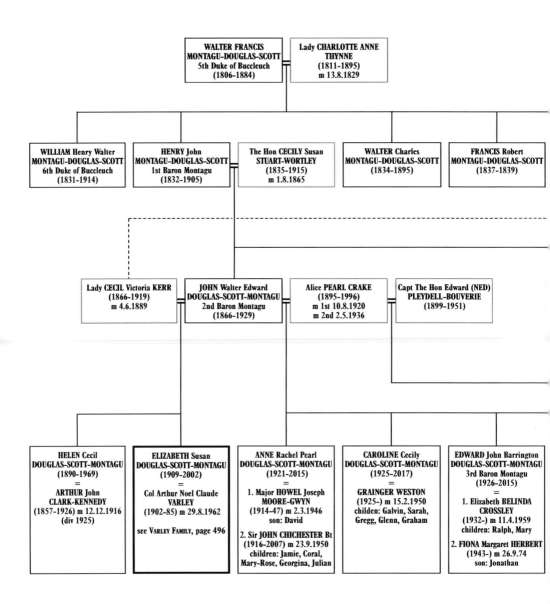

WALTER FRANCIS MONTAGU-DOUGLAS-SCOTT 5th Duke of Buccleuch (1806-1884)	Lady CHARLOTTE ANNE THYNNE (1811-1895) m 13.8.1829			

| WILLIAM Henry Walter MONTAGU-DOUGLAS-SCOTT 6th Duke of Buccleuch (1831-1914) | HENRY John MONTAGU-DOUGLAS-SCOTT 1st Baron Montagu (1832-1905) | The Hon CECILY Susan STUART-WORTLEY (1835-1915) m 1.8.1865 | WALTER Charles MONTAGU-DOUGLAS-SCOTT (1834-1895) | FRANCIS Robert MONTAGU-DOUGLAS-SCOTT (1837-1839) |

| Lady CECIL Victoria KERR (1866-1919) m 4.6.1889 | JOHN Walter Edward DOUGLAS-SCOTT-MONTAGU 2nd Baron Montagu (1866-1929) | Alice PEARL CRAKE (1895-1996) m 1st 10.8.1920 m 2nd 2.5.1936 | Capt The Hon Edward (NED) PLEYDELL-BOUVERIE (1899-1951) |

| HELEN Cecil DOUGLAS-SCOTT-MONTAGU (1890-1969) = ARTHUR John CLARK-KENNEDY (1857-1926) m 12.12.1916 (div 1925) | ELIZABETH Susan DOUGLAS-SCOTT-MONTAGU (1909-2002) = Col Arthur Noel Claude VARLEY (1902-85) m 29.8.1962 see VARLEY FAMILY, page 496 | ANNE Rachel Pearl DOUGLAS-SCOTT-MONTAGU (1921-2015) = 1. Major HOWEL Joseph MOORE-GWYN (1914-47) m 2.3.1946 son: David 2. Sir JOHN CHICHESTER Bt (1916-2007) m 23.9.1950 children: Jamie, Coral, Mary-Rose, Georgina, Julian | CAROLINE Cecily DOUGLAS-SCOTT-MONTAGU (1925-2017) = GRAINGER WESTON (1925-) m 15.2.1950 childen: Galvin, Sarah, Gregg, Glenn, Graham | EDWARD John Barrington DOUGLAS-SCOTT-MONTAGU 3rd Baron Montagu (1926-2015) = 1. Elizabeth BELINDA CROSSLEY (1932-) m 11.4.1959 children: Ralph, Mary 2. FIONA Margaret HERBERT (1943-) m 26.9.74 son: Jonathan |

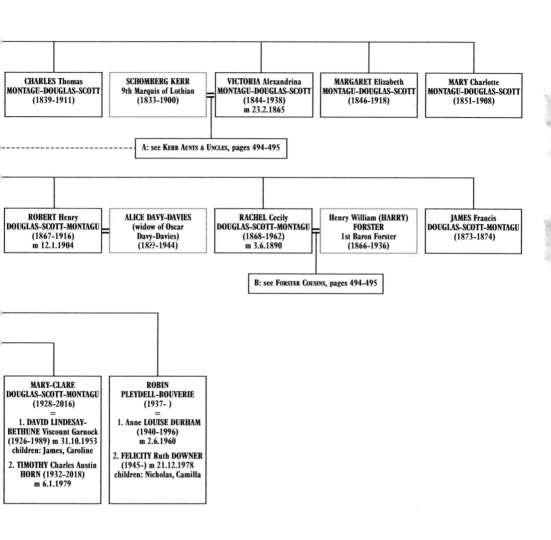

CHARLES Thomas
MONTAGU–DOUGLAS–SCOTT
(1839-1911)

SCHOMBERG KERR
9th Marquis of Lothian
(1833-1900)

VICTORIA Alexandrina
MONTAGU–DOUGLAS–SCOTT
(1844-1938)
m 23.2.1865

MARGARET Elizabeth
MONTAGU–DOUGLAS–SCOTT
(1846-1918)

MARY Charlotte
MONTAGU–DOUGLAS–SCOTT
(1851-1908)

A: see KERR AUNTS & UNCLES, pages 494-495

ROBERT Henry
DOUGLAS–SCOTT–MONTAGU
(1867-1916)
m 12.1.1904

ALICE DAVY–DAVIES
(widow of Oscar
Davy-Davies)
(18??-1944)

RACHEL Cecily
DOUGLAS–SCOTT–MONTAGU
(1868-1962)
m 3.6.1890

Henry William (HARRY)
FORSTER
1st Baron Forster
(1866-1936)

JAMES Francis
DOUGLAS–SCOTT–MONTAGU
(1873-1874)

B: see FORSTER COUSINS, pages 494-495

MARY-CLARE
DOUGLAS–SCOTT–MONTAGU
(1928-2016)
=
1. DAVID LINDESAY-
BETHUNE Viscount Garnock
(1926-1989) m 31.10.1953
children: James, Caroline

2. TIMOTHY Charles Austin
HORN (1932-2018)
m 6.1.1979

ROBIN
PLEYDELL–BOUVERIE
(1937-)
=
1. Anne LOUISE DURHAM
(1940-1996)
m 2.6.1960

2. FELICITY Ruth DOWNER
(1945-) m 21.12.1978
children: Nicholas, Camilla

KERR AUNTS & UNCLES

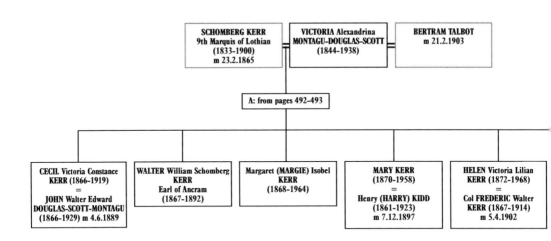

SCHOMBERG KERR
9th Marquis of Lothian
(1833-1900)
m 23.2.1865

VICTORIA Alexandrina MONTAGU-DOUGLAS-SCOTT
(1844-1938)

BERTRAM TALBOT
m 21.2.1903

A: from pages 492–493

CECIL Victoria Constance KERR (1866-1919)
=
JOHN Walter Edward DOUGLAS-SCOTT-MONTAGU
(1866-1929) m 4.6.1889

WALTER William Schomberg KERR
Earl of Ancram
(1867-1892)

Margaret (MARGIE) Isobel KERR
(1868-1964)

MARY KERR
(1870-1958)
=
Henry (HARRY) KIDD
(1861-1923)
m 7.12.1897

HELEN Victoria Lilian KERR (1872-1968)
=
Col FREDERIC Walter KERR (1867-1914)
m 5.4.1902

FORSTER COUSINS

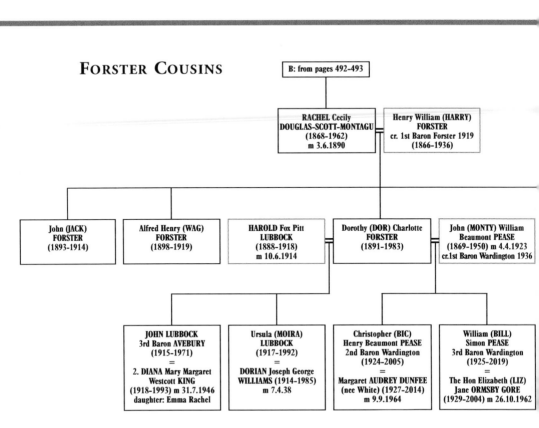

B: from pages 492–493

RACHEL Cecily DOUGLAS-SCOTT-MONTAGU
(1868-1962)
m 3.6.1890

Henry William (HARRY) FORSTER
cr. 1st Baron Forster 1919
(1866-1936)

John (JACK) FORSTER
(1893-1914)

Alfred Henry (WAG) FORSTER
(1898-1919)

HAROLD Fox Pitt LUBBOCK
(1888-1918)
m 10.6.1914

Dorothy (DOR) Charlotte FORSTER
(1891-1983)

John (MONTY) William Beaumont PEASE
(1869-1950) m 4.4.1923
cr.1st Baron Wardington 1936

JOHN LUBBOCK
3rd Baron AVEBURY
(1915-1971)
=
2. **DIANA Mary Margaret Westcott KING**
(1918-1993) m 31.7.1946
daughter: Emma Rachel

Ursula (MOIRA) LUBBOCK
(1917-1992)
=
DORIAN Joseph George WILLIAMS (1914-1985)
m 7.4.38

Christopher (BIC) Henry Beaumont PEASE
2nd Baron Wardington
(1924-2005)
=
Margaret AUDREY DUNFEE
(nee White) (1927-2014)
m 9.9.1964

William (BILL) Simon PEASE
3rd Baron Wardington
(1925-2019)
=
The Hon Elizabeth (LIZ) Jane ORMSBY GORE
(1929-2004) m 26.10.1962

495

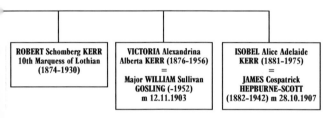

ROBERT Schomberg KERR
10th Marquess of Lothian
(1874-1930)

VICTORIA Alexandrina
Alberta KERR (1876-1956)
=
Major WILLIAM Sullivan
GOSLING (-1952)
m 12.11.1903

ISOBEL Alice Adelaide
KERR (1881-1975)
=
JAMES Cospatrick
HEPBURNE-SCOTT
(1882-1942) m 28.10.1907

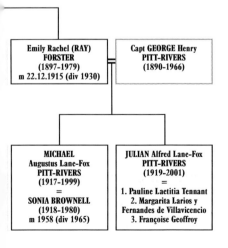

Emily Rachel (RAY)
FORSTER
(1897-1979)
m 22.12.1915 (div 1930)

Capt GEORGE Henry
PITT-RIVERS
(1890-1966)

MICHAEL
Augustus Lane-Fox
PITT-RIVERS
(1917-1999)
=
SONIA BROWNELL
(1918-1980)
m 1958 (div 1965)

JULIAN Alfred Lane-Fox
PITT-RIVERS
(1919-2001)
=
1. Pauline Laetitia Tennant
2. Margarita Larios y
Fernandes de Villavicencio
3. Françoise Geoffroy

496

VARLEY DESCENT

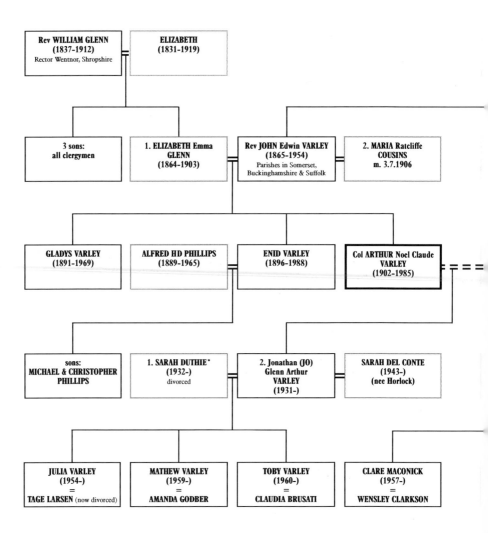

| Rev WILLIAM GLENN (1837-1912) Rector Wentnor, Shropshire | ELIZABETH (1831-1919) |

3 sons: all clergymen

1. ELIZABETH Emma GLENN (1864-1903)

Rev JOHN Edwin VARLEY (1865-1954) Parishes in Somerset, Buckinghamshire & Suffolk

2. MARIA Ratcliffe COUSINS m. 3.7.1906

GLADYS VARLEY (1891-1969)

ALFRED HD PHILLIPS (1889-1965)

ENID VARLEY (1896-1988)

Col ARTHUR Noel Claude VARLEY (1902-1985)

sons: MICHAEL & CHRISTOPHER PHILLIPS

1. SARAH DUTHIE* (1932-) divorced

2. Jonathan (JO) Glenn Arthur VARLEY (1931-)

SARAH DEL CONTE (1943-) (nee Horlock)

JULIA VARLEY (1954-) = TAGE LARSEN (now divorced)

MATHEW VARLEY (1959-) = AMANDA GODBER

TOBY VARLEY (1960-) = CLAUDIA BRUSATI

CLARE MACONICK (1957-) = WENSLEY CLARKSON

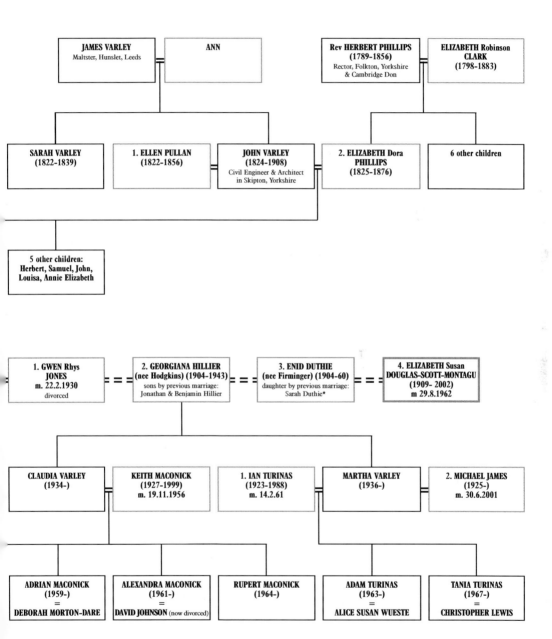

STOLEN IDENTITY

Whilst Elizabeth was working on the film 'Stolen Identity' in 1952, writer Robert Hill penned this affectionate and strikingly perceptive profile which is published here for the first time.

Dickie *is Liz Dickenson.*
Ghino *is Ghino Wimmer, Assistant Director.*
Robert *is Robert Turin who assisted Robert Hill.*
Ernst's wife, Adrienne Gessner, played the part of the housemaid, Mrs Fraser.

I first saw Liz in Dickie's office one day, just a glimpse of a handsome woman with a high colour and heard her very bright, clipped British speech. Ghino had talked of her... said she would be invaluable as our dialogue director. She was working then on a film being made by an American company in Vienna. A week or so later, as I was looking for Dickie, I was told she had gone to have tea with 'Miss Montagu' in the Kursalon in the Stadtpark. This was the end of summer and on Sunday afternoons the band played in the park, people sat on the terrace eating and drinking and the walks of the park, below, were crowded with people strolling under the trees or just listening to the music, seated on the park benches. Two swans sailed about on the surface of the lake and the band conscientiously worked its way through von Suppe and Strauss with occasional excursions into Verdi. Herr Hübner, the particular genius of the Viennese restaurant business, scurried about, greeting his patrons and speculating on the difficulties of being a restaurateur. He paused to greet Liz, to kiss her hand and inquire about her martini, just made of excellent gin but inferior vermouth by the travelling bar on wheels. As he did, I came up, greeted Dickie, and was introduced to Liz.

Dickie was very impressed. Liz was quite obviously a lady and quite obviously knew how to handle both herself and other people. She was also exceptionally pleasant to look at, very neat and with her warm summer colouring looking much younger than her years. She laughed and chatted and asked us both to have dinner with her later in the week. She was living out of town, but she had a car, a new British Ford, and she was going to move into town for the winter, she said. It was a very pleasant moment, the terrace was cool, the green leafed trees shaded us from the sun and the martinis were pleasant if not inspired. Through the iron pickets of the park we could see the tree-shaded Ring outside, and if the Russians were banging about rather too loudly in their motor-pool across the far side of the Ring, it was far too pleasant a day to take any notice of them. The great palais in which they were installed had a private park of its own and the tops of the trees in this were visible. The little Russian soldiers in their ill-fitting, badly dyed uniforms scurried around and about in this park, not unlike amiable little squirrels.

It was obvious, Dickie opined, we must get Liz to be part of our organisation. Because she was short of money, we'd have to help her. She worked out a plan whereby Liz would go on a sort of expenses basis, to get her salary when she went to work on the picture. At that time we were aiming for an October shooting date and the whole thing seemed a pleasant and amiable arrangement. Otherwise Liz would have to go back to England immediately, currency regulations being what they were.

The arrangement concluded, Liz began to come in fairly regularly to the office. She took an apartment, but its location was a deep secret for some reason. I asked her out for dinner and she wouldn't let me pick her up but drove by and picked me up. This was our first real meeting and we had a lot of fun, except she got rather sentimental over her drinks later in the evening and asked me, truly now, was I only taking her out because of her title? I was quite taken aback. I hadn't known she had a title, I said quite truthfully. Then it turned out her brother was Lord Montagu and she herself (with her sisters) was an 'Honorable' which in America means only that one is a Congresswoman or a Lady Mayor, but in England it has a definite place in the social strata.

Liz was not an outwardly sensual woman but she had some strange and potent attraction for men, and for women too. This was occasionally embarrassing as she had to keep a good two steps ahead of the men and three behind the women. Furtwängler used to chase her, and Dickie, of course, and later Robert, who was always trying to get in bed with her. This, and her shoe problem when the rainy weather set in (she didn't have enough shoes) and the difficulties of keeping up her liaison with her love, Ernst Lothar, plagued her. It was also hard to get coal and Ernst's wife found out where her apartment was and, ostensibly turning the other cheek, used to send her flowers to Liz's great embarrassment.

The apartment and its location I finally discovered too. After some weeks of deep secrecy on Liz's part she asked me up for tea or a drink or something. It was connected in some way with the Bristol Hotel and was rather pleasant and well-furnished. She had a piano moved in and was given to playing Chopin somewhat over-vigorously in rainy weather, looking down at the traffic on the Ring. Mostly because of her liaison, however, practically no-one came to visit her. She had to leave all her free time for Ernst. He could get away only at odd hours, for odd moments and when he thought no-one would see him.

Though it had been going on for three years, it was still a somewhat tempestuous affair and Liz would go to extraordinary lengths to effect a meeting with him.

"Darling," she said, "I've not been unfaithful to him once in three years. The first time that's ever happened," she added musingly.

Ernst was apparently an excellent lover. Her eyes would go very misty as she confessed he was, "terribly imaginative. It's different every time."

"Spends all his time thinking up new ways," I opined and Liz, a little surprised, agreed that was probably it. I wondered when he had time for it all for in the intervals of turning out books, he was also working on occasion for the State Department, and directing for the Burgtheater, as well as other activities. His wife, Adrienne, a famous Viennese stage star, demanded a certain amount of attention, though not in bed, as apparently due to some physical ailment, she was unable to comply there, much to her own chagrin.

Liz is terribly difficult to describe. Was it because I saw her alone most of the time, and not too often with other people? I don't know. She was elusive. We had lunch and dinner together quite often and we would talk at length about the ups and downs of the film company. Poor Liz, without enough money, keeping up the apartment mainly as a rendezvous for her life with Ernst, trying to keep that a secret when, after three years, it was becoming one of the town's best known secrets; it was all very difficult.

Let's look at her again. About forty, given to wearing rather hearty clothes, a touch of the male about her in some ways and, in her younger days certainly, she had had girl friends and Sapphic love affairs. She was pretty but now the Montagu nose, a fine, high bridged aristocratic feature, was becoming a little more prominent than it should, the lovely complexion was developing a tendency to flush a little too pink, and the waistline, always firm from having been captain of the girls' hockey team, had to be watched with care now. But still there was much admiration, much attention, and a girl had to be light on her feet and quick with her wits. And she was in love and beloved. Occasionally there were dark moments when she considered the future.

"Bob darling, what will happen when I'm sixty?" she would ask, staring despairingly at a green salad. "I'll still like men but I don't want to become one of those old women."

She decided she would become a nun and amused herself remembering other noble ladies who have renounced the world, after having given the flesh and the devil a run for their money, and become models of saintliness and propriety. This seemed an unlikely end for Liz, but it amused her to consider it pensively and she would stare at her reflection in the glass of restaurants, speculating mentally on how well she would look in black and white at sixty with no lipstick. And without her eyelashes dyed blue, a favourite cosmetic conceit of hers, which certainly made her blue eyes bluer.

What else would we do? We'd go sometimes to the hotel run by and for the French, the Hotel de France. They had a marvellous French cuisine there. We'd have lobster bisque and champagne (very good, very cheap) and for ten dollars have an amazing dinner. I was in the first flush of my newly won schillings and Liz would eye my prodigality enviously. Or we would go to the Drei Hussar, once the smartest restaurant in town and, after being closed for years, just reopened. Or to the Sacher, late in the year, where the waiters all referred to her as *'Gräfin'*, a title she had no right to, but enjoyed anyway. Indeed all through Vienna she was known as 'Lady Montagu' because in the Continental fashion, her father's and brother's title was automatically bestowed upon her.

PICTURE CREDITS

Pictures are reproduced by kind permission of the following individuals and picture libraries. Where not credited below, photographs are sourced from the archives of the Montagu, Pitt-Rivers and Varley families.

BIBLIOGRAPHY

Against the Law	Peter Wildeblood
A Journey to Vienna	Mrs Robert Henrey
Alexander Korda	Karol Kulik
Captured	Bessy Myers
In Search of England	HV Morton
In Search of The Third Man	Charles Drazin
John Montagu of Beaulieu	Paul Tritton
John Montagu of Beaulieu - A Memoir	Laura Troubridge & Archibald Marshall
Memoirs of a British Agent	Sir Robert Bruce Lockhart
Rosa Lewis of the Cavendish	Michael Harrison
Red Tape Not Withstanding	Yvonne Macdonald
Shadow Lovers	Andrea Lynn
The Autobiography of a Spy	Mary Bancroft
The BBC Symphony Orchestra	Nicholas Kenyon
The Celluloid Mistress	Rodney Ackland
The Envy of the World	Humphrey Carpenter
The Europe I Saw	Elizabeth Wiskemann
The Open Page magazine: A Spy's Cover	Julia Varley
The Parting of the Ways	Sheila Grant Duff
To the Bitter End	Dr Hans-Bernd Gisevius
What I Remember (unpublished)	Captain HER Widnell
Wheels Within Wheels	Lord Montagu of Beaulieu

EDITOR'S FOOTNOTES

These notes serve mainly to add information which came to light during the research process. Unless otherwise stated, the source is the Beaulieu Estate archive, or the accumulated knowledge of members of the Montagu and Varley families, including the diaries of Pearl Pleydell-Bouverie.

WIR *What I Remember,* the unpublished memoirs of Captain HER Widnell
JSM John Scott-Montagu (2nd Lord Montagu of Beaulieu)

CHAPTER 1 : THE SHOCK OF BEING A GIRL

1 Birth certificate states 5 Stanhope Street, which was later renamed.

2 In 2003, the Abbey Stores.

3 In 2003, Queensmeade Village Shop.

4 From 1923. (WIR p372)

5 Seville's Copse.

6 WIR p142.

7 Formerly the lay brother's dormitory, and one of only two abbey buildings to survive dissolution.

8. Widow of Archie Stuart-Wortley who painted the splendid portrait of Elizabeth's mother which hangs in Palace House.

9 WIR p366.

10 The site of what later became the Warden's Lodge.

CHAPTER 2 : NORTH OF THE BORDER

1 1887 - 1892.

2 Appointed 8th August 1914.

CHAPTER 3 : UPHEAVAL

1 He played for Hampshire 1885-95. (MCC)

2 Exbury was the Forster's parish church. Castings also exist in All Hallows by the Tower in London, St John's Catford and Christ Church Cathedral, Newcastle NSW.

3 JSM's diary for 6th July 1916 mentions 'Visit to Farnborough, Tudor Hart re camouflaging'. The first tank was used in action on 15th September 1916.

4 Parent National Education Union.

5   12th February 1917.

6   Under the powers of the Defence of the Realm Act or DORA.

7   When Ditton was put up for sale in 1897, the asking price had been £100,000. In 1908 it was put on the market again for £160,000. The compulsory purchase in 1917 was for £30,000 and £20,000 for the Park.

8   WIR p130.

9   Captain Widnell was initially engaged as an Assistant Agent to JSM, but quickly took on the full role of Agent.

10   article dated 20th September 1919.

11   12th December 1916.

12   Fees paid on 22nd February and 25th October 1910. (RADA)

13   *Trilby* ran from 19th December 1912 to 20th March 1913. (Theatre Museum Lib)

14   24th December 1914.

15   Helen lived at Monteviot for some time prior to the divorce (granted 11th July 1925) so that she was legally domiciled in Scotland. (Betty Haywood)

16   27th November 1926.

CHAPTER 4 : LITTLE FELLER

1   First published by Methuen in 1927, this passage and other references to JSM were omitted from editions after 1930, perhaps because he had died the previous year. Excerpt reproduced by kind permission of Methuen Publishing.

2   John Buchan was created First Baron Tweedsmuir of Enfield in 1935.
     Susie Grosvenor's mother was Caroline Stuart-Wortley.

3   WIR p489.

4   Created Baron Forster of Lepe on 12th December 1919, he departed for Australia on 21st August 1920. The timing of the wedding, less than a year after the death of Elizabeth's mother, was influenced by JSM's desire to hold the ceremony before his brother-in-law left for Australia.

5   WIR p276-7.

6   Sunday 23rd and Monday 24th July.

7   1st August 1922.

8   Arranged by Sir Alfred Mond, Chairman of ICI, who was a friend of JSM.

9   Lord Coke, later Earl of Leicester. Silvia's maternal grandmother was Mary Charlotte Montagu-Douglas-Scott, third daughter of 5th Duke of Buccleuch, and sister to Elizabeth's grandfather. She married Col Hon Walter Rudoplh Trefusis in 1877.

10   In 2003, the Upper Dining Room.

11   WIR p397-401.

12   An expert examination later determined the correct height as 5'7" to 5'8".
      (Report by Sir Arthur Keith, 4th October 1926).

CHAPTER 5 : COMING OUT

1   Then called 'By-the-Mill'.

2   Later the Earl of Malmesbury.

3   WIR p 464, 466.

4   Later Lady Wardington – see Forster family tree on page 520.

5   Actually the House on the Shore.

6   Not the same animal as Neddy, the Beaulieu donkey.

7   *The New Forest and its Old Woods,* a short book by JSM in the family archives, well
      illustrates his knowledge of, and views on, the New Forest.

8   Home of Lord Claude Hamilton, one of the King's equerries.

9   WIR p474.

CHAPTER 6 : LONG-HAIRED INTELLECTUALS

1   30th March 1929.

2   3rd April 1929.

3   9th June 1930.

4   The plane, which was one of the *Giant Moth* class, was built in 1928.
      Registration no G-AAAN, it was originally named *Canberra.* (Douglas Gregory)

5   Departed 21st February 1931.

CHAPTER 7 : TREADING THE BOARDS

1   21st November 1931

2   'That is the sort of thing which impels me to violent nausea or to join the Labour
      Party, or both…' wrote Reggie Hooper in *Bystander* magazine on 2nd December
      1931. '…I cannot congratulate those who go in for this sort of imbecile
      extravagance on their efforts to bring nearer a revolution from which they would be
      the first to run with lisping squeals.'

3   28th/29th November 1931.

4   Knighted in 1938.

5   Fees first paid on 22nd April 1932.

6. In 2003, Warner's Cinema, Leicester Square.

7   Letter dated 3rd March 1934.

8   Letter dated 25th March 1935.

9   Broadcast on the Regional Programme on 7th February 1935 and on the National Programme the following day. *(Radio Times)*

10 The PM was James Ramsay MacDonald (heading a National Government), Anthony Eden was Privy Seal (office not in cabinet), Sir John Simon was a Foreign Office minister, Stanley Baldwin was Privy Seal (office in cabinet). (House of Lords)

11 Published by Hodder & Stoughton, 1935.

12 *Glasgow Herald* 7th May 1935.

CHAPTER 8 : NEW FREEDOM

1   15th January 1936.

2   King George V died on 20th January 1936.

3   A rich chocolate cake.

CHAPTER 9 : ETRUSCAN PLACES

1   Dachau, the first official concentration camp in Germany, opened in March 1933.

2   Described in *Capri, Island of Pleasure* by James Money.

CHAPTER 10 : MEISTERSCHULE

1   Later promoted Captain.

2   Exiled Emperor Haile Selassie I.

CHAPTER 11 : MANNEQUINS MONDAINS

1   *Sturmabteilung* or Stormtroopers.

2   Winter Aid.

3   The Institute of Political Science in Paris.

CHAPTER 12 : THE MAESTRO AND FAMILY

1   Concert dates: 26th & 28th May, and 2nd, 4th, 15th & 16th June 1937. *(Radio Times)*

2   Now South Terrace, off Thurloe Square.

3   11th July 1937.

CHAPTER 13 : PARTING OF THE WAYS

1   Otto Christian Archibald, Prince von Bismarck (1897–1975) was a diplomat posted
     to the German Embassy in London 1928-1937; he was the grandson of the
     German chancellor Otto von Bismarck.

2   In 2003, the Mayflower Theatre.

3   Related to Elizabeth via Dor's first husband, Harold Fox Pitt.

4   See Sheila Grant-Duff's *The Parting of the Ways*.

CHAPTER 14 : DARK HORIZONS

1   See *Memoirs of a British Agent* by Sir Robert Bruce Lockhart.

2   9th August 1939.

CHAPTER 15 : SIGNING UP

1   MTC records at the Imperial War Museum show that Elizabeth's recorded date of
     enrolment was 16th September.

2   In September 1938, the War Office directed that all women's organisations should
     come under the umbrella of the ATS. The President of the Women's Legion, Lady
     Londonderry, advised her members to follow this advice, but Mrs Cook, the
     Commandant, disagreed. Anxious not to lose the identity and independence of the
     Corps, she re-formed it as the Mechanised Transport Training Corps. Despite its
     voluntary status, the MTC was given official recognition in November 1941 when
     it was placed under the Ministry of War Transport. (*Red Tape Not Withstanding* by
     Yvonne Macdonald)

3   First wife of south Hampshire landowner Peter Barker-Mill, of Mottesfont Abbey,
     Romsey. They were divorced in the mid-1930s.

4   Published by Hutchinson & Co in 1941.

5   A letter written by Beth Tregaskis to Elizabeth's doctor expressed similar concerns.

CHAPTER 16 : CONVOY

1   The Hadfield-Spears Unit was No 1 Company, and No 2 was devoted to home
     service. (*Red Tape Not Withstanding* by Yvonne Macdonald)

2   Writing to the editor in January 2003, Elena German-Ribon recalled her thoughts
     when Yvonne told her that she was to go to Angoulême with Elizabeth. 'We looked
     at each other suspiciously, and Elizabeth told me later that she had wondered how
     she would get along with a temperamental South American who would probably
     have hysterics and tantrums at the slightest thing; and I saw this tall Englishwoman
     in a trenchcoat, sensible shoes and a terrible cold and wondered if she could even
     speak any French. We soon discovered our mistake; I was placid, easygoing,
     unflappable and very British, and she was warm, amusing, romantic and spoke

perfect French. We enjoyed each other's company, read the same books (Mauriac, Maurois), enjoyed the same jokes and we both loved France and its traditions.'

3   An anti-insect powder.

4   Report dated 25th December 1939.

5   15th January 1940. As a consequence of her ill health, Elizabeth was transferred from No 3 Company to the Reserve. (MTC papers at Imperial War Museum)

6   Paquin was a famous ladies' fashion designer in Paris and London.

7   Passport stamp on entering Switzerland: 11th February 1940.

CHAPTER 17 : 'AUX ARMES CITOYENS'

1   Passport stamp on entering France: 29th May 1940.

2   The Head Messenger and Gate Porter remained with their wives to look after the embassy which was put under the protection of the United States. When the US entered the war, the Swiss agreed to take control of the building. (British Embassy, Paris)

3   Whilst some at Beaulieu regarded Elizabeth as a deserter, a conversation with Elena German-Ribon in November 2002 established that her MTC comrades took a more sympathetic view. Elena knew of Elizabeth's *affaire* with Roland, and felt that with her language skills, she was well equipped to make her way in Vichy France.

CHAPTER 18 : EAST TO BRAMAFAM

1   The Reynaud government resigned in favour of Pétain on 16th June. France signed an armistice with Germany on 22nd June 1940. (British Embassy, Paris)

     Roland departed Bordeaux on 22nd June, travelling to London via Madrid and Portugal. (Laure de Margerie-Meslay)

CHAPTER 19 : LIFE AS A SUBMARINE

1   Nina Alexandrowicz (Jean-Francois Thibault)

2   Het Kwiatkowska died in 1956. In a letter dated 27.1.57, Het's sister Jad wrote to Marcelle asking for the dimensions of the Montagu portrait which she wanted to offer to 'The' Warsaw Museum. A similar letter was sent on 23.11.57, indicating that, before she died, Het had intended to contact Elizabeth concerning the portrait (*son excellent portrait,* writes Jad) and that both Het and Jad Kwiatkowska considered it one of her best works of the period. (*Le plus representatif de son art*). The tone of the correspondence suggests that Marcelle resisted Jad's demands. The National Museum in Warsaw has no record of the portrait which remains untraced.

CHAPTER 23 : THE RITUALS OF ESPIONAGE

1   A secret British radio communications system.

CHAPTER 25 : THE GISEVIUS AFFAIR

1   Eduard Schulte, an anti-Nazi German industrialist was one of those who passed
     information to the allies concerning the development of Germany's secret weapons
     with details of the facilities at Peenemünde. He fled to Switzerland in December
     1943 after being warned by Eduard Waetjen, an associate of Gisevius, that the
     Gestapo had ordered his arrest.

CHAPTER 26 : CANDIDA

1   In practice, Therese was the director as Gordon Dickens was on stage.

2   *Some European Films* was broadcast on the Third Programme, 30th September 1946,
     just 24 hours after the launch of the new station.

3   Note in the front of Elizabeth's copy of the script reads: Film begun – November 7th
     1944, 8.30am. Tessin, Maggia River mouth.

4   Ignazio Silone's original script focused much more on Italy and the freedom fight of
     the partisans, but this was greatly reduced by Wechsler who scrapped several of the
     scenes which were to feature the *Partigiani*. (Peter Kamber in conversation with
     Ettore Cella in 2002. Cella had a minor role in the *The Last Chance*)

CHAPTER 27 : RETURN TO ENGLAND

1   21st January 1946.

2   From an article by Andrea Reimann.

3   Roland was Consul-General in Shanghai 1940-1944, then Chargé with the office of
     the French Embassy in Peking 1944-1946. Thereafter, he held a number of posts in
     Europe, the most important being the French Ambassador in Bonn 1962-1965.

CHAPTER 28 : LONDON FILMS

1   See *The Celluloid Mistress* by Rodney Ackland.

2   She later married Anthony Eden.

3   Stage name Mary Hinton; her part was too small to be credited.

4   Who played Princess Betty Tversky.

5   Who played Marietta the Nanny.

CHAPTER 30 : KORDA'S EMISSARY

1   Letter from Elizabeth to Korda of 8th March 1948 refers to telephone conversation.

2   Death from starvation.

3   Army stores and supplies; US equivalent of the NAAFI.

CHAPTER 32 : CHRISTMAS IN PARIS

1   One of the intelligence agencies with which Moura almost certainly had links was
     the Z Organisation. This was set up by spymaster Claude Dansey in the mid-1930s
     and worked in parallel with the British Secret Intelligence Service. Korda was one of
     Dansey's agents and allowed the Z Organisation to use the offices of London
     Films in England and America as covers for their activities. With Moura being a
     close friend of Korda, and later an employee of London Films, it seems likely that
     she was somehow involved with Z Organisation activities. (*Shadow Lovers* by A Lynn)

     Recently released papers have revealed that MI5 devoted huge resources to
     investigating Budburg. Their belief that she was a Soviet agent was never proved.
     Even if she did have ties with the KGB, her loyalty was evidently divided as she
     revealed Anthony Blunt's membership of the Communist party to a former MI6
     officer as early as 1951. The information was passed on to MI5, but ignored on the
     grounds that the source was unreliable. (*The Times*, article on Moura
     Budburg, 28th November 2002)

CHAPTER 33 : DIALOGUE DIRECTING

1   Published by JM Dent & Sons – rights applied for.

CHAPTER 34 : THE MONTAGU CASE

1   Later MP for Dulwich.

CHAPTER 35 : THE SCHOOL FOR WIVES

1   15th December 1955.

2   25th March 1958.

CHAPTER 36 : OH! MY PAPA!

1   Broadcast as a *Sunday Night Theatre* on 29th July 1956. *(Radio Times)*

2   3rd April 1957.

3   19th January 1958.

CHAPTER 37 : FRANCIS-MONTAGU IS BORN

1   10th March 1959.

2   Doreen and Freddie were never married, however Doreen changed her surname to
     Francis by deed pole (Freddie Francis: *The Straight Story from Moby Dick to Glory, a
     Memoir*)

3   Letter from Lord Montagu to Doreen Francis refers to shooting during the week
     beginning 2nd May 1960.

INDEX

italic numerals refer to photographs or illustrations

ELIZABETH MONTAGU

Elizabeth Montagu was born in 1909, the second daughter of John, 2nd Baron Montagu of Beaulieu. Initially groomed as heir to the family estate, she accepted the role dutifully, but was greatly relieved her half-brother Edward was born as this gave her the freedom to make her own way in the world.

Following her season as a reluctant debutante, she rebelled and went on the stage, soon appearing in London's West End. She spent much of the 1930s studying music in Switzerland and travelling across Europe; here she met many leading writers of the period and witnessed the rise of the Nazis in Germany. At the outbreak of war, she declined a job with *The Times* in favour of driving an ambulance in France, but when the British evacuated in June 1940, Elizabeth astonished her family by staying behind. After a period of living in hiding, she escaped to Switzerland, only narrowly avoiding arrest by the Gestapo.

In Switzerland she was recruited to work in intelligence, de-briefing a top Nazi double-agent. As a cover job, she formed a theatre group which led to work in the film industry as a script writer and dialogue director. This was the beginning of her post-war career. When Graham Greene visited Vienna in 1948, she acted as his guide, a trip which heralded the writing of *The Third Man*, on which she worked. In the late 1950s, she co-founded Francis-Montagu, an award winning television film company.

Music was an important thread running through Elizabeth's life. She was particularly proud of her libretto for Rolf Liebermann's *School for Wives* and Paul Burkhard's *Oh! My Papa!* Despite numerous suitors, Elizabeth remained resolutely independent until she met Colonel Arthur Varley in 1962. Her marriage to this leading figure from the world of advertising started a new chapter in her life. As Mrs Varley, she settled in Devon where she discovered she had a half-sister living just a few miles away.

To order more copies of this book, telephone 01590-614639
or e-mail: gift.shop@beaulieu.co.uk

Honourable Rebel, a film about the life of Elizabeth Montagu,
is available on DVD from www.thehonourablerebel.com